Pivotal
Response
Treatments
for Autism

Pivotal Response Treatments
for Autism

Communication, Social, & Academic Development

by

Robert L. Koegel, Ph.D.

and

Lynn Kern Koegel, Ph.D.

with invited contributors

·P·A·U·L·H·
BROOKES
PUBLISHING CO. ®

Baltimore • London • Sydney

Paul H. Brookes Publishing Co.
Post Office Box 10624
Baltimore, Maryland 21285-0624

www.brookespublishing.com

Typeset by Integrated Publishing Solutions, Grand Rapids, Michigan.
Manufactured in the United States of America by
Sheridan Books, Chelsea, Michigan.

The photographs in this book and on the covers are used courtesy of Rosy Fredeen,
Sharon Hawthorne, Eric Hotchandani, Blenda Montoro, Nicolette Nefdt,
Roz Romero, Eric Smyers, Grace Werner, and Patti Wilczek.

The stories in this book are based on the authors' experiences. Some of the cases
represent actual people and circumstances. In a few instances, real names and details
are used by permission. Other individuals' names and identifying details have been
changed to protect their identities.

Library of Congress Cataloging-in-Publication Data
Koegel, Robert L., 1944–
Pivotal response treatments for autism : communication, social, and academic devel-
opment / by Robert L. Koegel and Lynn Kern Koegel.
    p.   cm.
   Includes bibliographical references and index.
   ISBN-13: 978-1-55766-819-6 (pbk.)
   ISBN-10: 1-55766-819-1 (pbk.)
   1. Autism.   I. Koegel, Lynn Kern.   II. Title.
RC553.A88.K64 2006
362.196'85882—dc22   2005023288

British Library Cataloguing in Publication data are available from the British Library.

Contents

About the Authors

Robert L. Koegel, Ph.D., Director, Koegel Autism Center, Professor of Clinical Psychology, Professor of Special Education, Gevirtz Graduate School of Education, University of California, Santa Barbara, 1110 Phelps, Santa Barbara, California 93106

Dr. Robert L. Koegel is internationally known for his work in the area of autism, specializing in language intervention, family support, and school inclusion. He has published well over 150 articles and papers relating to the treatment of autism. He also has authored five books on the treatment of autism and on positive behavioral support. He has been the recipient of numerous multimillion-dollar research and training grants from the National Institutes of Health, the U.S. Department of Education, and the National Institute of Mental Health. Models of his procedures have been used in public schools and in parent education programs throughout California and the United States, as well as other countries.

Dr. Robert L. Koegel is Director of the Koegel Autism Center at the University of California, Santa Barbara, where he is also Professor of Clinical Psychology and Professor of Special Education. He has trained many health care and special education leaders in the United States. His doctoral graduates have been employed at major universities, including Harvard University; The Johns Hopkins University; University of Maryland; University of California, Los Angeles; University of California, San Diego; University of California, Santa Barbara; University of Oregon; University of Utah; and Yale University.

Lynn Kern Koegel, Ph.D., Clinical Director of Autism Services, Koegel Autism Center, Gevirtz Graduate School of Education, University of California, Santa Barbara, 1110 Phelps, Santa Barbara, California 93106

Dr. Lynn Kern Koegel is Clinical Director of Autism Services at the Koegel Autism Center at the University of California, Santa Barbara. She has been active in the development of programs to improve communication in children with autism, including the development of first words, development of grammatical structures, and pragmatics.

Dr. Lynn Kern Koegel is co-author and co-editor of major textbooks on autism and positive behavioral support and is co-author of the bestselling book *Overcoming Autism: Finding the Answers, Strategies, and Hope That Can Transform a Child's Life* (Penguin, 2004). In addition to her published books and articles in the area of communication and language development, she has developed and published procedures and field manuals in the area of self-management and functional analysis that are used in school districts throughout the United States and have been translated in most major languages used throughout the world.

Dr. Lynn Kern Koegel is actively involved in providing support and intervention services in school districts, both locally in California and throughout the United States. She has also been featured in news reports on television stations throughout the United States and is a consultant for—and is scheduled to appear on—the internationally broadcast ABC television series *Supernanny*.

Dr. Robert L. Koegel and Dr. Lynn Kern Koegel were joint recipients of the first annual Sunny Days Award, presented by Sesame Street Parents and the Children's Television Workshop for brightening the lives of children. They co-authored the book *Teaching Children with Autism: Strategies for Initiating Positive Interactions and Improving Learning Opportunities* (Paul H. Brookes Publishing Co., 1995) and co-edited, along with Dr. Glen Dunlap, the book *Positive Behavioral Support: Including People with Difficult Behavior in the Community* (Paul H. Brookes Publishing Co., 1996).

At the time that *Pivotal Response Treatments: Communication, Social, and Academic Development* went to press, the Autism Research and Training Center at the University of California, Santa Barbara, was undergoing a significant expansion and name change. As of late autumn 2005, this center that the authors co-founded will be known as the Koegel Autism Center.

Contributors

Mendy A. Boettcher
Yale Child Study Center
Yale University
New Haven, Connecticut 06520

Lauren Brookman-Frazee
Child and Adolescent Services
    Research Center
Department of Psychiatry
University of California, San Diego
San Diego, California 92123

Yvonne E.M. Bruinsma
Componistenlaan 195
2215 SR voorhout
NETHERLANDS

Cynthia Carter
Department of Neurosciences
University of California, San Diego
La Jolla, CA 92037

Cheryl Fisher
Ladybird Crossing
502 West Girard Street
Atlas, Pennsylvania 17851

Rosy Matos Fredeen
Koegel Autism Center
University of California, Santa Barbara
Santa Barbara, California 93106

Joshua Harrower
California State University, Monterey
Bay
Seaside, California 93955

Eileen F. Klein
Koegel Autism Center
University of California, Santa Barbara
Santa Barbara, California 93106

Amanda Mossman
Koegel Autism Center
Gevirtz Graduate School of Education
University of California, Santa Barbara
Santa Barbara, California 93106

Nicolette Nefdt
Koegel Autism Center
Gevirtz Graduate School of Education
University of California Santa Barbara
Santa Barbara, California 93106

Daniel Openden
Koegel Autism Center
University of California, Santa Barbara
Santa Barbara, California 93106

George H.S. Singer
Special Education, Disability and Risk
    Studies Program
University of California, Santa Barbara
Santa Barbara, California 93106

Jennifer B. Symon
California State University, Los Angeles
5151 State University Drive
Los Angeles, California 90032

Karen M. Sze
Neuropsychiatric Institute
University of California, Los Angeles
Los Angeles, California 90066

Jane Lacy Talebi
Koegel Autism Center
University of California, Santa Barbara
Santa Barbara, California 93106

Laurie A. Vismara
M.I.N.D. Institute
University of California, Davis
Sacramento, California 95817

Grace A. Werner
Koegel Autism Center
Gevirtz Graduate School of Education
University of California, Santa Barbara
Santa Barbara, California 93106

Quy H. Tran
Koegel Autism Center
University of California, Santa Barbara
Santa Barbara, California 93106

Acknowledgments

We appreciate the assistance of Ty Vernon, who helped greatly with the editorial process in the development of this book. As always, we would like to acknowledge the families of the children with whom we work, who are a major inspiration to us. We are also grateful for the assistance of the funding agencies that have made possible much of the research described in this book. A great deal of the research was funded by grants awarded to Dr. Robert L. Koegel and Dr. Lynn Kern Koegel by the U.S. Public Health Service, the National Institutes of Health, the California Children and Families Commission, the California State Council on Developmental Disabilities, the National Institute on Disability and Rehabilitation Research, the National Institute of Mental Health, and the U.S. Department of Education.

Introduction

The purpose of *Pivotal Response Treatments for Autism: Communication, Social, and Academic Development* is to describe intervention procedures and outcome data related to Pivotal Response Treatments (PRTs) for autism.[1] The approach focuses on core areas of the disorder of autism,[2] producing especially rapid and broad intervention outcomes. It is hypothesized that autism itself may be a much milder disorder than previously suspected and that many of the seemingly severe aspects of the disorder may be side effects resulting from abnormal development. If corrected early, especially significant gains may be possible. PRTs are aimed at the core areas of the disorder to put the children back onto a more normalized course of development, thereby eliminating these seemingly severe side effects and producing large and rapid intervention results.

Some of the core areas that, when treated, seem to produce especially large intervention gains are

- Motivation to engage in social-communicative interactions
- Social initiations (initiated by the child), especially those of shared enjoyment and joint attention
- Self-regulation of behavior

These pivotal areas are addressed through a focus on four important aspects of the intervention: 1) family involvement in the design and delivery of the intervention, 2) treatment in the natural environment, 3) treatment of key pivotal target behaviors as primary to the secondary goal of modifying individual behaviors, and 4) the implementation of intervention in both home and school contexts.

PRTs address family involvement in two crucial ways. First, it is important to realize that families are under stress and that interventions need to be developed in such a way that they not only help the child with autism but also take into consideration the needs of other family members, including siblings and parents. Because PRTs are highly efficient by nature and are integrated into everyday family routines, they can be implemented with considerable ease and negligible disruption to everyday life. In fact, when implemented properly, they should considerably improve the quality of life for all family members. This is considered a primary goal throughout the development of the interventions.

Second, family involvement is considered as critical in the design and implementation of treatment. Because parents know their child so well and are so highly motivated to improve their child's condition, it appears that they are able to make greater improvements in their child's condition, while still living their own lives, than a professional clinician working alone can do. Data from the authors' National Institutes of

---

[1]Many pivotal responses are described in this book. When the term is used in the singular (PRT), we are referring to one individual pivotal area. When the term is used in the plural (PRTs), we are referring to the approach as a whole.

[2]It should be noted that the terms *autism* and *autism spectrum disorders (ASDs)* are used interchangeably. However, the term *ASDs* generally covers a wider range of subcategories, including Asperger syndrome and pervasive developmental disorder–not otherwise specified (PDD-NOS), whereas *autism* refers to children who exhibit symptoms in all of the three classic areas (communication, social impairment, and restricted interests).

Health and U.S. Department of Education research grants have repeatedly shown that children make greater gains with less parental stress when parents (or primary caregivers) are able to take an integral role in the design and implementation of treatment. As such, the PRT approach recognizes that parents are key variables in child development, and the entire intervention is considered in that context.

Additional aspects of *Pivotal Response Treatments for Autism* focus on the improvements in individual primary characteristics of the disorder of autism (in addition to changes in the child's overall condition of autism). Particular attention is devoted to the areas of development communication, social interactions, and broader areas of child interests.

Particular attention is devoted to understanding how PRTs can be implemented in the context of normal child development settings such as school. This book, particularly Chapter 1, focuses on methods of infusing pivotal response teaching procedures into general education curricula. Variables are described and illustrated in both regular home and regular school contexts. Curriculum examples are provided, as are examples of ways in which home and school coordination can occur. Similarly, examples describe how homework can be designed and completed with a high degree of productivity and parent and child satisfaction.

The PRT approach, which focuses on normalizing child development for children with autism, recognizes that social development cannot readily occur without opportunities for normal social interactions. Therefore, considerable details and data are described relating to methods for carrying out play dates at home and for promoting positive social interactions in community settings. It is shown how such an approach has the potential not only to improve social skills but also to result in the formation of true friendships. Furthermore, data are discussed showing how certain types of social interactions can dramatically improve the long-term outcomes for children with autism, as well as improve the lives of children who do not have disabilities.

Development of appropriate and fluent communication is a critical aspect throughout the interventions. Thus, procedures are detailed for developing speech in nonverbal children, including children who are very difficult to engage and do not readily respond to adult prompting. Once speech is developed, the importance of fluent communication takes on increased performance. Methods of using self-management to improve the ease and fluency of communication are described, and outcome data are discussed.

Each of the preceding areas are described in relation to each other and in relation to research being conducted by a large number of research programs throughout the world. Throughout *Pivotal Response Treatments for Autism*, the goal is to describe an integrated and comprehensive approach to the treatment of autism that can improve the lives of both children with autism and their family members.

Pivotal
Response
Treatments
for Autism

I

Overview of Pivotal
Response Treatment

1

The Basics of Pivotal Response Treatment

Robert L. Koegel, Daniel Openden, Rosy Fredeen, and Lynn Kern Koegel

This chapter describes a comprehensive service delivery model that focuses on decreasing the core symptoms of autism using Pivotal Response Treatment (PRT). The chapter discusses PRT as it relates to and integrates with broader areas of behavioral, cognitive-behavioral, and developmental research. This chapter also includes a framework of the PRT curriculum that is embedded within typical family activities and within the general education curriculum so that children with autism may spend their days at school with their typically developing peers.

DEFINITION OF PIVOTAL RESPONSE TREATMENT

PRT is a comprehensive service delivery model that uses both a developmental approach and applied behavior analysis (ABA) procedures. PRT aims to provide opportunities for learning within the context of the child's natural environments (L.K. Koegel, Koegel, Harrower, & Carter, 1999; L.K. Koegel, Koegel, Shoshan, & McNerney, 1999). *Pivotal areas* (also referred to in the literature as *pivotal responses* or *pivotal behaviors*) are areas that, when targeted, lead to large collateral changes in other—often untargeted—areas of functioning and responding (L.K. Koegel & Koegel, 1995; L.K. Koegel, Koegel, Harrower, & Carter, 1999; L.K. Koegel, Koegel, Shoshan, & McNerney, 1999; R.L. Koegel & Frea, 1993; Matson, Benavidez, Compton, Paclawskyj, & Baglio, 1996; Mundy, Sigman, & Kasari, 1990; Mundy & Stella, 2000; Schreibman, Stahmer, & Pierce, 1996). Pivotal responses, once acquired, result in widespread and generalized improvements in children with autism.

Thus far, five pivotal areas have been studied: motivation, responsivity to multiple cues, self-management, self-initiations, and empathy (L.K. Koegel, Koegel, Harrower, & Carter, 1999; L.K. Koegel, Koegel, Shoshan, & McNerney, 1999; R.L. Koegel, Koegel, & Carter, 1999; R.L. Koegel, Koegel, & McNerney, 2001). It is important to note that the treatment consists of a coordinated effort by all relevant stakeholders (Carr et al., 2002) so that a consistent and ongoing intervention is implemented across people, settings, and environments. The PRT model emphasizes the importance of parents as primary intervention agents; however, siblings, teachers and school personnel, consultants, peers, and others who interact with an individual with autism also are included as intervention agents to ensure that the delivery of the model is both coordinated and comprehensive. The primary goals of PRT are to move individuals with autism toward a typical developmental trajectory by targeting a broad number of behaviors and providing children with autism the opportunity to lead meaningful lives in natural, inclusive settings.

CRITICAL FEATURES OF SERVICE DELIVERY MODELS

The following sections discuss variables that are considered critical features of service delivery models for children with autism (e.g., Dawson & Osterling, 1997; Hurth, Shaw, Izeman, Whaley, & Rogers, 1999; Iovannone, Dunlap, Huber, & Kincaid, 2003; National Research Council, 2001; Powers, 1992). The sections also discuss PRT's integration of these dimensions—early intervention, hours and intensity of in-

Pivotal Response Treatment (PRT) is a very naturalistic intervention model. In this photo, a clinician is easily able to incorporate PRT opportunities into an activity at the beach.

tervention, family involvement, and natural environments—and how they relate to broader areas of behavioral, cognitive-behavioral, and developmental research.

Early Intervention

The early studies that focused on identifying and defining pivotal areas were initially developed for elementary-age students (R.L. Koegel, O'Dell, & Koegel, 1987). Their applicability has been expanded to younger children, as children are being diagnosed at younger ages (L.K. Koegel, Koegel, Harrower, & Carter, 1999). There is a consensus among professionals, parents, advocates, and policy makers that early intervention can maximize long-term benefits and prevent developmental problems for children with developmental disabilities (Guralnick, 1997). More specifically, many children with autism who receive early intervention can make substantial developmental gains (Dawson & Osterling, 1997; Kasari, 2002).

During the first years of life, typical children display remarkable development with respect to communication. At approximately 9 months of age, children make the transition from preintentional to intentional communication, which is followed by the emergence of first words at approximately 12 months of age (Bates, 1976). Researchers have suggested that intentional communication emerges as parents and other communicative partners attribute meaning to their children's actions and infants begin to comprehend that other people are influential in helping them to achieve a goal (Bates, Camaioni, & Volterra, 1975; Prizant & Wetherby, 1987; Wilcox, Hailey, & Ashland, 1996). Thus, very young children begin to understand how their behavior produces desired consequences from others in their environment.

Cognitive-behavioral research in the area of motivation, however, suggests that children with autism have a difficult time learning the response–reinforcer contingency (R.L. Koegel & Egel, 1979; R.L. Koegel, O'Dell, & Dunlap, 1988). A study by R.L. Koegel and Egel (1979) showed that when children with autism repeatedly responded incorrectly to tasks, their responsivity and enthusiasm decreased to extremely low levels. It has since been hypothesized that because children with autism have so many areas that need intervention, well-meaning adults often help them excessively, resulting in a low percentage of responses that receive contingent reinforcement. This also appears to contribute to the phenomena of learned helplessness (Seligman, 1972). Seligman and colleagues suggested that learned helplessness results from learning that responding and reinforcement are independent, often delaying or extinguishing the initiation of later responses and producing greater difficulty in learning the response–reinforcer contingency (Miller & Seligman, 1975; Overmier & Seligman, 1967; Seligman, 1972; Seligman, Klein, & Miller, 1976; Seligman & Maier, 1967). Although participants in the learned helplessness studies were not children with autism, the R.L. Koegel and Egel (1979) study suggested that the behaviors were strikingly similar to those exhibited by the children with autism.

In contrast, typically developing children show an understanding of the response–reinforcer contingency at approximately 9 months of age with the emergence of intentional communication. Thus, children with autism require intervention early on that forces exposure to the response–reinforcer contingency, precisely the treatment for maladaptive behaviors associated with learned helplessness (Seligman, Maier, & Geer, 1968).

Researchers have indicated that reinforcing attempts and continuous prompting for successful task completion forces frequent exposure to the response–reinforcer contingency, helping to eliminate a state of learned helplessness in children with autism (R.L. Koegel & Egel, 1979; R.L. Koegel, O'Dell, & Dunlap, 1988). Furthermore, early research suggested that successful task completion may increase motivation to respond, documented by marked increases in both responses of and enthusiasm in children with autism (R.L. Koegel & Egel, 1979). Thus, further research in this area began identifying additional variables likely to heighten the motivation to respond, such as child-preferred activities (R.L. Koegel, Dyer, & Bell, 1987), reinforcing attempts (R.L. Koegel, O'Dell, & Dunlap, 1988), stimulus variation (Dunlap & Koegel, 1980), and direct response–reinforcer relationships (R.L. Koegel & Williams, 1980; Williams, Koegel, & Egel, 1981). These motivational components are incorporated into teaching opportunities, such that children with autism are motivated to respond and receive contingent reinforcement from communicative partners in their environment. In turn, learned helplessness may be reduced, allowing for characteristics associated with intentional communication to emerge.

Although there is variability with respect to an operational definition of *intentional communication* (Calandrella & Wilcox, 2000; Prizant & Wetherby, 1987), there is a general consensus among researchers that the emergence of joint attention is a critical characteristic in the development of intentional communication in typically developing children. Although there are numerous definitions of and behaviors associated with joint attention, much of the literature has discussed joint attention as a child's alternating attention between an object and communicative partner (Bakeman & Adamson, 1984; Carpenter & Tomasello, 2000; Mundy & Willoughby, 1998). In an early, seminal study on joint attention, Bakeman and Adamson (1984) showed that the frequency, duration, and amount of joint attention slowly increased and progressed with age. The importance of joint attention in predicting later language development and size of vocabulary (Baldwin, 1995; Markus, Mundy, Morales, Delgado, & Yale, 2000; Smith, Adamson, & Bakeman, 1988; Tomasello, 1988; Tomasello, Mannle, & Kruger, 1986; Tomasello & Todd, 1983), as well as its contribution to general social-cognitive processes, has been well established in the literature (Baron-Cohen, 1995; Bruner, 1975; Mundy, 1995; Tomasello, 1995).

A growing body of literature suggests that disturbances in joint attention may be a critical deficit of autism (Mundy, 1995; Mundy & Markus, 1997) and an important target for early intervention efforts (Mundy, Sigman, & Kasari, 1994; Mundy & Stella, 2000). Furthermore, Mundy and Stella (2000) suggested that a "cogent argument can be made for joint attention as a pivotal skill arena" (p. 69). Although it is not clear whether targeting joint attention will produce collateral changes in many behaviors as a pivotal area, preliminary research suggests that targeting motivation may produce changes in joint attention that in turn produce changes in measurable, observable behaviors (Bruinsma, 2004). Mundy (1995) theorized that joint attention deficits in children with autism may disturb systems that motivate young children to attend to and engage in their social world. This theory suggests that joint attention is linked to motivation and therefore fits within the framework of PRT. Thus, by targeting motivation as a pivotal area in children with autism, collateral changes are likely in behaviors associated with joint attention. The presence of joint attention, then, may further motivate children with autism to use social communication in natural environments.

Deficits in joint attention may also relate to stimulus overselectivity in children with autism. Specifically, researchers showed that children with autism seem to respond to irrelevant objects or cues in the teaching stimulus or elsewhere in the clinic environment rather than to appropriate and relevant cues for discriminating between objects. Thus, the child's tendency to respond to an irrelevant component of a stimulus rather than to select the appropriate component was referred to as *stimulus over-selectivity* (Lovaas, Schreibman, Koegel, & Rehm, 1971). Lovaas et al. (1971) speculated that stimulus overselectivity was the primary cognitive deficit in autism. In the experiments that followed, substantial evidence for the stimulus overselectivity hypothesis suggested that children with autism have difficulty responding to multiple cues (R.L. Koegel & Schreibman, 1977; R.L. Koegel & Wilhelm, 1973; Lovaas & Schreibman, 1971; Reynolds, Newsom, & Lovaas, 1974; Schover & Newsom, 1976; Wilhelm & Lovaas, 1976). Approaches to teaching children with autism to respond to multiple cues, therefore, have been identified (R.L. Koegel, Dunlap, Richman, & Dyer, 1981; R.L. Koegel, & Schreibman, 1977; Lovaas, 1977; Schreibman, Charlop, & Koegel, 1982; Schreibman, Koegel, & Craig, 1977) and further conceptualized as a pivotal area.

Thus, if children with autism fail to coordinate their attention between a communicative partner and an object, they may be overselecting to an irrelevant component (either the object or the partner). Changes in stimulus overselectivity, then, may produce collateral changes in joint attention as children with autism learn to respond to multiple cues and, perhaps, to both the object and the communicative partner.

Hours and Intensity of Intervention

In an important study, Lovaas (1987) reported that children with autism who received 40 or more hours per week of intervention for 2 or more years achieved substantially better outcomes than those in a control group receiving 10 hours per week of the same therapy. Although details of this study remain controversial (Gresham & MacMillan, 1998; Schopler, Short, & Mesibov, 1989), it comes as no surprise that comprehensive models of service delivery generally emphasize the number of hours of intervention as an important program dimension. Of the comprehensive programs reviewed by the Committee on Educational Interventions for Children with Autism, all report the need for at least 20–45 hours of intervention per week (National Research Council, 2001). However, researchers have suggested that many variables are confounded with intensity (Dawson & Osterling, 1997; Kasari, 2002). For instance, Kasari (2002) suggested that the teaching approach (i.e., one to one or small group) and the teaching content—as well as child, family, and therapist characteristics—are related to intensity of intervention and need to be studied empirically. In the PRT model, because intervention is delivered in natural environments and spread across intervention agencies (e.g., parents, school personnel, peers), the total number of hours of intervention the child receives is substantially high. However, PRT is both an hour-intensive and cost-efficient model of service delivery because the service delivery is spread across all the significant individuals and settings in the child's life.

In addition to intensity and number of hours of intervention, the literature has begun to emphasize teaching content, focusing extensively on areas central to the disorder of autism. Of particular importance are developmental skills (e.g., joint attention, pretend play) that children with autism often lack and that are important predictors of later language and social development in typically developing children (Baron-Cohen, 1995; Bruner, 1975; Mundy, 1995; Mundy et al., 1990; Tomasello, 1995). Although no comprehensive programs have been developed, a couple of studies have targeted and found improvements in joint attention (Lewy & Dawson, 1992; Whalen & Schreibman, 2003). Researchers have called for additional intervention strategies that will improve joint attention (e.g., Mundy & Crowson, 1997), a core deficit in children with autism and pivotal to deficits in language and social development (Mundy, 1995; Mundy & Markus, 1997; Mundy & Stella, 2000). Thus, teaching content—that is, *what* is being taught during intervention—is equally important. In the PRT model, target behaviors are addressed through intervention in pivotal areas such that improvements will occur across a large number of behaviors (L.K. Koegel, Koegel, Harrower, & Carter, 1999; R.L. Koegel, Koegel, & Carter, 1999).

In addition, intervention takes place in natural settings that provide a context for responding to come under the control of natural environmental stimuli (L.K. Koegel, Koegel, Harrower, & Carter, 1999). PRT has emerged from the Natural Language Paradigm (NLP), an intervention procedure that closely approximates the manner in which typically developing children acquire language (R.L. Koegel, O'Dell, & Koegel, 1987). In addition to combining the previously mentioned motivational procedures, the NLP represented a shift toward naturalistic procedures for language interventions and away from pull-out settings using imitation and drill procedures (Camarata, 1996). Naturalistic approaches have implications for delivering intervention in inclusive environments (Camarata, 1995), an important consideration as increasing numbers of children with disabilities are being educated in general education classrooms and require inclusive service delivery (Camarata, 1996).

Finally, intervention services are provided through a parent education model. Many comprehensive models of service delivery for children with autism include a parent education component to further increase the number of intervention hours the child receives (Dawson & Osterling, 1997; Kasari, 2002, National Research Council, 2001). Although services are coordinated with schools and various community programs, PRT focuses primarily on educating parents such that intervention can be provided during all of the child's waking hours and throughout the child's day. Parent education in the PRT model is discussed further in the following section.

Family Involvement

Families are recognized as a critical component in effective intervention programs. In the PRT model, parents are viewed as an integral part of their child's program and as primary intervention agents. Parent education is an important element of effective behavioral interventions for children with disabilities (Baker, 1989). Wolf, Risley, and Mees (1964) began working with parents of children from residential settings so that successful behavior programs could be transferred to home visits. In a follow-up study of children who had received 1 year of intensive behavioral intervention, Lovaas, Koegel, Simmons, and Long (1973) found that intervention gains were maintained if children were discharged to parents who had received similar training. Conversely, children discharged to facilities that did not employ behavior programs lost most of their treatment gains. Schopler and Reichler (1971) began using parents as "cotherapists"—that is, as the primary therapeutic agents—in a developmental therapy program. Among other findings, children tended to demonstrate better developmental skills with their parents than with therapists. Because parents were taught and participated in the intervention with a clinician, intervention could be continued at home. Since these studies, research has shown that parents can effectively implement intervention for deficits central to the disorder of autism, such as communication and social interaction (e.g., Charlop & Trasowech, 1991; Harris, Wolchik, & Weitz, 1981; R.L. Koegel, Bimbela, & Schreibman, 1996; Laski, Charlop, & Schreibman, 1988; McClannahan, Krantz, & McGee, 1982; McGee, Morrier, & Daly, 1999; Sanders & Glynn, 1981).

Parent education is a critical component of the PRT model, and it is important that delivery be within the context of ecocultural theory (Bernheimer, Gallimore, & Weisner, 1990). That is, when designing effective interventions, it is critical to consider the family's broader sociocultural environment as a value system and the family's daily routines. Similarly, research in the area of positive behavior support (PBS) has emphasized that behavior plans maintain a "goodness of fit" such that interventions fit within the existing family context to produce lasting, durable benefits in multiple settings and environments (Albin, Lucyshyn, Horner, & Flannery, 1996; Carr et al., 2002). Although the benefits of parent education have been well established (Singer,

Goldberg-Hamblin, Peckham-Hardin, Barry, & Santarelli, 2002), research has also indicated that a subset of parents do not benefit from behavioral parent training unless it is supported by family-focused supports and contextualized interventions (Lutzker & Campbell, 1994; Sanders, 1996; Singer et al., 2002; Singer & Powers, 1993b; Webster-Stratton, 1997).

For instance, Moes and Frea (2002) taught parents to implement functional communication training (FCT) to address the challenging behaviors in three young children with autism. Training consisted of two phases. In the first phase, parents were taught to implement FCT during a randomly selected routine observed during baseline. In the second phase, family interviews were conducted to gather relevant information on the family context and daily routines. Modifications were made to the intervention package such that the FCT was contextualized to address family goals, concerns, supports, and resources. Although problem behaviors decreased with the initial FCT treatment, they were eliminated completely or reached near-zero levels in the contextualized FCT phase. Thus, consideration of each of the family's daily routines and an assessment of the broader ecology and context within which they fit improved the success of the treatment.

In the PRT model, parent education is delivered in natural contexts, settings, and environments and within family routines such that families can implement the procedures throughout the day and effectively provide teaching opportunities within the context of natural parent–child interactions. In addition to child gains, then, collateral effects on parents who implement PRT have also been documented, including positive family interactions (R.L. Koegel, Bimbela, & Schreibman, 1996) and positive affect of parents toward their children (Schreibman, Kaneko, & Koegel, 1991).

Finally, from a developmental perspective, teaching parents to provide frequent, natural interactions with their children may have positive effects on the development of joint attention and subsequent language acquisition. For example, Siller and Sigman (2002) looked at the behaviors of caregivers of children with autism during play interactions. Specifically, the authors were interested in the extent to which a parent's behavior was synchronized with the child's focus of attention and ongoing activity. Following baseline, assessment of development and language skills were taken at 1-, 10-, and 16-year follow-ups. The results of the study indicated that parents who initially synchronized their interactions by entering their children's focus of attention during play had children who developed better joint attention and language at each of the follow-up assessments than caregivers who showed lower levels of synchronization. This study not only suggests the importance of parent–child interactions but also indicates the importance of following the child's lead. In fact, studies have shown that children "learn new words best in joint attentional interactions, in which children and adults coordinate their attention to each other and an object of mutual interest" (Carpenter & Tomasello, 2000, p. 33).

The emphasis on teaching parents to incorporate intervention procedures into their natural environment and throughout their child's waking hours relates to the transactional model of development (Sameroff, 1975; Sameroff & Chandler, 1975). According to this model, child development is understood as a transactional process that entails interplay among the child's behavior, caregiver responses to the child's behavior, and the broader environmental context that influences the behaviors of both the child and the caregiver (McLean, 1990; McLean & Snyder-McLean, 1978; Sameroff, 1987; Sameroff & Fiese, 1990, 2000; Warren, Yoder, & Leew, 2002). Thus, child development is greatly influenced by the reciprocal, natural interactions between caregiver and child. According to Wetherby and Prizant (2000), "The nature of the social, communication, and language impairments in autism can best be understood by reflecting on the acquisition process from a transactional developmental perspective" (p. 3). By addressing these impairments in a natural context, PRT fits within this model of development: Parents are taught to target core areas of autism by implementing procedures that motivate their children to respond to and engage in typical interactions, thereby moving their children toward a more typical developmental trajectory.

Natural Environments

An important area of concern for children with autism has related to issues of spontaneity, generalization, and maintenance of treatment gains (Gresham & MacMillan, 1998). Thus, there has been an increase in development of interventions that focus on strategies of PBS (Carr et al., 2002; Horner et al., 1990; L.K. Koegel, Koegel, & Dunlap, 1996), and improved generalization and maintenance that also can be delivered in natural settings and environments began to emerge (National Research Council, 2001). Indeed, at the heart of a core area of intervention is the generalization and maintenance of intervention gains, particularly as they relate to responding coming under the control of natural environmental stimuli.

In a study of NLP, R.L. Koegel, O'Dell, and Koegel (1987) compared the effects of a traditional teaching approach and NLP to produce generalized and spontaneous initial verbal responding in children with autism. The analogue condition consisted of language teaching that was clinician directed, incorporated drilling of target behaviors until acquisition was reached, and employed arbitrary reinforcement that was not functional within the interaction. In the NLP condition, motivational components were incorporated into standard discrete trial teaching opportunities such as stimulus items chosen by the child, maintenance tasks interspersed with acquisition tasks, rewarding attempts to respond, and natural reinforcers directly related to the task (see Table 1.1). The results of this study indicated that children in the NLP condition displayed a higher rate and accuracy of correct responding, demonstrated more spontaneous utterances, and generalized language outside of the clinic setting.

Further examination of the motivational components packaged in the NLP documented collateral improvements in nontargeted behaviors and generalized areas of responding. These areas include decreases in disruptive behaviors (R.L. Koegel, Koegel, & Surratt, 1992) (see Figure 1.1), improved child affect (R.L. Koegel, O'Dell, & Dunlap, 1988), improvements in speech intelligibility (R.L. Koegel, Camarata, Koegel, Ben-Tall, & Smith, 1998), improvements in academic learning (Dunlap & Kern, 1993; Dunlap, Kern-Dunlap, Clarke, & Robbins, 1991), decreases in stereotypic and restrictive behavior (Baker, 2000; Baker, Koegel, & Koegel, 1998), and improvements in social areas (Gaylord-Ross, Haring, Breen, & Pitts-Conway, 1984; L.K. Koegel, Camarata, Valdez-Menchaca, & Koegel, 1998a; R.L. Koegel, Dyer, & Bell, 1987; R.L. Koegel &

Table 1.1.   Differences between common discrete trial and Pivotal Response Treatment (PRT) conditions

	Common discrete trial	PRT condition (inclusion of motivational components)
Stimulus item	Chosen by clinician	Chosen by child
	Repeated until criterion is met	Varied every few trials
	Phonologically easy to produce, irrespective of whether it is functional in the natural environment	
Prompts	Manual (e.g., touch tip of tongue, hold lips together)	Clinician repeats item
Interaction	Clinician holds up stimulus item	Clinician and child play with stimulus item (i.e., stimulus item is functional within interaction)
	Stimulus item not functional within interaction	
Response	Correct responses or successive approximations reinforced	Looser shaping contingency so that attempts to respond verbally (except those involving self-stimulation) are also reinforced
Consequences	Edible reinforcers paired with social reinforcers	Natural reinforcers (e.g., opportunity to play with stimulus item) are paired with social reinforcers

From Koegel, R.L., O'Dell, M.C., & Koegel, L.K. (1987). A Natural Language Paradigm for teaching non-verbal autistic children. *Journal of Autism and Developmental Disorders, 17,* 191 (Table 1); Copyright © 1992 Springer Science and Business Media; adapted with kind permission of Springer Science and Business Media.

Frea, 1993). Thus, by targeting an area central to the disorder of autism, such as motivation, widespread improvements could be produced.

One of the key features of natural language approaches is that generalization and maintenance are essentially built into the intervention, making them readily applicable for natural settings and environments (Camarata, 1995, 1996). This is an important consideration for school systems as the push toward educating children with disabilities in general education classrooms becomes increasingly influential (Camarata, 1996). Perhaps more important, though, is that naturalistic approaches have implications for delivering treatment in home and community settings, providing families with a goodness of fit intervention (Albin et al., 1996). Indeed, this represents a core area of service delivery for children with autism: If the intervention fits naturally within the sociocultural context of the family system (Bernheimer et al., 1990), parents would be more likely to provide treatment across multiple settings and throughout the child's waking hours to produce rapid, generalized, and sustainable improvements in their child's behavior and development.

SPECIALIZED CURRICULUM

Curricula in the PRT model have been designed to relate to broader areas of behavioral, cognitive-behavioral, and developmental research. That is, treatment begins early, is intensive, and is delivered in natural environments through a parent edu-

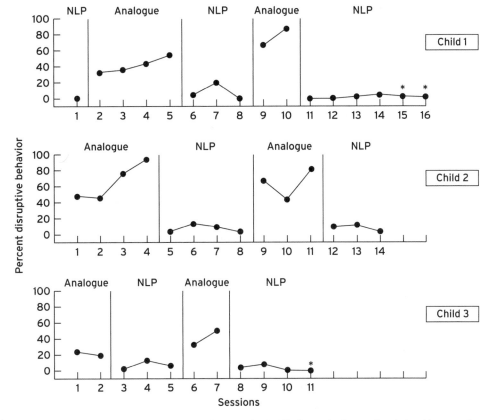

Figure 1.1. Language intervention and disruptive behavior. In this figure, *Analogue* refers to teaching opportunities using a standard discrete trial paradigm. *NLP* refers to Natural Language Paradigm. The NLP included motivational components of Pivotal Response Treatment. (From Koegel, R.L., Koegel, L.K., & Surratt, A.V. [1992]. Language intervention and disruptive behavior in preschool children with autism. *Journal of Autism and Developmental Disorders, 22*[2], 149 [Figure 1]; Copyright © 1992 Springer Science and Business Media; reprinted with kind permission of Springer Science and Business Media.)

cation model and a parent–professional collaboration model in the schools and in other settings. Teaching content and instruction is then specialized to address central deficits in autism—such as communication and social interaction—through a focus on core areas of intervention in autism, particularly motivation.

Generally, *curriculum* implies that the scope and sequence of a teaching procedure is well defined, such that it can be readily and effectively implemented and replicated. In addition, the National Research Council (2001), in an overview of comprehensive models for the treatment of autism, has referred to curriculum as the design of the environment, materials, and teaching interactions. Thus, the development of a comprehensive model should include a focus on clearly identifying the scope and sequence of treatment programs and describe how the environment, materials, and teaching interactions may be arranged, used, and implemented to produce widespread and generalized improvements. The following sections, then, discuss the goals and implications, environment, materials, and teaching interactions of a specialized curriculum. These are focused on core areas of intervention for children with autism and are embedded within the scope and sequence of the general education curriculum for typically developing children.

Goals and Implications of the Pivotal Response Treatment Curriculum

As indicated previously, the primary goals of PRT are to produce improvements that allow children with autism to move toward a typical developmental trajectory and to provide them with the opportunity to lead meaningful lives in natural, inclusive settings. To address these goals, the scope and sequence of the PRT curriculum is based on the general education curriculum for typically developing children rather than on an entirely separate curriculum. That is, components of the PRT curriculum focus on *how* to teach the general education curriculum by targeting motivation as a core area for intervention.

Adapting the general education curriculum to include motivational procedures has some important implications. First, although targeting motivation may be critical for children with autism, using motivational procedures may optimize the general education curriculum for all students. For instance, allowing preschool-age children to gain access to a preferred game by first dictating the letters on the box (e.g., for Mr. Potato Head) may have benefits for all children learning to identify letters of the alphabet. As children get older, baking desired items may be helpful when learning to add, subtract, multiply, and divide fractions. Thus, a focus on motivation as a core area for children with autism may allow for improvements in the general education curriculum and benefits for all children.

As stated previously, PRT does not require a separate curriculum for children with autism. Rather, the goal is to enrich the scope and sequence of the general education curriculum to include motivational procedures. Modifications to the general education curriculum, therefore, may be minimal, which in turn may be beneficial for ensuring a goodness of fit for both families and professionals (Albin et al., 1996). However, if the goal is to minimize the modifications necessary for children with autism to learn from the general education curriculum, the implication is that intervention should begin as early as possible. As detailed previously, the literature has overwhelmingly suggested the need for early intervention, particularly as it relates to broad developmental changes for children with autism. Thus, the sequence of PRT begins at a young age by targeting core areas of intervention that will motivate children with autism to become increasingly responsive to natural environmental stimuli and to acquire the scope of the general curriculum.

A third implication is that many children with autism do not begin receiving intervention at a young age. Likewise, some children who are provided with PRT early on may require additional modifications across the scope and sequence of the general education curriculum. Yet, the general education curriculum can still be used as a guide for what to teach while motivational procedures are infused into both the general education curriculum and the principle of partial participation (Baumgart et al., 1982). This principle suggests that some level of participation in an activity or instruction across the general education curriculum may be valuable for children with autism. Both researchers (Dunlap & Kern, 1993, 1996; Dunlap et al., 1991; Janney & Snell, 2004; Kern & Dunlap, 1998) and parents (Nickels, 1996) have discussed the conceptual and practical framework for modifying curriculum for individuals with disabilities (see Chapter 3). Many modifications include offering choices (Bambara,

Child choice is a key motivational component of the Pivotal Response Treatment (PRT) intervention model. This clinician is creating language opportunities around a game selected by the children.

Ager, & Koger, 1994; Dunlap, Foster-Johnson, Clarke, Kern, & Childs, 1995; Dunlap et al., 1991) and varying the size and duration of a task (Dunlap, Dyer, & Koegel, 1983; Dunlap et al., 1991; Weld & Evans, 1990) that relates directly to the motivational procedures described in the PRT model.

As discussed, the general education curriculum provides a useful model for identifying the direction of what is to be taught to children with autism in the PRT model. Although a discussion of the entire curriculum for typically developing children is beyond the scope of this chapter, it is important to describe how the environment, materials, and teaching interactions can be arranged to include motivational procedures across the scope and sequence of the general education curriculum. The following section provides examples from the scope of the general education curriculum for typically developing children and how the motivational procedures of PRT can be applied sequentially to optimize the curriculum for all children. It is helpful to keep in mind that the motivational procedures of PRT include using child choice, rewarding attempts, interspersing maintenance and acquisition tasks, and using natural and direct consequences.

Young Children   Social communication develops with little systematic teaching for typically developing children. Spradlin and Brady (1999) suggested, however, that children with autism often fail to comprehend the communicative efforts of caregivers. As discussed previously, cognitive-behavioral research in the area of motivation has indicated that children with autism have a difficult time learning the response–reinforcer contingency (R.L. Koegel & Egel, 1979; R.L. Koegel, O'Dell, & Dunlap,

1988), leading to low levels of responding and the phenomenon of learned helplessness (Miller & Seligman, 1975; Overmier & Seligman, 1967; Seligman, 1972; Seligman et al., 1976; Seligman & Maier, 1967). Thus, PRT's initial goal is to eliminate the hypothesized learned helplessness by using motivational procedures to force exposure to the response–reinforcer contingency and thereby develop intentional communication, first words, and expressive language.

For young children, both the environment and teachers (e.g., parents and family members, professionals, peers) are arranged to provide frequent opportunities to use, comprehend, and respond to the natural consequences of language. An overly structured setting is not necessary to implement PRT; rather, the focus is on arranging all environments to be readily accessible for natural language opportunities to occur. One of the advantages of teaching children with autism in natural environments is that environmental arrangements can be incorporated across settings. This provides a context for natural learning opportunities to bring responding under the control of natural environmental stimuli.

Generally, arranging the environment involves including in the setting preferred materials that the child is likely to find motivating across environments and routines. Until children reach preschool age, the majority of their time is spent at home. Thus, families will want to arrange the environment by placing highly preferred stimuli throughout their home; ordinary involvement of these stimuli in during daily routines will elicit natural language opportunities. Environmental arrangements that are often utilized by families and teachers include placing highly desirable items in sight but out of reach and "breaking up" preferred items (e.g., a child is provided with a part of a toy instead of an entire toy so additional opportunities for language can be created by the child's requesting additional items or pieces) (Kaiser, Hancock, & Nietfeld, 2000). These environmental arrangements and others are detailed in the following paragraphs.

In the PRT model, it is important to identify preferred items that are likely to motivate the child to respond. When intervening early with young children, materials generally include age-appropriate toys (e.g., trains, dolls, car ramps, musical toys), games or activities (e.g., chasing, being tickled or thrown in the air), and foods (e.g., snacks, favorite treats). Also, the natural environment provides a context for many child interests. For instance, a child may be motivated to gain access to a door to either enter or leave a room. Similarly, a child may be interested in getting down from his or her highchair following a meal.

Incorporating the child's interests is individualized, as desired items and activities vary for each child. One advantage of including family members in the intervention is that parents are viewed as the experts on their child. That is, parents are often very skilled at knowing which items and activities are likely to be of high interest to their child. Clearly, determining those motivating items and activities is critical to both the arrangement of the environment and to teaching interactions.

Teaching interactions in the PRT model incorporate motivational procedures (see Table 1.1) into discrete trials, wherein antecedents and consequences are systematically manipulated to produce a desired response or behavior. Components of the procedure include the following:

- The child is engaged in a natural environment—such as the home—that is arranged to stimulate interest through use of preferred items and desired activities.

- The caregiver follows the child's lead and allows the child to become interested in a particular stimulus (e.g., the child reaches for or points to a ball).

- The caregiver provides a clear opportunity to respond that is related to the child's interest (e.g., the caregiver asks, "Do you want the ball?").

- The caregiver immediately provides the preferred item contingent upon the child's attempt to verbally respond (e.g., the child replies, "Baa"). (See also Chapter 8 for more details.)

This approach to teaching language is consistent with multiple theoretical orientations, developmental approaches (e.g., Rogers, Hall, Osaki, Reaven, & Herbison, 2001), and naturalistic approaches such as incidental teaching at the Walden Preschool (McGee, Morrier, & Daly, 1999, 2001) and milieu teaching (Kaiser et al., 2000), which focus on producing broad developmentally crucial improvements by targeting core deficits and areas of intervention in autism. Often, preferred items are placed where the child can see a desired item but cannot obtain it (e.g., on a high shelf). This draws the child's interest to the item, creates opportunities for language, and motivates the child to produce a response in order to obtain the item.

In addition to placing preferred items in sight and out of reach, parents can arrange the environment by providing opportunities that break up a preferred item. Rather than allowing a child to gain access to an entire item, a child is provided with a piece or part of the item. For instance, instead of providing a box full of blocks, the child can receive one block at a time, creating multiple opportunities for language. During mealtime, the child can be given small amounts of juice, creating opportunities to continuously request more juice. Rather than tickling a child continuously, the child can receive tickles for short periods of time to allow for additional opportunities to ask for more tickling.

Finally, parents can modify their own behavior when anticipating what will motivate the child, especially during daily routines. Typically, this involves a short time delay so that the child becomes aware that the routine has been broken. For example, when walking into a dark room, the parent can wait in the dark to provide an opportunity for the child to request that the lights be turned on. Instead of opening bottles, jars, or containers, the parent can provide an opportunity for the child to use language to gain access to what is inside. Instead of simply dressing the child for a favorite activity, the parent can wait between providing items of clothing to give the child a chance to ask for assistance.

Preschool   In preschool settings, typically developing children are expected to apply social-communicative skills by responding to and initiating communication with new and unfamiliar adults (i.e., teachers and school personnel) and interacting with their peers. In addition, a preschool curriculum for typically developing children often includes preacademic tasks—such as letter identification, one-to-one correspondence, and color identification—that prepare children for the academic expectations of kindergarten and further schooling. For children with autism, impairments in communication and social interaction often lead to difficulties in interacting with adults and peers and in learning new tasks. Therefore, the goal of PRT during the preschool years is to coordinate implementation of the motivational procedures between home and school such that children with autism generalize social communicative skills to new environments (e.g., preschool classroom, playground) and people (e.g., teachers, peers) as well as acquire the preacademic skills necessary to enter kindergarten.

For preschool-age children, the environment and teachers are arranged just as they are for young children. That is, the goal of providing frequent opportunities to experience the natural consequences of language is coordinated across settings (home and preschool). Typical preschool classrooms are ideal settings for teaching children with autism because they often include highly preferred, age-appropriate toys and games; a relatively small adult–child ratio; and typically developing children to model appropriate behavior. Thus, many of the environmental manipulations necessary for the home are essentially built directly into the general preschool curriculum (e.g., in sight but out of reach, breaking it up). It becomes the responsibility of school personnel to take of advantage of the preschool environment by embedding natural learning opportunities into interactions between teachers (both professionals and peers) and children with autism such that responding comes under control of typical preschool stimuli.

As indicated previously, the preschool classroom generally includes various items that are likely to be of high interest for many children (with and without autism), such as toys, games, activities, and foods. In addition, preschool settings often include a context for child interests not commonly found in the home. For example, a child may be motivated to gain access to a swing or large playground equipment. For some children with autism who have limited interests, however, it may be helpful for school personnel to coordinate with parents to incorporate those items that are most motivating. For instance, if a child with autism finds musical toys to be highly desirable, it would be advantageous to have such toys readily accessible in the preschool classroom. With many children in the classroom, it is likely that other children will be interested in musical toys as well.

In preschool environments, an emphasis is placed on identifying materials that are interesting to all of the children. As such, social interaction and responsivity to others can be taught and encouraged. Coordination between school personnel and parents may help identify the items that are both popular among all children and appropriate for the classroom. Clearly, determining which items and activities that are motivating for all children is critical to the teaching interactions that take place among children with autism, teachers, and peers in the classroom.

As indicated previously, the transition to preschool represents three shifts for typically developing children that guide the teaching interactions in the PRT model. First, intervention is coordinated to a new setting—preschool—such that children with autism can generalize their skills and language with new adults (i.e., teachers and school personnel). As a result, components of the procedure are identical to those implemented by parents in the home, where motivational procedures are systematically incorporated into natural language opportunities. Also, preschool teachers and aides can create natural learning opportunities in much the same ways that parents do in the home for young children with autism. Specifically, they can place preferred items where the child can see them but cannot obtain them freely, provide "break-up" opportunities to create multiple interactions, and anticipate the child's motivation during daily routines. Again, the goal is to coordinate intervention such that children with autism become responsive to new environments and interactive partners and thereby generalize these improvements.

A second shift is to incorporate the motivational procedures into interactions between children with autism and their typically developing peers. Thus, components of the procedure are modified to include the following:

- Children are engaged in either the classroom or on the playground, which is arranged to stimulate interest through use of preferred items and desired activities.

- The teacher follows the children's lead and allows the children to become interested in a particular stimulus (e.g., the children reach for or point to a container of blocks; the children walk toward a swing set).

- The teacher prompts one of the children (either the child with autism or a peer) and provides a clear opportunity to respond that is related to the item or activity of interest to the child with autism (e.g., "Do you want to play blocks?", "Do you want to swing?").

- The teacher prompts one of the children to immediately provide the preferred item contingent upon the child's attempt to verbally respond (e.g., "Blocks," "Sw-ee").

Thus, the teacher shifts his or her role to a facilitator such that peers become the intervention agents for children with autism and assist with teaching age-appropriate language, social, and play skills. In addition to targeting language, then, interacting with typically developing peers addresses the socialization needs of children with autism. Furthermore, the previously listed components may also be used to help children with autism learn age- and classroom-appropriate social skills, such as sharing and turn taking. This approach to teaching language by using peers in preschool environments is consistent with many preschool programs for children with autism (Handleman & Harris, 2001), including the Walden Preschool (McGee et al., 1999, 2001) and the LEAP program (Strain & Cordisco, 1994).

Although much of the general preschool curriculum centers on play, a third shift during the preschool years is a focus on preacademic tasks. Motivational procedures can be incorporated into natural interactions to teach all children various academic skills. For example, children begin learning and are expected to accurately identify the names of colors. Opportunities to name colors can be incorporated into interactions with either a teacher or a peer. Thus, if a child is interested in playing with blocks, he or she can be provided with one block at a time, contingent upon an attempt to name the color of the block. Similarly, a child can obtain his or her choice of crayon or marker after making a verbal attempt to request the color. During snack time, children can name the colors of M&Ms before eating them.

Another preacademic task may be learning the names of body parts. Certain preschool games—such as Silly Faces and Mr. Potato Head—have some natural learning opportunities for naming body parts. Thus, a teacher or peer would get control of all of the pieces and have the child ask for a preferred part (e.g., eyes, nose, mouth). If a child likes to be tickled, he or she can request the part of the body to be tickled (e.g., by saying, "Tummy or feet"). Finally, opportunities to name body parts can be interspersed into interactions. For instance, if a child is playing with blocks, the teacher or a peer can vary the task by placing the block on a body part (head), asking the child where the block is, and allowing the child obtain to the block after naming the body part.

Prereading skills—such as letter identification—are also frequently taught in preschool. Many games and toys that come in boxes have their names written on the box. Thus, a child can say or point to the letter to obtain the game. At lunchtime, a child can identify the letters on a milk carton or bag of potato chips to have either one opened.

Finally, preschool-age children also begin learning how to count with one-to-one correspondence. To obtain preferred items, such as toy cars, children can count the number of cars and then be provided with an opportunity to play with them. On the playground, children can request the number of pushes they want on a swing from an adult or a peer. During lunchtime or snack time, children can count the number of pretzels, carrot sticks, or apple slices to obtain a desired food.

Elementary School   Social-communication skills continue to develop as typical children make the transition from preschool to kindergarten to grade school. Responsivity, initiations, and social conversations become increasingly sophisticated as children consistently interact with family members, school personnel, and peers. An elementary school curriculum includes academic subjects—such as reading, writing, spelling, mathematics, science, and social studies—that increase in difficulty from year to year. Impairments in communication, social interaction, and behaviors may make it difficult for children with autism to achieve socially and academically. Thus, the goal of PRT during the elementary school years is ongoing collaboration between home and school such that motivational procedures allow children with autism to benefit from the social and academic aspects of the general education curriculum.

With the exception of kindergarten, classroom environments for elementary-school age children are much less likely to include toys and games than preschool classrooms. However, the goal of providing frequent opportunities to experience the natural consequence of language continues to be critical for the social and academic development of children with autism. Therefore, some simple arranging of the environment remains necessary. First, teachers can easily design the classroom such that students are afforded many choices (discussed in the following paragraph). Next, it may be helpful to organize seating arrangements into small groups rather than rows. Grouping students into clusters of four, for example, may increase the likelihood of peer interaction and support among all students.

Because highly preferred toys and games are not commonly found in elementary school classrooms, the materials teachers use should include many choices that are likely to increase interest for children with autism to attempt and complete various tasks. For instance, bookshelves can offer many different titles, topics, and genres of books. Students can also choose among various writing instruments: pencils, pens, crayons, markers, or colored pencils. Similarly, choice can be incorporated into work that is assigned. For example, during study periods, children can choose the order of either the work assigned or the order in which they complete a task. Also, children can choose the book that is read to the class or the color of the dry-erase pens that a teacher uses to write on a whiteboard. Choices can also be made on the playground during recess and lunchtime that may foster social interaction between children with autism and their typically developing peers. These include choosing a game or activity or a lunch table. Similar to both young and preschool-age children with autism, it may be helpful for school personnel to coordinate with parents such that the number of motivating choices can be maximized in the classroom. Again, incorporating materials that offer children choices has implications for the learning of all children.

For typically developing children, the transition from preschool to elementary school is similar to the one from home to preschool in that the children generalize their skills to new settings (e.g., a new school, a new classroom, the playground) and are expected to interact with both school personnel and peers. Thus, components of the procedure used to modify the curriculum for younger children with autism remain applicable during the elementary school years. The major shift for typically developing children during the elementary school years is increased attention to academics. Thus, teaching interactions in the PRT model during the elementary school years are guided by an additional focus on embedding the motivational procedures into the academic curriculum such that children with autism develop a wide range of academic skills.

Throughout the day, task variation and reinforcing attempts should be incorporated across tasks and assignments. That is, the size, duration, pacing, and difficulty of assignments, lessons, and lectures can be varied to increase motivated responding. Likewise, it is important to reward children with verbal and/or written praise for attempting to complete a task. In addition to these techniques, the following suggestions provide examples of how to supplement the general academic curriculum with additional motivational procedures.

Reading is a core academic subject that typically developing children begin learning early in the elementary years. Motivational procedures can be used to optimize the reading curriculum for all students. In addition to choosing books, children can be prompted to read information throughout their environment. For instance, children can be asked to read words printed on a bag of cookies before opening it. When coloring, children can read the words printed on a box of markers.

Similar modifications can be made to increase motivation for writing and spelling. For example, children can write a letter to a friend or a postcard to a grandparent. Instead of copying printed words on a writing worksheet, children can choose the writing instrument of their choice (e.g., pen, pencil, marker) and write the title of the book they choose to read. In order to go to recess, children can first write a couple of sentences indicating with whom they are going to play or what they are going to play.

During math, children can add, subtract, multiply, and divide to obtain the number of chips, pretzels, or cookies they want. Similarly, when learning about money, children can "purchase" small treats or snacks. When teaching children to work with fractions, it may be helpful to bake a cake or brownies that involve fractions for specific ingredients (e.g., $2\frac{1}{2}$ cups of sugar, $\frac{1}{2}$ stick of butter).

Middle School and High School   For typically developing children, the emphasis on academics continues as they make the transition first from elementary to middle school and again from middle school to high school. Thus, the goals of PRT during the middle and high school years remain the same as they were during the elementary years: home–school collaboration to ensure that the general curriculum includes motivational procedures to produce meaningful benefits for children with autism. The materials used in middle and high school may continue to require similar modifications as the materials used during the elementary school years (incorporating a wide range of choices). Also, implementing the motivational procedures into the teaching interactions across academic subjects will be quite similar to the elementary school years.

If a child has been receiving a specialized curriculum since preschool or earlier, it is possible that very little special arrangements, if any, may be necessary by middle and/or high school. When modifications are necessary, the major shift during the middle and high school years is the design of the environment, which may already be inherently optimal for children with autism as typical middle schools already contain elements that are optimal for an autism curriculum. First, the change from elementary school to middle and high school represents a change from a single teacher in one classroom to multiple teachers in multiple classrooms. Thus, there are multiple environments and multiple intervention agents. In coordinating implementation of the motivational procedures into the curriculum, each teacher, with help from special education staff, becomes responsible for modifying teaching interactions for only one academic subject (rather than one teacher for all subjects across a child's day). However, not all children require specialized intervention.

A second environmental advantage during the middle and high school years is an arrangement that is already set up for heterogeneity. That is, middle and high schools often include various academic tracks and subtracks to meet individualized needs for a wide range of student abilities. As children with autism get older, they may excel in some subjects and need additional support in others. The typical design of the middle and high school environments, then, supports the individualized needs of children with autism as it does for all children.

Curriculum for Clinical Intervention

The previously described curriculum options describe how one might implement a PRT intervention within a general education curriculum if a child begins intervention at a very young age. In many cases, however, children with autism receive clinical intervention outside of their schools. Also, some children do not receive early intervention but begin intervention at a much older age. The examples in Table 1.2 might be helpful, although the sequence may vary from child to child. These examples show illustrations of how one might begin intervention at a variety of different ages, then progress from beginning to intermediate to advanced intervention targets. It should also be noted that all targets and objectives listed below should be individualized to children's particular needs. The following case history illustrates how a comprehensive PRT intervention plan was implemented for one child who began intervention at a young age.

Case Example

At the age of 2 years, Peter was diagnosed with autism by a developmental pediatrician. His parents reported that they had heard him say seven words; however, these words were not used functionally or consistently.

In addition to communication delays, Peter engaged in a number of inappropriate behaviors. He regularly engaged in tantrums and aggression to request desired items, to terminate interactions, and to protest when he was denied access to a desired item or activity. Also, he generally used nonverbal communication, such as leading his parents to desired objects. Transitions were becoming increasingly difficult for Peter and were often accompanied by crying and disruptive behavior.

Socially, Peter did not demonstrate any joint attention behaviors, did not show an interest in his peers, and did not engage in simple interactive games or pretend play. Rather, Peter preferred to engage in repetitive and restricted interactions with items — such as spending unusual amounts of time playing with public pay telephones — that were followed by tantrums when his mother, Lisa, tried to leave the pay telephone or engage him in appropriate activities.

Consistent with the features of a comprehensive model of service delivery, intervention began early (2 years, 2 months) and focused on reducing the core symptom areas of autism — beginning with teaching Lisa procedures to improve his motivation — to address Peter's behavioral excesses and deficits. Specifically, initial goals of the program were directed toward increasing Peter's motivation to respond, increasing his production of functional verbalizations, and replacing his challenging and inappropriate behaviors with functionally equivalent behaviors.

In order to maintain a high level of intensity, procedures were coordinated with all of Peter's care providers across all of his daily environments. Because Peter spent the most time throughout each day with his mother, Lisa began participating in a parent education program that could be implemented across the family's daily activities and routines. Lisa was introduced to the motivational procedures of PRT, as highlighted in *How to Teach Pivotal Behaviors to Children with Autism: A Training Manual* (R.L. Koegel et al., 1989), and was taught how to incorporate their use into interactions with Peter throughout the day and in natural environments (e.g., home, the park, restaurants, the grocery store).

At first, Peter did not respond to his mother's attempts to implement the motivational procedures and elicit language; instead, he engaged in tantrums that included crying, screaming, hitting, and pulling his mother's hair. Within a couple weeks of implementing PRT, however, Peter's tantrums decreased in both frequency and intensity, and he gradually began to use verbal attempts to communicate.

Lisa was taught to provide natural reinforcers (i.e., preferred toys, activities, and foods) contingent upon Peter's attempts to verbally communicate. Initially, all of Peter's

Table 1.2. Illustrations of the progression of intervention started at different stages

Area	Objective	Example
Beginning		
Communicative intent	Teach the child the relationship between his or her vocalizations and reinforcement/consequences.	Sally loves her Elmo doll. Her mother models saying, "Elmo." Sally reaches for doll and says, "Ooo." Her mother reinforces the attempt by giving Sally the Elmo doll.
First words	Teach the child that each object has a specific label and how to increase spontaneous/independent use of expressive language.	Francisco and his father are playing with a toy box of favorite toys. Francisco's father takes out a car and asks, "What's this?" Francisco says, "Ca," and his father reinforces this attempt. Francisco's father then takes out a ball and asks, "Now what do you need?" Francisco responds, "Ball." Francisco's father has him label each toy presented while his son remains motivated by this activity.
Two-word combinations	Expand length and variety of child's utterances. Introducing this step is recommended after the child uses at least 50 single words spontaneously/independently.	Timmy's mother is pushing him on a swing. His mother pauses the swing and asks, "More swing?" Timmy says, "Mo swing." His mother pushes several more times and then asks, "What do you want?" Timmy replies, "Mo swing," so his mother continues pushing.
Beginning question asking	Introduce the child to beginning queries (e.g., "What's that?" "Where is it?"), and extend the child's ability to independently learn new information from the environment.	Luke's grandmother places his favorite candy into an opaque bag without him seeing. She prompts him to ask, "What's that?" Luke looks up and says, "Dat?" His grandmother pulls out the candy and as she gives it to him, she says, "It's a piece of candy."
Beginning initiations with peers and siblings	Teach the child to initiate expressive language (e.g., requests) with siblings and peers.	While taking turns playing with a ball ramp toy, Andrew's mother prompts him to ask his sister for the ball. Andrew looks at his sister and says, "Ball." His sister then gives Andrew the ball, and he gets to roll it down the ramp.
Intermediate		
Multiple cues	Teach the child to attend to multiple features/attributes of an object and to expand the complexity of his or her receptive and expressive language.	During snack time, Sila's father tells him he can choose either a green apple or a red apple. Sila requests, "Green apple," and correctly retrieves the green apple from the plate.
Verbs	Expand the length, variety, and complexity of the child's utterances. Following the developmental sequence of verb acquisition is recommended.	While playing with bubbles, Spencer pops all of the bubbles. His grandfather then asks Spencer if he wants to blow more bubbles. Spencer replies, "Blow bubbles," and gets to blow more bubbles into the air.

Multiple-word utterances (three or more words)	Continue to extend the child's length of utterances.	David and his father are playing ball. David's father asks, "Throw ball up or kick ball fast?" David replies, "Throw ball." His father asks, "Throw ball where?" David says, "Throw ball up." His father then throws the ball up, and David runs after it.
Question asking	Extend the child's repertoire of queries to include remaining "wh-" questions (e.g. "Whose is it?" "Who is it?" "When?"), and increase the sophistication of question asking. Also use queries to target language structures such as prepositions and past tense verbs.	Addie and her teacher are playing with balloons. Addie closes her eyes while her teacher hides the balloon. Addie then opens her eyes and asks, "Where is it?" Her teacher replies, "Where is what?" Addie uses a longer question and asks, "Where is the balloon?" Her teacher says, "It's under the table." Addie quickly runs to get the balloon from under the table.
Initiations with peers and siblings	Broaden the child's complexity of initiations toward peers and siblings to include longer utterances, directives, comments, and more sophisticated play.	During art, Monica needs a new marker. She tries to get one but cannot reach it. Her preschool aide says, "Ask your friend who has the can of markers. Remember, use her name." Monica then gestures toward the marker can and says, "Maria, I need a marker." Her peer gives her the marker can. A few moments later, Monica's aide walks over and prompts Monica to show her drawing to her neighbor. Monica turns to her peer and comments, "I made a sun." Her peer replies, "I made flowers and they're growing."
Initial play dates	Develop the initial set of skills necessary for successful play dates, including responsivity, turn-taking, and sharing. Use priming to familiarize the child with the activities/games to be done during the play date.	Nate and his mother review how to make fruit smoothies and play several board games the night before his play date. The next afternoon, his friend comes over. Nate's mother has Nate ask his friend what kind of fruit and ice cream he wants to use. Nate's mother also has him show his friend how to make the smoothie in the blender and pour it in the cup. Nate and his friend then play several of Nate's favorite board games.
Preacademics	Target kindergarten readiness skills, including number, letter, color, and shape identification; counting; letter-to-sound correspondence; sight reading; and basic letter formation.	During lunch, Richie's father has him practice counting. Before giving Richie a handful of French fries, Richie's father asks him to count them and reminds him to use his index finger. Richie begins counting, "1, 2, 3, 4. Four fries." Richie's father gives him the plate of fries, and they enjoy lunch.

(continued)

Table 1.2. (continued)

Area	Objective	Example
Initial social conversation	Build the child's ability to participate in simple reciprocal social conversations with others, including on-topic question asking, on-topic comments, and on-topic initiations. Self-management is often a helpful tool for building these skills.	Jack loves to talk about airplanes but has difficulty making appropriate on-topic initiations when conversing with others about different subjects. His teacher is using self-management to help Jack learn to make appropriate on-topic initiations. Each time Jack makes an on-topic initiation following a subject introduced by his teacher, he gives himself a point and gets to trade it for a favorite candy. His teacher says, "Today I ate vanilla ice cream." Jack replies "I also like ice cream," and gives himself a point.
Advanced		
Reading	Facilitate all reading skills being taught at school, including sight words, phonics, and reading comprehension. Home–school coordination is very helpful in meeting this goal.	Before playing on the computer, Sadie's mother has her select the right word from an array of three different words. After Sadie picks the word computer, she gets to play her favorite computer game. Sadie's mother has her practice her list of sight words from school throughout the day using natural reinforcers (e.g., when Sadie wants to ride her bike, she has to identify the correct sight word).
Writing	Target all age-appropriate writing skills, including letter formation, word formation, and sentence formation. Home–school coordination is very helpful in meeting this goal.	Tyrone loves to color. Each time he wants a different crayon, his grandfather has him trace the name of the color before getting to use the desired crayon. This is helpful because in kindergarten Tyrone is currently learning to trace words and do some independent writing.
Priming	Support the child's ability to attend to, participate in, and succeed in the activities, instructions, content, and so forth presented at school. Priming is not a tool limited to advanced skills or upper grades; using it throughout intervention when appropriate, including during the preschool years, is recommended.	Each day after school, Eric's teacher has his mother review the storybook to be read during circle time the next day. This helps Eric become familiar with the story, facilitates his ability to stay focused during circle time, and facilitates his ability to make appropriate on-topic questions and comments.

Modifications/accommodations to the school curriculum	Facilitate the child's ability to master the school curriculum and participate to the best of his or her ability.	Math is one of Max's less preferred subjects, and he often becomes frustrated with the number of problems he needs to complete on a given worksheet. Instead of requiring Max to complete all 12 problems on the math worksheet, his teacher has him choose 6.
Homework	Enable the child to learn homework's content and participate in homework to the best of his or her ability.	Leslie's mother identifies natural reinforcers that she can incorporate into homework to help keep Leslie motivated to complete her assignments. Tonight, Leslie has to write five sentences about red objects. Leslie's mother collects an array of red objects that Leslie really likes (e.g., red licorice, a red ball, red nail polish). Each time Leslie writes a sentence about a preferred red object, she then gets to use that particular red item.
Advanced play dates	Expand the child's repertoire of skills necessary for successful play dates. Increase the child's independence in sustaining more sophisticated and longer play dates. Continue the use of priming as needed.	The day before her play date, Madison and her aide went to the bowling alley and practiced using the score board and cheering for each other. The next day, Madison's aide reminded her and her friends to take turns and to cheer for each other. Madison's aide then faded her presence and provided minimal prompting, only when necessary.
After-school/extracurricular/ sports activities	Further support the child's friendship development and social network. Also, continue to include the child in community settings with typically developing peers.	Andre loves to swim. His parents enroll him in the neighborhood swim team, of which many of Andre's classmates are also a part. Andre's aide participates as one of the swim assistants not only to build Andre's swimming skills but also to ensure he and his peers practice showing each other how to do specific strokes, cheer for each other, and work in teams.
Advanced social conversation	Extend the child's ability to participate in more elaborate and sophisticated reciprocal social conversations with others, including peers.	Todd experiences difficulty in sustaining conversations with peers for long periods of time without returning to a perseverative topic of interest. Todd practices expanding the length of time he stays on topic with his cousin.

verbal attempts to use expressive communication to request desired items were a single vowel sound: /a/. Thus, whether he was requesting a ball or a toy car, Peter demonstrated his motivation to respond by reaching out his hand and saying, "Aaaaaaaaaahhhh." In time, Peter's attempts to communicate more closely approximated the label of the desired items. That is, Peter began saying, "Ba" for ball, "Ca" for car, and "Uh" to be picked up. As his word attempts increased and his word differentiation developed, joint attention also emerged; Peter began to consistently and spontaneously use single words to request desired items and communicate his needs while looking at his mother or other familiar adult. Shortly after, Peter began combining two words (e.g., "Open door," "Blue ball," "All done") and occasionally using three-word utterances (e.g., "More cookie please").

Lisa also incorporated the motivational procedures of PRT in various community settings, allowing Peter to be exposed to the same stimuli, events, and people that typically developing children encounter. For example, Lisa created numerous learning opportunities for Peter at the park, beach, and playground. At the beach, for example, she taught Peter how to dig in the sand by providing natural reinforcers contingent upon Peter's attempts to say words such as *sand, water,* and *shovel.* Peter also was taken on trips to the grocery store and to meals with his family in restaurants. At the grocery store, Peter added preferred food items to the grocery cart by attempting to verbalize the label of each item (e.g., cookies, juice, crackers). Thus, Lisa implemented PRT throughout daily activities such that Peter was motivated to respond across all natural settings and environments.

Consistent with the breadth of the comprehensive model, Lisa also enrolled Peter in a full-inclusion preschool at age 3 so that Peter would benefit from socially interacting with typically developing peers. Lisa played an integral role in coordinating services with the preschool by assisting the teachers and instructional assistants in ensuring that the intensity of intervention remained high. Thus, the preschool staff was taught to incorporate the motivational techniques throughout the day such that Peter would benefit both socially and academically. For example, the staff optimized the preschool curriculum for all children by incorporating the motivational procedures of PRT to facilitate interactions between Peter and his peers. For example, during an art activity, the preschool staff prompted both Peter and his peers to request items (e.g., paper, glue, crayons) from one another. By the end of his first year of preschool, Peter consistently requested items from his peers, participated in age-appropriate games with his classmates, and had several friends with whom he commonly interacted both in the classroom and on the playground. In addition, he learned to name a variety of shapes, to label colors, to identify all of the letters of the alphabet, and to count up to 20 with one-to-one correspondence. Peter's language also continued to improve such that he was within the range of a typically developing 4-year-old child.

Today, Peter is 5½ years old. He is about to enter kindergarten and has no syntactical delays. He socially communicates with his peers and plays appropriately with them. He no longer requires special education services, and Lisa reports that he is one of the most popular students in his class. Peter has a best friend and a number of close friends, attends birthday parties, has regular play dates, and loves to make believe with his friends that they are popular television characters.

DISCUSSION OF CHAPTER CONCEPTS

This chapter has attempted to describe the development of a comprehensive approach to service delivery for children with autism in three ways. First, the key features of PRT—one such core treatment approach—were briefly defined. Second, a rationale for PRT has been described that demonstrates both the model's integration of critical intervention components and its relationship to broader areas of behavioral, cognitive-behavioral, and developmental research. Finally, a specialized curriculum has been discussed to systematically embed the motivational procedures of PRT into the scope and sequence of the general education curriculum by modifying the environment, materials, and teaching interactions.

DIRECTIONS FOR FUTURE RESEARCH

In discussing both a rationale for the PRT model and its implementation into the general education curriculum, some remaining implications have emerged that warrant future research. Although it has been emphasized throughout this chapter, the importance of intensive intervention from a young age for children with autism cannot be understated. The previously described curriculum addresses the scope of what is to be taught across a sequential continuum of a child's life. Yet, the PRT curriculum is optimized when children begin intervention early on this continuum. By beginning intervention early, in the home, and with families, modifications to the general education curriculum may be minimized, especially once children reach middle and high school. Clearly, this depends on the early identification of children with autism. More research in this area, focusing on early diagnosis and early implementation of intervention, is critical.

A second implication related to early intervention is that once intervention has commenced in the home, preschools are an optimal mechanism to implement the PRT curriculum for young children with autism due to the minimal demands and large number of opportunities for social interaction with peers. This is consistent with many other comprehensive models of intervention, many of which are considered preschool education programs (Handleman & Harris, 2001). Because PRT fits well within natural environments, one implication is the desirability of dissemination of the model to preschools where the curriculum can be implemented to affect large numbers of children from a young age.

A third implication is the need for schools to emphasize the social curriculum across the sequence of students' education. For children with autism, a social curriculum is implemented within the interactions between parents and young children and is inherent to the general preschool curriculum. As children enter elementary, middle, and high school, however, the general curriculum increases in the amount of academics required. Although academics are essential to education, a social curriculum continues to be important for all students and systematic intervention remains critical for children with autism.

Finally, there is the need to disseminate comprehensive models of service delivery so that they may be implemented on a larger scale. The most efficient ways to disseminate information and provide training for large numbers of families and professionals while maintaining a high fidelity of implementation warrants further research. As discussed previously, preschools may be one mechanism for broadly implementing the curriculum. Some literature also has indicated that educational interventions, such as the Direct Instruction model, can be brought to a larger scale (Englemann, 1980; Englemann, Becker, Carnine, & Gersten, 1988). Similar efforts have been made in the field of positive behavior support (PBS), including the training of institutional support staff and human service supervisors (Parsons & Reid, 1995; Parsons, Reid, & Green, 1996; Reid et al., 2003) as well as schoolwide systems change methods (Horner et al., 2004; Sugai et al., 2000; Sugai & Horner, 2002). Overall, this chapter has suggested that a focus on core areas of autism provides a comprehensive intervention resulting in broad improvements in the children's development with large improvements in quality of life for the entire family. Details of specific aspects of this model are provided in the following chapters.

2

A Screening, Training, and Education Program

First S.T.E.P.

Lynn Kern Koegel, Nicolette Nefdt,
Robert L. Koegel, Yvonne Bruinsma, and Rosy Matos Fredeen

The prevalence of autism spectrum disorders (ASDs) continues to increase at an alarming rate (Croen, Grether, Hoogstrate, & Selvin, 2002). Although studies have shown that the majority of parents report that symptom onset occurs before 2 years of age (Baghdadli, Picot, Pascal, Pry, & Aussilloux, 2003), autism is often not diagnosed until 2–3 years after the symptoms begin to appear (Filipek et al., 1999). This is despite the fact that screening tools can be used to reliably identify children at risk for autism as young as 18 months of age (Baron-Cohen & Allen, 1992). This need for earlier diagnosis is especially critical in light of a growing body of literature that suggests remarkable positive effects of early intervention (Connor, 1998; Lovaas, 1987; R.L. Koegel, Koegel, Frea, & Smith, 1995; Rogers, 1998). Specifically, empirical evidence suggests a much more positive developmental trajectory if intervention begins well before age 5 and even greater gains occur if intervention begins before age 3.

This chapter discusses the implementation of First S.T.E.P. (Screening, Training, and Education Program), an outreach program through the University of California, Santa Barbara's Autism Research and Training Center (ARTC). First S.T.E.P. addresses the issue of early identification and intervention with a three-part package to help increase the number of children identified as at risk for ASDs at an earlier age and, most important, to ensure these children's access to appropriate intervention services. The first component of this three-part package is First S.T.E.P.'s outreach project for pediatricians and health care workers, educators, parents, and community members to increase awareness of early signs of ASDs, such as social and communication delays. The second component consists of developmental screenings offered to families with concerns about their children's development. Finally, the third component involves a family support package for families whose children are at risk or meet the criteria for a developmental disability. Included in the package is specialized guidance in locating and obtaining services and case management as well as a workshop that is provided almost immediately after a developmental disability is detected. This workshop involves several hours of parent education and is designed to provide the parent with some initial skills and to bridge the gap between diagnosis and commencement of intervention services. This chapter discusses each of the project's components in greater detail and provides some data on the outcomes of the project.

PART I: OUTREACH

The goal of the outreach project is to increase the knowledge and awareness of the early behavioral indicators of ASDs in order to decrease the age at which children at risk for ASDs are referred for evaluation and, subsequently, to decrease the age at which specialized intervention services are begun. Unfortunately, even with evidence that children with ASDs can be reliably identified at 18 months (Baron-Cohen & Allen, 1992), the average age of diagnosis for children with autism in the United States is 3–4 years of age (Filipek et al., 1999). When considering early diagnosis, it is also noteworthy that many studies suggest that children with autism may start exhibiting symptoms before or near 12 months (cf. Osterling, Dawson, & Munson, 2002) and that parents notice symptoms much earlier than professionals. On average, there is a

12-month gap between the time a parent is first concerned about his or her child and the time at which the child receives an evaluation regarding these concerns (Siegel, Pliner, Eschler, & Elliot, 1988). In fact, children frequently do not receive a diagnosis of autism until 2–3 years after the onset of their symptoms (Filipek et al., 1999). This finding suggests that parents and/or pediatricians have not acted upon parental concerns over behavioral symptoms, possibly due to a lack of awareness about early signs or available options (Shah, 2001).

To identify children with disabilities at a younger age and, consequently, to begin intervention earlier, the outreach project targets awareness of early signs of autism and related developmental delays. The following methods were used for increasing awareness and referrals. Each area listed is discussed in detail.

- Presentations to health care providers, child care providers, families, and so forth on red flags for autism

- Radio, newspaper, and movie theater advertisements

- Notices in church newsletters

- Distribution of posters and flyers in English and Spanish

- Printed information in local resource directories

- Mailings of flyers with cover letters to doctors and other health care providers

- Exhibits at local festivals

- Presentations to pediatricians and their staff as well as other health care providers

Presentations on Red Flags for Autism

The project's primary method of increasing awareness is through presentations to pediatricians (see also "Presentations to Pediatricians and Their Staff" for more details), health care workers, preschool teachers, parents, and child care providers. Presentations address the early signs and characteristics of autism in very young children, are individualized for the type of audience (e.g., technical language and details for health care providers, a focus on typical development for parents), and are scheduled at the host's convenience. In previous situations, presentations were given approximately once per week and had anywhere from 2 to 40 attendees. Each presentation includes an overview of the incidence, etiology, and symptomatology of autism, with a focus on research-based "red flags" for the areas of communication, socialization, and restricted area of interests. See Table 2.1 for a list of red flags used in presentations.

The presentations provide videotape examples demonstrating symptoms in each area in very young children. These are shown after reviewing the various symptoms seen in young children. Text is superimposed on the bottom of each videotape clip with the symptom that is being demonstrated. That is, videotape clips of approximately 1 minute each are shown, with various symptom areas labeled on the clip (e.g., lack of communication, restricted interests, lack of socialization, no joint attention).

In addition, information about the importance and effectiveness of early intervention is covered, including quotes from parents whose children were identified. For

Table 2.1.   "Red flags" for autism, as reviewed during presentations

Social	Communication	Behavior
Atypical eye contact	Echolalia	Obsession with objects, interests, or routines
Not orienting when name is called	No babbling by 12 months	Inappropriate or unusual toy play
Preferring to be alone/ ignoring others	No single words by 16 months	Repetitive body movements/unusual body postures
Limited imitation (e.g., not waving hello or good-bye)	No two-word spontaneous phrases by 24 months	Attachment to unusual objects
Not initiating social games (e.g., Peekaboo)	Peculiar use of language	Over- or undersensitivity to sensory stimuli
Little interest in being held	Lack of pretend play	• Inconsistent response to sound
Delay/deficits in joint attention	Failure to attract attention to self	• Unusual visual interests
Limited pointing/ gestures	Use of early forms of communication	• Insensitivity to pain, cold, or heat
		• Hypersensitivity to taste

example, one parent said, "Set aside your fears and act now. Early intervention gives your child the chance to be the best that he can be." Each presentation ends with the screening information, sample clips of various children's improvement following a short intervention package (described next), and an opportunity to ask questions or make comments.

It is important to note that although presentations are done for clinics around the United States, the project makes a special effort to reach community clinics that primarily serve low-income populations that may not have the resources to seek specialized intervention services. In California, the program also focuses on cities with a high density of migrant farm workers who are generally monolingual Spanish speakers and rarely use public health systems. This step is important, as research shows that paucity of regular care, which is common in populations with low socioeconomic status, may reduce the likelihood that symptoms of ASDs are noticed (Mandell, Listerud, Levy, & Pinto-Marti, 2002).

Radio, Newspaper, and Movie Theater Advertisements

Another successful method of outreach has been the use of a variety of media outlets including radio announcements, newspaper advertisements, and advertising slides preceding movies in theaters. To simplify the referral process, only one symptom (communication) is targeted. Communication was selected because research suggests that it is the symptom that is largely responsible for parents' concern about a possible developmental disability. Furthermore, 12–18 months (the approximate onset of spoken words) is well below the age at which most children are referred.

Large advertisements with the statement, "If your child is 18 months and not talking, call for a free screening" with large pictures of children are placed periodically in the local newspaper. This part of the program has been responsible for a large number of referrals (it forms the third-largest referral source). In addition, a similar color slide is run in movie theatres quarterly, particularly around holidays, when children are out of school and parents are likely to spend more time with them at the movies. Public announcements are made by radio stations, and advertisements are also placed in religious newsletters. Again, efforts are made to reach Spanish speakers by placing Spanish-language advertisements in local Spanish newspapers, announcements in church newsletters for churches with primarily Spanish-speaking congregations, and announcements on Spanish-only radio stations.

Distribution of Posters and Flyers in English and Spanish

Another important outreach strategy is the use of posters and flyers in Spanish and English. The colorful 11″ × 17″ posters feature photos of young children and use large letters to relay the text from the newspaper advertisements. Small business-size cards, featuring a number for the First S.T.E.P. telephone line, are attached to the poster for adults to tear off and take. Posters and flyers have been distributed to anyone providing services to children and their families, such as doctor's offices, public health clinics, hospitals, child care centers, county programs, toy stores, delicatessens, grocery stores, and preschools. Furthermore, thousands of brochures, in both Spanish and English, were printed and distributed. Although this was a time-intensive process, as brochures were hand delivered and explained on a one-to-one basis as often as possible, this provided opportunities to develop rapport with community members, thereby increasing the likelihood that when children with developmental concerns cross their paths, referrals will be made.

Exhibits at Local Festivals

Equally important has been the project's presence at fairs and festivals. This involves setting up a table with a poster detailing the project. Usually balloons and candies are provided to entice families, and flyers are available. At these booths, a sign-up sheet is available for those interested in a more in-depth screening. Usually there is a small fee for using such spaces. The festivals and fairs are carefully selected to enable networking with other local organizations, including those with a potential need to refer families (e.g., local music schools for toddlers) and those that can offer support or services to families and children who have been through the project and demonstrated needs (e.g., parent support groups).

Presentations to Pediatricians and Their Staff

One of the project's most important outreach goals is to target professionals who have the earliest and most consistent access to young children. This group includes pediatricians and their office staff members, as well as emergency medical treatment staff and other health care providers. During the project's initial year, there was a focus on working with preschool teachers. However, it was determined that parents of very young children with autism often do not send their children to preschool because their children's communication is limited, they do not appear interested in socialization, they often have behavior problems, and they generally are not toilet trained. A focus on pediatricians and health care providers has been particularly ef-

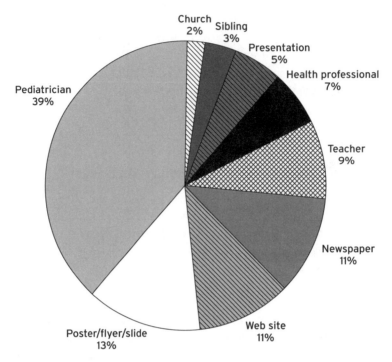

Figure 2.1.   Breakdown of referral sources during the last 3 years of the outreach project at the Autism Research and Training Center at the University of California, Santa Barbara.

fective, as preliminary data indicate that the majority of referrals have been made by pediatricians (see Figure 2.1).

As previously noted, approximately a year passes between the point at which parents are first having concerns and the point at which their children are evaluated, even though most parents first voice their concerns to the family pediatrician (Siegel et al., 1988). Staff at First S.T.E.P. hypothesized that most young children visit their pediatrician somewhat frequently during the first few years of life. Therefore, if these professionals were trained to recognize early symptoms of autism or developmental delays and to make appropriate referrals, then the average age of diagnosis could be decreased.

In the hope of increasing referrals, First S.T.E.P. created a presentation specific to pediatricians. This presentation considers some of the variables that may be contributing to their reluctance to refer, including limited time spent with patients, limited time for training about ASDs, outdated training (Shah, 2001), concerns about creating anxiety in the family, concerns about misdiagnosing, and a lack of information about resources for children and families. The project's first task was to gain access to pediatricians, who are not only very busy but also have demands on their time by other disability groups, drug companies, and so forth.

First S.T.E.P.'s efforts have indicated that certain components are important for successful outreach to pediatricians:

- Scheduling presentations during preexisting training times

- Providing meals

- Presenting succinct, updated material
- Using video examples
- Leaving materials

Presentations are scheduled during already existing training times so that pediatricians do not need to find time in their already full schedules. It is especially important to provide an incentive, typically a meal, for attendance during presentations, especially if physicians were scheduled during lunchtime or at the end of the workday. The meal reinforces attendance. In addition, if physicians are not required to attend the training, they seem more likely to do so to receive a lunch rather than going off site to get their meal.

The problem of outdated training is addressed by presenting the latest research on the early characteristics of autism, which is summarized into the three affected areas: communication, social, and behavior. The focus is on informing physicians about typical processes of child development, especially social and communicative development, while comparing specific examples of typical and atypical behaviors. For example one of the highlighted areas is joint attention because of its strong predictive ability for children with ASDs (Lewy & Dawson, 1992; Mundy, Sigman, Ungerer, & Sherman, 1986). Symptoms are behaviorally described. For example, the rate of gaze alternation (i.e., alternating between looking at one's mother and an item of interest) in typically developing children is approximately six times per minute, or once every 10 seconds (Whalen & Schreibman, 2003). The fact that this behavior is often absent or extremely depressed in children with ASDs is discussed. Furthermore, a child's not pointing or not responding to his or her name is discussed as a possible reason for concern. It was important to provide this information succinctly, with the most important points emphasized to show respect for the physicians' time. It is interesting to note that many referrals from pediatricians come because of a lack of eye contact by the child, which suggests that areas such as joint attention, response to name, and eye gaze during social interactions may be particularly salient characteristics to share in presentations.

Another area addressed in these presentations is the reluctance of pediatricians to alarm parents, given that there is great variability in developmental rates. It is understandable that if one in a position of authority may be anxious about providing potentially incorrect diagnostic information about a patient. Furthermore, it may be difficult to inform parents of a developmental problem without being able to provide information about a cause and adequate resources and treatment.

Concerns about misdiagnosis are addressed by informing pediatricians that First S.T.E.P. can diagnose and refer for any developmental delays or symptoms that they or parents notice in addition to autism. Essentially, they can refer children about whom there is a concern without making a formal decision of whether autism is present. In addition, it is suggested that when physicians refer families to the First S.T.E.P. project, they need not mention autism if they feel uncertain; rather, they can present the project as a screening to assess a child's developmental level and whether a further evaluation would be warranted. First S.T.E.P.'s philosophy of welcoming all families with concerns about their children, regardless of how trivial the concerns appear, is portrayed to the pediatricians; it is hoped that physicians will share this philosophy with parents and thereby feel at ease about making referrals. In addition, a component of the presented screening process includes intervention and further referrals for appropriate intervention so that any child with a developmental delay can be assisted.

The video examples emphasize the range of symptoms that may be present in very young children with autism and the importance of noting the absence of typical behaviors rather than focusing on the presence of atypical behaviors. For example, instead of showing children with severe and blatant symptoms—such as hand flapping, rocking, or spinning objects—video examples show children who exhibit a lack of typical social and communicative behaviors. That is, the clips show children playing with a toy while their parents are trying to engage with them. During this play, the children do not exhibit typical behaviors for their age: They do not use eye gaze appropriately, do not babble, do not share enjoyment, and lack interest in their parents.

Finally, it is of utmost importance to emphasize the availability of intervention services and to discuss treatment outcomes for children with autism. Concerns about the lack of treatment options for children with autism are foremost for most pediatricians. This issue is addressed first by describing research-based outcomes for children with autism who have had intervention, suggesting substantial language gains and decreases in symptomology. In addition, intervention data are presented, demonstrating changes in communication scores that move children with ASDs toward a more typical developmental trajectory and emphasizing that children with ASDs who receive intervention early in life can overcome many (or in some cases all) symptoms of the disability (see Chapter 7).

It is also important to leave brochures with the physicians to increase the likelihood of referral. This way, they do not have to remember the First S.T.E.P.'s telephone number but instead can simply hand parents a brochure with the contact information. Since the onset of the targeted outreach to pediatricians, the number of referrals from pediatricians more than doubled in just over 1 year after the start of the project (see Figure 2.2). These data suggest that targeting pediatricians and related

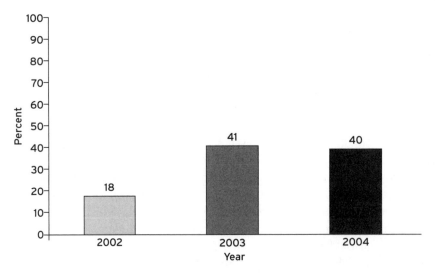

Figure 2.2. Rates of pediatrician referral from 2002 to 2004.

health care professionals, such as their office staff and nurses, appears to be critical in decreasing the age of referral for very young children with ASDs.

PART II: SCREENINGS

Following the initial awareness and training outreach program, there was an increase in the number of children referred. Part II of First S.T.E.P. involves screening the children for developmental disabilities. Consistent with other components of the project, a collaborative, family-focused approach, in conjunction with research-based practices, is applied.

Following referrals (generally a pediatrician referral or a self-referral), parents call to schedule an appointment. If parents call after regular office hours, an answering machine plays a message in both English and Spanish. The message indicates that someone from First S.T.E.P. will return telephone calls within 2 business days.

During the initial telephone contact, parents are asked about the age of their child and to describe their concerns. Next, the screening process is described in detail in order to eliminate any potential anxiety. Specifically, parents are told that staff will be playing with their child with a variety of toys and activities. Parents are also told that there is no formal testing and that their child will not be required to participate in any activity in which he or she does not desire to take part. Furthermore, as parents describe their child's needs, staff attempt to discuss various interventions that may be effective for each particular concern so that the parents do not feel a sense of hopelessness. Finally, an effort is made to schedule an appointment no later than a week from the initial telephone call, in order to relieve the anxiety that the parents may be experiencing (Siegel et al., 1988) and to reduce the length of time before the child can obtain services.

Each screening is conducted at the ARTC and is attended by a child's primary caregiver, the child, and various family members. In addition to screenings conducted at the ARTC, screenings are also conducted at the homes of families or at community agencies and clinics for individuals who cannot travel to the university. Many families from remote farming areas or families without means of transportation take advantage of off-site screenings.

In a research phase of the project, screenings were conducted by two advanced doctoral students, one of whom was studying special education and the other of whom was studying clinical psychology. Both had advanced training in applied behavioral analysis, several years of experience providing parent education to parents of children with autism, several years of experience in testing for and diagnosing autism and related disabilities, and an in-depth knowledge of the literature regarding early characteristics of ASDs. In addition, all sessions were videotaped with signed parental consent, and the tapes were reviewed by two doctoral level supervisors specializing in autism.

The actual screenings begin with the screeners informally greeting the child and taking him or her to a playroom and parents completing paperwork, such as consent forms, grant agency forms, and an initial intake form. The latter is a questionnaire about parent concerns in the areas of socialization, communication, and behavior and also includes other more general questions about the child's development, the child's first symptoms, and the referral process. Consistent with the literature, most of the parents report that the first symptom they notice was abnormal, or a complete lack of, speech development (Siegel et al., 1988).

Although approximately 65% report that they also have concerns about their child's social development, it appears that communicative delays are the easiest to recognize because they have such clear established developmental benchmarks. That is, by 16 months of age children should express single words, and by 24 months they should begin to combine words. Unlike communicative development, social development is not as well defined, and there is considerable individual variability; therefore, delays in this area appear to be more difficult for a parent to recognize. However, if the goal is to diagnose a child before 16–18 months of age, efforts will need to be made to increase awareness about atypical social development, sensory sensitivity, repetitive behaviors, restricted interests, delayed receptive communication, behavior problems, differences in pragmatics, and other symptoms of autism that may appear well before the onset of verbal communication concerns arise.

Screening Protocol Developed by the Autism Research and Training Center

Following completion of the consent forms and related paperwork, parents are asked to play with their child for a short time period. This is videotaped and is helpful for observing parent–child interactions and assessing the child's communication. After this initial taping, parents are interviewed about their child's development and concerns using the Vineland Adaptive Behavior Scales (Sparrow, Balla, & Cicchetti, 1984). In addition, a semistructured interview and direct behavioral observations of the children are conducted using a protocol developed by researchers at ARTC. This protocol (see Figure 2.3) incorporates items from the Modified Checklist for Autism in Toddlers (M-CHAT; Robins, Fein, Barton, & Green, 2001), the Autism Diagnostic Observation Schedule (ADOS; Lord et al., 1989), and the text revision of the *Diagnostic and Statistical Manual of Mental Disorders, Fourth Edition* (DSM-IV-TR; American Psychiatric Association [APA], 2000). Observational analysis, along with information from the parent interview, is used to determine if the child shows symptoms that put him or her at risk for ASDs.

Researchers at ARTC believed that it was important to include several particular areas in the protocol. Specifically, research indicates that specific behaviors, some of which are even evident starting at approximately 12 months of age, are suggestive of being at risk for ASDs (Baranek, 1999; Baron-Cohen & Allen, 1992; Osterling & Dawson, 1994). Such behaviors in the social domain are limited eye contact and delays in joint attention (Osterling & Dawson, 1994). Those in the communication domain include not orienting when one's name is called, delays in language development, the presence of echolalia, and a lack of symbolic play (Charman et al., 1997; Lord, 1995).

The ARTC's protocol was comprised of items that could be evoked during the screening from each of the three diagnostic areas: 1) qualitative impairments in reciprocal social interaction; 2) qualitative impairments in communication; and 3) restricted, repetitive, and stereotyped patterns of behavior, interest, or activity (APA, 2000). In addition to probes designed to assess the three diagnostic areas of autism, the protocol focused on certain areas known to be predictive of ASDs: lack of joint attention, communication delays, lack of pretend (or symbolic) play, and repetitive or restricted interests. ARTC analyzed program data (collected from July 2002 until November 2004) in these and other areas; findings are presented in the following subsections as applicable.

Lack of Joint Attention   The lack of joint attention behaviors—such as alternating gaze between a communicative partner and an object of interest, showing, and pointing—has been consistently related to the development of ASDs, especially with regard to the use of these behaviors to share enjoyment (Mundy et al., 1986). Unlike joint attention to request, which is sometimes intact in children who develop ASDs, this ability and/or motivation to use gaze and/or gestures to communicate enjoyment to another person is generally not present in children who are at risk for ASDs (Osterling & Dawson, 1994).

Thus, in First S.T.E.P. screenings these joint attention behaviors are intentionally probed. The child is given numerous opportunities to exhibit joint attention behaviors. During free play, novel toys that are likely to instigate sharing of enjoyment are scattered around the room. Furthermore, motivating items (e.g., cookies, chips) are placed in tightly sealed containers and out of children's reach. In addition to naturally occurring elicitations of these behaviors, children are probed for joint attention throughout the screening in a variety of ways. For example, intentional pauses and interruptions during motivating activities are incorporated so that a child has to request for the continuation of the activity. Specifically, one of the probes administered is a task in which the clinician blows bubbles for the child, periodically pausing before resuming the activity; this situation provides opportunities for joint attention behaviors (e.g., gaze alternation, pointing), requesting, and sharing enjoyment (ADOS; Lord et al., 1989). Paralleling previous research, none of the children screened by First S.T.E.P. who were diagnosed as having autism showed the use of joint attention to share enjoyment during the screenings. As indicated in Figure 2.4, only 45% used joint attention to request desired activities.

Communication Delays   Communication delays are typically the main reason for referral to First S.T.E.P. In addition to gathering information through parent report about a child's communication development, data is also collected from a probe of a parent–child interaction in which the parent is asked to have his or her child communicate to the best of the child's ability. During this interaction and throughout the screening, several areas are assessed and noted, including the child's vocabulary or language, the presence of echolalia, and the child's use of nonverbal communication (e.g., gestures). These findings provide screeners with information on the child's functional use of communication, which can be supplemented by the parental report data.

Lack of Pretend Play   In addition to deficits in social communicative behaviors, a lack of symbolic play is also noted in children with autism (Baron-Cohen & Allen, 1992; Wing & Gould, 1979). Here again, children screened at First S.T.E.P. are given multiple opportunities in both structured and unstructured activities to demonstrate their play level. For example, toys likely to elicit pretend play (e.g., dolls, toy

Child's name: _____

Child's age: _____   Date: _____

Notes

Introduction		
Did child make eye contact?		Y N
Did child exhibit social smile?		Y N
Probes		

Response to name:
    Parent
    Clinician
		Y N
		Y N

Pretend play? (M-CHAT)		Y N
Point with his or her index finger on demand? (M-CHAT)		Y N
Follow a *point*? (M-CHAT)		Y N
Did child engage in a *social smile*? (ADOS)		Y N
Balloon: *Initiation* of repetition of the social routine? (ADOS)		Y N

Bubbles (ADOS)
    Did child use *joint attention*?
    Repetitive motor mannerisms?
	Vocalization/nonverbal request	*Request* Y N
		Share Y N
		JA for other item:
		Y N

Observations		
Does child explore area?		Y N
Does child play appropriately with toys?		Y N
Does child play with a variety of toys?		Y N
Does child *show any toys to parent*? (With or without JA)		Y N
Overall responsivity		Appropriate Mild Moderate Severe

Did child coordinate gaze, facial
    expressions, vocalizations,
    and/or gestures?
		Y N

Use gestures?		Y N
Does child point?		*Request* Y N *Share* Y N
Appropriate pragmatics?		Y N
Appropriate eye contact?		Y N
Stereotypic or repetitive play with toys?		Y N
Stereotypic, repetitive, restrictive behaviors?		Y N

Figure 2.3.   Screening protocol developed by researchers at the Autism Research and Training Center at the University of California, Santa Barbara. *Key:* ADOS = Autism Diagnostic Observation Schedule (Lord et al., 1989); M-CHAT = Modified Checklist for Autism in Toddlers (Robins, Fein, Barton, & Green, 2001); JA = joint attention.

Parent Report		
Does child have history of ear infections?		Y N
Has a hearing test been conducted?		Y N
Sensory problems?		Y N

*Mark **O** for observed and **P** for parent report. Leave blank if neither.*

Social interaction and reciprocity:

_____ Poor imitation
_____ Abnormal eye contact
_____ Poor relating or interactions
_____ Underresponsive/ignores others
_____ Little interest in social games
_____ Preference for being alone
_____ Little interest in being held
_____ Little smiling/bland facial expression

Communication:

_____ Speech delays
_____ Little use of gestures
_____ Failure to attract attention to own activities

Restricted and repetitive interests and behaviors:

_____ Motor stereotypies/unusual postures
_____ Inappropriate use of objects/unusual play
_____ Attachment to unusual objects
_____ Unusual visual interests
_____ Inconsistent response to sounds/seems deaf
_____ Insensitive to pain, cold, or heat
_____ Hypersensitive to taste/smells/sounds

Type	Age range	Observed	Definition
Attention seeking	12–18		Solicits attention to self
Request object	13–17		Demands desired tangible object
Request action	13–17		Commands other to carry out action (incl. req. help)
Request information	24		Finds out about object or event, include wh-q or if with question intonation
Protest	13–17		Commands stop of undesired object or action
Comment on object	13–17		Direct other's attention to object (pointing, showing)
Comment on action	12–18		Calls listener to the movement of object or action
Greeting	13–17		Hi/bye/please/thank you
Answering	9–18		Responds to question
Acknowledgement of other's speech	9–18		Acts or utterances that indicate the other was heard
Other	9–18		Tease, warn, alarm, exclaim or convey humor

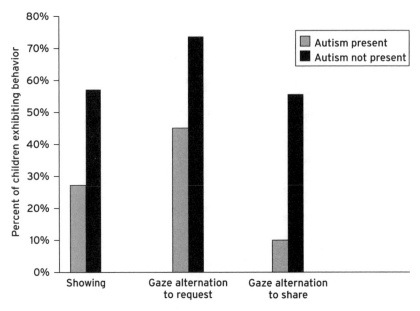

Figure 2.4. Differences in joint attention behaviors between children with autism and children with other disabilities.

vehicles, pretend food and utensils) are available during parent–child interactions and throughout the screening. In the structured setting, a clinician presents a child with either a pretend doctor's kit or tea set and, after observing the child's natural inclinations, scaffolds play, providing a hierarchy of prompts, to probe for symbolic play. Results from these probes indicated that only 20% of First S.T.E.P.'s sample of children who were diagnosed with ASDs engaged in pretend play.

Repetitive or Restricted Interests   The presence of repetitive behavior or motor mannerisms, restricted interests, or abnormal sensory behaviors may indicate autism. Parents are also asked if they have noticed any play that is repetitive. It has been suggested that children who develop autism may not yet exhibit repetitive behaviors at ages as young as 2 years (Lord, 1995); in ARTC's sample, however, 81% of the children under 2 years of age exhibited either repetitive behavior or restricted interests.

Summarizing the Screening for the Parent

After all observational and reported data are collected for a child, the clinician provides the parent with clinical impressions in terms of the child's strengths and weaknesses regarding the three areas associated with ASDs and any other developmental delays that may not specifically be in the autism spectrum. Based on this information, if the child exhibits delays, then the family is referred to an appropriate agency for intervention. Finally, a parent follow-up call is placed approximately a week after the screening to further help the parent obtain appropriate services. In addition, a letter is sent to relevant state agencies (see Figure 2.5) if the parent wants to accelerate the process of beginning intervention, and a letter regarding the screening results is sent to the referring pediatrician (see Figure 2.6) or agency.

UNIVERSITY OF CALIFORNIA, SANTA BARBARA

BERKELEY · DAVIS · IRVINE · LOS ANGELES · RIVERSIDE · SAN DIEGO · SAN FRANCISCO   SANTA BARBARA · SANTA CRUZ

GRADUATE SCHOOL OF EDUCATION
FIRST S.T.E.P.

To Whom It May Concern:

We received a referral from you regarding one of your patients. _____ (DOB:_____) was seen on _____ for a screening at the UCSB Autism Center-First S.T.E.P. program. In addition, his mother, was interviewed about her child's development and skills. It should be noted that this visit was a brief screening and not a comprehensive evaluation.

The following behaviors were observed during the screening:

Social	o Abnormal eye contact o Not orienting when name is called o Preferring to be alone/ignoring others o Failure to attract attention to self o Delay/deficits in joint attention o Limited pointing o Lack of gestures o Not responsive to social games
Communication	o Echolalia (Immediate/Delayed) o No single words by 16 months o No 2-word spontaneous phrases by 24 months o Peculiar use of language o Lack of pretend play o Unconventional communication o Use of early forms of communication
Behavior	o Obsession with objects, interests, or routines (Attachment to unusual objects) o Inappropriate or unusual toy play o Repetitive body movements/unusual body postures o Over or under sensitivity to sensory stimuli

Based on the results of the screening we have referred _____ to Tri Counties Regional Center for further evaluation for **Autism Spectrum Disorder / Developmental Concerns**. As always, we will follow up with the family to ensure that the child has been able to access services for this disability.

As you are the child's primary physician, we feel it is important for us to collaborate with you regarding your patient. Thank you for your concern.

If you have any further questions, please feel free to contact us at (xxx) xxx-xxxx.

Nicolette Nefdt, M.A., First S.T.E.P. Clinician   Eileen Klein, M.A., First S.T.E.P. Clinician

_____   _____

Lynn Koegel, Ph.D., Clinical Director

_____

Figure 2.5. Letter used to refer children to state agencies following a screening. Circles are checked where behavior excesses or deficits occur.

Analyzing Overall Data from a Selected Screening Period

Analysis of screening data collected from July 2002, until November 2004, indicate that within the relatively small area of Santa Barbara County, 114 previously unidentified children and their families participated in screenings. Of this sample, 48% were families from underserved minority backgrounds and approximately 35% of the children were age 24 months and younger. Of the 114 children, 39% received a diagnosis of ASD (which was confirmed by an outside agency). Less than 2% of the chil-

---

UNIVERSITY OF CALIFORNIA, SANTA BARBARA

BERKELEY · DAVIS · IRVINE · LOS ANGELES · RIVERSIDE · SAN DIEGO · SAN FRANCISCO   SANTA BARBARA · SANTA CRUZ

GRADUATE SCHOOL OF EDUCATION
FIRST S.T.E.P.

SCREENING REPORT

Child:
D.O.B.:
Mother's Name:
Phone:

To Whom It May Concern:

_____ was seen on _____ by **First S.T.E.P.** at the UCSB Autism Research and Training Center.   A parent interview in addition to screening measures, were conducted and behavioral observations were recorded.   Based on this brief screening we are referring this child to **Tri-Counties Regional Center** regarding the following behavioral deficits:

  o   Impairment in communication

  o   Impairment in social interaction

  o   Restricted, repetitive, stereotyped behavior, interest or activities

  o   Impairment in Daily Living Skills

  o   Impairment in Motor Skills

We are referring _____ for:

  o   Parent education workshop provided by UCSB (at no cost to family)
  o   Further evaluation by TCRC
  o   Further evaluation by County Schools
  o   Other_____

Please contact us at xxx-xxxx with any questions

_____
Nicolette Nefdt, M.A.
First S.T.E.P. Clinician
Autism Research and Training Center

_____
Lynn Koegel, Ph.D.
Clinical Director
Autism Research and Training Center

Figure 2.6. Letter used to provide feedback to a referring physician or agency. Circles are checked to indicate behaviors noted and steps taken.

dren referred had no diagnosable disability, suggesting that the majority of the referrals were indeed appropriate. Finally, the data indicate a decrease in age at referral of all children referred following the implementation of the project (see Figure 2.7). Thus, as a whole, this screening project has been effective in providing an earlier diagnosis for children with ASDs and in finding children with other types of developmental delays. Table 2.2 presents the characteristics found among children participating in the project.

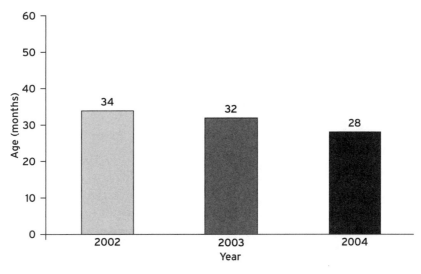

Figure 2.7. Decrease in average age of all referred children from 2002 to 2004.

PART III: FAMILY SUPPORT

An equally important part of First S.T.E.P. is providing support for families immediately after their child is diagnosed with autism or another developmental disability. Families dealing with autism undergo considerable stress, especially at the time of diagnosis, so the development of a family support package is of utmost importance. Helping children with disabilities obtain early appropriate intervention is the underlying goal of the entire project. Efforts to provide families with resources and support are detailed next.

As discussed previously, family support begins during the first telephone conversation. A referral from a pediatrician, from a family member, or because of the parents' suspicion that there is a disability is extremely stressful; therefore, ARTC makes a substantial effort to ensure that families feel welcomed and at ease with the process. Parents are provided with an opportunity to take as much time as necessary to describe their concerns in detail, and they are told exactly what to expect during the screening. All questions and concerns are addressed empathetically and honestly,

Table 2.2. Characteristics of children with autism in the First S.T.E.P. project

Average age	29 months (range: 16 months–55 months)
Sex	86% male
Ethnicity	52% Caucasian
	31% Latino
	8% Asian
	6% African American
	3% Other

and parents are assured that the screening is a collaborative process. During the initial intake, all information gathered via parent report is considered important and valid (Glascoe, 1998; Glascoe & Dworkin, 1995). Also, it is made clear to parents that they are the experts on their child and that the project staff are simply there to help them obtain services and to facilitate and improve on the excellent care that they already have been providing for their child.

Referral and Recommendations

In addition to the feedback provided in screenings, following consultation with the directors of the program, parents are called with any additional feedback. For children demonstrating symptoms of ASDs, all feedback is presented to parents with regard to strengths and weaknesses, within the framework of the three diagnostic categories (i.e., communication, socialization, and repetitive or restricted behaviors). Some parents experience sadness and depression after learning that their children have severe developmental disabilities; therefore, all feedback is provided with extreme sensitivity and awareness of potential parental concerns.

Because the telephone call is typically made approximately 3 days after the initial screening, parents are asked if they have been able to contact the intervention agencies to which they have been referred, and they are asked how the referral process is progressing. Typically, parents are successful at connecting with intake coordinators and making appointments for their children to be evaluated or to begin intervention through agencies that provide intervention at no cost to families. If this is not the parents' experience, our clinicians directly contact the relevant agencies to help facilitate the process.

For children who are referred to a specific center, such as a state agency, for further evaluation, a brief screening report is given to parents and is faxed to the agency. Figure 2.6 shows how this report specifies recommendations and summarizes the behavioral observations by indicating the area(s) of concern regarding communication, socialization, and behavior. It is helpful to communicate directly with agencies, particularly state agencies, to whom ARTC refers families, as this seems to speed up the intake process. Furthermore, although parents are thoroughly informed about the reason for referral, because of their high stress levels resulting from concerns about their child, they may have trouble remembering specific information and relaying it to other service providers.

Case Management

All children who participate in screenings are followed for a period of time to ensure their access to appropriate intervention services. In addition, families are encouraged to call with any questions or updates about their children. An important step in reducing anxiety and depression in parents is the provision of information about what the diagnosis means and what to expect for their child's future (Randall & Parker, 1999). Therefore, ARTC attempts to provide as much information as possible about what to expect and about the potential long-term outcomes for children with autism. This information is critical for families because, unfortunately, many state diagnosing

If a screening indicates that a child shows signs of a communication delay and/or possible autism, parents are provided with a free workshop designed to familiarize them with Pivotal Response Treatment techniques.

agencies provide little information relating to etiology, the course of the disability, and intervention options. Many families maintain contact until their children begin receiving services and then continue to call with specific questions for years after the screening.

Workshops

In addition to follow-up telephone calls and information about the screening and referrals, a 2-hour parent education workshop is offered, at no cost to the family, for all children who exhibit a developmental disability. Preliminary data from the project suggest that even such short workshops can be dramatically helpful. Workshops are scheduled as soon as possible after the screening, usually within a month, and are typically conducted in families' homes. The workshops are designed to teach parents ways to accelerate their children's development, and they help to bridge the delay between identification of a developmental delay and the onset of specialized services.

Each workshop begins with a 15–20 minute discussion of the Pivotal Response Treatment (PRT) principles. During this time, parents are provided with a copy of *How to Teach Pivotal Behaviors to Children with Autism: A Training Manual* (R.L. Koegel et al., 1989), which describes specific techniques of PRT, and a copy of *Teaching First Words* (Koegel, Koegel, Bruinsma, Brookman, & Fredeen, 2003), which describes the use of PRT to teach first words to children who are nonverbal. A diagram is then used to explain how the techniques relate to antecedents and consequences. Then, presenting clinicians spend 15–30 minutes demonstrating the use of PRT procedures with the children who have autism. During the remainder of the time (ranging from 60–90 minutes), parents implement the PRT techniques with their children while receiving feedback from clinicians.

Typically, the first hour takes place in a somewhat structured setting, such as in a clinic room on the university campus or one room in the child's house, whereas the second hour of therapy is done in more naturalistic settings, such as the kitchen, the garden, or a playground. A variety of settings are incorporated to encourage parents to provide opportunities for communication and other behaviors throughout their children's day in a variety of environments. At the completion of a 2-hour workshop, a follow-up appointment is scheduled to provide additional feedback to parents. In addition, parents are encouraged to maintain contact through telephone calls and e-mails. After 2–3 weeks, families are seen again, either at the clinic or at home. At this time, probes are taken of parents using PRT techniques with their children, feedback on their use of the strategies are given, and next steps regarding the child's communication and behavior are suggested. In addition to discussing the child's progress, clinic staff inquire about services that the children are receiving to ensure that the referral process is proceeding properly.

These brief intervention workshops appear to be a successful way to begin teaching parents some initial strategies for improving their children's use of expressive communication. In fact, the analyzed research indicates that most of the children began showing improvement during the first 2 hours and continued to show increases in both the total number and diversity of functional verbalizations, including at follow-up. Figure 2.8 shows data collected prior to intervention and at follow-up, which ranged from 1–9 weeks for each child. These data suggest that a short initial workshop that focuses on teaching parents (through practice with feedback) is likely to result in some initial improvements in children's use of expressive words.

These workshops are a vital part of the family support package because they provide parents with immediate strategies to begin tackling their children's challenges. Not only do the workshops give parents tools to help their children, but they also give parents an opportunity to see their children learning and succeeding, thus restoring their hope for their children's future.

DISCUSSION OF CHAPTER CONCEPTS

The primary focus of First S.T.E.P. has been to decrease the age at which children with ASDs are identified and, in turn, to begin the intervention process at an earlier age. The project's outreach methods to pediatricians and the community appear to be an effective means of reaching the desired goal of early identification. Prior to the start of this program, data for California suggested that children with ASDs were beginning services between the age of 4 and 5 years. After implementation of this project, however, the average age of children diagnosed with ASDs was 29 months (range: 16 months–55 months). Furthermore, these families received a workshop within 1 month of the screening, and most were enrolled in community intervention programs within 1–2 months. This part of the outreach program also greatly reduced the age of diagnosis for children with autism and related developmental disabilities.

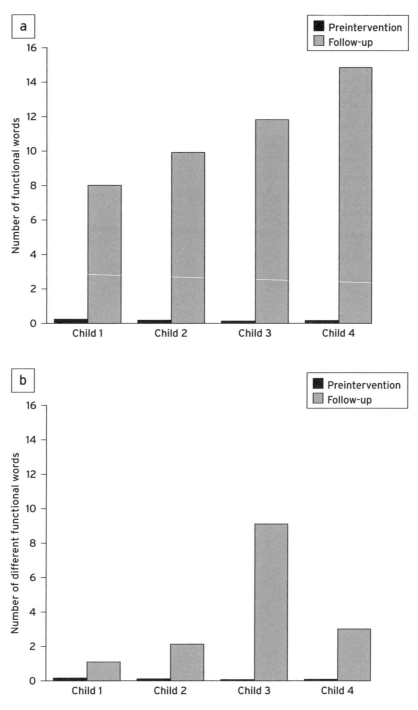

Figure 2.8. **a)** Increases in total number of functional verbalizations from preintervention to follow-up following a 2-hour intervention workshop; **b)** Increases in diversity of functional verbalizations from preintervention to follow-up following a 2-hour intervention workshop.

It should also be noted that the success of this project has been largely due to a collaborative effort with pediatric offices, preschools, county programs, and local community organizations. Collaborative partners continue to display information, such as posters and flyers, at their sites. In addition, they continue to include information in their newsletters and to host presentations (for community professionals and families) on the early signs of autism or a developmental disability. Many collaborating agencies, particularly those in remote areas, continue to coordinate and host screening days for community families concerned about their children's development. It is hoped that as pediatricians and community members begin to become more familiar with the symptoms of autism, formal training will not be necessary to make a diagnosis and, in turn, early developmental screenings will become an integral part of a toddler's health care.

DIRECTIONS FOR FUTURE RESEARCH

The positive effects of early intervention have been well-documented and are described in details in other chapters of this book. Although education appears to be critical in increasing the numbers of children who are referred for early intervention services, diagnosis in the first year of a child's life is rare. Preliminary research suggests that some symptoms may exist during the first few months of life (Adrien, Faure, Perrot, & Hameury, 1991). Further research regarding that area may result in even earlier intervention, if warranted.

On a related note, most parents first report concerns about their child's development to their pediatrician. Research is critically important regarding training of pediatricians, maintenance of diagnostic skills following training, and best practices for developmental screening by pediatricians.

Finally, methods for reducing the delay between screening and diagnosis and the onset of intervention is crucial. Many families face long wait periods for intervention following a child's diagnosis of autism. Research on the most effective types of intervention, and critical components of programs that may be implemented while a family waits for services, may be extremely helpful for children with autism.

3

Interventions in General Education Classrooms

One Boy's Story as Seen by His Mother

Cheryl Fisher

DARK DAYS: UNCERTAINTY AND FEAR

Alex's birth was uneventful. The first weeks of his life were delightful and just as we anticipated. Yet in the early months, I began to feel a vague uneasiness about his development. Alex's physical milestones were late. He was not holding his head up, rolling over, sitting, drinking from a cup, or crawling within expected timeframes. He had a persistent drool, and he was 18 months old before he started to toddle. Strangely, Alex also began to parrot words at that time, leaving me confused yet somewhat hopeful that all would be fine.

When Alex was 20 months old, his sister Rachel was born. In the weeks following her birth, I noticed that Alex gradually stopped repeating my words. My uneasiness returned. As we had done several times before, the doctor and I spoke again about Alex's development. Though he was puzzled, the doctor noted that it was not unusual for a child to slip back a little when a new sibling is born. The doctor observed that although Alex was delayed in achieving milestones, he did, in time, reach them. Perhaps Alex was just on a "slow clock" and he would right himself in time.

Time, however, was not our friend. My concern only deepened as the months passed. A change was occurring in my beautiful, blue-eyed, blond-haired little boy. It was gradual but it was real. Beyond the late milestones, something new and frightening was happening. I sensed in Alex a full emotional retreat. If he was in a room alone and someone joined him, he left to find an empty room where he could be by himself again. When I tucked him in at night and gave him a goodnight hug and kiss, he turned his face from me and I felt his little hands on my chest pushing me away. At the church nursery, he no longer separated easily from me but cried inconsolably when I tried to leave him and resisted contact with other children, refusing to join in games and group activities. When company came to the house, Alex became extremely anxious, wrapping himself in my skirt, clinging to my legs crying softly, or retreating into a room alone.

Alex was not developing the usual play patterns of a young child. Rather, his favorite activity was watching videotapes on television. With all the things he was not learning to do, he quickly learned how to operate the VCR. Alex had a preferred collection of superhero movies and selected cartoons he loved to watch over and over. He often rewound the video to a favorite spot, watching it repeatedly.

Perhaps most perplexing, Alex was developing tantrums with a capital "T." Sometimes the tantrums were predictable. If I interrupted his video selection, I was met with a huge tantrum. Alex prostrated himself on the floor, screaming and pounding his feet and hands. When I tried to direct his attention to learning something, such as dressing himself, the response was a tantrum. When trying to get him into the car to go somewhere, I was met with a tantrum. Other times the tantrums seemed to come from nowhere. I was hopelessly baffled. Alex was my fifth child. I thought I knew something about raising children, but Alex challenged everything I knew.

A version of this chapter previously appeared in Nickels, C. (1996). A gift from Alex—The art of belonging: Strategies for academic and social inclusion. In L.K. Koegel, R.L. Koegel, & G. Dunlap (Eds.), *Positive behavioral support: Including people with difficult behavior in the community* (pp. 123–144). Baltimore: Paul H. Brookes Publishing Co.; adapted by permission.

With each passing month, the gaps in Alex's development widened. He was not responding to toilet training. He was not learning to feed or dress himself. He was not learning letters or numbers or how to cut, paste, or color. Language was not developing. I seemed unable to teach him. I found his behaviors completely bewildering and unresponsive to traditional discipline.

I was deeply concerned but had no clue what was happening or what to do about it. Looking for answers became an urgent priority. I took Alex to a child development center for an evaluation. From the moment he entered the room, Alex showed the evaluator why I was concerned. He refused to sit down or attend to the examiner's materials. He paced back and forth, cried without stopping, screamed when pressed to attend, tried to escape the room, and spent most of the time clinging tightly to the doorknob. The center staff gave us no reason for Alex's delays and behaviors, but they stated that he qualified for their services and recommended we enroll him. We enrolled Alex in the program with high hopes that their intervention would produce positive results.

In the meantime, my search for some sort of explanation for Alex's developmental puzzle expanded to a well-respected community pediatrician, a speech-language therapist, child psychologist, and geneticist. Their opinions ranged from "profound, severe mental retardation" to "he's just marching to a different drum; he'll be okay in time."

Alex's behaviors continued to deteriorate. I had lost all behavioral control. Excursions into public places were becoming more and more challenging. Trying on an article of clothing in a store enraged Alex. If I attempted to try a coat on him in the aisle of the store, Alex did his "fall on the floor and have a major fit" routine. In a dressing room, he pounded and kicked the walls, bringing a concerned clerk more than once to check what was happening. Having to take a seat in a restaurant was met with a major outbreak of resistance.

My anxiety continued to deepen with the passing months. Alex was 4 years old. He was making very little progress at the child development center. One day he seemed to know a color; the next day, this knowledge was gone. He developed no language, only gibberish. He knew no letters or numbers, had no cutting or coloring skills, did not dress himself, and was not toilet trained. He seemed content only when absorbed in his own preferred activities.

Alex's father and I talked often of our serious concerns about Alex's development. It was urgent, constantly nagging from the shadows of my mind. Alf steadfastly reassured me that Alex would be all right, that he would outgrow all this—just give him time. I clung to that little string of hope, but it was getting thinner by the day. One day that thin thread of hope finally broke, too.

It was a lovely summer morning. Alex was 5 years old. Alf was taking a group of Boy Scouts on an overnight trip to an amusement park. I had been busy that morning helping Alf get things together and ready to leave. I had not yet attended to getting Alex dressed or paid much attention to what he was doing. Alf was just pulling out the driveway as Alex came running into the dining room and saw his father's RV disappear down the road. He immediately started to cry, looking up at me, then out the window and back at me again, almost frantically. Although Alex had no words, what he wanted could not have been more obvious. Furthermore, I noticed Alex had dressed himself. His clothes were on inside out and crosswise but Alex did have his clothes on and in his hand he carried his pajamas. It often seemed Alex paid no attention, as if he did not know what was happening, did not care, was not interested, and did not comprehend the activities that surrounded him. Yet in that instant I knew better. It was a lesson I never forgot. Alex knew what was going on.

Alex knew his father was going someplace, and Alex wanted to go with him. It was the first time Alex communicated something he wanted in that manner. It tore me up to realize that he had wanted to go with his dad and I had not even thought to consider the possibility. I walked to the telephone and started calling Boy Scouts' homes until I found one Alf had not yet been to. I asked to have Alf call me when he came to pick up their child; I said it was an emergency.

When Alf called, I told him he must come back to pick up Alex. Alex had to go with him. Alf was confused but said he was on his way. I straightened Alex's clothes and packed a little bag. Alex gave me no resistance. There was none of the usual combat as I rearranged his clothing. That sent a powerful message to me about Alex's motivation.

The next morning, the one little thread of hope I had been holding onto snapped. Alf called me and said, "Cheri, there's something wrong with Alex. I don't care where we have to go or who we have to take him to, just find someone who can tell us what's going on here!" After spending 24 hours nonstop with Alex, he suddenly felt the same sense of urgency I did.

That afternoon I made an appointment with the pediatrician. I would not settle for "I don't know" or "Give it a little more time." I had to get answers. I left the appointment with the name and telephone number of a former colleague of the pediatrician at an out-of-state university medical center. By the end of the next day, an evaluation for Alex was scheduled.

Frustrated by the lack of progress Alex had made at the child development center during the previous 2 years, I withdrew him from the program. In August, Alex entered Acorn School, a preschool, with his little sister Rachel. The school followed a Montessori approach in its curriculum, and although Alex remained distant and aloof, I sensed immediately he seemed more comfortable here. Subtle changes became apparent instantly. The morning battles to get Alex dressed, ready, and off to school dissipated as soon as Alex realized he was going to the new school with his sister. Without resistance, he walked willingly into the classroom with Rachel each morning.

In the following weeks, I discreetly watched Alex from time to time in the classroom. Alex was given the same work as other children. Rather than trying to avoid the task, he turned to see what his neighbor was doing. Then, he attempted to do what the other child did. Although his teachers were not specially trained, they did "common sense" kind of things to support him. Dotted lines were provided for him to trace, projects were partially cut out, and hand-over-hand assistance was provided. Alex accepted the assistance and attempted the tasks.

In early November, Alex brought home a Halloween project that he had made at school. The children had made a booklet of a Halloween witch with a colorful wardrobe. Each day they made a different colored piece of clothing for the witch to wear until her wardrobe was complete. The witch sported a red skirt, a purple shirt, a pink hat, and so on. Alex, who had never demonstrated color identification before, now plopped down on the kitchen floor, opened his little booklet, and pointed at each piece of her clothing; he identified the colors, one after another. Then he closed his Halloween book and looked up at me. I was trembling with excitement when he finished. I fell to my knees on the floor beside him. Opening the book, I asked Alex to show me again but he refused. He picked up his little book and walked away. He told us the colors again, but only when *he* wanted to. For the first time in years, I began to hope again that my child could learn.

I did not know it then, but those first years of dealing with Alex's development taught me two important concepts of both positive behavior support (PBS) and Pivotal Response Treatment (PRT): 1) placement in a natural setting with typical peers can diminish negative behaviors and be a source of motivation and 2) a child will attempt to do a hard task when sufficiently motivated by a desired outcome—for example, the day Alex dressed himself because he wanted to go to the amusement park with his dad.

SEEDS OF HOPE

In November 1985, Alex's father and I sat quietly in a small room in the university medical center, awaiting the report of the team who had spent the previous 3 days evaluating our son. My fears were confirmed as the doctor said, "Your son has autism."

Traveling home with Alex, my mind sifted through the prognosis the doctors shared with us. Among other things, they told us that generally behaviors become so difficult to manage that by the time children with autism are between 8 and 12 years of age, it is necessary to place them in settings outside the family home. In my mind I resolved that somehow, some way we would gain behavioral control. Alex would not be placed outside our home.

We found tremendous advantage in having the diagnosis of autism. For the first time, we had something tangible on which to base our search for help. It was not long until we uncovered the work of Lovaas and Koegel. Therein I found at least some justification for hope. I also realized that in Idaho, we were going to have to build an intervention program from the ground up.

By March 1986, I had located and observed the Core Behavior Management Program. This program was designed to teach children with autism the most elementary skills of learning—skills that typical children seem to develop naturally but children with autism do not innately possess and do not gain unless provided with specific interventions. Through this one-to-one program, I was told that Alex would learn to sit quietly, maintain eye contact, visually tract objects, imitate actions, and comply with simple directions consistently and in a timely manner.

I brought this program to our school district, which agreed to implement it with Alex during the summer school session. A veteran special education teacher who had some experience with children with autism joined us to work with Alex. By the end of the summer, when Alex had completed the program, he had made great progress. He was responsive and cooperative with his teacher and had gained skills that I believed would allow him to move forward and learn.

It had been a hard summer, but it also had been a very good one. It seemed to me that there was definitely reason for hope, and I rejoiced in that hope.

SEEDS MAKE FLOWERS

In February 1986, we initiated discussions with the school district about Alex attending a general education first-grade classroom in the fall. However, we were unable to reach agreement with the school about Alex's placement and his educational plan. When school started that fall, Alex was placed in a corner of a resource room in the basement of the school. Alex's response to this placement was immediate and interesting. The morning battles of getting Alex dressed, ready, and off to school returned. Instead of the summer session reports of cooperation and progress, we were told of a boy who was crying, crawling under tables to escape work, and kicking teachers. Alex had mounted a campaign of all-out resistance.

Our search for effective strategies led us to Dr. Mike Day in Boise, an educational consultant who might be able to assist us in designing a program for Alex in a general education classroom setting if the school would agree. In December, at a team meeting convened as a final attempt to avoid a due process hearing, the school district agreed to work with Dr. Day and give Alex a chance in a general education classroom. In January 1987, Alex joined typical children in a general education first-grade classroom. The battles to get Alex to school ended immediately, and he willingly climbed the stairs to his classroom each morning. There was no more scooting under tables or kicking teachers. Alex sat quietly at his desk. There were still challenges, but they did not include constant and overt tantrums.

Alex was now in a position to use the skills he had acquired in the Core Behavior Management Program to begin learning and developing the ability to navigate in the real world. Dr. Day came to the school several times to teach the staff how to guide Alex to success. During the next couple of years, we learned methods and strategies to effectively work with Alex.

These methods served Alex well at home, at school, at church, at scout camp—everywhere. They supported Alex's participation in the various environments of his community from first grade to high school graduation. They are still used to support Alex as an adult. These are some of the strategies, carried out in general education classrooms by general education teachers, that made a difference in Alex's life.

1. Place children in natural settings. We observed dramatic differences in Alex's behavior and learning depending on his placement in inclusive versus segregated environments. Through his behaviors, Alex communicated that he did not like to be in isolated, segregated settings, limited in his interactions only to others who also had disabilities. In inclusive settings, Alex's motivation and cooperation seemed to increase dramatically. His resistant behaviors decreased. He responded to the peer pressure of typical children, observing their behaviors and trying to do as they did. Rather than being surrounded by atypical behaviors of other children who were also struggling with disabilities, Alex was able to attempt to imitate the behaviors of the typically developing children who surrounded him in general education classrooms. We found that inclusive placements yielded cooperation and attempts at learning; segregated placements yielded resistance.

2. Use sound instructional techniques. All those who worked with Alex were carefully and deliberately taught sound teaching methods such as gaining Alex's attention before giving instructions, using concise and clear task-related language when giving instructions, combining verbal instructions with modeling, and ensuring that instruction had an obvious beginning and ending.

3. Embed reinforcers into the daily program. Reinforcers were an essential component of Alex's program. Using intrinsic reinforcers built into the teaching activities worked best. With them, Alex gave us the sun, the moon, and the stars. Without them, he gave very little. Initially, reinforcers had to be immediate, obvious, and frequent. Each day, a preferred item (e.g., a Hot Wheels car) lay on the corner of Alex's desk. Alex knew when he finished the task, the item on his desk belonged to him. Over time, as Alex became highly motivated by the reinforcer of task completion, the reinforcer changed to a paper grid attached to the corner of his desk. With each completed task, Alex earned a check mark or sticker for the grid. When the grid was filled, Alex exchanged it for his choice of an item from the reward box in the teacher's desk. We ensured the items in the box were of high value to Alex.

Alex's peer partner sat in the desk across the aisle. The partner rotated every few weeks. The partner observed Alex at work, rewarding him when appropriate with checkmarks. Alex earned marks by looking at the teacher or chalkboard, retrieving the needed textbook from his desk, turning to the correct page in his book, listening to and following directions, completing his worksheet, and so forth. The grid spaces gradually became smaller, requiring Alex to work longer and earn more checkmarks to claim his reward.

As Alex grew older, he was prompted to place the checkmarks on the grid himself. In time, he learned to monitor his activity independently. He knew when he had earned a mark. Teachers commented on how honest Alex was in his self-monitoring.

Over time, the nature of the rewards changed to reflect Alex's age. Rather than earning toys, Alex worked for comic books for older readers; videos; and books and magazines about planes, movies, superheroes, military history, and other areas of interest to him. At that point, he worked a week or more to earn rewards. We also tracked Alex's "earnings" in the journal that went from school to home on a daily basis for me to review. This increased the value of the system because Alex also earned money at home for his progress. This was our first step in weaning Alex off getting rewards at school. Eventually Alex's rewards were mainly received at home.

Critics observe that such reinforcement programs are nothing but bribery systems. My answer to their opinion is "So? What's your paycheck?" People spend their lives doing hard things to earn paychecks so they can get what they want. Alex's reinforcement program is not bribery; rather, it is his "paycheck" for working hard.

Concern was also expressed that Alex's program was unfair to other children in the classroom who did not have a toy on the corner of their desk. I knew a few adults who had a problem with that, but I never knew children who did (especially when they could join Alex in playing with the toy). We spent time with Alex's classmates each year talking about Alex and autism, explaining why Alex was "weird," and yet how he was very much like them. We validated their fears and answered their questions about Alex in open and frank conversations. We talked about why Alex needed a toy on the corner of his desk. We discussed how classmates could help Alex, and help him they did! The children also learned that when Alex earned his reward, they could join him in playing with it. That was an added bonus of the rewards. The rewards facilitated interactions between Alex and his classmates. The goal is find out what a child really, really likes or wants and will work for. Then use it.

4. Recognize when the child is shutting down and know how to help. Sometimes Alex shut down and stopped responding. He started to have tantrums again and to become very resistant to certain activities. When pressed to respond, he grabbed and tightly squeezed or pinched the teacher's arm in an effort to end her demands. On several occasions, Dr. Day visited to troubleshoot because we were losing Alex and could not get him back. Each time, the consultant was able to help us refocus and regroup to bring Alex back. It is instructional to note that the solutions the consultant brought us were not found in new strategies. Almost always, the key lay in reemphasizing one or more of the techniques he had already taught us but from which we had slid away over time. He reminded us to clean up the instruction; get back to clear, concise language paired with modeling; make sure that Alex knew and understood what was wanted; beef up the reinforcers; increase positive consequences; make sure rewards were of high value to Alex; fall back to easier tasks at which Alex was successful; and move gradually back into the newer or more difficult tasks. After a time, we learned to recognize and make those corrections without a consultation.

5. Prepare the child for changes ahead of time. We prepared Alex for upcoming activities or changes in various ways. The first was to make a picture or a word story of a new event and discuss it with Alex before it happened to help him "learn" the new activity. We had him use the picture or word story later as a guide while participating in the actual activity. The second method was to write or draw pictures on a calendar, time line, or paper clock to show Alex what was coming up and when. A third approach was to walk Alex through a new or changed activity alone with the teacher before it happened (i.e., to "prime" activities). Experiencing something new with the teacher or parent alone is a much safer way for a child with autism to process and deal with a change than trying to sort it out for the first time while experiencing the commotion of the entire class.

6. Embed supports into the daily schoolwork itself by adapting the materials or task to the child's skills *and* by preparing the child. We had to make sure that Alex was familiar with the work he was given by pre-practicing or "priming" him. He needed to know what was expected and to have the skills needed to successfully do the task asked of him. In some cases, Alex's resistance was sparked because the work he was given was too difficult, he did not know what to do with the work, he did not know what was expected, or he was not processing our instructions or understanding what we were asking of him.

Much positive intervention can be carried out by supports embedded into a child's task, activity, or work. One method for doing this is to make a picture or word story that shows the child the order of a task and prompts him or her what to do next. Another method is to adapt the work so that it is consistent with the child's skills. This reinforces the child's attempts to work with a more challenging curriculum. Many educators question how this can be done when a child with lesser skills than those of same-age peers is placed in an inclusive setting with curricular materials beyond the child's beginning skill level. (See the appendix at the end of this chapter for guidelines on modifying advanced curricula to accommodate a child's lesser skills.) A third approach is to provide the child with alternative methods to demonstrate and share what he or she knows. For example, instead of expecting verbal responses, provide a visual or manipulative method to enable the child to respond. Several picture or word cards placed on the child's desk during a class discussion will enable the child to answer the teacher's question by pointing to the correct card rather than by giving a verbal answer. Again, a possible approach is to try to preteach or prime the task or worksheet in the safe environment of a one-to-one setting at school with a teacher or at home with the parent the day or night before the activity. Using familiar and similar formats for the child's work is a helpful approach as well. When a new format is necessary, it should be introduced in a one-to-one setting in advance. Another method is to increase the relevancy of the task, when possible, by including something in the task the child likes, knows about, or is interested in. That is, use the child's choices to increase motivation. Finally, it is important to adjust the amount of material the child is expected to complete or the time the child is required to work. Be flexible. Know when enough is enough.

7. Create an accepting, embracing community and a safe place for the child, where he or she can risk new and difficult challenges. Some of the previously described strategies were used to help Alex feel secure in his surroundings. Our efforts needed to extend further, however. One of the most significant aspects of building a safe situation for a child lies in building support in the "people" part of the child's environment, including the child's peers and his or her teachers and staff.

It is not acceptable for children to be tormented, teased, ridiculed, or ignored, and this need not happen. It is important to reach out to typically developing children, teach them, inform them, touch their hearts and minds, join them in frank and open conversation about disabilities, listen to them, and let them express their fears and questions. Acknowledge their concerns and reassure them that it is okay to be apprehensive. Give them the information they need to get past their fears. Then, involve them in the child's life and solicit their assistance. They will rise to the invitation in surprising and heartwarming ways. Typically developing children provide the support, assistance, and guidance needed to create a warm, embracing environment for children with autism.

Typically developing children coaxed Alex into their circles. They taught him how to play, how to talk, how to take turns, how to touch appropriately, and how to feel safe in a world that was frightening. Even today, Alex's behavior in "people-prepared" environments is dramatically different from his behavior in environments that are not prepared. In a safe environment, Alex is outgoing, confident, and "less autistic." (See Fisher-Polites, 2004 for a lesson plan and activity guide for building support among typically developing children.)

Sharing information and knowledge about the child and the program with teachers and staff is equally important. Preparing teachers and staff to provide PRT is an essential part of building a successful program for children. As with classmates, the capacity to create such support among the child's teachers lies in sharing insight and vision with them. Tables 3.1 and 3.2 give helpful ideas and hints about important information that should be shared with teachers and staff at in-service trainings. The tables use examples from in-service handouts actually used by Alex's teachers. This material illustrates how a picture of a child can be drawn to provide teachers and staff with the information that will enable them to provide necessary positive supports.

Table 3.1.   Prepare staff to support the child by sharing the vision with them: Examples from Alex's staff training handout

Ensure the entire team has the answers to these questions:

Who is this kid anyway?

Why is he in my classroom?

What exactly is the nature of his disability and challenges?

What are his strengths and needs?

What techniques and strategies do I need to have to teach him, support him, respond to him, and gain his cooperation?

What are his unique behaviors and learning abilities?

What is my role?

How do I grade his work?

What are his goals? What does it say on his individualized education program (IEP)?

Why is Alex in the general education classroom?

To learn to *attend*

To learn to *participate* (partially)

To learn to be *engaged*

To learn to *cope* with new settings, situations, and people

To learn to *comply*

To learn to *interact* with a wide circle of people

To learn to *live and function* in the natural settings of the real world

How can you, as the general education teacher, help?

Be outgoing with Alex. Say hi; speak to him about things he likes.

Inform his parents in advance of your weekly lesson plans and activities (by Thursday, if possible) so they can prepare adapted materials and preteach when necessary.

Draw Alex into your class activities and discussions as per the IEP goals.

Consciously monitor Alex's participation. (See the Weekly IEP Goal Checklist.)

Follow through with use of reinforcers in order to gain Alex's compliance and participation. (Use peers to help!)

Meet with Alex's parents regularly to identify needs, concerns, successes, and problems.

Do not be fearful. Although outbursts do occasionally occur, they are not difficult to manage. Alex's parents can support you and help you learn how to address such behavior.

Table 3.2.   Prepare staff to support the child by helping them know and understand the child: Examples from a staff training handout for suggestions on working with Alex

Take time to get to know Alex.

Ask Alex to show you one of his books or magazines.

Ask him about Power Rangers, The Shadow, Zorro, Batman, or planes.

Spend a few minutes with him to watch part of one of his videotapes about Pearl Harbor, military equipment, a favorite plane, or a favorite superhero.

Ask him about Sean, Byron, Larry, Tara, or Rachel or about Christmas or Halloween.

By doing these things, you will more quickly gain Alex's confidence and friendship. This will increase his comfort level and, hence, his cooperation and participation.

Speak to Alex in clear, concise language.

Simple directives are best; they are easier for Alex to process. Eliminate unnecessary words.

Couple verbal directions with "showing" when possible.

Preface directives or questions with Alex's name to get his attention.

Be prepared for initial strange responses.

As Alex eases into new situations with new people, there is an increase in unusual, "autistic" behavior. When first meeting people, Alex might call them "chicken" or "peck" or talk about his brother Sean, his grandfather, or something that seems totally irrelevant.

Initially, Alex is generally resistant in new situations.

These behaviors will fade as the situation and people become more familiar to Alex.

Alex will not be working at grade level.

He generally will, however, be working with grade-level materials that have been modified.

The objective is *not* that Alex will master all the concepts of grade-level math, English, science, and so forth. Do not become anxious when this does not occur.

Alex's goals are different.

Alex's goals in your classroom are different than those of your typical students. See Alex's individualized education program (IEP).

While other students are working to master Algebra, the goal for Alex may be that he will respond when asked.

Define your role as the general education teacher.

It is *not* your role to design Alex's program or prepare the materials but, rather, to administer his program in your classroom.

Your role is to draw Alex into discussions, lectures, and activities. Keep Alex tuned in, attending, participating, and following directions. See his IEP.

Initially, due to the newness of the people and situation, Alex may resist or be silly because he is uneasy and unsure of his new surroundings. Be patient with and supportive of Alex while he works through this adjustment period.

Assist Alex to respond by making it easier for him. Ask questions for which he knows the answers, provide nonverbal response strategies, and reinforce him as he responds.

The greatest contribution of the general education teacher lies in his or her *awareness* of Alex in the classroom and in being thoughtful and creative in developing questions and strategies that draw Alex into classroom discussions, lectures, and activities.

Use the teacher's assistant as the liaison between you and the special education teacher and Alex's parents. She is in regular communication with them.

(continued)

Table 3.2.   *(continued)*

Alex's greatest strength is nonverbal.

Because language is difficult for Alex, provide nonverbal methods for him to demonstrate what he knows. As Alex responds nonverbally, model the verbal response for him and have him repeat it to you.

Use manipulatives, flannel boards, diagrams, pictures, and labels to facilitate Alex's responses.

Peers are a great resource.

Peers are Alex's greatest teachers and resource. Use them to model, prompt, assist, and reinforce.

Many times peers can get Alex to do what adults cannot.

The importance of reinforcement is significant.

Use check mark and sticker grids, which will be turned in later for a desired item such as a "magazine peek," cash, or a treat at school or at home.

Peers can assist in providing reinforcers.

Communicate with Alex's parents about help with difficulties and identifying and providing reinforcers that might help.

Keep Alex busy.

Alex should be provided with sufficient materials to keep him busy.

Monitor this and let his parents and the special education staff know if more material is needed.

Looking at favorite magazines or books should be used as a reward, not as a time-filler.

Monitor social interactions and IEP goals that are to be implemented in your classroom.

Use the IEP Checklist to monitor Alex's goals. Return the checklist to the special educator each week. This allows special education staff and Alex's parents to follow his progress and identify areas of need quickly as they arise.

Watch social interactions to ensure that they are remaining positive and rewarding for both Alex and the other students.

Provide opportunities to discuss Alex's social strengths and needs with his classmates as needed.

Notify special education staff and parents of concern about any checklist goal.

What about touching?

If Alex gets "grabby," prompt him with, "Where do you put your hands, Alex?" Lift your arm slightly between Alex and yourself and prompt him to touch your lower arm by tapping your hand on your arm and saying, "Touch me here, Alex."

If Alex attempts a full-body hug, raise your arm between you and him, turn sideways, and verbally and physically prompt him to give a shoulder hug.

Help students to remember and use these strategies with Alex also.

It is okay to correct Alex!

If Alex behaves inappropriately, he needs to be corrected. Alex can understand and respond to correction.

Alex can be required to call others by name and to be polite.

If Alex behaves inappropriately, teachers and students can say, "Alex, that's not nice," "Alex, do that this way," or "Alex, I don't like it when you do that."

Alex's fellow students need to know that it is okay to correct Alex. If he behaves inappropriately, they should use these response strategies with Alex in a calm, simple manner linked with a verbal and/or physical reminder of how to respond more appropriately.

In response to inappropriate behavior, Alex occasionally sits in a chair in a time-out format. This method is rarely needed at school and should be used only sparingly. Results are usually achieved with positive measures.

Get in touch with Alex's parents if any problem persists.

8. Make sure the pronoun in the child's support plan is _WE._
People comment on my use of the word _we_ when I talk about Alex's program. They want to know to whom "we" refers and ask whether there is a "we" at their school. _We_ refers to families and schools working together. The importance of schools and families working in concert for children with autism cannot be overstated. It is critical to communicate with each other, compliment and support each other's efforts, be on the same page, listen to each other, teach each other, learn from each other, and respect each other. There is no room in this business for turf, rivalry, competition, antagonism, or jealousy.

The accomplishments made while working together for children with autism cannot be matched by those of individuals working alone. I have the deepest respect and regard for Alex and other children and adults like him. I am in awe of how hard Alex works, of the effort he makes to put autism to the side and to make a real run at life every day. Children with autism deserve that the adults in their lives, the parents and teachers, be just that: _adults,_ working together and putting aside the petty grievances they sometimes allow to grow between them. Those grievances must be weeded out so that adults can work together to do what is best for individuals with autism. These brave children and young adults who make such valiant efforts deserve to live their lives to the fullest potential possible. This can happen only as educators and parents work together.

9. Finally, remember that intervention is not a bunch of "stuff" done to a child to make him or her stop doing something. Rather, it is a carefully structured, well thought out series of strategies and supports put in place to help a person get on in the world. PRT includes any techniques used to help people with disabilities make sense of their world; pay attention to and understand what is happening around them; understand what is expected of them; participate in what is going on around them; live in an environment that is friendly, embracing, and "risk safe"; and enable them to share their knowledge, needs, desires, and responses in the community in which they live. PRT is something done with, for, and around a person, not something done to a person.

FLOWERS ARE BEAUTIFUL

In 1998, at the age of 19, Alex graduated from high school with his friends. As the senior class marched out on the far side of the field, I recognized Alex by his notable and unusual gait as he made his way, in cap and gown, onto the grass. My mind danced back across the years, through the valleys of fear and discouragement, across the plateaus when movement slowed and seemed to stop, and up the mighty summits when victory was with us. I lived again the journey we had taken with this incredible young man.

When Alex walked across the platform to receive his diploma, my eyes filled with tears: His classmates rose as one in a proud salute to a dear friend they had helped rescue from a time when Alex exhibited many challenging behaviors. Words fail to express what I felt that day for each person, child and adult, who had helped make that wonderful moment possible. Without the keys of intervention, Alex would not be the young man he was on that memorable graduation day.

DISCUSSION OF CHAPTER CONCEPTS

Interventions have not cured Alex; they have not made him "normal." Sometimes Alex still paces and hums and pounds his hands together. Sometimes he still gets frustrated and upset. Sometimes, rarely, he still has an outburst. However, the strategies give Alex tools he can use to navigate through the real world. What a wonderful gift that is for Alex! As these strategies have been implemented in our family, school, and community, not only has Alex gained skills, but also the attitudes and behaviors of the people he has touched have been profoundly modified and changed. That is quite an accomplishment and another wonderful gift of the process of providing support and intervention to people with autism.

Appendix

Guidelines and Examples for Modifying Advanced Curricula

An important part of building positive supports for a child with autism and ensuring his or her success is preparing and providing work suitable for the child's skill level. When children are placed in settings with same-age peers, many parents and educators have concerns about how work compatible with the children's lesser skills can be provided given the advanced curricula.

Using techniques of modification and adaptation, grade-level curricula and activities can be utilized to prepare work that is suitable to the individual skills and abilities of each child. The cardinal guiding principal of such modifications is partial participation. Keep in mind that the child does not have to learn or do the entire task in order to participate in it. It is critical to study the grade-level curriculum and activities to identify the *part or parts* that a particular student can do. Then, using the basic guidelines of modification and adaptation that follow, modify the remaining material to that child's abilities. Using such methods, Alex's schoolwork was drawn from and based on general education curricula from first grade to high school.

1. Identify which part(s) of the task the child can do.

2. Simplify the task, make it easier, and reinforce attempts.

3. Identify and limit the concept(s) to be learned.

4. Provide orientation cues.

5. Make the task more concrete.

6. Make the task more relevant to the child's interests and experiences.

7. Adapt the task to the child's skill level.

8. Use tape recordings, a calculator, a computer, and so forth to enhance the child's skills.

9. Preteach materials and activities when helpful.

10. Provide peer support as needed.

Examples of Guidelines 1–7 are found in Figures 3.1–3.11 of this appendix. Note that several guidelines are used to modify a single worksheet. The main guideline used is identified immediately following the figure number. Other guidelines utilized are listed at the end of each description. Guidelines 8–10 should be used whenever they will help the child succeed.

NOTE: The activity of modifying and adapting materials and activities was a completely collaborative process between the teaching staff and me. The teacher's assistant gathered the materials from the classroom teacher. The assistant and I then reviewed the materials and divided them between us to prepare the modifications. The general education teacher was not responsible for adapting Alex's work.

Use with Lesson C, Unit 5
Beginning sounds

NAME *Alex*

Beginning Sounds

Name the key picture.
Which word starts with the same sound?
Put an X in the right box.

1. frog
   - [ ] fan
   - [X] fruit
   - [ ] foot

2. train
   - [ ] table
   - [ ] toe
   - [X] tree

3. gloves
   - [ ] gum
   - [X] glass
   - [ ] green

4. snowman
   - [X] snake
   - [ ] shoes
   - [ ] sheep

5. chair
   - [ ] cat
   - [X] cherry
   - [ ] cap

6. flower
   - [X] flag
   - [ ] fire
   - [ ] fish

Initial consonant digraphs   26

Figure 3.1.   Example of Guideline 1: Identify which part(s) of the task the child can do. In addition, reinforce academic curriculum attempts. If the child is unable to complete the entire task, find a way for him or her to participate partially. At the time the class did the worksheet presented in Figure 3.1, Alex could not identify and match sounds aurally. He was, however, learning to match letters visually. Therefore, this worksheet was adapted to reinforce that concept. By writing the name of the picture at the top of the word group, Alex could visually identify the word that started with the same sound and successfully complete this worksheet with the rest of the class. Overall, this process incorporated Guidelines 1, 2, 3, and 7.

NAME *Alex Nickels Zorro*

CHAPTER 6   How Your Body Works

| VOCABULARY | Use with Sections 3 and 4, pages 60 - 72 |

Skill: Recognizing Vocabulary Words

Read the clues found in the ACROSS and DOWN lists. Find the answers in the term box below and use them to complete the crossword puzzle.

cells	cartilage	joint	ligaments	marrow	organs
pelvis	skeleton	tissues	vertebrae	body systems	

ACROSS

4. organs
9. vertebrae
10. joint
11. ligaments

DOWN

1. cell
2. body system
3. tissues
5. cartilage
6. skeleton
7. pelvis
8. marrow

1. joint
   a. two bones connect
   b. hip and bone
2. marrow
   a. eyes and nose
   b. tissue in bone
3. skeleton
   a. toes and fingers
   b. body framework
4. cell
   a. smallest part
   b. hair

vocabulary practice **34**

Figure 3.2.   Second example of Guideline 1: Identify which part(s) of the task the child can do. Again, reinforce attempts as well. For this worksheet, Alex could not learn all the "across" and "down" clues and match them with the words in the box. However, Alex could learn a few of the words, and he could write the answers correctly in the crossword puzzle. To facilitate this, we covered the clues with blank sticky labels and wrote the crossword numbers and answers over them. The numbers on the puzzle were very small. We wrote large numbers and circled them to help Alex locate them. We identified four words for which Alex would learn the definitions. A box for those words was placed in the corner of the worksheet. Overall, this process incorporated Guidelines 1, 2, 3, 4, 5, and 7.

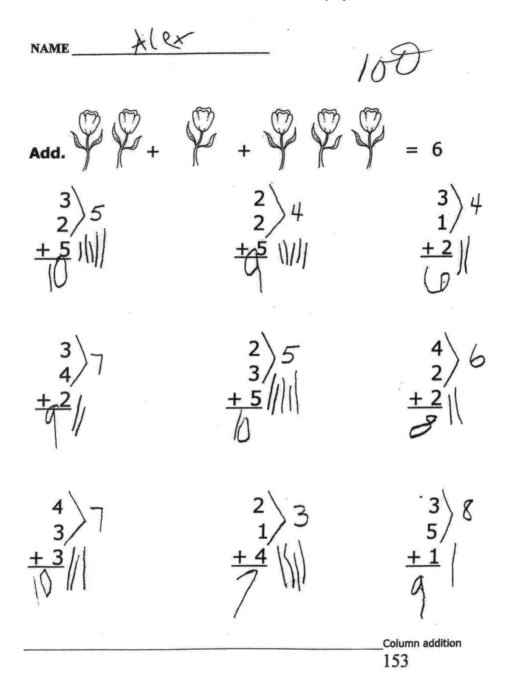

Figure 3.3. Example of Guideline 2: Simplify the task, make it easier, and reinforce attempts. Alex worked slowly so we used blank sticky labels to cover six of the problems. Although Alex could add problems with two addends, he faltered when the problem contained three addends. To simplify the task, we grouped the top two addends and placed their sum to the side of the problem. In a preteaching session, we showed Alex that he needed only to add the number to the side and the third addend. We also taught Alex to make counting sticks to help him add the problem. Of course, we continued to work on three addend addition problems in pull-out time, and Alex eventually did learn to do them without modification. Overall, this process incorporated Guidelines 1, 2, 5, and 7.

Name Alex hickels

CHAPTER 7

PLANTS

Section 7-1. Plants & Animals Help Each Other

Plants and animals share a relationship called the oxygen-carbon
dioxide cycle. Animals breathe in oxygen and breathe out carbon
dioxide. Green plants take in the carbon dioxide. As the plants
produce food, they give off oxygen. The steps of this cycle are listed
below. The words of each step have been scrambled. Put the words
in the correct order.

1.   in oxygen animals breathe   a b x o

     animals breathe in oxygen

2.   breathe out dioxide carbon animals   a b a c d

     animals breathe out carbon dioxide

3.   carbon dioxide in plants take/   p t i c d

     plants take/carbon dioxide

4.   make food plants   p m f

     plants make food

5.   off oxygen plants give   p g off o

     plants give of/oxygen

Figure 3.4.   Second example of Guideline 2: Simplify the task, make it easier, and reinforce attempts. Alex
did not have the skills to unscramble the sentences used for this worksheet. We simplified this task and
made it possible for him to complete it by putting the first letter of each word in order for him. By matching the letter to the word, he could put the words in order. In a preteaching session, we taught Alex to cross
out each letter and word as he used it to help him keep track of where he was in the task. Because Alex's
handwriting was very poor, he used a label maker to type and print out the words. The label backs were
adhesive, so they could easily be placed in the answer blanks. Overall, this process incorporated Guidelines 1, 2, 3, 5, and 7.

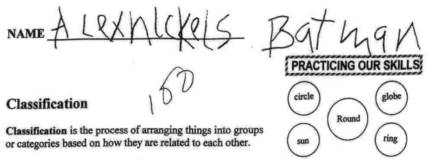

NAME _Alexnickels Batman_

Classification

Classification is the process of arranging things into groups or categories based on how they are related to each other.

PRACTICING OUR SKILLS

circle   Round   globe

sun   ring

Directions: Read each group of words below the box. Look at the words in the box and choose one that shows how the groups of words are related. Write it on the line above the words. Then find another related word in the box and write it on the line at the bottom of the group. The first heading is given for you.

Community Helpers	store	horse	Farm Animals
fish	Beach	Birds	blue jay
Buildings	waves	Pets	teacher

1. Community Helpers

fireman
policeman
doctor   f i r e m a n

4. _____

barn
house
garage   h o u s e

2. _____

cow
sheep
chicken   c h i c k e n

5. _____

cat
gerbil
dog   c a t

3. _____

bird
parrot
woodpecker   b i r d

6. _____

sea gulls
sand
sea shell   s e a   s h e l l

15

Figure 3.5. Example of Guideline 3: Identify and limit the concept(s) to be learned. Once again, reinforce attempts as well. While typically developing children were directed to classify the groups of words, Alex was learning to read the words. His task was to look at each picture on the worksheet; find and mark the word for the picture; and, using his label maker, type out the word and place it on the appropriate line. Overall, this process incorporated Guidelines 1, 2, 3, and 7.

NAME ___Alex___

Vocabulary Activity: Word Search

The words in the lists below can be found in the big box of letters. Find each word in the box and circle it. Find the words by reading across and up and down.

100% Good Job! ☺

BLUFF   ESCAPE   MOAT
BOW   GOLDFINCH   STERN
CARDINAL   HICKORY   TUNNELS

C	A	R	D	I	N	A	L	R	A	F	T	CARDINAL
F	L	E	X	I	B	L	A	B	O	W	U	BOW
Y	M	A	Q	B	Z	O	R	R	O	L	N	ZORRO
B	A	T	M	A	N	T	R	E	U	E	N	BATMAN
B	A	D	L	U	T	E	S	C	A	P	E	ESCAPE
T	X	S	P	I	D	E	R	M	A	N	L	SPIDERMAN
G	O	L	D	F	I	N	C	H	E	O	S	GOLDFINCH
T	H	I	C	K	O	R	Y	S	O	R	P	HICKORY

Figure 3.6. Example of Guideline 4: Provide orientation cues. Alex did not have the skills to discriminate the words in the maze of letters for this worksheet. By choosing only the words that read from left to right and by cuing him to those words by writing them at the side of the box, we oriented Alex's attention to the relevant letters—thus enabling him to find the words. In the lines that had no words, we changed the letters to include words of high interest to Alex (e.g., Zorro, Batman, Spiderman), making the task more inviting to him. Overall, this process incorporated Guidelines 1, 2, 4, 6, and 7.

Typical student assignment for each short story in literature class:

Using your glossary, look up the words below and write their definitions. Write a sentence using each word.

undulate	throttle	squadron
rivet	delirious	obsession

Alex's task for this activity:

Alex is given a worksheet that has each word, a multiple-choice answer, and the page number in the glossary where he can find the definition. With each new story, Alex receives a clean copy of the text glossary. In the glossary, a box is drawn around a group of words that contain the definition Alex is looking for. Alex searches in the box to find the word and definition that match one of his answers. He circles the correct answer and using his label maker, he types out the answer and sticks it in the blank.

Example:

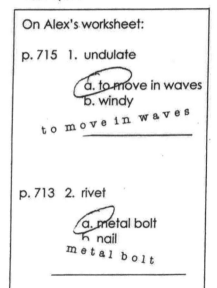

On Alex's worksheet:

p. 715   1. undulate

    a. to move in waves
    b. windy

    to move in waves

p. 713   2. rivet

    a. metal bolt
    b. nail

    metal bolt

In the glossary:

(on page 715)

undermine	to weaken or injure
uncowed	not timid or afraid
undoing	the cause or ruin
undulate	to move in waves
unfilial	not like a loving son
unfledged	lacking experience

(on page 713)

rhetoric	showy language
rigorous	harsh, strict
ritual	a religious ceremony
rivet	metal bolt
rosette	ornament like a rose
rowdy	rough, disorderly person

Figure 3.7. Second example of Guideline 4: Provide orientation cues. For this worksheet, Alex would have been lost if given an entire glossary in which to locate definitions. Therefore, we provided orientation cues to help him find his way. We noted the page number on which he could find the word. Then, by boxing in a group of words that contained the definition he was looking for, we oriented his attention to a smaller area so he could successfully locate the word and the definition. Overall, this process incorporated Guidelines 1, 2, 4, and 7.

Language Arts   Pronouns

Name _A L ex h i cke l s z o r ro_

Chapter 4 — Masculine and Feminine Pronouns

Read the sentences below and choose from the pronouns in the box to fill the blank with the correct masculine or feminine pronoun.

| he   her   herself   she   himself   his |

(M)asculine   (F)eminine
he   she
his   her
himself   herself

(M)
1. Lee studies math because ___(he)___ wants to become a scientist.

(F)   her   she
2. Karen lent ___his___ bicycle to Mike.

(M)   herself
3. Bill found ___(himself)___ amazed by how easy cooking really was.

(M)   her
4. Mr. Chang washed ___his___ hands after working in the garden.

(F)   she
5. When Melissa was younger, ___he___ loved reading mysteries.

(F)   himself
6. Rebecca called ___(herself)___ Becky, but her mother wouldn't.

Skills Practice   89

Figure 3.8. Example of Guideline 5: Make the task more concrete. For this worksheet, it was important to add an information key with relevant clues at the top of the activity for Alex's reference. Separating the clues into two lists identified the masculine and feminine pronouns. Each pronoun in the sentence was marked with *F* or *M*. With that assistance, Alex could independently complete the worksheet. For Alex, the purpose of this exercise was not to learn the pronouns but to pay attention to the task, follow directions, match the items, complete his work, and participate in the classroom activity with his peers. Overall, this process incorporated Guidelines 1, 2, 4, 5, and 7.

Name _Alex nickels_   Batman

section **10** - learning about fractions

Directions: Circle the fraction that correctly represents the object.

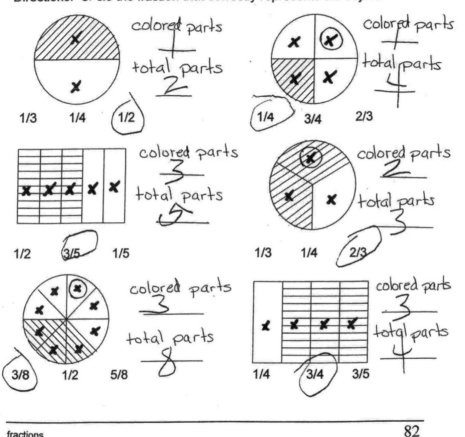

1/3   1/4   (1/2)   (1/4)   3/4   2/3

1/2   (3/5)   1/5   1/3   1/4   (2/3)

(3/8)   1/2   5/8   1/4   (3/4)   3/5

fractions   82

Figure 3.9. Second example of Guideline 5: Make the task more concrete. To help Alex visualize fractions on this worksheet, we added the activity of counting the colored and total parts of the objects. The X mark made each portion of the object more concrete and helped Alex count the parts more successfully. Circling one X in each circle helped Alex know where to begin counting and when he was finished. Time was taken in a preteaching session to familiarize Alex with this worksheet so he would know what to do when he received it in class. Overall, this process incorporated Guidelines 2, 4, 5, and 7.

Facilitating participation in class discussions.

Based on the teacher's lesson plans and in a pre-teaching session, information about tomorrow's class discussion was previewed with Alex. Several simple, concrete questions that Alex could answer were identified. The answers to the questions were written on note cards. Alex practiced the questions. A list of the questions was given to the teacher at the beginning of the class. Alex brought the cards with him to class and laid them out on his desk. At the appropriate time during the class discussion, the teacher asked Alex the questions. He responded by pointing to the correct answer card.

Example:

List of questions given to teacher for class discussion of short story "Mother in Manville".

1. Who is this story about?
2. What was the boy's name?
3. Where did the lady live?
4. What did Jerry do for the lady?
5. How much did the lady pay him?
6. What animal did he like?

Answer cards to be placed on Alex's desk.

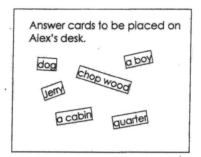

Supporting Alex in writing a research paper.

Knowing that Alex would be more cooperative and interested in a subject of interest to him, he was allowed to choose his own topic. Alex chose "Batman". Since Alex was very active in following his favorite movies on Internet web sites, it seemed natural to make use of these sites as his research source. With assistance from the teacher's assistant, Alex used "cut and paste" to develop the research note cards required for his paper. "Cut and paste" was also used to obtain text and pictures to build the body of his paper. Alex was very excited and involved in creating his research paper and very proud of the completed product. Two samples pages are shown below.

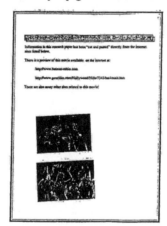

Figure 3.10. Examples of Guideline 6: Make the task more relevant to the child's interests and experiences. Figure 3.10a addresses class participation while following the child's lead and choices. The questions and answers from the story were chosen because they had some relevance to Alex's experience. Alex's family owned a cabin, and he knew about chopping wood. Alex could relate to a boy, a dog, and a quarter. Although Alex could answer verbally, chances are he would not, especially at the beginning of a school year when he was in a new class with a new teacher. Giving him a nonverbal way to respond allowed him to participate, share what he knew, and develop confidence in the new environment so that he could respond verbally later. Figure 3.10b addresses the assignment of completing a research paper. Superheroes are a high-interest area for Alex, so choosing this for a paper topic was a plus. Using Alex's ability to find information about movies on the Internet enticed his participation immediately. Overall, the processes addressed in both parts of this figure incorporated Guidelines 1, 2, 4, 5, 6, and 7.

Note taking during lectures becomes an increasingly important skill as students progress into higher grades.

Below are two of several adaptations provided for Alex:

The science teacher provided us in advance with the outline he used which contained key words he wrote on the board as he lectured. Typical students made notes from these key words the teacher wrote on the board. Alex was provided with a skeleton outline of the teacher's outline and sticky labels that contained the keywords, which the teacher wrote on the board. Alex watched as the teacher wrote the keyword. Alex's task was to choose and place the sticky labels in the correct place as the teacher lectured.

Example of teacher's outline:

Sources of Water from the Earth
1. Spring
   a. water flows from rock to surface
   b. comes from caverns
   c. comes from faults and fractures
   d. example: Thousand Springs in Snake River Canyon
2. Aquifer
   a. body of rock through which water can move
   b. dig wells to reach water
   c. water table depends on dry and wet seasons
3. Artesian well
   a. aquifer between 2 shale beds
   b. water rises above the surface

Example of Alex's note taking paper:

Sources of Water from the Earth
1. Spring
   a.
   b.
   c.
   d.
2. Aquifer
   a.
   b.
   c.
3. Artesian well
   a.
   b.

page of sticky labels

When studying the American Indian tribes, the teacher used a large chart on the board on which she placed key words as she lectured. The students made their own chart in their notebooks and filled in the keywords as the teacher discussed them. Alex was given a blank pre-made chart with keywords written on sticky labels. As the teacher placed the keywords on the chart at the front of the class, Alex watched, listened, and chose the correct label and placed it correctly on the chart. (boxed words represent sticky labels)

NORTHWEST COASTAL PEOPLE						
Location	Climate	Vegetation	Food	Clothing	Transportation	Housing
British Columbia	Mild	Trees	Elk	Weaving	Long Boats	Long Houses
Canada Coast	Cool	Ferns	Deer	Skins		
Oregon	Wet	Vines	Fish	Hides		
Washington		Berry Bushes	Berries			

Figure 3.11. Examples of Guideline 7: Adapt the task to the child's skill level. This guideline once again aims to reinforce attempts. By taking inventory of what a child can do, activities can be modified and adapted so he or she can participate using available skills. These examples of how Alex was able to "take notes" demonstrate that with a little creativity based on what he could do, it was possible to identify ways for him to participate in some way, at some level, in virtually any curricular activity.

4

Incorporating Motivational Procedures to Improve Homework Performance

Robert L. Koegel, Quy Tran, Amanda Mossman, and Lynn Kern Koegel

The literature suggests that academic performance, especially in homework, can be a serious problem for children with autism and that motivational techniques such as those used in Pivotal Response Treatment (PRT) are an effective intervention for ameliorating the language, social, behavioral, and academic deficits associated with autism spectrum disorders (ASDs; L.K. Koegel, Koegel, Harrower, & Carter, 1999). This chapter discusses techniques to improve motivation to complete homework assignments and presents a parent education model to facilitate homework performance among children with autism who have severe cognitive and behavioral deficits. Using these motivational techniques has the potential not only to improve children's motivation and performance in relation to homework by decreasing disruptive behaviors but also to increase children's affect and positive statements surrounding homework and parent–child interactions during homework.

BACKGROUND

There is currently a lack of research discussing homework issues among children with autism. However, numerous studies in related areas have described the problems that parents and students with a variety of learning disabilities have in completing homework tasks. Students with various types of learning disabilities and motivational deficits are more likely to have problems completing homework assignments than typically developing peers, adversely affecting academic performance and achievement (Bryan, Burstein, & Bryan, 2001). Baumgartner, Bryan, Donahue, and Nelson (1993) found that homework time can be a source of frustration, aggravation, disappointment, and self-doubt for parents and students with such disabilities. Bryan and Nelson (as cited in Bryan et al., 2001) summarized the beliefs of parents of children with various learning disabilities; this included beliefs that the children find homework to be too hard, frustrating, and overwhelming and that homework is an added burden because of their children's existing organizational and motivational problems.

Cooper and Nye (1994) reviewed literature on homework for students with various learning disabilities. It was suggested that homework policies and practices for students with various learning disabilities should emphasize simple, short assignments; careful monitoring by teachers; and parental involvement. The concept of simple, short assignments was supported with the idea that homework should help reinforce skills and class lessons, not integrate and extend class material, at the elementary level. This concept was supported by Muhlenbruck, Cooper, Nye, and Lindsay (2000), who reported that homework at the elementary level was related less to student achievement and learning than to developing time management and study skills. The support for parental involvement in homework for students with learning disabilities was based on the idea that these students had less developed self-management and study skills than other students. Empirical evidence suggests that parental involvement should be sustained, not discrete. Cooper and Nye (1994) concluded that when homework functions properly, the benefits for students with learning disabilities can be numerous, with the development of both academic and life skills. Improperly functioning homework can lead to frustration, stress, and negative attitudes about school among students who already struggle in the classroom. Keys to success include 1) assignments that are appropriate for the skill and motivation level of students and 2) appropriate involvement and/or education of parents in the homework process.

In particular, the lack of motivation characterized among children with autism, which is likely to impede learning and may appear as a learning disability, has been well established (R.L. Koegel & Egel, 1979). R.L. Koegel and Egel (1979) reported that when children with autism completed activities (typically in an incorrect fashion), their motivation (i.e., their attempts at responding and enthusiasm) for those tasks decreased to low levels. That study found that intervention procedures designed to increase motivation led to increases in level of responsivity. Numerous studies have noted that motivational procedures such as those used in PRT (see Chapter 1 for more information) form an effective intervention that improves areas such as language, pragmatics, self-help, and academics by increasing child motivation to initiate and respond to complex interactions. Empirical evidence supporting the use of PRT has shown improvement in areas such as language, play, affect, parent–child interactions, and overall development (R.L. Koegel, Koegel, & Brookman, 2003). Specifically, Moes (1998) suggested that using the motivational procedure of child choice improved the homework performance of children with autism who had relatively mild impairments, and Hinton and Kern (1999) showed that incorporating student interests (i.e., using child choice and natural reinforcers) increased homework completion among typically developing fifth graders from a school with a history of low standardized test scores. In addition, R.L. Koegel, Koegel, and Surratt (1992) demonstrated that PRT results in simultaneous decreases in problem behavior such as aggression and tantrums, producing more rapid intervention gains. Such literature suggests that having parents implement PRT during homework time may prove beneficial.

PARENT EDUCATION MODEL FOR ADDRESSING HOMEWORK ISSUES

The chapter authors conducted an evaluation to examine the effectiveness of specifically applying PRT in a parent education model to school-assigned tasks for children who have particularly severe cognitive and behavioral issues. It was hypothesized that PRT would improve these children's attitudes toward and performance on homework by decreasing their disruptive behaviors, increasing their affect and positive statements surrounding homework, increasing the number of correct responses on homework tasks, and facilitating homework completion.

Intervention

Intervention included a review of designated PRT techniques and examples of how to apply them to homework. The parent was then instructed to implement the strategies while receiving brief interspersed feedback from the educators. See Table 4.1 for examples on how the motivational procedures of PRT were adapted to homework.

Table 4.1.   Examples of Pivotal Response Treatment (PRT) techniques applied to homework assignments

PRT technique	Explanation of technique	Examples of application to homework
Child attention	Get the child's attention before providing opportunities.	Tap the child's shoulder or gain eye contact before providing instructions.
	Use brief and clear instructions.	Use fewer words, and give the child time to process the instructions.
Child choice	Use child-preferred or child-selected materials, topics, and toys, and follow the child's lead during interactions.	Allow the child to choose the location, materials, order of completion, and so forth.
Natural direct reinforcers	Use reinforcers that are functionally and directly related to the task.	Use M&Ms along a number line to count, and give the child an M&M if he or she counts the numbers correctly.
		Have the child spell the name of a favorite cartoon character, and give the child a sticker of the character for a correct/attempted answer.
		Have the child add and subtract by using balloons; blow up a balloon for the child to play with if he or she answers homework questions sufficiently.
Interspersing maintenance trials	Intersperse previously learned tasks/responses with acquisition tasks.	Mix simple addition problems with new subtraction problems.
		Have the child spell a word that he or she knows and/or likes while learning to spell new words.
Reinforcing attempts	Reinforce reasonable attempts at responding that are clear, unambiguous, and goal directed.	If the child has difficulty beginning the assignment, reinforce him or her for writing his or her name on it.
		Reinforce the child for tracing a word before having him or her independently write it out.
Contingent reinforcement	Provide reinforcement immediately after a correct response.	Let the child eat one Skittle immediately after completing a math problem that uses Skittles.

Measurement

The following measures were used to determine the program's effectiveness. An effective program should yield improvements in all five of these areas:

1. *Amount of homework completed:* Children with autism complete very little—if any—of their homework assignments. Samples of their work can be collected to track progress. Either the percentage of each assignment completed or a child's incidences of on-task behavior during homework can be recorded.

2. *Degree of disruptive behavior: Disruptive behaviors* can be defined as any behaviors that impede the progress of homework completion, including whining, crying,

protesting, destroying materials, leaving one's seat, using delayed echolalic speech or singing, and not complying with instructions. Time engaged in disruptive behavior, or incidents of disruptive behavior, can be calculated.

3. *Child affect:* Child affect can be scored by completing three, six-point rating scales in reference to the child's enthusiasm, interest, and happiness during the homework session. The affect scales are located in Chapter 8. Scores of 0 and 1 indicate negative affect, 2 and 3 indicate neutral affect, and 4 and 5 reflect positive affect. Prior studies have shown each scale to be reliable in measuring levels of affect (Dunlap, 1984; Dunlap & Koegel, 1980; R.L. Koegel & Egel, 1979; Moes, 1998). Affect can be rated periodically or during each session.

4. *Parent affect:* The same scales used for child affect can be used for parent affect. It is also important that a child's parent enjoys the homework sessions, as this increases the likelihood that the parent will continue to work with the child on future assignments.

5. *Positive statements:* The number of positive statements by a child and his or her parent during the homework assignment can be counted. Examples of positive statements by the child include comments about him- or herself, such as, "I did a great job!" or "I'm good at this!" Examples of positive statements toward the homework include, "This is a good story!" "I like math" or "That was a fun problem!" Positive parental statements such as, "You're doing a great job!" or "You got it right!" can be tallied as well.

Case Example

Billy and Mark Lopez were 8-year-old twins who had autism and were fully included into general education classrooms. When working with the Lopez family, the daily stress and struggles that ensued (due to the family's unique circumstance of having twin boys with autism and a younger daughter with cerebral palsy) was readily apparent. In addition to difficulties encountered during daily routines with three children with disabilities, Mr. and Mrs. Lopez met serious challenges on a daily basis with homework completion. Mr. Lopez was a firefighter, which meant he would be away from home for days at a time, leaving Mrs. Lopez to care for the children independently several days of the week. However, when Mr. Lopez was home, he helped considerably with the children. Mrs. Lopez also worked part time while her children were at school.

Aside from wanting to improve Billy and Mark's communication and social skills, one of the major concerns presented by Mr. and Mrs. Lopez was their difficulty with getting Billy and Mark to complete their homework assignments without having to address disruptive behaviors. Mrs. Lopez reported that homework time was filled with protests, whining, crying, avoidance, and extreme frustration. Homework often was incomplete due to the high level of stress that it caused in the home. Mrs. Lopez also reported that she experienced much pressure from Billy and Mark's teachers for the homework assignments to be completed, with the interest of Billy and Mark's academic development. This made improving homework time a priority in Billy and Mark's intervention program.

Prior to intervention, the chapter authors observed the children at home during homework time. Observations before intervention revealed much resistance from the twins, while the parents experienced much frustration in trying to help their children. Billy and Mark both engaged in yelling, whining, crying, making negative statements about the assignments and their own performance, and destroying homework materials. Mr. and Mrs. Lopez tried withholding rewards and taking away privileges to get their children to complete homework, with very little success.

The next step was to implement the intervention program designed to improve this challenging time. Through instruction and practice with feedback, Mr. and Mrs. Lopez were taught how to apply the PRT points to homework with their children. For example with Mark, Mr. and Mrs. Lopez were first asked to offer Mark choices (i.e., letting him choose which utensil to write with, where he wished to complete his homework, what order of problems to follow, and so forth). Mr. Lopez began this first lesson by turning to his son and saying, "Okay Mark, which assignment do you want to do first?" Mark gave his answer along with a smile, which led Mr. Lopez to offer additional choices. Mark's father also offered him a choice of writing implements, such as colored markers, colored pencils, pens, or regular pencils. When Mr. Lopez offered Mark a choice, Mark would answer his father and begin to engage in his homework simply because he got to choose. This was highly effective because it immediately helped Mark to stay in his seat and gain interest in the homework process. In addition to providing a variety of choices, Mark continued to enjoy his assignments much more when they incorporated items and topics that interested him, such as counting with his favorite animal figures and writing names of his favorite television characters along with his usual weekly spelling words.

With Billy, introducing choices, incorporating motivating items and topics, and reinforcing his good attempts helped him to maintain his focus during homework time and developed his eagerness to participate. One lesson involved use of a number line. Before the intervention was implemented, Billy would simply guess at answers until his mother corrected him, and he did not show an interest in learning how to use the number line independently. As part of the intervention, Mrs. Lopez used an M&M (Billy's favorite treat) to help Billy learn to add and subtract on a number line. Mrs. Lopez demonstrated a problem of "9 + 8" for Billy by taking the M&M and placing it on the number 9, then scooting the M&M up 8 spaces for Billy to see, arriving at the answer 17. Then Mrs. Lopez popped the candy in her mouth and said, "I get to eat this because I got it right." Immediately, Billy smiled and asked for a turn. Billy immediately got the remaining math problems correct by using this strategy. Eventually, such interventions made the homework process increasingly enjoyable and motivating for the twins. Fewer applications of PRT were needed as time progressed, and increased homework success seemed to make homework time naturally reinforcing.

After PRT techniques were applied to homework, improvements were seen immediately. See Figures 4.1–4.4 for an illustration of the results obtained for all study participants, examining rate of disruptive behavior, child affect, number of positive

This sequence of photos exemplifies how to incorporate motivational procedures into homework. The mother provides her twin sons with a choice of writing materials to increase their interest in the assignment (first photo). During the homework session, she maintains their interest by praising their attempts (second photo). The ultimate goal is the increased ability to complete assignments independently (third photo).

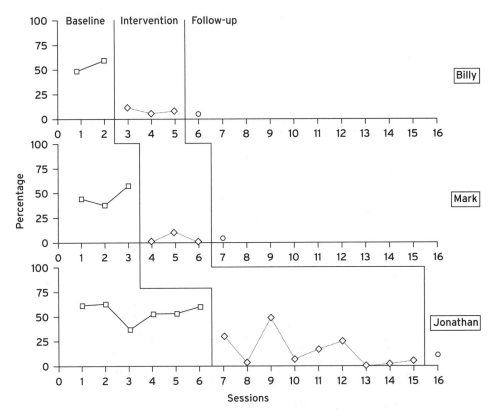

Figure 4.1. Percentage at which disruptive behaviors occurred across sessions for each participant.

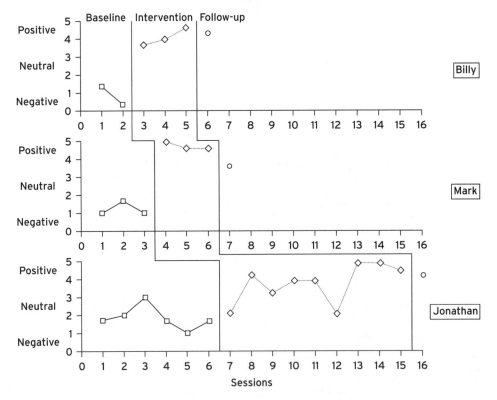

Figure 4.2. Composite child affect ratings on a six-point scale across sessions for each participant.

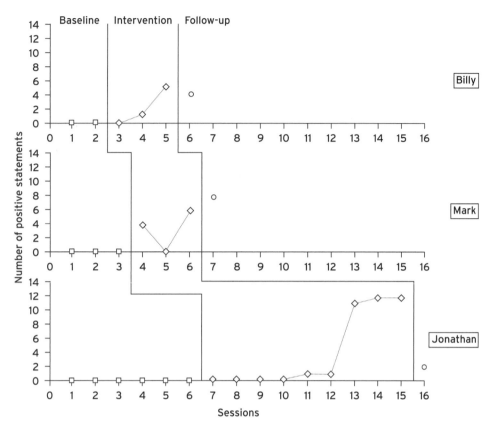

Figure 4.3. Number of positive statements made by each child across sessions.

statements made toward homework task or child's self, and percent of homework problems completed correctly. Applying PRT procedures helped to make homework time more motivating and enjoyable for Billy and Mark, which resulted in decreases in disruptive behavior, improvements in child affect from negative to positive, increases in the number of positive comments made, and improved homework performance. After the introduction of intervention, Billy and Mark completed assignments daily and made comments such as "I'm doing well!" "That was a great story!" or "I want to try another one!"—comments that were never heard during preintervention observations. Mr. and Mrs. Lopez also enjoyed themselves, as evidenced by their increased praise of and positive affect toward the twins throughout homework time. Improving the experience of homework time for the Lopez family made a positive difference in the family's daily routine, as well as in the twins' homework completion.

DISCUSSION OF CHAPTER CONCEPTS

The application of PRT's motivational procedures to homework assignments among children with autism generates positive effects on child performance, motivation, and nature of the parent–child interaction during school assigned tasks. This is consistent with studies reviewed by L.K. Koegel and colleagues (1999), who reported that the

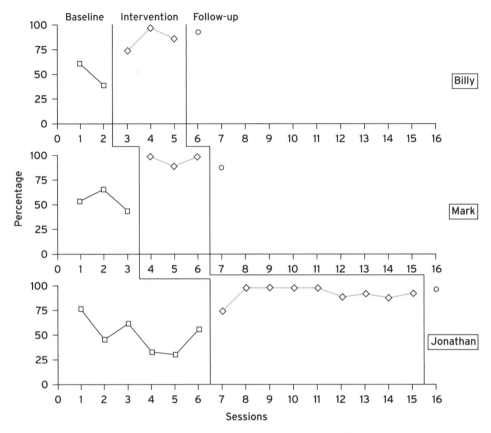

Figure 4.4. Percentage of correct performance on homework tasks for each participant across sessions.

use of PRT to focus on core pivotal areas such as increasing motivation to initiate and respond to complex interactions improved peripheral features of autism in areas such as language, pragmatics, self-help, and academics.

The combination of motivational techniques in PRT may be effective in reducing extreme levels of disruptive behaviors, negative affect, and lack of enjoyment during homework tasks. Moes (1998) found that applying choice alone can improve the homework performance of children with autism who had mild impairments. Yet children with more significant delays in cognitive and behavioral functioning can also benefit by showing reduced levels of disruptive behavior, greater homework completion, and positive comments about their ability. In addition, parents showed improved affect and gave their children more positive statements when the procedures were implemented. This is consistent with R.L. Koegel et al. (1992), who reported that the use of PRT resulted in a decrease of problem behavior such as aggression and tantrums, allowing more rapid gains. This further relates to the study conducted by Baumgartner and colleagues (1993), who reported that homework time can be a source of frustration, aggravation, disappointment, and self-doubt for parents and students. Reductions in disruptive behavior can be explained by an increase in motivation to respond by using PRT techniques, such as providing child choice, varying the tasks, reinforcing the child's attempts, and providing natural and contingent reinforcement in relation to homework.

As children progress in age, homework assignments grow more complex, and students may be stigmatized and have fewer opportunities to work with peers if they are not doing their homework assignments (Bryan et al., 2001; Vaughn, Schumm, & Kouzekannani, 1993). Applying intervention strategies that help children with autism develop motivation and academic abilities through homework assignments has positive implications for improving their academic achievement and social development trajectory, especially within inclusive classrooms. The chapter has addressed this need for academic interventions among children with autism by describing a PRT-based strategy that focuses on improving motivation to do homework, which has implications for improving the level of homework completion and performance as well. Cooper and Nye's (1994) literature review recommended that homework policies and practices for students with various learning disabilities emphasize parental involvement. The study described in this chapter addressed the importance of parental involvement; clinicians worked with parents to incorporate PRT effectively in homework situations. The improvement in child responses helped to make homework time more enjoyable for both the students and their parents. Evidence of maintained improvements, as seen through follow-up probes, supports the use of parental involvement to uphold progress for each participant.

DIRECTIONS FOR FUTURE RESEARCH

The effectiveness of using PRT during homework lends support for continued research into other ways of applying the procedures to motivate children with autism to make more rapid academic gains. This may include examining specific areas independently, such as reading, writing, and math skills. It may also be helpful to look at other common activities that are less motivating, such as household chores and daily self-care tasks. Applying PRT to such activities so that children with autism are more motivated to learn and practice them is likely to prove beneficial for families and their daily routines.

5

Parent Perspectives on Parent Education Programs

Jennifer B. Symon, Robert L. Koegel, and George H.S. Singer

Bradley, a 5-year-old boy with autism, lived with his mother, father, and 7-year-old sister in a suburb of a Southwestern city. Bradley's mother worked part time, and his father worked full-time in a small business. With both parents working, the family was lucky to have support from their maternal grandmother, who provided a significant amount of caregiving while Bradley's mother was working.

Bradley spoke in single words and short phrases to have his needs met. He also engaged in disruptive behaviors (e.g., screaming, tantrums, grabbing) when he was told "no" or when making the transition from a preferred activity (e.g., playing video games) to a nonpreferred activity (e.g., getting ready for school). In the area of play, he showed some interest in several toys, but his play often became repetitive (e.g., saying the same words after pushing a button, repeatedly landing on the same square of a board game). Socially, he showed some interest in other children, but he did not interact or play appropriately with them.

These behaviors prompted Bradley's mother to contact the Autism Research and Training center (ARTC) at the University of California, Santa Barbara, to participate in an individualized parent education program. She hoped to gain skills to increase Bradley's motivation to communicate, to reduce his aggressive and noncompliant behaviors, and to improve the family's interactions with him. Bradley's mother and babysitter participated in the program. During the week-long, intensive program, Bradley's mother learned techniques to address his motivation and to improve his social communication. She mastered the use of the motivational teaching techniques and identified teaching opportunities that could be transferred to the family's typical routines (e.g., meals, bath time, play time) at home and in the community. Most important, she became hopeful that her son would make progress in his communication skills and was eager to share her new experience and skills with others who interacted frequently with Bradley (e.g., Bradley's grandmother, teachers, and therapists).

When the family returned home, Bradley's mother successfully taught his father how to use the Pivotal Response Treatment (PRT) strategies with Bradley during play interactions. When the family visited with Bradley's grandparents shortly thereafter, Bradley's grandmother commented on the improvements in his language as well. The family has maintained a relationship with the parent educator through e-mail and telephone contact. Three years after the family participated in the program, Bradley's mother still shares Bradley's progress through anecdotal stories about his academic and social success as a student in an inclusive elementary school classroom:

Just wanted to say "Hi" and brag about my son. . . . He has a wonderful teacher and incredible "first grade friends". . . . [Bradley] is included full time—he doesn't even leave for special ed. He receives all his instruction in the regular class and is performing at or above grade level in all areas. His teacher tells me there are days at recess you would never know he has special needs. . . . [During a school game] he shouted, "I'm a winner!" and EVERY kid in that class cheered for him. They were all truly excited for him. It was one of those moments I just wanted to cry.

OVERVIEW OF THE PARENT EDUCATION PROGRAM

Although the majority of services at the ARTC are provided to nearby families, ARTC's parent education program provides services to children with autism and their families who live far from the center. With the growing number of children becoming diagnosed with autism spectrum disorders (ASDs) and a limited number of specialized centers, more families are searching for services for their children (Bryson, Clark, & Smith, 1998; Burton, 2002; Fombonne, 2003b; Gillberg, Steffenburg, & Schaufman, 1991; R.L. Koegel, Koegel, & Carter, 1999; Yeargin-Allsopp, Rice, & Karapurkar, 2003). ARTC's parent education program provides an innovative service delivery system that expands existing resources and gives children and families access to specialized services. This chapter describes the program and describes a project that provided some initial findings through qualitative outcome data. The goal of this project was to begin to understand the types of support and experiences that families encountered as a result of participating in a parent education program. Although the findings are specific to ARTC's program, the experiences that participating families have are likely similar to those of many other families who receive parent education as part of their child's intervention plan. The purpose of this chapter is to discuss an intensive parent education program and the effect it can have on the families of children with autism.

BACKGROUND

A body of literature discusses the challenges that many parents face if their child is diagnosed with a disability such as autism. Parents of children with disabilities can endure high levels of negative stress, often reported to be in the clinical range as scored on standardized measures. This heightened stress can be due to the unknown prognosis for the child's future and the family's challenged expectations. It can also be related to obtaining high-quality specialized resources that the children often need. Children with ASDs require special education resources, as well as ongoing and intensive intervention and support. In regard to obtaining effective and appropriate support, researchers have identified common barriers that family members face (Ruef, Turnbull, Turnbull, & Poston, 1999; Turnbull & Ruef, 1996). Through focus group meetings, these authors obtained feedback from individuals with disabilities, their family members, and others who support them. They found that a lack of effective resources was a widespread barrier to effectively supporting families. This lack of resources was associated with a limited amount of services, lack of sufficiently trained staff members, high staff turnover, negative staff attitudes, and use of negative practices. Again, realizing the discrepancy between the specialized services available to families of children with autism as compared with the growing number of identified children, it is clear why families may struggle to find support for their children and themselves. In order to obtain these necessary services for their children, parents may be faced with excessive financial burdens and stress (Birenbaum & Cohen, 1993; Singer & Powers, 1993a).

In addition to the emotional and financial stress of trying to obtain appropriate services, parents of children with autism often deal with the stress caused from managing their children's challenging behaviors. In children who have a diagnosis of autism, social communication is delayed and stereotypic behaviors are common. Many of these children rely on using early forms of communication, specifically disruptive behaviors, to get their needs met. They also engage in repetitive and stereotypic behaviors that also present challenges to parents who find it strenuous to successfully interact with their children in more prosocial ways. Research has shown elevated levels of stress for parents of children with autism due to the children's scattered skills and engagement in repetitive and antisocial behavior (Moes, 1995; Plienis, Robbins, & Dunlap, 1988). Parents of children with autism reported greater stress related to caregiving responsibilities, cognitive impairment, disruption in daily activities, and long-term care for their children as compared with parents whose children did not have disabilities. Specifically, findings suggest that parenting a child with a disability increases stress in the areas of everyday management of disruptive behaviors, heavy caregiving responsibilities, and concerns about the child's future when the parents are no longer able to care for the child (R.L. Koegel, Koegel, & Schreibman, 1991). Heavy caregiving responsibilities and problem behaviors can affect the family's daily living situation by limiting engagement in leisure or recreational activities. For example, if a child has tantrums in public areas (e.g., a restaurant, the grocery store), the family may avoid taking their child into the community.

For these reasons, families can develop feelings of social isolation and choose not to engage in such activities. For a family that enjoys spending time in community settings, having a child who engages in disruptive and stereotypic behaviors can be embarrassing, stressful, and overwhelming. This lifestyle alteration can serve as a source of stress for families. In turn, these areas of family stress can inevitably lead to a lowered quality of life for the children and for their family members. The increased stress for parents of children with autism was found to be consistent across family characteristics including geographic location, child's age, and severity of impairment (R.L. Koegel, Koegel, & Surratt, 1992).

In an effort to enhance program outcomes and to support families, many intervention programs for children with autism include a parent education component. Given that children with autism typically spend time engaged in self-stimulatory or other socially avoidant behaviors, they miss many natural opportunities to learn from their environment. Therefore, it has been suggested that they receive intensive intervention throughout the day and during their waking hours (L.K. Koegel, Koegel, Kellegrew, & Mullen, 1996; Lovaas, 1987). There is a large body of literature supporting the inclusion of parents as active team members for their children with autism, and the results of many studies have shown the benefits of this model. Unlike professionals, teachers, and service providers, parents typically spend more time with their children throughout the days and evenings or on weekends. Therefore, they can provide "round-the-clock" intervention for their children (R.L. Koegel, Koegel, Frea, & Smith, 1995). Educators and other service providers most likely provide support to children based on a set weekday schedule, during specific and regular periods of time, and in a particular setting such as a clinic room, classroom, or even in a room at the child's home. Conversely, parents are natural teachers for their children through-out the week and on the weekend. They are often with their children in numerous settings such as homes, stores, restaurants, airports, parks, beaches, museums, and movie theatres. In addition to the various settings in which parents are frequently with their children, parents also provide teaching opportunities across various daily routines such as mealtime, car rides, bath time, running errands, shopping, and bed-time. Therefore, a benefit of parent education is the likelihood that children's skills will more likely generalize because teaching occurs in many settings.

Although there has been a great deal of work demonstrating the positive effects of including parents into their children's rehabilitation process, the roles of the par-ents have been only slightly diversified. The majority of literature in this area involves including parents as therapists in their children's intervention program. This model in-creases the amount of support through a cost-effective model of service delivery, and it contributes to the children's rate of progress (Cordisco, Strain, & Depew, 1988; Cun-ningham, 1985; R.L. Koegel, Schreibman, Britten, Burke, & O'Neill, 1982; Lovaas, Koegel, Simmons, & Long, 1973; McClannahan, Krantz, & McGee, 1982; Sanders & Glynn, 1981). Parents have effectively learned strategies to reduce problem behaviors (R.L. Koegel, Koegel, & Surratt, 1992; Lutzker, Huynen, & Bigelow, 1998; Lutzker & Steed, 1998; Lutzker, Steed, & Hunyen, 1998; Sanders & Dadds, 1982; Sanders & Glynn, 1981), to improve their children's nonverbal (Anderson & Romanczyk, 1999; Krantz, MacDuff, & McClannahan, 1993) and verbal (Charlop & Trasowech, 1991; L.K. Koegel, Koegel, Harrower, & Carter, 1999; R.L. Koegel, Symon, & Koegel, 2002; Laski, Charlop, & Schreibman, 1988; McGee, Jacobs, & Regnier, 1993; McGee, Mor-rier, & Daly, 1999) communication skills, and to increase appropriate play skills (Stah-mer, 1995; Stahmer & Schreibman, 1992).

Researchers have studied the positive outcomes from including parents as thera-pists in their children's intervention process to increasing the quantity and availabil-ity of intervention for the child (Iacono, Chan, & Waring, 1998; R.L. Koegel et al. 1991; R.L. Koegel, Bimbela, & Schreibman, 1996; McClannahan et al. 1982; McGee et al., 1993) and also to support the family (Clarke, Dunlap, & Vaughn, 1999; R.L. Koegel et al., 2002; Moes, 1995; Santelli, Turnbull, Lerner, & Marquis, 1993; Singer & Powers, 1993a). Research has shown parents of children with autism as effective implementers of behavioral, social, and communication programs for their children (R.L. Koegel et al., 1996; R.L. Koegel et al., 1991, Laski et al., 1988; McClannahan et al., 1982; Sanders & Glynn, 1981; Stiebel, 1999; Vaughn, Clarke, & Dunlap, 1997).

In a study by R.L. Koegel et al. (1982), the authors compared a clinical model of direct treatment for children with autism with a parent education model. The results showed that all of the children improved their levels of appropriate behaviors after participation in the program. However, 3 months after the termination of the pro-gram, the group of children whose mothers received parent education continued to improve their skills, whereas the children who received services from a clinician only decreased in appropriate behaviors. In addition, large differences were found be-tween the groups of parents in the amount of leisure time that families reportedly en-gaged in following intervention. The mothers who received parent education re-ported dramatic increases in the amount of time that the family spent engaged in leisure activities, whereas the mothers in the clinician group only reported no difference after the program. These findings support the benefits of parent education over a traditional clinician model of intervention. Including parents in the intervention process resulted in maintained gains in the children's behavior during interactions with their mothers and contributed to the generalized benefits of family functioning. An additional finding reported in this study was that the children's skills did not generalize during their interactions with others (e.g., strangers). Rather, for both groups of children, the treatment provider (i.e., mother or clinician) needed to be present in order for improvements to be maintained. Nonetheless, the study's overall results highlight the limitations of traditional behavioral intervention programs—that is, those that do not include parent education.

Similar conclusions have been proposed by others who assessed generalization of treatment gains to new settings following parent education programs. For parents of children with disruptive behaviors, implementing a self-management program for the parents following parent education was necessary for maintenance and generalization of treatment gains (Sanders & Glynn, 1981). Another study conducted with parents of children with autism (Cordisco et al., 1988) concluded that training may need to occur in multiple settings in order for parents to generalize the use of techniques into new settings.

The Individuals with Disabilities Education Act (IDEA) of 1990 (PL 101-476), its 1997 amendments (PL 105-17), and its 2004 reauthorization (PL 108-446) have included parents in their children's education (Taylor, 2001; Wood, 1995). Parents have particularly been empowered through individualized education program (IEP), individualized family service plan (IFSP), and individual transition plan (ITP) meetings, whereby they can be active participants in the assessment, development, and evaluation of their children's school programs (Fine & Gardner, 1994; Wood, 1995). These positive changes have increased the amount of coordination among children, their families, agencies, and schools. This collaboration between families and service providers also supports the powerful role of parents in their children's education and enhances intervention plans for the children (Fine & Gardner, 1994; Mullen & Frea, 1995).

Parent education can be beneficial not only for children but also for their parents and family members (Baker, Lander, & Kashima, 1991; R.L. Koegel et al., 1996). Several parent education programs have included teaching parents to advocate for their children (McGee et al., 1993) and to provide information and support to other parents and caregivers (Ainbinder et al., 1988; Santelli et al., 1993; Symon, in press; Turnbull, Blue-Banning, Turbiville, & Park, 1999). For example, parents of children with autism can learn techniques for working with their children to overcome socially avoidant behaviors. This positive behavioral change has potentially high reinforcement for parents (McClannahan et al., 1982).

One purpose in designing interventions for parents of children with autism is to reduce the amount of stress that the parents experience resulting from their child's special needs. Various researchers have investigated the effects of social support interventions on families (Ainbinder et al., 1998; Albanese, San-Miguel, & Koegel, 1995; Dunst & Trivette, 1990; Koegel, Schreibman, et al., 1992; Minnes, 1988; Pierce, Sarason, & Sarason, 1996; Plienis et al., 1988; Singer et al., 1999). Social support has been viewed as a multidimensional model whereby different types of stress can be optimally alleviated with certain types of support (Cutrona & Russell, 1990; Dunst, Trivette, Gordon, & Pletcher, 1989). In other words, to best meet the needs of an individual in distress, the support provided should match the type of stress that he or she experiences.

One theoretical model of loneliness, proposed by Weiss (1974), suggests that different interpersonal relationships can meet different "social provisions" and deficiencies in any area can cause specific types of distress. In his theory, Weiss defined six "provisions" of social support (Russell, Cutrona, Rose, & Yurko, 1984):

1. *Attachment*—providing safety and security

2. *Social integration*—a social network of activities and interests

3. *Reassurance of worth*—providing acknowledgement and praise for skills or accomplishments

4. *Reliable alliance*—available under all circumstances

5. *Guidance*—providing advice

6. *Opportunity for nurturance*—feeling responsible for another person

According to this typology, each provision is typically offered through a specified relationship, although these connections are not rigid. Attachment is most typically provided by a spouse or significant other through a close, intimate relationship. Social integration, along with shared vales and concerns, are commonly provided through relationships with friends. Reassurance of worth is notably provided by co-workers or colleagues and may enhance self-esteem or lead to personal empowerment. Reliable alliances, which are usually formed with close family members, provide assistance and can be used during emotional distress. Mentors or other teachers traditionally provide guidance, and children usually provide the opportunity for nurturance.

These provisions have been directly applied to the stresses particular to parenting. Everyday stressors of parenthood are complex and vast and therefore affect each family member in a variety of ways. Parent support systems offer coping strategies to confront the daily hassles that parents may experience. Social support from a variety of sources can also reduce the stress that parents experience. However, the strength of the support has been shown to depend on the individual need (Albanese et al., 1995; Singer, Irvine, & Irvin, 1989), and a body of literature documents the positive effects of providing social support that matches the individual families' needs (Dunst et al., 1989). Examples of positive outcomes include enhanced quality of life, positive perceptions of the child, fewer time demands by the child with a disability, and improved interactions (Dunst et al., 1989).

In applying Weiss's (1974) provisions of social support to parenting a child with autism, one can understand the importance of matching an individual's needs to the types of support offered. Professionals have assisted individuals in obtaining support for themselves through providing opportunities for involvement in support groups and developing skills to build support networks (Singer & Powers, 1993a). The types of support, however, vary by individual. Dunst and Trivette (1990) distinguished between formal and informal systems of support. Examples of informal support systems include family members, friends, and social groups (Albanese et al., 1995). Examples of formal support systems include receiving services from professionals and service agencies. Formal and informal social support can be delivered through a variety of models. One-to-one interactions (e.g., counseling, talking to a friend), support groups (e.g., attending professionally mediated focus groups, attending unstructured meetings), professional support services (e.g., receiving parent education), family gatherings, or friendship networks are just a few examples.

The role of the reliable ally has been discussed as an important provision of support for parents of children with disabilities (Singer & Powers, 1993a). This relationship usually develops through a history of repeated contact with an individual who is viewed as trustworthy, and it often consists of common or shared experiences. Self-help support groups and parent-to-parent groups are examples of service systems whereby the individuals are grouped or matched with others who share similar experiences and attitudes surrounding their experiences. Through these interactions, participants receive direct support and, at the same time, work together to increase advocacy.

INTERVENTION

The intervention program described in the remainder of this chapter focuses on teaching parents (i.e., primary caregivers) the skills of PRT to target their children's motivation and improve their children's social-communication skills. This work follows a programmatic line of research to assess and identify the effects of participation for families and their children. A previous work by R.L. Koegel and colleagues (2002) presented quantitative results from five participant families who lived in various areas of the United States prior to, during, and after they participated in the program. The results showed that each of the primary caregivers learned how to incorporate motivational techniques of PRT after a 25-hour parent education program. Each participating primary caregiver mastered the use of the PRT techniques and then successfully incorporated them into their use during natural daily routines at home (e.g., mealtime, bath time). The parents' skills were shown to maintain for 3 months to 1 year following participation. Improvements were shown in the children's social-communication skills as well. The children's functional, social communication improved substantially and continued to improve as their caregivers persisted in utilizing the techniques. Aside from the improvement in learned skills, a rating of social validity was included to assess parental affect during play interactions. The results showed that after participation, the parents appeared happier, more interested in interacting with their children, and less stressed. These encouraging findings illustrate how parents can effectively learn strategies in a relatively short period of time and, by improving their own skills, can improve communication—a key area of functioning in their children.

Findings from a follow-up study with three other participant families presented additional quantitative data whereby parents not only learned the intervention strate-

In this photo, a mother is being taught how to create Pivotal Response Treatment opportunities with her child. Intervention education helps to increase positive affect and decrease stress levels among participating parents.

gies but also each trained an additional caregiver (Symon, in press). The primary caregiver, along with the target child and possibly other family or team members, received individualized support to incorporate skills into their interactions with their child. Upon returning home, however, each primary caregiver also taught another significant care provider (e.g., spouse, grandparent, babysitter) who could not participate in the week-long training program how to incorporate the PRT techniques into their daily routines with the child. Results indicated that the primary caregivers mastered the use of the PRT techniques, as in the previous study, and effectively trained others to implement the procedures. Similar to the findings from the initial study, the children demonstrated gains in their communication skills not only with their primary caregivers but also with the additional care providers. The data showed that compared with findings from before caregivers learned PRT techniques, children increased their social language, as shown by talking and attempting to communicate more with their other significant caregivers. In this way, the parent education program was shown to expand the amount of services that children were receiving and to increase the spread of effect of the intervention. By training primary caregivers in specific strategies and then having them train other important caregivers, children can potentially receive many more valuable teaching opportunities.

Although the findings from these previous studies clearly documented some of the benefits of training parents through a short, yet intensive, individualized program, this chapter presents work from a project aimed at developing a better understanding of the parents' experiences after they participate in such programs. Little is known or is documented regarding parents' experiences when they receive parent education. In an attempt to add to the quantitative body of knowledge presented through the previous studies (i.e., R.L. Koegel et al., 2002; Symon, in press), this study adds to the literature by searching for common experiences of parents who participated in the parent education program with their children. The components of the caregivers' experiences relate to their quality of life and may not have been captured by quantitative methods.

According to Lincoln and Guba (1985), qualitative methodologies are suitable for use in the early stages of analysis or to describe phenomenon that is unclear. Through qualitative evaluation, patterns and clearer understandings of broad concepts can emerge and ultimately lead to new hypotheses and theories in new areas of study (Patton, 1990). Therefore, these methods were used to examine whether components of the clinician–parent relationship may have influenced the quantitative outcomes and also to identify the aspects of the program that could not be measured by quantitative methods.

Description of Participants, Settings, and Clinicians

Each participating primary caregiver was the mother of a child with autism. All three of the primary caregivers were Caucasian. All had completed college, and two had graduate degrees. None of the primary caregivers had previously received parent education in PRT strategies.

Most of the parent education sessions were conducted in ARTC's clinic playrooms, which contain a table, chairs, a video camera, and a variety of toys. Additional sessions were conducted in nearby community settings such as restaurants, stores, and parks. For all participating families, approximately 80% of the intervention hours took place in the center playrooms and the remaining 20% took place in community settings.

The parent educator/clinicians were doctoral candidates in the university's Gevirtz Graduate School of Education and were pursing degrees in educational psychology and/or counseling/clinical/school psychology. The clinicians had between 3–6 years of experience working with children with autism and providing behavioral interventions to families. They received frequent and ongoing training and supervision from the center director and graduate program advisor, who each had expertise in autism, research, behavioral intervention, and parent education.

Preintervention Procedures

Prior to their participation in the parent education program, rapport between the parents and the parent educators began through telephone conversations. Through the telephone contact, the parent educators obtained information about the child and family, and they provided the parents with an overview of the parent education program. The Vineland Adaptive Behavior Scales (Sparrow, Balla, & Cicchetti, 1984) were administered to obtain information on each child's functioning level, and specific information for each child was obtained in the areas of communication and language skills, social skills, adaptive behavior, challenging behaviors, school placement, and additional services that the child had received.

Intervention Procedures

One family per week participated individually in the parent education program. For each family, the child's primary caregiver, the child with autism, and the parent educator attended all sessions. Additional family members (e.g., father, grandparents, siblings) and educational team members (e.g., speech therapist, teacher, school or home therapist) attended with some of the families as well. The clinical director (a licensed speech pathologist with a doctoral degree in psychology and expertise in autism) observed and attended the sessions for approximately an hour each day.

Parent education intervention sessions took place for 5 hours per day over 5 consecutive weekdays, for a total of 25 hours. In addition, during the week, each family was offered respite care for one or two evenings, which was provided by undergraduate students who assisted in ARTC and had experience in looking after and working with children with autism.

The intervention program began with an informal meeting between the parents and the parent educator, and possibly other attendees, to observe the child's interactions, discuss target behaviors, and become familiar with the family. Following this brief initial meeting, the parents were provided with a copy of *How to Teach Pivotal Behaviors to Children with Autism: A Training Manual* (R.L. Koegel et al., 1989), which describes specific PRT techniques. The motivational techniques described in the manual were presented to the primary caregivers as they related to their own children.

The clinician initially modeled the use of the PRT strategies during interactions with the child for 1–2 hours on the first day of the program and then gradually included the primary caregiver (i.e., the child's mother) in the intervention. The parent educator then began to point out social-communication opportunities and provided the mother with continuous feedback while she practiced using the techniques herself. During the subsequent 4 days of the program, the parent educator modeled the PRT techniques for approximately a half hour each day and continued to provide feedback to the primary caregiver during her interactions with her child. The PRT techniques were implemented in the context of everyday activities (e.g., playing with toys, playing games, teaching skills, eating meals, going to the park) to demonstrate the techniques and encourage caregivers to use them on an ongoing basis whenever opportunities arose.

Although the primary goal of the intervention program was to provide the primary caregiver with an overview and training in PRT techniques, parents were invited to ask questions regarding their children's educational programs, behaviors, social skills, or other related topics. Questions arose intermittently throughout the program. Approximately 80% of the program consisted of direct parent education; the remaining portion consisted of troubleshooting; answering questions; discussing topics related to the child and family such as the child's general development, educational programming, and family issues; and building a relationship between the clinician and parents.

Depending on the individual needs of the children and the parents, additional suggestions or reading materials were provided to the family to assist them in addressing other concerns that they voiced. All of the families were presented with additional reading materials based on the specific needs of their children. Because all of the children engaged in disruptive behaviors, each family was provided with *Understanding Why Problem Behaviors Occur* (Frea, Koegel, & Koegel, 1994), which describes the steps for conducting a functional assessment. The families were also provided with *Increasing Success in School Through Priming: A Training Manual* (Wilde, Koegel, & Koegel, 1992). Two of the families received manuals on toilet training.

Postintervention and Follow-Up

During the final hour of the parent education program, a meeting was conducted with the primary caregiver (and other attendees), parent educator, and clinical director to summarize the teaching strategies practiced, provide additional recommendations for future target behaviors, and answer any remaining questions (e.g., regarding school placement or IEP goals). Parents were provided with the parent educator's e-mail address and the clinic's telephone number and were encouraged and invited to maintain contact. At that time, parents completed a Consumer Satisfaction Questionnaire (described in the following section). Throughout the follow-up period, parents and parent educators maintained contact via e-mail and telephone. In addition, parents sent videotaped segments of their children at home during typical family routines, and parent educators provided feedback, comments, and suggestions to the families.

Measurement

In addition to child measures such as gains in communication and appropriate behavior, data were collected on parental fidelity of implementation (see Chapter 8 for more information). Furthermore, generalization measures in regard to spread of effect were collected from significant others in the child's life. Because these measures are discussed at length in other chapters in this book, this chapter focuses on the qualitative measures that were collected.

Qualitative methodologies were used to explore and to develop a better understanding of the parents' experiences, aside from direct feedback and instructions that were provided during the intervention. Methods of triangulation were used to ensure consistency and dependability in the analysis of the qualitative data. Triangulation is a method of merging multiple sources of information to verify findings and to strengthen the design of the data collection procedures (Patton, 1987; Singer & Powers, 1993a). Several types of triangulation were included in the methodology of this study. Methodology triangulation, including multiple sources of data, was achieved by including session notes, telephone conversation notes, e-mails, and answers to questions on the Consumer Satisfaction Questionnaire. In particular, the Consumer Satisfaction Questionnaire included four open-ended questions that generated qualitative responses: 1) What types of changes, if any, do you foresee in your child?; 2) What part of the program was most helpful to you?; 3) What did you like most about the program?; and 4) How could the program have been improved to help you more? Table 5.1 presents examples of each source of data included in the methodological triangulation.

Table 5.1. Examples of data included in methodological triangulation

Source of data	Example
Session note	Day 3. Mom asked if parent educator or center director know of anybody who lives [near the family] to consult or work directly with kids. Center director suggests that they [could] come back even for a few days or . . . could hire people and show them how to do the techniques.
Telephone conversation note	Mom called. [Child] started to increase his spontaneous language. [Significant caregiver] noticed an increase too. [Child] still tries to grab but will talk when [provided] an opportunity.
E-mail	[Parent,] Hi. How is school going for [your son]? How are you? Did the functional assessment idea help? You can call me. . . . I can explain more. . . . [Parent educator]
Answer to question on the Consumer Satisfaction Questionnaire	Question: What types of changes, if any, do you foresee? Parent answer: Increased speech and social interaction

As shown in Table 5.1, parent educators maintained detailed session and telephone conversation notes throughout the program to describe the questions, responses, and other communications that took place during and after the program. The data were collected and analyzed without a specific focus or predetermined expectation of where the information would lead (Lincoln & Guba, 1985). This inductive approach is most useful to explore, without preconceived notions, areas of study that have not previously been understood.

Document analyses were conducted on the session notes, telephone conversation notes, and e-mails. Initially, each continuous thought or idea within a document was read, and a set of codes was developed to organize the data (Miles & Huberman, 1994). This process of analysis resulted in the emergence of many codes.

Next, investigator triangulation, which included a variety of evaluators, was achieved through discussions between two coders and careful review and analysis of the codes. The two coders carefully read the documents, discussed and redefined the codes, and collapsed the codes into major themes. These documents were read, reviewed, and discussed by the two coders until discovery of repeated experienced and common themes emerged.

Data triangulation (i.e., the use of different data sources) was achieved by conducting member checks with parent and clinician participants. Member checks were then conducted with one of the primary caregivers and one of the parent educators to ensure accuracy and validity of the themes that emerged. Member checks consisted of short, directed telephone interviews based on the five themes that arose from the document analysis and coding. Members were provided with a brief description (approximately three sentences) for each theme and then were asked if the description fit with their own personal experience of participation in the program. Both the clinician and participant parent were very satisfied with the themes that emerged. They believed that the themes strongly reflected their experiences and only made minor changes or additions to confirm the themes. This program provides clinical services to many families aside from those who participated in this project. To further enhance the methods of triangulation, session notes, telephone conversation notes, and e-mails from additional families (who participated in this program but did not participate in this study) were added to strengthen the support of the qualitative findings.

Case Examples

Isak   Isak was a 3-year, 2-month-old boy who lived with his mother and father in a small Northwestern city. He received 30 hours per week of one-to-one behavior intervention in his home. Isak was nonverbal prior to beginning the program; however, he could repeat a few early developing speech sounds following an adult model, including /m/ and /b/. Isak did not have any consistent word labels, and he frequently engaged in disruptive behaviors (e.g., screaming, having tantrums, grabbing) and aggressive behaviors (e.g., hitting, kicking) to get his needs met. His age equivalent on the communication domain of the Vineland Adaptive Behavior Scales (Sparrow et al., 1984) was 1 year, 2 months. Isak showed some interest in several toys, but his appropriate play with toys was limited (e.g., he often looked at sticks or tapped crayons on his lips). He displayed self-stimulatory behaviors including jumping up and down, twirling his hair, and making repetitive verbal noises that were incompatible with learning opportunities. He was not toilet trained, and he neither interacted with nor showed interest in other children.

Jerry   Jerry was a 5-year, 4-month-old boy who lived with his mother, father, older sister, and younger brother in a suburban area of the Southwest. He attended a special education preschool 4 days per week for 2½ hours each day. He also received 12½ hours of one-to-one intervention and 1 hour each of individual speech therapy and occupational therapy in his home weekly. Prior to the intervention program, Jerry primarily communicated his needs verbally using short phrases and complete sentences, and many of his utterances were immediately echoed after an adult. The majority of his language served the function of making requests, and many of his utterances were protests (i.e., saying "no") to avoid or escape interactions with others or to escape demands. The communication domain of the Vineland Adaptive Behavior Scales (Sparrow et al., 1984) yielded an age equivalent score of 2 years, 9 months. Jerry engaged in inappropriate behaviors to gain access to items (e.g., grabbing items from others) and in disruptive behaviors (e.g., yelling, whining, hitting) when demands were placed on him, when he was told "no," or during transitions. He was interested in a variety of toys and activities such as markers and board games. He played appropriately with them; however, his play became repetitive after several minutes (e.g., he made his game piece land on the same position over and over, he recited a single phrase after each spin of the spinner).

Shad   Shad was a 2-year, 10-month-old boy who lived in a suburban area of the East Coast with his mother, father, and older sister. He received 22 hours per week of one-to-one intervention in his home. He also received 40 minutes of speech therapy and 45 minutes of occupational therapy weekly. Shad said several words and made several approximations to refer to all items that he wanted (e.g., /opie/ for *open* and *bubble*). He primarily repeated vocalizations and word approximations following an adult model or a carrier phrase. For example, an adult said "all" and Shad completed the statement by saying "done," or the adult said "need" and Shad responded with "help." The Vineland Adaptive Behavior Scales (Sparrow et al., 1984) yielded an age equivalent score of 1 year, 7 months. Shad frequently engaged in self-stimulatory behaviors including running in place, flapping his arms, and making repetitive verbal noises (e.g., /mumumu/) He also occasionally engaged in aggressive behaviors (e.g., biting others) and self-injurious behaviors (e.g. biting his hand) when verbal demands were placed on him. He showed interest in several toys and social games, yet the majority of his play was repetitive (e.g., putting stickers on and pulling them off his hands, toys, furniture, or other items).

Themes Underlying Parent–Clinician Communication

The results from the qualitative analysis show that five major themes emerged that describe the communication between the parents and clinicians throughout the program. A description of each pattern or theme is presented next, along with examples to verify it.

Theme 1: Parent Educators Viewed as Credible Sources   Based on communication between parent educators and program participants, the parents viewed the clinicians as credible resources for general information regarding their children as opposed to resources specifically related to the techniques of the training. This theme emerged for all of the families, as they asked the parent educators a variety of questions about their children aside from those specifically related to learning the techniques of PRT. Throughout the program, parents asked for suggestions in areas such as changing the children's behaviors (e.g., learning toilet training, learning independent skills, completing bathroom routine, sitting for mealtimes, reducing disruptive and self-stimulatory behaviors, receiving a haircut, going to the doctor, responding to name when called), school placement (e.g., full inclusion, home schooling), IEP goals, and peer or sibling interactions. For example, one mother asked for suggestions regarding formulation of IEP goals for her son. An upcoming IEP meeting was scheduled shortly after their participation in the program, so she asked the clinician to review the goals and then requested assistance in developing communication, social, and self-help goals for her son.

Two additional examples of parents viewing the clinicians as credible resources were exemplified by the follow-up requests for assistance. One mother requested assistance to address a bothersome behavior that emerged after the intervention program and for which she could not determine the cause. Another mother requested additional assistance with her son's challenging behaviors that he engaged in during care routines. She described her son's previous tantrum behaviors during these events and requested suggestions to improve his behaviors to accomplish these tasks. Furthermore, she requested assistance on how to prioritize behaviors that she wanted to teach her son.

These examples show parents turning to clinicians for suggestions on their children's overall intervention program, not just those related to PRT techniques. Thus, session notes and follow-up e-mails demonstrate that the parents viewed clinicians as credible sources of broad information.

> [My son] started sucking on his fingers a lot lately. I lent out the behavior book that you gave me, so I haven't had a chance to see if that can help, but maybe you have some suggestions. I haven't pinpointed anything that sets it off; sometimes I see it when he's bored but also when he's playing on the computer [or other things that don't require both hands]; also he will even play with the food in his mouth when he's eating. Anyway, if you've got any bright ideas on that. . . .

Another mother not only requested assistance on how to teach behaviors but also requested support to prioritize behaviors that she wanted to teach her son. In an e-mail she wrote,

> How important is teaching [my son] to broaden his food horizons? There is just so much he needs to learn: language, obviously. Also, dressing himself, eating with a fork, toilet training. Do I tackle and master one at a time, or work on all, slowly, at once?

This mother requested additional assistance with challenging behaviors that her son engaged in while taking a bath, having his nails cut, and getting a haircut. She described her son's previous tantrum behaviors during these events and requested suggestions to improve his behaviors to accomplish these tasks. The information from session notes and follow-up e-mail quotations demonstrates his parents turning to the clinician for suggestions on the child's overall educational program, not for items specifically related to the program's teaching techniques.

These results were verified through responses on the Consumer Satisfaction Questionnaires. In response to the question, "What did you like most about the program?" the second mother noted that it worked with each child's unique needs and answered all of her questions. To that same question, another mother wrote that she liked being able to ask questions and to have experienced clinicians observe and provide feedback on parent–child interactions.

Theme 2: Parents Experienced Positive Changes in Perceptions   During the program, parents reported noticeable improvements in their children's targeted behaviors. Families often shared anecdotal stories that occurred during or immediately following the week-long program to demonstrate that they saw improvements in their children's behaviors. For example, one mother initiated a follow-up telephone conversation and shared that her son had started to increase his spontaneous language (the targeted behavior). Another mother reported that her son was "doing really well with his speech." Through an e-mail, she later shared her success of taking him for a haircut after receiving recommendations from the clinician. She mentioned that incorporating those suggestions helped her son to remain still and quiet during the haircut, which was previously a difficult experience:

> I had forgotten that two weeks after [the parent education program], I had primed [my son] to "cut hair." He really did well—sat in the chair by himself (not on my lap), sat mostly still, and screamed [during] the entire haircut. After talking with you last week, I did better this

time. . . . Saturday, he sat alone, still, and silent for the entire haircut! The hairdresser was delirious [during] that last haircut: I think she held her breath for this one!

This theme of changed perceptions of the child was verified by another mother's response to a question on the Consumer Satisfaction Questionnaire: She wrote that what she liked most about the program was "seeing results."

Further evidence to support this theme was demonstrated by comments that other significant caregivers made to those who participated in the program. Each mother in this study reported through follow-up communication that she received verification of her child's noticeable improvements through comments from others, namely therapists or relatives. One mother commented that her child's grandparents noticed an improvement in her son's targeted behaviors, such as verbally requesting items and using complete sentences. In an e-mail she wrote, "While we were [visiting my parents], my mom commented on how well [he] was asking for things, using complete sentences, etc." Another mother commented in a telephone conversation that a significant caregiver noticed an increase in her son's spontaneous language shortly after their participation in the program. In a later telephone conversation, this mother told the clinician that her son's speech therapist, who was reluctant to incorporate PRT techniques into intervention sessions, eventually commented that "his word labels were coming quicker and more spontaneously. He was talking clearer and quicker in general." The third parent reported that home therapists noticed improvements in her son's functional language when the family returned home from the parent education program. In an e-mail, she wrote, "[He] is doing great. . . . Even his Lovaas program tutors said, 'Wow, he's talking up a storm!'"

Theme 3: Parents Initiated Questions Related to Training Others and Were Provided with Nondirective Responses

A theme that emerged through careful analysis of the session notes was that all primary caregivers initiated questions related to training others and recognized their desire for treatment to extend across settings for their children. In response, they were provided with nondirective comments rather than directed feedback. For example, one mother commented that no one in her family's area knew PRT techniques. Twice during the program, this mother initiated questions about how she and her husband could find individuals living in their area to work with her son and incorporate the techniques.

A second parent recognized that she would need to increase the amount of respite care that she received at home and mentioned that she planned to teach the respite providers how to implement the PRT techniques. In addition to those parent initiations, two parents in the study independently requested training videotapes, consisting of short segments of them with their children, that were collected during the program. One mother wanted to use the videotape to train the child's father at home so he could incorporate the techniques; the other mother requested the videotape to show her child's speech therapist the techniques that were presented during the training.

For all of the participant parents, nondirected responses were given to their questions regarding training others. For example, in response to one mother's questions about finding professionals who work in her family's area, the clinic director suggested simply finding people interested in working with her son and then training them in PRT techniques. In response to a second parent's question about training others who interact with the child, the clinician recommended that the mother show the other caregivers how to use the techniques. For all of the families, the clinicians and the center director suggested that parents train others who work with their children, but no specific recommendations for how to deliver the training were provided.

Theme 4: Parents Experienced Challenges in Integrating Services   After the parents experienced changed perceptions of their child's potential by seeing progress during the program, they expressed some dissatisfaction with their services when they returned home. Parents commonly report the challenge of integrating the newly learned skills into the child's educational programming and difficulties in collaborating with preexisting service providers. For example, through a follow-up telephone call, one mother stated that she experienced difficulties in coordinating services with her son's speech therapist. Another participant described her dissatisfaction with the services available in her family's area, commenting that the existing service providers seemed "intimidated" by new intervention techniques. The third participant seemed content with her son's teacher at school but expressed dissatisfaction with the summer services available to her child.

The challenge of program integration was further supported by several other mothers who participated in the parent education program but did not participate in this study. For example, a few days after one family returned home, a mother contacted ARTC because her child's existing therapists did not want to incorporate PRT techniques.

> I wanted to speak with you because I'm having problems with the [current therapists]. They don't want to do what I've learned and I'm going to have the meeting with the boss and she does not want to do it. So, basically, I have to find another program but until then I have to stay with them. I wanted to know if you know of any other programs that work the way you taught me.

This frustration was shared by yet another mother just after returning home. In a distressed voice, she left a message asking whether the home therapist's style of increasing her son's speech could be integrated with the PRT techniques that she had learned.

> I'm calling you because I really need your help. I really need help. The thing is that my behaviorist working in my home . . . they have another feeling of how to work with [my son]. I was trying to convince them that we need to work harder in his speech. . . . So, I am very confused now because they want to do their own style and I want another style and I don't know if we can combine [them].

Another mother described her frustration with her son's services at his school, which had him engaging in meaningless tasks in an attempt to foster independence. Her son's IEP meeting was approaching, and she wanted advice on which tasks she should ask the school to address. In an e-mail she wrote,

[My son's] IEP meeting is 7:30 a.m. Monday. The other day I came to pick him up from school for an appointment and they had him putting clothespins in a bowl to teach him independent tasks. He looked pathetic. He was slumped in his chair looking around as he did it. I can't see how they'll transition this into the regular education room or into anything in life. What tasks should they be teaching him at school to do independently?

Despite these evident challenges as stated in the document analysis, the parents generally resolved these issues in a variety of ways. A participant mother, after faced with resistance from her son's speech therapist, requested materials from the parent educator, including an additional copy of the training manual and videotaped segments from the program. In a follow-up telephone conversation, this mother reported that the speech therapist did in fact incorporate the techniques after reviewing the materials and seeing progress in the child's behavior. Verification of the child's progress by the speech therapist was previously reported under the heading for Theme 2. Another participant mother resolved her frustration by searching for different services. These responses demonstrate the parents' empowerment in coping with the obstacles of integrating their new skills with the previous services.

Theme 5: Parent Educators Provided Social Support to Parents   A final and salient theme that emerged through the qualitative analysis was that the parent educators provided social support to the families. Following Weiss's (1974) six provisions of support, the data suggest that several types of support were provided through the parent education program. First, the parent educators appeared to form a reliable alliance with the parents as evidenced throughout the program documents. For example, one mother stated that she always felt better after talking with her parent educator: "Thanks for your phone call. I always feel better after I talk with you." She added during the member check that the clinician provided support by talking to her every so often and by pointing out the child's progress. This mother also believed that she could call for any reason. This provision of support was further evidenced through the member check with a clinician who added that the parents were provided with e-mail addresses and strongly encouraged to contact ARTC at any time for any reason.

A second type of social support that was evident from analysis of the documents coincides with Weiss's (1974) reassurance of worth component. E-mail correspondence showed that the clinicians praised the parents on their use of the PRT techniques and on their general parenting skills. Throughout the program, the clinicians frequently encouraged the parents with general praise such as, "Keep it up! You and [your husband] are both great with him and will get him lots of opportunities." After viewing a videotape sent for feedback, a clinician wrote to another participant mother

Every time I watch your tapes I think that you are just the BEST mom!! . . . [Dad] also looks like such a great dad—the kids love playing with him and he's so much fun. I'll give you specific feedback later.

In addition to these general statements, the clinicians also provided specific, detailed positive feedback regarding the parents' use of PRT techniques. In the session notes, one clinician described the feedback that she gave to the mother: "Good prompts—good following lead and trying to interest him when he's not motivated." Another clinician described her feedback as follows: "Parent doing great at PRT on the swing, providing very clear instructions, being contingent, and following his lead. Also teaching him to hold onto the swing independently."

Another example of specific feedback related to the implementation of PRT procedures was provided to parents through telephone conversations. In her notes, one clinician wrote, "Talked to mom on the phone with feedback. Significant Caregiver is doing such a good job at PRT. She really follows his lead and has him request what he wants (i.e., get down, swing, push, cut hot dog, etc.)." Similar comments were made to another parent in a follow-up e-mail. The clinician wrote, "You are really having him talk more during looking through books. He is answering your questions perfectly and only needing a bit of prompting. The whole interaction looks so natural like you are not working. . . ."

The third type of support that emerged through the qualitative analysis was characterized by Weiss's (1974) guidance component. Throughout the program, the clinicians provided the parents with advice. As previously mentioned, the parents asked the clinicians a host of questions regarding their children's development, behaviors, services, and so forth. Following are examples of some of the recommendations that the clinicians provided to the families.

In response to one parent's question about how to introduce a variety of foods, the clinician suggested that the mother could introduce new foods gradually. For instance, the clinician recommended having the child take one bite of something new before getting to eat one of his favorite foods. Eventually, the mother could increase the number of bites required, thereby increasing the variety of foods her son ate.

The provision of guidance was also supported by the correspondence between clinicians and the additional families not involved in this study. Six months after participation, one mother requested assistance in developing goals for her son. She and the clinician exchanged several e-mails and had a brief telephone conversation to discuss ways of including her son in a general education classroom during challenging academic activities. After this troubleshooting process, the mother sent an e-mail expressing her enthusiasm for the advice received—that is, to have the school first engage her son in functional skills and then adapt more difficult aspects of the curriculum so he could do purposeful class activities. She then requested further advice for what to do if that approach did not work or if the school district refused to implement it:

> Thanks so much for all the help you're giving me! I am thinking if they get him doing [functional skills during class] like you suggested, then in time they could adapt [more difficult curriculum]. Do you have any ideas for a back-up plan if this doesn't work, or if the district doesn't go for it? I want [my son] to be doing purposeful, functional things that will do him some good and not just waste his time.

Summary of Themes   In summary, the theme of providing social support emerged for many of the families and was supported by a variety of sources. A review of the documents made clear, and the process of triangulation strengthened, the idea that social support was an important component to the program.

DISCUSSION OF CHAPTER CONCEPTS

As demonstrated, several themes emerged to describe how parents experienced their participation in a parent education program. Although the program focused on teaching parents specific strategies to improve their children's skills in areas of need, many other components of the program seem to be unknown and yet very important to understand. The findings, expressed through five themes, provide some insight into how families may feel about participating in a program such as the one described in this chapter.

Parent participants viewed the clinicians as credible resources. This theme highlights the individuality of children with autism and the need for more qualified and well-trained professionals in the field. Because each child and family is unique, caregivers had many specific questions about their children's needs. This information is not provided in any one manual, web site, or textbook. Rather, the strategies and suggestions need to fit for the particular child and with the child's family and school system (Albin, Lucyshyn, Horner, & Flannery, 1996; Bailey, 2001).

The parents commented on their observations that the children all demonstrated progress in their skills after participating. This finding is important for parents as consumers and collaborators to notice the gains that their children are making. Many parents question which type of services to select when provided a choice of services, and by seeing improvements in their children's skills, they can feel more confident with their services. In addition, the participant caregivers may have felt more confident or empowered by being able to improve their children's skills. Further research is needed in this area to assess the particular components of parent education programs that could result in increased parent empowerment; programs should strive to provide services that incorporate those components.

Another finding was the type of feedback and suggestions that the parents received when they asked the parent educator about training others. Placing the parents in the role of experts or trainers has been uncommon in the parent education literature (Symon, in press). However, this program aimed to do exactly that. It is interesting to note, however, that the focus of the program was not to teach this role to parents but, rather, to collaborate with them and concur with their suggestions for training others. With only minimal input from the parent educators, the parents trained other caregivers when they returned to their home settings.

The challenge of integrating services is common for many parents of children with autism. Many children with autism often need intensive intervention, so they often have an educational team comprised of specialists from a variety of disciplines. Parents often struggle to coordinate services among the different service providers and sometimes feel confused when team members' opinions are at odds. Even with the movement to include parents in the assessment, goal development, and implementation processes (IDEA 2004 reauthorization), collaboration continues to be a challenge. Although it has been well documented that parents play a critical role in their children's lives, and therefore should play a critical role in their children's education (Bailey, 2001; Soodak & Erwin, 2000), this philosophy has not been practiced consistently (Lake & Billingsley, 2000; Soodak; & Erwin, 2000; Taylor, 2001). It appears that despite efforts to encourage collaboration and development of amicable relationships between parents and providers, achieving such partnerships is a complicated process that still remains a challenge. To address these issues and challenges, programs have aimed to promote parents from the position of involved participants to that of partners by including parents in writing IEPs (Taylor, 2001), designing or coordinating programs (Bailey, 2001; Epstein, Munk, Bursuck, Polloway, & Jayanthi, 1999), and participating in group action planning (Blue-Banning, Turnbull, & Pereira, 2000). Another method of including parents in the forefront of their children's education has been through the use of training models. Parents have been included in a trainer-of-trainers model to increase the amount and availability of support and services. These researchers demonstrated that parents could effectively train other parents (Jenkins, Stephens, & Sternberg, 1980; Timm, 1993), support other parents (Singer et al., 1999), collaborate with speech therapists, train additional caregivers (Symon, in press), and train community outreach partners (McConkey, Mariga, Braadland, & Mphole, 2000). In the best interest of children and their families, educational teams should collaborate and compromise when adopting intervention strategies.

A final component of the parent education program that emerged through this qualitative analysis was that of social support for families. Some literature documents the provision of social support as a mediating variable for families (Bristol & Schopler, 1984; Dunst & Trivette, 1990; Minnes, 1988; Pierce et al., 1996). According to Weiss's (1974) provisions of support, parents in this study received social support through their relationship with the clinicians in three forms: guidance, formation of a reliable ally, and reassurance of worth.

DIRECTIONS FOR FUTURE RESEARCH

A deeper exploration of these results yields an interesting finding regarding the provisions of support and the clinician–parent relationship. As previously noted, Weiss (1974) suggested a typical, although not absolute, source that provides each type of support. According to this typology, guidance is typically provided by a mentor. This finding would have been expected through a parent education program whereby the clients (parents) sought advice and mentoring from the service provider (clinicians). This relationship was also supported by the documented theme of the parents viewing the clinicians as credible sources. In other words, the parents viewed the clinicians as valuable sources of knowledge and looked to them for guidance and advice. A second type of support provision that emerged was that the parents viewed the clinicians as reliable allies. It is interesting to note that Weiss (1974) aligned this type of support with close family members. It has been stated in previous literature that a reliable alliance is more likely to develop through casual discourse as opposed to formal, technical communication (Singer & Powers, 1993a). As shown in the communication documents presented, the communication style between the parents and clinicians was informal. On the contrary, the relationships between parents and many service providers, particularly school personnel, are often formal. Typically, and historically, a hierarchy exists in the delivery of services for children with disabilities, particularly in schools. Likewise, unilateral relationships typically exist between professionals and clients or advisors and advisees. In these cases, the formation of a reliable alliance would seem unlikely. However, the results from the present study provide contrary evidence. More research in this area is warranted.

Based on the findings, the third type of support provided to the parents was reassurance of worth, or providing praise for accomplishments. This type of support is most commonly provided by colleagues or co-workers (Weiss, 1974). Rather than maintaining a hierarchical relationship, the parent–clinician teams worked together as a team to address the child's behaviors and to develop the appropriate interventions for the child—that is, interventions that matched the value system of the family. This finding brings the discussion back to the importance of the role of parents and family members in the intervention process and also in establishing their value in this process. These findings propose that the supportive relationship established between the parents and clinicians may have served to assist the parents in overcoming challenges that they faced after their participation in the program.

Research shows that social support from a variety of sources may lead to greater parent satisfaction and more positive parent–child interactions (Crnic, Greenberg, Ragozin, Robinson, & Basham, 1983). Perhaps additional measures could be collected in a future study to examine these types and sources of caregiver support, including spouses, extended family, friendships, co-workers, group networks, and so forth. Ideally, researchers would discover critical variables for families' stress reduction and aim to provide these factors for future programs.

The findings added breadth to the previous quantitative analyses through several sources of documented communication; however, they did not provide all of the details of the parent–clinician relationship, such as personal communications and exchanges of anecdotal information. It also could not capture the experience of every family who participates in a parent education program. To further understand the components of the clinician–parent relationship and the experiences for families, additional research is needed. It is suggested that future researchers use elaborate qualitative methods to capture the details of the relationship in order to fully understand parent education from the parents' viewpoint and to enhance programming for these families and their children.

This study described the experiences of parents who participated in a very individualized program to learn the motivational teaching strategies of PRT. Parent education has long been considered an important component in effective programs for children with autism, and the information from this study supports parents as valuable educators for their children. We believe in the importance of supporting family values, empowering parents, and collaborating. In our continuous quest toward improving outcomes for children with autism and their families, we have begun to search for and understand the parents' experiences as participants in a parent education program.

6

Ecocultural Theory and Cultural Diversity in Intervention Programs

Karen Sze and Robert L. Koegel

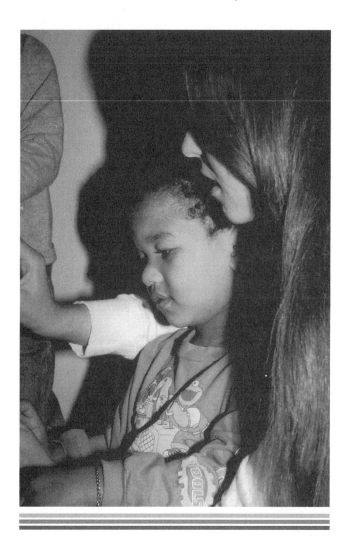

Since Leo Kanner's description of the syndrome, autism has been recognized as a disorder that occurs in every region of the world with remarkable consistency in its essential features. The literature from cross-cultural psychology (e.g., Segall, Lonner, & Berry, 1998) suggests that the extent to which key variables are related to serving individuals with a particular disorder may vary widely across cultures. Such is the case with autism; although the disorder imposes universal problems, cross-cultural differences are found in the attitudes of professionals and parents, as well as the ways in which they and their societies deal with autism (Everard, 1987). This chapter discusses ecocultural theory with examples related to intervention for culturally and linguistically diverse families.

OVERVIEW OF ECOCULTURAL THEORY

The application of ecocultural theory has extended beyond families of typically developing children to include families of children with differing lifestyles (Weisner & Garnier, 1992) as well as other exceptional children. This discussion focuses on a specific adaptation of ecocultural theory as a framework for understanding severe childhood disabilities such as autism (Gallimore, Weisner, Kaufman, & Bernheimer, 1989).

The Ecocultural Niche

Families create their own ecocultural niche as a result of their adaptive task of establishing meaningful daily routines (described in the following section). As its name suggests, the ecocultural niche (or *econiche*) reflected in families' account of daily routines is a mix of culture and ecology that delineates the larger sociocultural environment surrounding the child and family. A family's econiche takes into account the material environment and ecology, such as housing and space, income, public health conditions, transportation, and distance from relatives or services. Another dimension of the econiche reflects cultural influences, which are used by individuals to understand and organize their everyday lives (Gallimore et al., 1989). Furthermore, niches are hierarchical and interconnected in nature, in which some features (i.e., mortality, subsistence, and moral-cultural training) are more powerful than others (Bernheimer, Gallimore, & Weisner, 1990). Econiche variables offer insight into the origins of parental beliefs about goals for a child's development (Schneider & Gearhart, 1988) and changes in relation to socioeconomic constraints, resources, and family accommodations (Gallimore et al., 1989).

Activity Settings   Ecocultural theory proposes that the activity settings of daily routines in the home should be the primary unit of analysis (Bernheimer et al., 1990; Bernheimer & Keogh, 1995; Gallimore et al., 1989; Kellegrew, 2000), as they are created and sustained by ecocultural influences. In this framework, daily routines are viewed as the central adaptive task that families actively strive to construct and sustain (Gallimore, Bernheimer, & Weisner, 1999). In addition to providing structure to family life, daily routines provide natural and deliberate opportunities to promote children's learning and development throughout the day. As articulated by Gallimore and colleagues (1989), the value of activity settings to families lies in the fact that they occur naturally—they are familiar parts of a family's day, the "architecture of every-day life" that constitutes adult–child interactions. Examples of daily routines specific to families of children with disabilities include fostering independent self-help skills by having a child make his or her bed and reading storybooks with the child to promote cognitive and linguistic development. The literature suggests that daily routines are mediated by the ecological and cultural system in which a child is raised. As documented in classical ethnographic studies, the cultural context reveals potent information on the meaning and values that a family assigns to activity settings (Harkness & Super, 1995; Whiting & Whiting, 1975). The fact that powerful cultural beliefs and personal values affect the organization and types of daily routines unique to each household underscores the social-constructivist perspective adopted by ecocultural theorists.

The Accommodation Process   Families in the ecocultural framework make proactive efforts (i.e., accommodations), both at the individual and collective level, to adapt, exploit, counterbalance, and react to competing and contradictory forces (Gallimore et al., 1989). Accommodation occurs in response to econiche variables, factors over which families only have partial control (Schneider & Gearhart, 1988), within the context of a larger ecological system. Furthermore, accommodation is mediated by cultural goals and values unique to each family (Gallimore, Weisner, Bernheimer, Guthrie, & Nihira, 1993). Studies on the accommodation process in families of children with disabilities reveal that family accommodation need not be activated by stressful events: it is theoretically presumed to be occurring in response to both serious concerns and mundane problems of daily life (Gallimore et al., 1993). Accommodation is an ongoing process that is believed to have costs and benefits to each individual in the family and to the family as a whole (Gallimore, Coots, Weisner, Garnier, & Guthrie, 1996).

An Ecocultural Approach to Treating Children with Disabilities   An ecocultural approach to treating children with disabilities focuses on enhancing the quality of life of the entire family through the modification of daily routines. Consistent with the ecocultural literature, daily routines should be the primary unit of analysis for planning intervention programs because they provide an accurate picture of the family's valued goals and activities that sustain family life (Bernheimer & Keogh, 1995). Daily routines provide much-needed structure for the lives of families of children with disabilities and provide deliberate learning opportunities to enhance the children's development of skills that are meaningful. In attempting to understand the family's social construction of meanings, intervention should focus on the sustainability of these routines (Gallimore et al., 1999). When individualizing treatment using the ecocultural approach, there are a number of factors that affect the sustainability of routines: ecological features of the family's econiche, the family's goals and values, and personal characteristics of family members. In addition, interventions are more likely to be sustained if contextual fit is secured (Albin, Lucyshyn, Horner, & Flannery, 1996). *Contextual fit* refers to interventions that are compatible with the individual child, the values and goals of family members, and the existing routines and everyday living patterns in the surrounding environment. Specifically, a family ecol-

When designing an effective treatment program, the family's individual needs, goals, and values must be taken into account.

ogy assessment may be conducted through interviews and discussions with family members in order to identify and understand family characteristics, family values and goals, and the ways in which the family has constructed meaning (Albin et al., 1996; Gallimore et al., 1989).

The effectiveness of interventions depend on the family's adjustment to the child's disability and the interventionist's understanding of the family's perspective in dealing with the child's disability within the context of its routines. As noted by Bernheimer et al. (1990), ecological interventions extend beyond a traditional family needs assessment, which only focuses on demographics and other descriptive interventions, to include family beliefs and values. A successful example of a contextual intervention was provided by Moes and Frea (2000), who reported decreases in disruptive behaviors and increases in adaptive behaviors in a child when treatment was contextualized. It is suggested that the sustainability of behavior support plans contributed to the generalization and maintenance of treatment gains. The same authors (2002) extended this line of research by demonstrating that the adaptation of validated behavioral interventions, such as functional communication training (FCT), to incorporate the individual needs and values of families contributed to the stability and durability of reductions in challenging behaviors in children with autism. Similarly, Lucyshyn, Albin, and Nixon (1997) noted improvements in child behavior and routine completion of activities when functional assessment procedures were used in conjunction with a comprehensive ecological assessment. Collectively, family members are more likely to implement and sustain interventions if the interventions fit into the family's daily routines and are compatible with the parents' goals and values.

The importance of understanding the meanings, goals, and values that a family has assigned to daily routines, ecocultural niche, and the accommodation process becomes particularly salient when the family comes from a culturally and linguistically diverse (CLD) background. The following section shifts to the discussion of ecocultural theory as applied to treatment of CLD children with severe disabilities such as autism.

Following the extensive empirical support for the standard implementation of Pivotal Response Treatment (PRT) procedures, a large part of PRT research is now shifting to individualizing treatment to meet each family's and child's needs (R.L. Koegel, Koegel, & Brookman, 2003). When working with CLD families of children with autism, literature suggests one future area for exploration may relate to increased participation from families when additional cultural variables, such as those involved in the formation of parent–professional collaborative partnerships, are incorporated into the PRT program (Brookman-Frazee, 2004). Specifically in terms of PRT implementation, motivational components may be easily individualized in ways that are consistent with cultural variables. For example, selecting tasks, activities, or natural reinforcers to use with a family that fit with its cultural background and ethnic customs will likely increase both the child's performance and the family's participation in the use of PRT. It also may influence the family's motivation to collaborate with professionals. It is especially important to consider the PRT model from a culturally sensitive perspective, as cultural differences may affect the ways in which parents perceive, evaluate, and use an intervention program (Schreibman & Koegel, 2005).

ECOCULTURAL THEORY AND FAMILIES OF CULTURALLY AND LINGUISTICALLY DIVERSE CHILDREN WITH DISABILITIES

The current emphasis on cultural diversity in the disability literature permeates through the disciplines of psychology and special education. Several dimensions of culture are fundamental to understanding disability in the context of CLD families. First, the literature suggests the importance of examining cultural definitions and interpretations of disabilities, which are socially constructed according to group norms and expectations (Harry, 2002; Kalyanpur & Harry, 1997). Professionals should be aware that families from different cultures might attach different meanings to a condition, with some conditions being perceived as more or less stigmatizing in other societies. Rogers-Adkinson, Ochoa, and Delgado (2003) explored the differing interpretations of disability for several cultural groups. For example, in Navajo culture, children with disabilities participate in all traditional aspects of child rearing instead of receiving segregated services, due to the cultural belief that the person with a disability is a teacher to the clan. This is not the case with other cultures, which may be more likely to segregate children with disabilities. Collectively, when working with CLD families, professionals should take into account culturally appropriate developmental norms and recognize family interpretations of and attitudes toward disability.

Second, professionals need to be aware of culturally mediated child-rearing practices. This includes parents' expectations for their child with a disability and methods of discipline (Chen, Downing, & Peckham-Hardin, 2002; Kalyanpur & Harry, 1997). Although mainstream American culture typically focuses on the development of autonomy and independence, some families may place more value on interdependence and caring for each other. For example, in traditional Asian and Latino families, early self-help skills are given less emphasis, and parents tend to be more protective of their children than in European American families (Chen et al., 2002). Furthermore, different cultures may have different expectations of what constitutes "appropriate behavior" for a child with a disability. For example, Puerto Rican, Mexican, and Columbian parents coming from a strong religious belief system may be more accepting of a child's limitations and functioning level (Rogers-Adkinson et al., 2003). Similarly, discipline methods are also mediated by cultural variables. Chen et al. (2002) suggested that methods that families use to discipline their children may influence their participation in the development and implementation of behavior support plans. For example, discipline methods such as shaming, which may be considered abusive by members of the mainstream American culture, may be viewed as culturally appropriate in traditional Asian families (Ho, 1987; Sue, 1981).

Finally, professionals should recognize the role played by the cultural interpretation of family systems, its impact on families' participation in a child's intervention program, and its impact on their relationship with service providers (Chen et al., 2002). For example, traditional Asian, Latino, African, Native American, and Middle Eastern families tend to be multigenerational and extended in structure. Family characteristics such as clear roles and responsibilities, filial obligation, and extended family may affect the family's participation in the child's treatment and their relationship with professionals. Overall, the issue of cultural diversity in the study of disability calls for the need of a contextualist approach, which emphasizes the embeddedness of all contexts (Harry, 2002). In essence, culture brings extra dimensions to the process of treatment planning for children with severe disabilities.

In a review of trends and issues in serving culturally diverse families of children with disabilities, Harry (2002) identified two major barriers to the study of these families: ethnocentrism and the subsuming of cultural identity into disability as the master status. The ecocultural approach offers various ways to address these barriers. Consistent with a contextualist approach to the study of diverse families, an ecocultural approach to treatment utilizes the activity setting as the basic unit of analysis, thus allowing a shift from the larger context to a microanalysis of family contexts. It provides professionals with a useful framework to analyze the impact of culture and context on families' accommodations for their child's disability.

Addressing the Cultural Component of Ecocultural Theory

In examining the cultural component in ecocultural theory, it is helpful to refer to the theory's origins. From its inception, ecocultural theory has been distinguished by its applicability to families in all cultures and its intention to be cross-culturally valid

(Bernheimer et al., 1990). As discussed in the classical ethnographic literature on culture and parenting by Whiting and colleagues (Whiting & Edwards, 1988; Whiting & Whiting, 1975), culture acts as the "provider of settings" while parents act as "organizers of settings" for their children's development (Whiting & Edwards, 1988, p. 35). Bernheimer and colleagues (1990) discussed several reasons that support the meaningful, nondiscriminatory, and nonjudgmental nature of ecocultural theory. In particular, they proposed that ecocultural theory provides an empirical basis to prevent the dangers of comparisons that always favor the dominant groups.

The field of psychology has become increasingly concerned with the issue of cultural diversity within culturally complex societies (Segall et al., 1998). It may be inferred from the preceding discussion that in theory, the ecocultural approach provides a practical and meaningful framework to inform treatments for CLD children with severe disabilities and their families. However, it is interesting to note that because the theory was conceived entirely from examining the family life of a particular cultural group in its own immediate context (e.g., native Kenyans in Kenya), further work needs to be done to evaluate ecocultural theory of family life in terms of cultural contact with other groups (e.g., Kenyans in the context of the mainstream American culture). This may be quite challenging in a complex plural society such as the United States. Berry (1997) defined a *plural society* as one where people of many cultural backgrounds come to live together in a diverse community. Acknowledging the complexities of a culturally diverse society means that the characteristics of the econiche in CLD families of children with disabilities need to reflect the unique experience of cultural minorities in a plural society.

Ecocultural Niche of Culturally and Linguistically Diverse Families

Most studies have focused on applying an ecocultural framework to study the adaptation of European American, middle-class families to having a child with a severe disability. In general, there is limited research on children from CLD backgrounds with severe disabilities and none on working with CLD families of children with autism (Zhang & Bennett, 2003). However, there have been a few promising studies examining the ways in which CLD families respond to the challenges associated with raising children with disabilities. For example, Skinner, Rodriguez, and Bailey (1999) interviewed Latino parents of children with mental retardation and suggested that the implementation of interventions that fit parents' cultural/religious interpretation of their child's disability was a critical component of success. Another emerging line of research examines the experiences of immigrant families of children with disabilities in the United States as compared with those in their country of origin. For example, Raghavan, Weisner, and Patel (1999) compared patterns of accommodation to children with developmental delays of South Asian families living in California with similar European American families. Both groups of families were found to share similarities regarding hope for improvement, active service use, educational and medical issues, and work/child care problems. Although the families positively appraised the services they had received, as compared with those they may have received if they had not immigrated, South Asian families lamented the loss of support from extended family members had they remained in their country of origin. Similarly, Cho, Singer, and Brenner (2000, 2003) compared adaptation and accommodation responses from Korean and Korean American parents and found that despite the common adaptive task of actively making accommodations for a child with a disability, parents in Korea experienced more difficulties than their immigrant counterparts due to dramatic differences in social policy, public policy, and resources available in the two nations.

Findings from this line of research appear to support the universal assumption of ecocultural theory that all families seek to make meaningful accommodations to their ecological niches through the construction of sustainable routines of daily living (Cooper & Denner, 1998). However, it also appears that some aspects of the ecocultural niche of having a child with a disability may be unique to CLD families in pluralistic societies. Specifically, in addition to the three basic components to the theory, these families' ecocultural niche appears to be mediated by the combined forces of acculturation and oppression. As different cultural groups come into contact in a pluralistic society, a family's acculturation strategies—including assimilation, separation, integration, or marginalization (Berry, Kim, Power, Young, & Bujaki, 1989)—will produce different effects on their receptivity to or involvement in their child's intervention plan. The acculturation process has a powerful effect both on parenting styles and on parental beliefs about child development (Harry, 2002): CLD families become immersed in the dominant culture over time, their behavior may adapt in response to social, political, and demographic changes. For example, Cho and colleagues (2000) found that in contrast to their Korean counterparts, immigrant Korean mothers in their study worked outside the home and were amenable to giving their children fast food for meals. This shift in family values and accommodation responses has resulted from corresponding social changes that accompany acculturation in American society. In addition to acculturation, families' ecocultural niche is also influenced by the unique oppression or discrimination experienced by their cultural group in relation to the material environment and ecology. For example, in a study examining African American families' perceptions of cultural sensitivity within the special education system, Zionts, Zionts, Harrison, and Bellinger (2003) found strong relationships between cultural differences (discrimination) and satisfaction with services as related to issues of cultural respect and levels of comfort.

It is noted that the importance of taking culture into consideration when formulating interventions for children with disabilities is bound by the extent to which the particular family embraces its original culture (i.e., enculturation). Historically, second- and third-generation families are more likely to assume the values of the dominant culture in thinking and behavior (Rogers-Adkinson et al., 2003). Therefore, culturally modified treatments for CLD children with disabilities may not be necessary for these very acculturated families. From this perspective, ecocultural theory in its original form does not take into account the subtle complexities of culture in pluralistic societies, such as acculturation and oppression, and their effects on formulating treatments specifically tailored for CLD children with disabilities.

Despite the limited literature on the application of ecocultural theory as it relates to CLD children with severe disabilities in the context of culture contact, there is a growing body of literature on the use of positive behavior support (PBS) techniques with culturally diverse families. These intervention procedures take into account the experiences of immigrant families in a plural society. PBS is a professional, behaviorally based movement that shares many theoretical perspectives of ecocultural theory. For example, it shares an emphasis on good contextual fit with family life, the use of family activity setting as a unit of analysis; person-centered values; comprehensive lifestyle change; and value of the family's beliefs, needs, and preferences (Lucyshyn, Horner, Dunlap, Albin, & Ben, 2002). Ecocultural theory provides a useful framework for understanding PBS. The following section provides a discussion of ecocultural theory in the context of providing PBS to CLD families of children with disabilities.

Ecocultural Theory in the Context of Positive Behavior Support for Culturally and Linguistically Diverse Families

As noted by Lucyshyn and colleagues (2002), although attaining goodness-of-fit (Albin et al., 1996) in the collaborative process of conducting a functional assessment or designing a behavior support plan is sufficient for some families, a more in-depth understanding of family ecology may be required to ensure contextual fit for families of culturally diverse backgrounds. Recognizing that the diverse values, child-rearing practices, and behavioral expectations of CLD families may affect the implementation of behavior support plans, many PBS researchers have developed excellent guidelines for using culturally responsive practices during functional assessment and behavior support plan development.

Chen and colleagues (2002) suggested that for CLD families, information concerning family ecology should be gathered prior to or concurrent with the completion of a functional assessment. Operating within an ecocultural framework, they point to the importance of obtaining information about daily routines in designing interventions that are consistent with cultural patterns and lifestyles in order to increase the likelihood of the plan being implemented consistently over time. Continuing this line of research, Salend and Taylor (2002) addressed the need for differential treatment of culturally diverse children in functional assessment procedures. They proposed a number of guidelines for conducting culturally sensitive functional assessments: creating a diverse multidisciplinary team, using culturally sensitive ways of selecting and defining target behaviors, collecting information about students and their behaviors, analyzing data and formulating hypothesis statements, and developing culturally responsive behavioral intervention plans and evaluating their impact on students' cultural perspectives.

Santarelli, Koegel, Casas, and Koegel (2001) applied the ecoculturally informed idea of contextual fit to a behavior therapy parent education program for a Spanish-speaking family of a child with autism. Specifically, the ecocultural barriers and cultural values targeted were providing therapy in the family's native language, providing therapy in the home (to address the constraint of transportation), allowing flexibility in scheduling to suit the needs of the family, and incorporating the extended family into intervention sessions (cultural values). The authors reported that once these barriers were overcome, there was consistent implementation of intervention in the home by family members, positive reception of the intervention by the family, and child improvement. Likewise, Callicott (2003) developed culturally sensitive guidelines for the person-centered planning process and noted that cultural differences can affect the communication of success outcomes.

In essence, the literature on PBS-based interventions suggests the need to modify some key components in order to meet the needs of CLD families of children with severe disabilities. Emerging literature on ecocultural theory has provided professionals with a useful framework to understand these families' lifestyles, goals and values, and accommodation processes. In order to address the need to tailor ecoculturally informed interventions to meet the needs of families of CLD children with disabilities, the PBS literature on cultural diversity offers culturally sensitive guidelines for professionals who work with these families.

When implementing PRT with CLD families of children with autism, various aspects of treatment may be modified to better meet their needs. In terms of creating opportunities to use language during natural, ongoing activities, clinicians may provide a context for language learning that is relevant to CLD families' values and needs. For example, when working with an Asian American family that values traditional foods, it may be more appropriate to provide the child with language opportunities for preferred snacks such as noodles, toasted seaweed, and shrimp crackers instead of Doritos or Oreos. Given the emphasis of PRT on increasing the child's motivation to communicate (L.K. Koegel, Koegel, Harrower, & Carter, 1999), creating a culturally relevant context for language acquisition will facilitate the use of the most powerful and relevant reinforcers and, therefore, the development of increased motivation as a pivotal response. In contrast, if the context for establishing language opportunities does not include such cultural considerations, the intervention may not be effective in targeting the pivotal area of motivation.

DISCUSSION OF CHAPTER CONCEPTS AND DIRECTIONS FOR FUTURE RESEARCH

Ecocultural theory has proven to be extremely instrumental in its use of culture as an adaptive tool to understand children's development in the context of the family and to modify interventions for children with severe disabilities. In examining the origins of ecocultural theory, it appears that the theory evolved out of studying family life in its local or immediate cultural context. However, there is still a need for research that takes cultural contact between diverse cultural groups into consideration. Although ecocultural theory is well recognized for studying individuals in their own cultural context, future studies need to examine families in the context of culture contact, where cultural groups interact in a pluralistic, "melting pot" society such as the United States.

Emerging research examining the ecocultural niche of CLD families of children with severe disabilities reveal two critical findings: 1) these families share the common universalistic assumption of ecocultural theory that families are driven by the adaptive task of making accommodation through the creation of meaningful daily routines and 2) their econiche features incorporate the culture-mediated variables of acculturation and oppression that are unique to CLD families. It is noted that the extant literature on the application of ecocultural theory to families of children with disabilities have neither fully nor explicitly addressed the effect of these variables on the accommodation patterns of these families.

Systemic data on the implementation of PRT with CLD families of children with autism are likely to be an especially important area for future exploration. At present, clinical information suggests that PRT is especially effective with CLD families when several treatment variables are incorporated into its implementation: 1) a collaborative parent–professional partnership, 2) individualization of motivational components according to cultural needs, and 3) a culturally relevant context for language learning. Given the pivotal role of cultural variables such as acculturation and oppression, future research may continue to investigate the feasibility of using an ecocultural approach to design treatment for CLD children with disabilities within these culturally defined parameters.

II

Development of Communication

7

Developmental Trajectories with Early Intervention

Robert L. Koegel, Yvonne E.M. Bruinsma, and Lynn Kern Koegel

The literature suggests that early intervention is crucial to the development and prognosis of young children diagnosed with autism. This chapter discusses the communicative progress for five children younger than 3 years of age who initially were essentially nonverbal. Intervention was implemented in the context of a parent education program using motivational procedures described by Pivotal Response Treatment (PRT). As a result of this early intervention, all five children demonstrated substantial gains. For three of the children whose data were analyzed in greater detail, developmental trajectories accelerated to near the typical range after the start of intervention.

BACKGROUND

Once considered a relatively rare disability (Lotter, 1966; Ritvo et al., 1989), estimates on the incidence of autism spectrum disorders (ASDs) now suggest a geometrical increase (Filipek et al., 1999; Fombonne, 1998; Gillberg & Wing, 1999). By the late 1990s, autism was most frequently diagnosed between ages 3 and 4 (Azar, 1998; Filipek et al., 1999). However, advances in screening and diagnosis suggest that children as young as 18 months of age can be reliably identified by individuals with expertise in autism diagnosis (Baron-Cohen, Cox, Baird, Swettenham, & Nightingale, 1996; Bristol-Power & Spinella, 1999; Robins, Fein, Barton, & Green, 2001). Some research even suggests that a diagnosis may be possible as early as 8–12 months of age (Baranek, 1999; Gray & Tonge, 2001; Osterling & Dawson, 1994; Osterling, Dawson, & Munson, 2002).

The importance of early diagnosis has been emphasized by researchers and practitioners, who recommend starting intervention as early as possible in the child's development, preferably before age 3 (Dawson & Osterling, 1997; McGee, Morrier, & Daly, 1999; Mesibov, Adams, & Klinger, 1997; National Research Council, 2001; Rogers, 1998; Schreibman, 2000). However, advances in diagnosing children at very young ages are not yet reflected in the existing literature regarding early intervention outcomes. Reviews by Dawson and Osterling (1997) and Smith (1999) of early intervention outcomes for children with autism reveal that although some programs and studies included participants under age 3, the overall mean age at start of intervention was older than 43 months. In general, research including very young children with autism is limited.

As a whole, the literature supports the need for early intervention data. That is, studies focusing on preschoolers with autism have documented the positive short and long-term effects (e.g., Anderson, Avery, DiPietro, Edwards, & Christian, 1987; Campbell et al., 1998; Dawson & Osterling, 1997; Fenske, Zalenski, Krantz, & McClannahan, 1985; Lovaas, 1987; McClannahan & Krantz, 1997; McEachin, Smith, & Lovaas, 1993). These outcomes have ranged from partial to nearly complete remediation of symptoms in as many half of the young children diagnosed with autism (e.g., Anderson et al., 1987; Dawson & Osterling, 1997; Fenske et al., 1985; Handleman, Harris, Celiberti, Lilleheht, & Tomchek, 1991; Harris, Handleman, Gordon, Kristoff, & Fuentes, 1991; Hoyson, Jamieson, & Strain, 1984; Lord & Schopler, 1989, 1994; Lovaas, 1987; McEachin et al., 1993; Sheinkopf & Siegel, 1998). Such

Functional speech is a vital part of social interaction and a critical component of an individual's overall quality of life.

studies lay the groundwork for the importance of measuring developmental trajectories as they relate to the trajectories of typically developing children. Specifically, an important question is whether the learning curves of young children with autism are accelerated when intervention begins before age 3. The trajectories of communicative development, particularly in the area of expressive verbal communication, may be especially important because lack of communicative competence is a hallmark of autism (Lord & Paul, 1997; Wetherby & Prizant, 1999). Families often view communication deficits as one of their greatest sources of stress (Bristol, 1984), and parents frequently note that a lack of communication is their first indication that their child may have a disability (Lord & Paul, 1997; Lord & Pickles, 1996; Siegel, Pliner, Eschler, & Elliott, 1988). In addition, deficits or delays in verbal expressive communication have been hypothesized to be the underlying cause of secondary maladaptive behaviors, such as self-injurious behavior or aggression, that create even more stress for families (L.K. Koegel, Valdez-Menchaca, & Koegel, 1994). Finally, the presence of functional speech before age 5 is reported to be associated with more favorable clinical outcomes (DeMyer et al., 1973; Freeman, Ritvo, Needleman, & Yokota, 1985; Garfin & Lord, 1986; McEachin et al., 1993). Therefore, determining interventions that have a positive influence on the children's early development is of critical importance.

INTERVENTION

Parents of the children who participated in the intervention described in this chapter received ongoing parent education. The goal of this intervention component was having parents evoke communication from their children on an ongoing basis through-out the day. Parent education sessions were conducted for 5 hours each week (with reported follow-through by the parents during the remainder of the week). At least one parent (usually the mother), the child, and the parent educator attended each session. All sessions were held in the families' homes and were implemented once to twice weekly. It should be noted that there also was usually a spread of effect to other treatment providers and educators, with the parents working collaboratively to coach these other intervention providers.

The parent educator had a master's or higher-level degree, with advanced train-ing in applied behavior analysis and at least 2 years of experience in providing parent education to families of children with autism. In addition, two doctoral-level super-visors (one of whom was also a speech-language pathologist) met weekly to review videotaped sessions.

During intervention sessions, parents were shown how to increase their child's re-sponsivity by using a modified discrete trial format (stimulus–response–consequence) with motivational factors in the context of natural activities. Motivational factors were based on the PRT procedures described in detail in the earlier chapters of this book and in a variety of professional journals (L.K. Koegel, Koegel, Harrower, & Carter, 1999; R.L. Koegel, Bimbela, & Schreibman, 1996; Schreibman, Kaneko, & Koegel, 1991) and included

- Following the child's lead and interest in the choice of stimulus materials
- Regularly varying the task to keep the child's interest
- Interspersing maintenance (previously mastered) tasks among acquisition (new) tasks to create behavioral momentum
- Reinforcing correct responses as well as the child's reasonable attempts
- Providing direct and natural reinforcers–that is, reinforcers that were an intrinsic part of the task (e.g., opportunity to play with the item requested by the child)

The parent educator used modeling and ongoing positive feedback to actively en-gage parents in the use of the techniques. Parents practiced during typical daily rou-tine activities (e.g., mealtime, bath time, dressing) as well as during play, with the goal of encouraging the use of the techniques throughout the day.

Measurement

Parent questionnaires and observational data were collected for each family. In ad-dition, fidelity of implementation measures were collected to ensure that each parent reached a minimal 80% level of correct implementation of the previously listed mo-tivational procedures. Measures were as follows:

1. *Observations:* Observational measures were collected, either by scoring videotapes or directly observing the child with his or her parent(s) in a playroom or in the living room of the family's home. These settings contained a large variety of age-appropriate toys with which the child could play. Short representative samples

were collected while the parent attempted to evoke communication from the child. From these observations, the following analyses of the child's communication were made:

- Total number of words: All words that the child said were recorded. It was noted whether the utterances were spontaneous, prompted, or echolalic in nature. *Echolalic utterances* were defined as nonfunctional imitative utterances. For example, if the mother said, "Do you want a cookie?" and the child said, "You want a cookie?" in return, the utterance was coded as echolalic. Echolalic utterances were excluded from the sum of the total number of words used by the child (Miller, 1981). If an utterance was unintelligible, it was also excluded from analysis. *Prompted responses* were defined as any appropriate functional verbal response to a verbal or nonverbal stimulus by the parent. Examples might include the mother saying, "What do you want" and the child answering, "Ball" or the mother holding up a bottle of bubbles and the child saying, "More bubbles." *Spontaneous speech* was defined as any appropriate functional verbal response without a verbal or nonverbal stimulus by the parent. An example might be if the mother and her child were playing with an animal puzzle and the child looked over to the ball and said, "Ball." Each type of word was subsequently summed to obtain a total number for each category.

- Vocabulary diversity: It was also important to calculate the child's vocabulary diversity—in other words, how many different words the child said. Again, echolalic and unclear utterances were excluded from the count.

2. *Parent measures:* In this study, the parent measure consisted of the Vineland Adaptive Behavior Scales (Sparrow, Balla, & Cicchetti, 1984), which includes parent interviews about the child's communication skills.

Findings

Prior to specialized intervention, the children with autism younger than age 3 used no or very few expressive words. Following intervention that focused on incorporating motivational procedures, however, most children made very rapid gains. In fact, in this analysis of five young children, four of whom said no words prior to intervention, all children showed considerable progress after receiving this short intervention. The range of words that the children said in a representative 10-minute sample while their mothers were evoking expressive communication was from approximately 16 to up to more than 200 words per typical sample. Furthermore, their vocabulary was marked by both diversity and spontaneity. That is, the children's diversity of words ranged from approximately 3 different words to approximately 93 different words within a typical 10-minute sample. Finally, the children were able to use their new words spontaneously, ranging from approximately 2 to 30 spontaneous words per typical 10-minute sample. As can be seen in Figure 7.1, data from the Vineland Adaptive Behavior Scales (Sparrow et al., 1984) Communication Domain age equivalences for five children demonstrate that scores for all of the children with autism fell well below the expected norms for their ages prior to intervention. How-

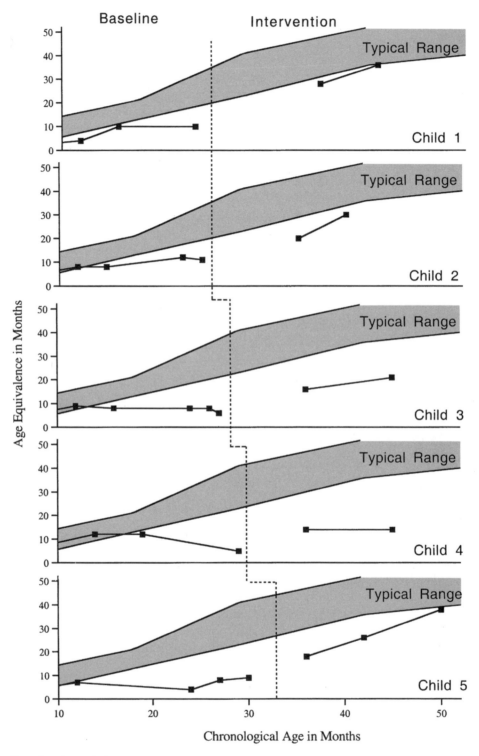

Figure 7.1.   Age equivalences on the Vineland Adaptive Behavior Scales Communication Domain (Sparrow, Balla, & Cicchetti, 1984) for five children prior to and during intervention. The shaded area represents the range (plus or minus 1 standard deviation; Sparrow et al., 1984) for typically developing children.

ever, following the short intervention, strong and steady gains occurred. The children's chronological ages are depicted on the abscissa (x-axis), while their age equivalence scores are depicted on the ordinate (y-axis). The shaded area in the graph represents the range in development of communication skills in typical children in terms of age equivalence scores on the Vineland Adaptive Behavior Scales Communication Domain (average development plus or minus 1 standard deviation; Sparrow et al., 1984). The data depicted in the graphs are consistent with the trends that were observed for the children's gains in speech, with Child 1, Child 2, and Child 5 making very strong steady gains and Child 3 and Child 4 having slower, less dramatic trajectories. Of particular note is the fact that three of the five children's developmental trajectories accelerated to near the level for typically developing children.

Case Example

Just before his second birthday, Andrew received a diagnosis of autism. At that time, he was nonverbal. According to his parents, he had on several occasions said a word such as *duck* or *Dada*; however, he did not use any words consistently with a clear intent to communicate. Andrew lived with his parents in a two-bedroom apartment that was part of a large complex. Many young families lived in the complex and shared the facilities, including a laundry room, a children's playground, a bike path, walkways, and community yards.

Andrew enjoyed certain activities and items, including kicking balls, playing with cars and trucks, building blocks, and watching television; however, he spent a great deal of time outdoors engaged in repetitive behaviors such as placing leaves inside a small drain hole and running back and forth along a fence. To communicate his needs, he reached for items that he wanted, made brief eye contact, and occasionally vocalized (e.g., saying, "Dadada"). He also engaged in a greater number of tantrums than appropriate for his age. These often occurred when Andrew was told "no" or when he wanted certain items. Sometimes his tantrums lasted for up to 40 minutes.

Andrew's interactions with other children were discouraging. Many young children lived in the apartment community; however, Andrew showed no interest in them. When passing by other children in the walkways or on the playground, Andrew typically turned and walked the other direction. When approached by other children in closer proximity, such as during a play group or in the laundry room, Andrew screamed to terminate the interactions. His interactions with other children brought a painful look to his mother's face and a tear to her eye.

Andrew's parents were very loving and caring toward each other and toward Andrew. Their interactions with Andrew were typical of those recommended by early childhood educators to foster and encourage emotional, social, and communicative development. They read to him. They tickled and introduced him to social games. They responded to all of his communicative attempts and talked to him. Yet, he was not learning language. Their initial goals for their son were for him to learn how to talk and to enjoy playing with other children. They hoped that he could attend the neighborhood preschool. They hoped that Andrew would start closing the increasing gap between his development and that of other children his age and that one day he would no longer need intervention.

Andrew qualified for early intervention services, and his parents received 5 hours per week of individualized intervention. A clinician who had several years experience working with young children with autism and experience in parent education introduced Andrew's parents to PRT's motivational strategies and gave suggestions for incorporating the strategies into their daily routines. Andrew's parents were very dedicated to working toward improving Andrew's behaviors, and within several sessions, they began to master the techniques. Sessions took place in the home as well as in the shared community setting as opportunities arose. Andrew's parents also consulted with other intervention providers so that the PRT techniques could be integrated into much of Andrew's intervention and teaching throughout the day. Within weeks of instating the program, Andrew said his first new word, "cah" (for *car*). During the walks in the neighborhood, Andrew showed interest and excitement as he pointed to cars on the road and in the parking lot and proudly said, "Cah."

Soon after his first clear word approximation for *car,* several words were taught based on Andrew's favorite items and activities (e.g., *ball, swing, television, banana*). Each day when Andrew's mother came home, she prompted Andrew to say "mama" before picking him up. When Andrew said, "Dadada," she rewarded his attempt. She will probably always remember the day that she prompted him and he clearly said "mama." Shortly after that, Andrew said "mama" nearly every minute, as many typically developing toddlers do.

Over the next few months, Andrew's vocabulary continued to grow, and as he learned to talk, he no longer needed to use his less appropriate challenging behaviors. He improved from saying single words to saying word combinations. His articulation improved, and he recognized the letters of the alphabet and began initiating communication. His play had also improved. Rather than putting leaves in the drain or running back and forth, he became more interactive with adults. As a next step, intervention addressed his interactions with peers.

Although Andrew was not initially interested in other children, he learned to tolerate them. First, he was taught to say "bye" rather than scream to terminate interactions. From there he was taught to share items and to show interest in what other children were doing. When he turned 3, his parents enrolled him in the neighborhood school. He occasionally initiated interactions with the other children and enjoyed the activities. He began to spontaneously comment on all the interesting items in his environment by saying things such as, "Look, there's a butterfly." As Andrew accelerated his trajectory, his goals changed to reflect the increased interactions with his peers, and interventions focused more on facilitating play with peers (as discussed in Chapter 11).

Andrew is now 5 years old and fully included in a regular kindergarten classroom. His language development is continuing to progress. He asks questions about topics that he finds motivating (e.g., "Where is Spiderman?" "What is Spiderman doing?"), and his clinicians are continuing to target question asking about nonpreferred topics. Andrew loves playing with typically developing peers at school. He plays Chase, Hide-and-Seek, Follow the Leader, and other simple games. He has learned how to maintain an interaction when he wants to move to a new activity (e.g., by asking a friend to engage in the new activity with him instead of just running away). Because Andrew is playing appropriately when he is with one other child, a new intervention goal is to help him interact appropriately with a group of peers. The behavior support plan in place consists of priming the group activity, prompting Andrew to engage in appropriate interactions with the support of an aide, and gradually increasing the amount of time he plays with a group of children before leaving the area. Andrew's parents are thrilled with his progress and look forward to new social, behavioral, and academic accomplishments in his first year of elementary school.

DISCUSSION OF CHAPTER CONCEPTS

Accumulating data indicate the importance of early intervention, and this chapter emphasizes the benefits of beginning intervention before the age 3. That is, the study's data suggested that the children's developmental trajectories for communication prior to the start of specialized services remained stable with little improvement, resulting in an increasing gap with the expected trajectories of typically developing peers. However, following the start of specialized services focusing on autism and parent education, all of the children improved. Specifically, the trajectories for children changed direction, with three children making progress toward the range of typical developmental trajectories at their latest available intervention point. In addition, four of the five children showed steady increases in both the total number of words and in their vocabulary diversity, and all children engaged in both prompted and spontaneous speech at the latest intervention probe.

There is no doubt that specialized intervention services for children with autism should begin as early as possible (Dawson & Osterling, 1997; McGee et al., 1999; National Research Council, 2001; Rogers, 1998). Findings discussed in this chapter demonstrate that children's developmental trajectories for communication prior to intervention deteriorated or at best remained somewhat stable at age-inappropriate levels. Based on the preintervention trajectories, it is likely that the gap between typical developmental trajectories and the trajectories of these children would have widened without intervention, providing even more support for the importance of identifying autism and providing specialized intervention at an early age.

These data also point out the importance of parent education early intervention on the acquisition of functional expressive language. Many studies have documented the effects of intensive early intervention (e.g., Dawson & Osterling, 1997; Smith, 1999); however, this study extends the literature by providing support for interventions that rely heavily on parent education to deliver treatment that can be both cost-effective and empowering for families (Kaiser, Hancock, & Nietfeld, 2000; R.L. Koegel, Schreibman, Johnson, O'Neill, & Dunlap, 1984).

Finally, these data support other articles in the literature that have suggested that an increasing number of children are learning expressive verbal communication when motivational or incidental teaching procedures are used. That is, at least as many as 85%–90% of children with autism can learn to use functional speech if intervention begins in the preschool years (L.K. Koegel, 1995, 2000; McGee, Daly, & Jacobs, 1994).

DIRECTIONS FOR FUTURE RESEARCH

Given these optimistic results, it may be important to further investigate potential mediating parent, child, and intervention variables. Parent variables that have been identified in the literature as potentially influential include the amount of stress that a parent is experiencing as a result of the child's disability (Robbins, Dunlap, & Plienis, 1991), following the child's lead (Siller & Sigman, 2002), family socioeconomic status, and maternal education status (Yoder & Warren, 2001). It may also be important to measure parent follow-through and parental mastery of the motivational procedures taught in this study. Important child variables may include the child's cognitive skills prior to the start of intervention (Gabriel, Hill, Pierce, Rogers, & Wehner, 2001; Harris & Handleman, 2000), age at start of intervention (Fenske et al., 1985; Harris & Handleman, 2000), motor imitation skills (Stone & Yoder, 2001), and certain joint attention behaviors (e.g., Mundy, Sigman, & Kasari, 1990). Intervention variables may include length and intensity of intervention (Stone & Yoder, 2001).

A further potential area of future research in this area is whether it would be possible to predict eventual child outcomes from children's developmental trajectories prior to the start of intervention. Some work in this area has already suggested that age and IQ score at program entry may be indicative of outcome (Gabriel et al., 2001; Harris & Handleman, 2000). Furthermore, L.K. Koegel, Koegel, Shoshan, and McNerney (1999) demonstrated that child initiations at program entry predicted highly favorable treatment outcomes. It may be that the slope of a child's developmental trajectory after the start of early intervention is a function of such child variables (e.g., age, IQ score, initiations), with environmental variables such as family functioning carrying less weight (Gabriel et al., 2001).

In summary, these results appear to support the recent focus in the literature on the earliest possible identification and start of intervention for children with autism. Furthermore, these data may be able to provide hope to parents whose newly diagnosed children have very minimal expressive abilities by showing that substantial progress is possible.

8

First Words

Getting Verbal Communication Started

Robert L. Koegel, Karen Sze, Amanda Mossman, Lynn Kern Koegel, and Lauren Brookman-Frazee

The literature suggests that increasing numbers of nonverbal children with autism are able to acquire verbal communication with systematic intervention procedures. This chapter discusses researched strategies to teach first words to nonverbal children with autism. In addition to describing the procedures, the chapter discusses techniques for coordinating these procedures in the context of a parent education program. Active participation of parents in the intervention process can result in consistency of procedures across the child's waking hours in addition to more opportunities for language use under a variety of conditions and settings. Consequently, faster acquisition and increases in generalized communication can be seen. Although these procedures are effective for the large majority of nonverbal children (up to 90% if intervention begins in the preschool years), there is a small subgroup of children who may experience challenges in the acquisition of a functional vocabulary. Strategies are described for these children, who may have difficulties producing clear words or who inappropriately overgeneralize sounds or words.

BACKGROUND

Historically, acquisition of expressive communication only occurred in about half of the children diagnosed with autism. Largely, this was due to the extreme difficulty and time commitment associated with implementing intervention procedures (Carr, 1982; R.L. Koegel, O'Dell, & Dunlap, 1988; Lovaas, 1977; Lovaas, Berberich, Perloff, & Schaeffer, 1966). In addition, procedures for teaching words often did not incorporate semantic intent; therefore, speech was not used functionally. In contrast, research on naturalistic, motivation-based language interventions, such as Pivotal Response Treatment (PRT; R.L. Koegel et al., 1989) and incidental teaching (McGee, Krantz, & McClannahan, 1985), has documented substantial improvements in the prognosis of speech acquisition for an increasing number of nonverbal children. Specifically, outcome studies suggest that when children begin naturalistic, motivation-based types of intervention before the age of 5 years, approximately 85%–90% can successfully acquire some level of verbal communication (L.K. Koegel, 1995, 2000; McGee, Morrier, & Daly, 1999). If intervention begins before the age of 3 years, as many as 95% of the children appear to be able to learn expressive verbal communication as their primary mode of communication.

On a related note, research has demonstrated that motivational techniques lead to improvements in imitation and spontaneous speech, lead to generalization across settings, and can easily be implemented by parents (e.g., R.L. Koegel et al., 1988; R.L. Koegel, O'Dell, & Koegel, 1987; Laski, Charlop, & Schriebman, 1988; Moes, 1995). In addition, researchers have reported collateral decreases in the levels of untargeted disruptive behaviors with this type of teaching (R.L. Koegel, Camarata, & Koegel, 1994; R.L. Koegel, Koegel, Frea, & Smith, 1995; R.L. Koegel, Koegel, & Surratt, 1992). Thus, accumulating evidence suggests the importance of early intervention using motivational procedures for expressive communication.

METHOD

The specific procedures for teaching first words were described by R.L. Koegel et al. (1987) and incorporate the following motivational principles into the intervention:

1. *Provide child choice:* Child choice of stimulus materials is used to evoke verbal communication. This variable is especially critical in the context of teaching first words and should include the use of toys and activities (e.g., favorite routines and physical games) that are extremely motivating to a child while providing opportunities to evoke expressive communication. To assess child choice, a child's team must look at his or her interests and focus on the toys and activities in which the child engages. If a child initiates an interaction with a particular toy or activity, it is important to use that item or activity for intervention. The child's team can determine the activities and toys in which the child spends the most time engaged and have those available. In addition, it is important to consider that the child's interests may change day by day or even minute by minute. Think about what the child is particularly motivated by at every moment—for example, drinking a cup of cold water may be especially motivating after the child has eaten potato chips or another salty snack. These findings can be recorded on a form such as the Pivotal Response Treatment (PRT) Fidelity of Implementation Scoring Sheet (see the fifth column of the appendix at the end of this chapter).

2. *Intersperse acquisition and maintenance tasks:* For a child who is learning his or her first words, interspersing maintenance tasks may include balancing opportunities between easier words that he or she has already mastered with opportunities for acquiring words that are more difficult for the child. For example, a child who is consistently capable of producing attempts of /ba/ for *ball* may be given several of these maintenance opportunities before being provided with an acquisition opportunity for a less familiar word such as *cookie*. Members of the team may want to ask themselves, "Which words are easier for your child to use?" and "Which ones are more challenging?" If the child is completely nonverbal, the team may want to include nonverbal activities that the child has mastered, such as playing with a particular toy. Remember to do a mixture of these to help the child feel successful, thereby keeping the child motivated to learn. Refer to the third column of the Pivotal Response Treatment (PRT) Fidelity of Implementation Scoring Sheet.

3. *Reinforce attempts:* In the early stages of teaching a child his or her first words, it is important to reinforce any functional verbal attempts even if they do not sound exactly like the adult pronunciations. For example, if a child who is learning his or her first words says "i" while reaching for the milk, he or she should be given immediate access to the milk. For a child who is first learning to communicate verbally, it is important to reward attempts so that the child understands the connection between verbalizations and the desired outcome of obtaining the requested item. Initially, the child may go through his or her repertoire of skills and

When attempting to teach first words, it is important to use stimulus materials that the child finds very motivating. In this photo, the clinician is using a highly desirable toy to elicit a verbal response.

use early forms of communication, such as crying or whining, but soon the child will figure out that attempting to say the word will result in access to the desired item or activity. Also remember only to reinforce functional verbalizations that are free of inappropriate behaviors, such as self-stimulatory behavior or disruptive behaviors. See the last column of the Pivotal Response Treatment (PRT) Fidelity of Implementation Scoring Sheet.

4. *Provide natural contingent reinforcement:* Providing natural consequences involves the use of natural and contingent reinforcers following any word or attempt. In the context of teaching early expressive communication, this includes providing immediate access to rewards that are directly related to the language opportunity. For example, if the child makes attempts to say "ball," he or she should be given the ball immediately so that a clear connection is made between the child's vocalization and the desired object. Again, this will help the child learn that vocalizations are tied to a consequence, thus making verbal communication meaningful. Refer to the sixth and seventh columns of the Pivotal Response Treatment (PRT) Fidelity of Implementation Scoring Sheet.

PARENT EDUCATION

As mentioned previously, research suggests that parents are a critical component of the intervention process, and their active participation is essential. In our programs, staff at University of California, Santa Barbara's Autism Research and Training Cen-

Parent participation has long been associated with a highly favorable long-term outcome. Here, the parent is learning about the contingent delivery of a reinforcer for communication attempts. This father is waiting for his child to make an attempt at saying "cookie" before rewarding him with a snack.

ter (ARTC) have a variety of ways parents participate. Parents are provided with a copy of the manual *How to Teach Pivotal Behaviors to Children with Autism: A Training Manual* (R.L. Koegel et al., 1989) prior to starting intervention. During the intervention sessions, clinicians model the techniques and provide opportunities for the parents to work with their children while offering them systematic feedback relating to their use of the procedures. Learning trials are incorporated into naturally occurring opportunities in order to facilitate their children's use of functional verbal communication in their daily routines and environments. Sessions are held in playrooms, in the child's home, and in a variety of community settings. Consistent with ARTC's previous research suggesting that parent-implemented interventions might be especially powerful, ARTC's current preliminary data indicate that when parents have a potent intervention tool (e.g., PRT) at their disposal in addition to their unique knowledge of their child's characteristics, the effect on their child's expressive communication can be quite dramatic.

MEASUREMENT

Scoring the Parent or Clinician

It is important to regularly assess whether the parents, clinicians, and others working with the child are correctly implementing the intervention procedures. This can be accomplished either by taking direct data while working with the child or via video probes of parents and clinicians implementing the motivational teaching procedures. Specifically, the use of each category of teaching procedures discussed in the "Method" section (i.e., provide choice, intersperse acquisition and maintenance tasks, reinforce attempts, and provide natural contingent reinforcement) can be scored from representative probes. With the scorer observing in 10 1-minute intervals, the findings can be recorded on the Pivotal Response Treatment (PRT) Fidelity of Implementation Scoring Sheet, with a plus indicating correct use and a minus indicating incorrect use. Fidelity is attained when each of the eight PRT categories listed in the scoring sheet's chart are performed correctly by the parent/clinician 80% of the time during the probe intervals.

Child Measures

In addition to measuring the parent's or clinician's use of the procedures, it is important to assess the child's progress on a regular basis. For children who are progressing slowly, weekly or biweekly probes may be adequate. If children are progressing quickly, child measures may be collected more frequently. If daily probes are collected, these should be videotaped and analyzed later so that they do not interfere with the natural social interactions between the child and adult. Some areas to assess regularly include acquisition of words, behavior, affect, phonology, and pragmatics.

Acquisition of Words   The acquisition of words is further assessed in terms of total number of words and vocabulary diversity.

Total Number of Words   Because the goal is to measure the changes in a child's expressive communication, it is important to keep track of total number of functional words verbalized by the child during interactions. Functional words are noted when the child verbalizes distinctly recognizable functional words and appropriately uses them in context. For example, if the child says "ba" while reaching for a ball, that would be counted as a functional word attempt. If the child says the word "ba" 10 times and the word "fish" twice in context during an observation, the total number of words would be recorded as 12.

Vocabulary Diversity   In addition, it is important to assess the diversity of the child's functional word use. Specifically, it is necessary to measure the number of different functional words verbalized appropriately in context by the child. For example, if the child produces a word such as *ball* four times when a context for the word *ball* is appropriate, the verbalizations would be counted as one word. If the child says "ball" and "go" functionally in appropriate contexts, the verbalizations would be counted as two different words. It is important, particularly during this early stage of word acquisition, to ascertain whether the child understands that each item has a different label. All children tend to overgeneralize their first words (e.g., anything with four legs is a "doggie"), but children with autism sometimes use their first initial sounds or words for all requests. Therefore, assessing word diversity is critical during these early stages.

Behavior   As mentioned previously, a collateral benefit of motivational procedures is that they provide naturally rewarding consequences and result in rapid acquisition of first words, as well as a reduction in challenging behaviors. Hence, it is important to assess changes in a child's behaviors by measuring whether the child engages in any disruptive behaviors during PRT interactions. Initially, all preverbal children use forms of communication such as crying to make their needs known. As time goes on and children learn more effective ways to communicate (i.e., words, phrases, and sentences), the disruptive behavior decreases. Furthermore, research shows that the motivational procedures used in PRT result in lower levels of disruptive behavior compared with more traditional drill-type exercises (R.L. Koegel et al., 1987; R.L. Koegel et al., 1992). Thus, behaviors such as screaming, kicking, hitting, and biting should be considerably lower if the procedures are being implemented correctly. Measuring challenging behaviors also helps in evaluating the possible implications of the intervention for the family's functioning and quality of life and for communicative areas to target.

Affect   The goal is for children to be enjoying their interactions while learning their first words. Therefore, it is useful to measure a child's interest, happiness, and general behavior with a five-point affect scale (see Figure 8.1; R.L. Koegel & Egel, 1979). Doing so is helpful in assessing whether the intervention is producing clinically significant changes.

Phonology   As a child begins to acquire words, it is helpful to assess whether the words are intelligible. Some children with autism demonstrate perfect articulation, even using later developing sounds correctly, whereas others need more practice before the words become intelligible. Keep track of a child's articulation errors to determine if articulation should be targeted. Research shows that even sounds can be taught by using the previously described motivational procedures.

Semantics   Typically developing children usually have some difficulty with the meanings of their first lexicon, but this occurs only with a very small percentage of their words. That is, they tend to use some of their initial words in restricted or loose ways. For example, some children may say "Dada" only in the context of their own father, whereas others may say "Dada" to refer to any male. Because some children with autism occasionally overgeneralize a large number of their first words and word attempts, consideration of their semantic understanding throughout the teaching process is important. Initial words of children with autism tend to be concrete and can be assessed by determining whether a child is reaching toward the requested item, is looking at the requested item or action, or chooses the requested item in a choice situation. In this manner, semantic knowledge can be improved by providing opportunities with a variety of exemplars for a given word.

Pragmatics   Children with autism often have difficulties in pragmatic areas, such as using appropriate eye contact, intonation, and body movements that accompany communication. However, because intervention involves providing direct, natural reinforcers, rewarding appropriate pragmatics can easily be incorporated into the intervention. For instance, if a child wants to be picked up, the mother can wait until the child looks into her eyes while making the request. Likewise, if a child wants a desired item that is high on a shelf, he or she can be prompted to point to the item

Low interest (0-1)	Neutral interest (2-3)	High interest (4-5)
Looks bored, uninvolved, and not curious about or eager to participate in the activity Yawns or tries to avoid the activity Spends little time attending to the task A long response latency when there is a response (Score as 0 or 1, depending on extent of lack of interest)	Neither particularly interested nor disinterested Seems to passively accept situation Does not rebel but is eager to continue (Score as 2 or 3, depending on extent of interest)	Readily attends to the activity Is alert and involved in the task (Score as 4 or 5, depending on level of alertness and involvement)
Unhappy (0-1)	**Neutral happiness (2-3)**	**Happy (4-5)**
Appears to be sad, angry, or frustrated Cries or engages in tantrums Seems not to be enjoying self (Score as 0 or 1, depending on extent of unhappiness)	Appears to be neither decidedly happy nor particularly unhappy Smiles or frowns occasionally but seems rather neutral in this situation overall (Score as 2 or 3, depending on extent of happiness)	Seems to be enjoying self Smiles or laughs appropriately (Score as 4 or 5, depending on level of enjoyment)
Disruptive behavior (0-1)	**Neutral behavior (2-3)**	**Well behaved (4-5)**
Engages in disruptive behavior (e.g., has tantrums; attempts to leave the room; interrupts the adult's instructions and/or prompts; shows aggression toward adult, self, or objects) Is generally off task (e.g., fidgets and squirms, shows inappropriate/off-task vocal or motor behavior) Shows little attention to task Is noncompliant (Score as 0 or 1, depending on extent of disruptiveness)	Is neither very disruptive nor exceptionally attentive Fidgets and appears inattentive but is not aggressive or rebellious Generally complies with instructions or responds to prompts but may not do so readily (Score as 2 or 3, depending on extent of attentiveness)	Attends quietly to adult or task Responds to prompts or instructions (e.g., is compliant, appears to try to perform successfully) Laughs or shows other emotional behavior under appropriate circumstances (Score as 4 or 5, depending on extent of attention and compliance)

Figure 8.1. Scale for rating a child's affect on the dimensions of interest, happiness, and general behavior. (From Koegel, R.L., & Egel, A.L. [1979]. Motivating autistic children. *Journal of Abnormal Psychology, 88*[4], 418–426. Copyright © 1979 by the American Psychological Association. Adapted with permission.)

while making the request. Associated appropriate pragmatics can be incorporated early on the intervention. Regular assessment of the child's pragmatic skills is important.

CHALLENGES IN LEARNING FIRST WORDS: MAKING LEARNING EASIER

It bears repeating that the large majority of young children with autism (approximately 90%) will rapidly acquire words using the previously described motivational procedures. However, a small number of children seem to have difficulty with the acquisition of first words. The following section presents some interventions that are particularly helpful for those children.

Using Familiar Verbal Routines

As described previously, PRT's motivational procedures consist of rewarding attempts, but occasionally a child will get stuck on a particular sound or word or may alternate between just a few sounds or words for labeling a variety of objects. That is, the child understands the connection between vocalizing for communicative purposes but has not learned that every item has a distinct label. Such difficulties can often be reduced through careful planning of initial target words for teaching. It is important to consider the context of the language learning opportunity: The more familiar and predictable the learning opportunity, the easier it will be for the child to succeed. Research suggests that imitation within familiar contexts is easier for children to learn (Masur & Ritz, 1984; McCabe & Uzigiris, 1983; McCall, Parke, & Kavanaugh, 1977) and, more specifically, that routines facilitate various aspects of language acquisition, from comprehension to production (Kim & Lombardino, 1991; Yoder & Davies, 1992; Yoder, Spruytenburg, Edwards, & Davies, 1995), as the predictable context is presumed to make the interaction less demanding for the child (Nelson, 1986). Therefore, if a child is exhibiting this problem, opportunities to evoke new and different words can be designed using familiar verbal routines or carrier phrases. For example, the parent/clinician may want to model "ready, set, go" before providing the child with an opportunity to engage in a favorite activity. Once the child can anticipate this situation, the parent/clinician must provide a pause, and the child must verbalize to complete the sequence, such as the opportunity to vocalize "go" after the parent/clinician says "ready, set." This can be instrumental as a maintenance task and can provide an easy opportunity for the child to develop the idea that a different word needs to be used. More detailed steps for using this procedure follow.

Step 1: Prepare Verbal Routines   The parent/clinician is asked to think back to previous interactions with the child. He or she may consider certain routines that are always done in a particular way (e.g., saying "one, two, three" when picking up the child). Books and songs that the child enjoys form another area of consideration. The parent/clinician then records his or her interactions with the child over several days. Questions such as, "What activities utilized verbal routines?" "Does the child already tend to vocalize more during certain routines or games?" should be used to analyze the findings. All of these routines, games, or items can be used during intervention.

Step 2: Select Opportunities for Teaching   At this point, the parent/clinician assesses which activities will be most motivating for the child. For example, using "one, two, three" because it is associated with getting a piggyback ride is likely a better choice than using "up, up, and away," which is said during a diaper change. Again, if there are activities in which the child already tends to vocalize more, it may be more effective to establish routines and opportunities in the context of these tasks.

Step 3: Plan the Opportunity   The clinician decides which part of the verbal routine to provide for the child and which part he or she will expect the child to complete. In the early stages of learning, the parent/clinician should provide the entire routine; then, when the child is able to anticipate that the reward is about to be provided, the parent can say just the beginning of the routine, leaving the end of the routine "open" for the child to complete. For example, if the activity of choice is swinging, the parent/clinician might tell the child "one, two . . . " and then wait expectantly for the child to approximate the appropriate response of "three" before swinging the child to reinforce the vocalization.

Step 4: Measure Program Effectiveness   The primary goal of this intervention technique is to provide a language opportunity that is familiar and easy for the child. Therefore, this can be a useful tool for children who are slow to develop a functional vocabulary or begin to overgeneralize first word attempts. In addition, as the procedure is easier for children and often involves a highly enjoyable activity, the routine-based opportunity can function as a maintenance task to improve motivation. Both a child's quality of word attempts as well as his or her motivation during learning are essential in teaching early communication. It is recommended that program effectiveness be measured in the following areas: object–label correspondence, correct responding, and affect.

Object–Label Correspondence   A primary goal of this intervention is for the child to demonstrate label discrimination in expressive communication. This variable is expressed as the presence of a one-to-one relationship between the child's vocalization (label) and a desired referent (object). For example, the child only vocalizes /da/ to obtain a toy dog and does not vocalize /da/ for any other objects. Total functional vocabulary can be measured as the number of vocalizations that the child uses only for a given referent.

Correct Responding   Because the overall intervention package (PRT) targets a child's core motivation, it is important to consider the number of learning opportunities in which the child demonstrates success. Tracking the percent of opportunities in which the child responds with correct verbalizations is recommended. A *correct response* can be defined as a response that approximates the correct pronunciation of the target word. For example, if the child vocalizes /ba/ or /all/ for *ball,* this would be scored as correct. Conversely, if the child vocalizes /car/ or /miflglix/ for *ball* or does not respond, this would be scored as incorrect.

Affect   It is important to assess the child's affect to further establish that the child is motivated by the learning process. For more information, see Figure 8.1 and the previous discussion on using an affect scale.

Findings   Preliminary data from several nonverbal children with autism in this early intervention program support the effectiveness of incorporating verbal routines as language opportunities into the implementation of PRT. Prior to the introduction of verbal routines in learning opportunities, these children had difficulty developing a functional vocabulary—that is, they would use a variety of word approximations interchangeably across referents. In addition, the children demonstrated a low rate of correct responses and presented with low affect during intervention sessions.

After the incorporation of familiar verbal routines into teaching, these children showed dramatic increases in vocabulary development, correct responses, and affect. Specifically, the children began to consistently complete the carrier phrase when the routine-based opportunity was introduced, and later the children mastered more distinct labels. Eventually an acceleration in vocabulary development was noted. Hence, routine-based opportunities can be instrumental in facilitating object–label correspondence for the children and thereafter can function as a maintenance task to further motivate and stimulate vocabulary development.

Case Example   Tara was a 3½-year-old girl diagnosed with autism who was nonverbal prior to participation in the parent education intervention program. When Tara and her father, Bill, attended an intake meeting, Tara did not exhibit any functional expressive speech, nor did she use gestures to communicate her needs. Bill reported that in order to communicate, Tara often engaged in disruptive behaviors, such as hitting, hair pulling, and biting. In addition, Bill reported that Tara had received a variety of different therapies and that he "had little faith in a new approach."

The primary goal of Tara's intervention program was to facilitate the development of a functional expressive vocabulary, utilizing PRT, via a parent education model. Language opportunities were based on Tara's main interests, which were balls, cars, and cookies. Within the first 2 weeks, it was clear that Tara understood that she needed to vocalize during teaching opportunities to receive the desired items. However, producing clear word attempts was rather difficult for Tara, as evidenced by her infrequent attempts. In addition, Tara did not consistently use the same vocalization to communicate. Sometimes she would say "ba" for *ball,* but more often than not, she would say "ma" or "da." Bill was pleased with Tara's early progress and offered her the item she appeared to be requesting contingent on any vocalization.

However, over the next months of treatment, Tara did not progress in her ability to discriminate various labels for objects; instead, she tended to use the same word approximations for all objects (e.g., saying "bababa").When Bill would wait for the appropriate vocalization for a given item, Tara would engage in a tantrum or lose interest. She was not able to consistently and correctly label desired objects in her environment.

One thing that Tara had enjoyed since she was a baby was listening to her father read her favorite books and sing her favorite songs. The clinician explained to Bill how books and songs could also be good opportunities for Tara to use her language. Bill first tried this approach with the song "Five Little Ducks." He sang, "Five little" and then paused, at which point Tara immediately filled in "ducks." From that point on, Bill continuously used Tara's favorite books and songs for language opportunities. As Tara became more successful during these routines, she was soon able to consistently and appropriately imitate words in a variety of other contexts and developed 10 distinct words within 2 weeks of introducing the routines.

Selecting Words Using Sounds that a Child Already Uses

As mentioned previously in this chapter, it may be necessary to increase the motivational properties of the language opportunities in order to evoke appropriate functional verbal responses from children who have particular difficulty learning their first words. One approach is to create a language opportunity that is predictable and easier for the child to respond to, such as one that is routine based, as described in the previous section. Similarly, another approach is to carefully and systematically select initial target words for teaching. Specifically, special consideration should be given to the sounds that the child is already producing, as it will be easier for the child to learn to use these sounds for functional communication purposes, rather than targeting a sound that is absent or infrequently produced by the child. As nonverbal children often already produce sounds without communicative intent, it may be worthwhile to choose target words that are similar to these sounds. For example, if the child often says "mmm" while playing, a target word for teaching could be one that uses the phoneme *m* for a request, such as "music" to request having music played. The steps for this process are detailed next.

Step 1: Establish a Baseline   It is important to establish a baseline by first asking the basic question, "What sounds does the child make?" The parent/clinician should watch the child play and observe what kinds of sounds he or she makes. Any of the following should be noted:

- Certain contexts in which the child makes sounds more than others
- Times when the child makes a particular sound more often
- Instances in which it seems like the child makes a sound for certain purposes

Step 2: Select Target Words for Teaching   Based on observations of the child's play interactions, the clinician selects the sounds that the child seems to make most frequently as the initial target words for teaching. It is necessary to find out if these sounds resemble anything that might be motivating for the child. For example, if the child says "ooo" quite readily and enjoys trains, one might want to make an association between that sound and "choo-choo." In addition, one could also teach the child to say "ooo" for help with opening doors and containers.

Step 3: Pair Child's Vocalizations with Motivating Reinforcers   Vocalizations and reinforcers can be paired by using an "incidental" approach or by establishing opportunities based on existing vocalizations.

"Incidental" Pairing of Target Sounds   Because the child may not consistently make the targeted sound upon request, it can be helpful to pair the child's usage of a sound with an item. That is, when the child happens to produce the target sound, he or she should immediately be given the corresponding item. Building on the previous example, while playing with a train set, the child may begin saying "ooo-ooo" noncontingently. Immediately providing the child with the train can reinforce the relationship between his or her vocalization and obtaining the train.

Establish Language Opportunities Based on Child's Existing Vocalizations   Another method involves establishing language opportunities that incorporate items or stimulus materials that are consistent with the child's repertoire of existing vocalizations. For example, if the child often vocalizes "ooo" and is motivated by the train set, one may model saying "choo-choo" instead of "train" as the target word to evoke a functional and appropriate verbal response from the child.

Step 4: Measure Program Effectiveness   Measures of program effectiveness are required to demonstrate improvements in expressive communication. Two approaches measure object–label correspondence and percent of overgeneralized responses.

Object–Label Correspondence   A primary goal of this intervention is for the child to demonstrate improvements in expressive communication. This variable is defined as the presence of a one-to-one relationship between the child's vocalization (label) and the desired referent (object). For example, the goal is that the child only vocalizes /ca/ for a car and does not vocalize /ca/ for any other objects. It is recommended that total functional vocabulary be measured as the number of vocalizations that the child uses only for a given referent.

Percent of Overgeneralized Responses   In order to determine the extent to which the child is utilizing an identical response across referents, calculating the percentage of overgeneralized responses the child makes is recommended. An *overgeneralized response* is defined as one that is used by the child in a contextually inappropriate manner across referents. For example, if the child said "bu" for the ball and also said "bu" to request ice cream, "bu" would be considered an overgeneralized response.

Findings   Preliminary outcome data on several nonverbal children with autism from the early intervention program support the use of pretreatment vocalizations in circumventing the problem of overgeneralization of first word attempts or sounds. Prior to using pretreatment vocalizations to select target words for teaching, these children produced the same overgeneralized responses across a variety of items (e.g., vocalizing /baba/ for everything). That is, they did not acquire label discrimination in expressive communication (object–label correspondence) and produced no functional speech.

However, when their existing vocalizations were incorporated into target words for teaching as part of the intervention, the children showed an immediate and significant improvement in their object–label correspondence and no longer produced overgeneralized responses to labeling opportunities. Hence, an inverse relationship was found between the children's ability to discriminate object labels and overgeneralized responses to labeling opportunities. That is, as the children developed a consistent functional vocabulary, they no longer overgeneralized the use of a single vocalization across different referents. Overall, using the children's pretreatment vocalizations to guide the selection for target words appeared to be an effective strategy for eliminating the problem of overgeneralization in the subgroup of nonverbal children who have difficulty acquiring first words.

Case Example   Stephanie, a 3½-year-old girl diagnosed with autism, was non-verbal prior to participation in the early intervention parent education program. At the beginning of intervention, she did not exhibit any functional expressive words or appropriate nonverbal gestures of communication (e.g., pointing) but occasionally produced machinery sounds when looking at picture books about cars and trains. In order to have her needs met, Stephanie frequently engaged in severe disruptive behaviors, including crying and screaming for communicative purposes. Her parents reported that the intensity of Stephanie's "meltdowns" had increased since the birth of her younger sister. A few months before their participation in the program, Stephanie's parents received numerous complaints from neighbors in their housing complex about the noise from Stephanie's tantrums.

The initial goal of the intervention program was to establish a functional vocabulary of expressive single words for Stephanie through a parent education model, using PRT procedures. Target words for teaching were selected based on Stephanie's interests. Within the first week of intervention, she established a single functional vocalization, /eh/, which she consistently used to request a variety of her favorite items (e.g., candy, tickles, toy dog). Although these vocalizations did not represent a phonologically accurate production, Stephanie's mother was excited about her daughter's emerging communication skills and provided Stephanie with desired objects contingent upon her verbal attempts.

As Stephanie acquired communicative intent, the subsequent goal of intervention was the discrimination of object labels. However, over the next 4 months of intervention, she demonstrated a great deal of difficulty progressing beyond the establishment of the same vocalization across different referents. More specifically, Stephanie did not appear to grasp the concept that each referent had a distinct label (i.e., object–label correspondence) and continued to overgeneralize the use of a single vocalization as a request for any desired item or activity. For example, although Stephanie's general verbal attempt changed from saying "eh" to "ba" and "da" over time, she did not differentiate her use of these sounds; instead, she used the same sounds across referents. When she was prompted to produce a sound other than her overgeneralized attempt, Stephanie would continue to produce the same vocalization and engage in tantrum behaviors when adults tried to prompt her to use sounds that more closely approximated the adult word.

Stephanie's mother and a clinician discussed an intervention procedure using pretreatment vocalizations to help Stephanie eliminate this overgeneralization. The procedure consisted of systematically selecting target words for teaching through establishing language opportunities that incorporated items or materials that were consistent with Stephanie's repertoire of pretreatment vocalizations as well as her interests. Her clinician compiled a list of pretreatment vocalizations by speaking with Stephanie's mother and watching early videotapes, which revealed that Stephanie randomly produced a variety of machinery sounds while playing alone with her toys, including engine and train track noises. Stephanie's mother began incorporating machinery sounds into PRT language opportunities for her by using cars and trains that made similar sounds when a button was pushed. For example, she would show Stephanie a car and contingently reinforce the engine sound by pushing the button and giving Stephanie the car. Similarly, she would also incorporate Stephanie's existing machinery sounds with her favorite car and train pop-up books. For example, she would manipulate the pop-up tab for the train after Stephanie produced an attempt for *train*.

Within a few sessions of PRT involving the selection of target words based on these pretreatment vocalizations, Stephanie no longer overgeneralized her use of a single verbal attempt and established object–label correspondence. Specifically, she discriminated the labels for cars and trains and began acquiring labels expressively for other objects. For example, instead of resorting to her general, identical vocalization across multiple referents, Stephanie learned a variety of functional, in-context first words, including *mama, ball, dog, go,* and *car.* At this point of intervention, Stephanie was rapidly developing a functional vocabulary so that target words for teaching could be selected solely on the basis of motivation and did not have to necessarily incorporate machinery sounds.

Within fewer than 5 months, Stephanie acquired an expressive vocabulary of hundreds of words, which she used spontaneously and functionally both for requesting and commenting purposes. She was consistently using multiple cues (e.g., colors, sizes) in her utterances and was combining words to form three- to four-word phrases. Soon afterward, she began to speak in full sentences. In addition, Stephanie's parents have reported that her disruptive behaviors have decreased significantly since her expressive communication has improved.

Improving Consistency Across Settings

As mentioned previously in this book, parents are potentially powerful intervention agents for children who are in the early stages of learning expressive communication. This is most probably due to their specialized knowledge of their children's unique characteristics. In addition, most parents are highly motivated to implement programs that will help to ameliorate their children's symptoms of autism. In the context of teaching first words to children with autism, it is critical to ensure that motivational procedures are being implemented correctly and consistently across a variety of settings (e.g., in the clinic setting, at home, in the community). When starting a parent education program for teaching first words, the initial focus is on consistency across a child's day. This is accomplished by using the following steps.

Step 1: Establish a Baseline   In order to assess parents' acquisition of motivational procedures, it is important to conduct information regarding parent–child interactions prior to starting the parent education process. This may mean providing the parents with a variety of toys and having the parents try to get their children to communicate. That is, clinicians can observe parent–child play interactions and identify specific areas in which motivational procedures may be implemented and capitalized on to facilitate expressive communication.

Step 2: Implement Parent Education   After going over the PRT manual (R.L. Koegel et al., 1989) with the parents, clinicians discuss opportunities for adults to provide concrete opportunities for evoking expressive communication while incorporating motivational procedures. Clinicians focus on providing these opportunities during typical routines, as busy parents experience increased levels of stress if they have to set aside periods of time during the day to work with their children. Clinicians can model the use of intervention procedures, then provide opportunities for the parents to work with their children while offering systematic and positive feedback relating to the parents' correct implementation of the procedures. In order to track progress that parents' have made, it is helpful to collect ongoing data, either during the sessions or from representative video probes. The Pivotal Response Treatment (PRT) Fidelity of Implementation Scoring Sheet (found in the chapter appendix) can be used as a criterion measure of parent skill acquisition. Is the parent providing clear language opportunities while his or her child is attending? Is the parent following the child's lead? Is the parent providing natural and immediate reinforcement? Is the parent interspersing a mixture of new and already learned tasks? Is the parent reinforcing the child's reasonable, goal-directed attempts? It is important to recognize that at this introductory stage of the parent education program, many parents will need a great deal of practice before attaining the criterion level for correct use of intervention procedures.

Step 3: Train According to Parent Need and Increase Consistency   Depending on the characteristics of the individual child and the style of parent–child interaction, the parent may initially experience difficulty reaching criteria on correct use of the specific motivational component. As the parent continues to receive parent education, he or she may initially reach the criterion level for correct use of motivational procedures based on the procedures for the Pivotal Response Treatment (PRT) Fidelity of Implementation Scoring Sheet, but may be implementing the intervention inconsistently. That is, although the parent may initially and briefly maintain criteria for correct use of interventions, it may be difficult for him or her to maintain this level of accuracy over time.

At this intermediate stage of parent education, it may be helpful to offer more systematic training by addressing the specific area of parent need according to ongoing assessment data from the Pivotal Response Treatment (PRT) Fidelity of Implementation Scoring Sheet. Knowing whether the parent is at the 80% criterion level for each motivational component is necessary in order to determine which specific components need to be practiced more thoroughly.

After determining specific areas of need, the clinician reviews these identified areas of need with the parent and provides more in-session opportunities for the parent to practice the specific components with the child. At this point, the goal is to encourage the parent to implement the intervention in a more fluid and consistent manner across a variety of settings.

Step 4: Measure Program Effectiveness   The parent education program's outcome data for several representative families with nonverbal children suggest that over time, a significant relationship exists between parents' correct and consistent use of motivational procedures and the very rapid acquisition of functional first words in nonverbal children with autism. In addition, there are positive collateral changes in the reduction of children's disruptive behaviors.

Findings   As parents were exposed to PRT techniques but had not yet attained criteria for correct implementation in all areas (see Phase I in Figure 8.2), the children showed some minimal improvements in their functional word use. Improvements in speech continued at a very slow rate when the parents briefly and initially attained criterion level but were implementing intervention inconsistently (Phase II). In contrast, when parents were given systematic training based on their specific areas of need, the children demonstrated very rapid increases in their functional word use (Phase III), as recorded by naïve observers (i.e., observers who were unaware of the purpose of the research). Such improvement continued throughout their participation in the intervention program. Specifically, improvements in vocabulary diversity (the number of different words used in a given probe) were seen, as well as improvements in the children's total number of words used. These gains were especially significant because the children were nonverbal prior to their participation in the intervention program

Furthermore, it is important to assess whether the consistent use of the procedures resulted in any collateral (untreated) changes in the children's level of disruptive behaviors as related to their acquisition of functional first words. Overall, the

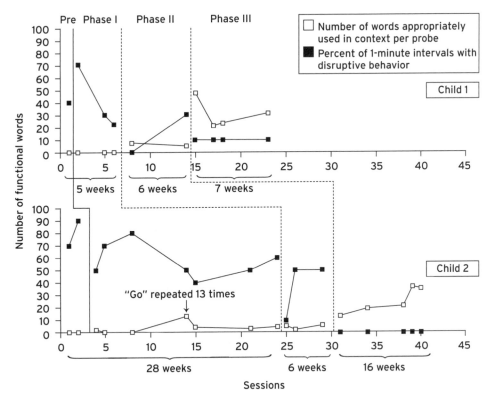

Figure 8.2. Number of functional words for two children whose parents received parent education in Pivotal Response Treatment (PRT), with corresponding reductions in disruptive behaviors in a multiple baseline design.

level of disruptive behavior was observed to have an inverse relationship to each child's word use. The children had frequent and severe disruptive behavior prior to intervention. During the introductory and intermediate periods of parent education, before the procedures were being implemented consistently, the children learned a few words, which were infrequently and inconsistently emitted, but disruptive behavior continued to remain at high levels. However, when the parents began using motivational procedures correctly and consistently, the children showed rapid increases in their word use with concomitant decreases in their disruptive behavior.

Case Example   Alistair, a 4½-year-old boy diagnosed with autism, was nonverbal prior to participation in the parent education program. At the beginning of intervention, Alistair did not exhibit any functional expressive words but occasionally engaged in repetitive vocalizations (i.e., babbling to himself in a noncontingent manner), particularly when he heard familiar songs or nursery rhymes. In order to communicate his needs, Alistair frequently engaged in several forms of disruptive behaviors, including screaming, hitting, hair pulling, throwing objects, and kicking. His parents reported numerous concerns about the severity of Alistair's behaviors at home and in the community, as these challenging behaviors also posed safety concerns (e.g., running away from his parents to protest or to escape from demands, hitting his siblings in protest).

Intervention consisted of 1-hour parent education sessions once per week over approximately 10 months. The initial goal of the intervention program was to establish a functional vocabulary of expressive single words for Alistair using PRT procedures. Target words for teaching were selected based on Alistair's interests. For example, soon after the first session, he began using his first word (*go*) at varying but low levels for toys that could be turned on. However, it was noted that although his mother prompted communication for the specific targeted toys, she rarely required communication for other activities, and Alistair continued to demonstrate high levels of disruptive behavior.

As training continued, the clinician focused on expanding the consistency of prompting for word use beyond his initial word *go*. Following this expanded focus for approximately four sessions, the clinician saw additional improvements in Alistair's production of functional words, but his progress was still slow and he continued to communicate through disruptive behaviors. At this point, Alistair's mother was using motivational procedures with him most of the time but still not consistently. Therefore, it was decided that more thorough training should continue until Alistair's mother fluidly and consistently implemented the procedures.

As a result of his mother's correct and consistent use of motivational procedures, Alistair showed rapid increases in his functional word use and vocabulary diversity. For example, after nine more sessions, he used a total of 35 words, consisting of 17 different functional words, in a single probe. At the same time, as Alistair acquired this rapid increase in functional communication skills, he no longer engaged in disruptive behaviors.

Following the intervention, Alistair had an expressive vocabulary consisting of hundreds of single words, which he used spontaneously and functionally for the purpose of requesting. He was beginning to use multiple cues (e.g., colors, sizes) in his utterances and was combining words to form three- to four-word phrases. In the most recent session, Alistair ran over to the session room table and requested lunch items that his mother had brought with her (e.g., "I want more sauce"). In addition, Alistair's parents reported that his disruptive behaviors had remained at low levels and that he no longer ran away or took off his clothes at inappropriate times. Alistair's mother continued to incorporate motivational procedures into his daily routines and had begun training his older siblings and other significant adults (e.g., school aide, teacher) to use these procedures during their interactions with him.

DISCUSSION OF CHAPTER CONCEPTS

As noted previously, using motivational teaching procedures results in significantly more children with autism acquiring verbal expressive communication. However, there is still a subpopulation of nonverbal children who do not appear to acquire functional expressive language with available intervention techniques (i.e., they are intervention nonresponders; R.L. Koegel, Koegel, & Brookman, 2003). For example, in teaching first words, some nonverbal children may initially overgeneralize the use of one or more first word attempts or alternate between several first word attempts across referents.

In such rare cases, one possible mechanism to alleviate difficulties in the acquisition of a functional vocabulary is available through careful selection of language opportunities and target words with a naturalistic, motivational learning context. Specifically, carrier phrases, routines, selection of specific words containing sounds that a child already produces, and consistent implementation of intervention procedures can be helpful in facilitating many aspects of language learning. These methods also can provide easier opportunities for the child to imitate a target word. Furthermore, it can be helpful to consider the targeted words chosen for teaching. As these strategies continue to evolve, one can anticipate more rapid and fluent acquisition of first words for nonverbal children with autism.

DIRECTIONS FOR FUTURE RESEARCH

With a growing number of previously nonverbal children with autism successfully acquiring speech, it is critical to further assess ways to enhance the motivational components of a language intervention package for an individual child. In particular, future research should examine the characteristics of the subgroup of nonverbal children who have difficulty acquiring functional speech even with the intervention technologies that are currently available. It is important to continue exploring added motivational strategies that are especially effective for this subgroup of children. Furthermore, given the benefits of using a parent education model to facilitate speech acquisition in children with autism, future research may need to examine different approaches to parent education to further increase parent participation in the intervention process and improve child outcomes.

Appendix

Pivotal Response Treatment (PRT) Fidelity of Implementation Scoring Sheet

Pivotal Response Treatment (PRT) Fidelity of Implementation Scoring Sheet

1-Minute interval	Child attending	Clear opportunity	Maintenance tasks	Multiple cues	Child choice	Contingent	Natural	Contingent on attempts
1								
2								
3								
4								
5								
6								
7								
8								
9								
10								
%								

INSTRUCTIONS

1. Score fidelity in 10 1-minute intervals. After each 1-minute interval, score each of the eight PRT components.

2. Score each category as

    + (plus): The person being observed utilized this component of PRT.

    – (minus): The PRT component was not demonstrated.

    N/A (not applicable): The child is not at an appropriate level for this PRT component (e.g., multiple cues), or the scorer is not familiar with the child (e.g., to know which activities are maintenance tasks).

3. The performance of the person being observed should be independent of child's response.

4. Intervals that have no opportunities are scored as "−" (minus) in all categories. The person being observed must actively seek opportunities.

5. The person being observed must score 80% (8 out of 10) in *each* category to meet fidelity.

Definitions

Child attending: The person being observed must have the child's attention prior to presenting an opportunity.

Clear opportunity: The question/instruction/opportunity (discriminative stimulus, or S^D) for the child to respond must be clear and appropriate to the task.

Maintenance tasks: The person being observed should intersperse maintenance tasks (ones the child can already perform) with acquisition (new) tasks. This category cannot be recorded if the scorer is not familiar with the child.

Multiple cues: If appropriate to the developmental level of the child, the question/instruction should involve the use of multiple cues (e.g., asking the child if he or she wants the blue ball or the red ball if the child is at an appropriate level to begin learning colors).

Child choice: To a large extent, the person being observed should follow the child's choice with tasks and activities. However, the individual must assume control if the child engages in hazardous activities (e.g., self-injury) or inappropriate activities (e.g., self-stimulation). If child does not show interest in the current task, the individual should attempt to change the activity.

Contingent: Reinforcement must be contingent upon the child's behavior. The response of the person being observed (e.g., giving the child a toy) must be dependent upon the child's response (e.g., saying "toy").

Natural: Reinforcement should be natural or directly related to the desired behavior.

Contingent on attempts: Any goal-directed attempt to respond to questions, instructions, or opportunities should be reinforced. Although an attempt does not necessarily need to be correct, it has to be reasonable.

9

The Pivotal Role of Initiations in Habilitation

Rosy Matos Fredeen and Robert L. Koegel

This chapter discusses the literature on child initiations as they pertain to language development in typically developing children and children with autism. It provides a brief overview of definitions, followed by an outline of empirical studies of prelinguistic, verbal, and social interaction initiations. Furthermore, empirical studies documenting initiations in children with autism in comparison with other children with disabilities are also described. Finally, future lines of research in the area of initiations for children with autism are identified and discussed with respect to their potentially critical role for excellent intervention outcomes.

BACKGROUND

A core feature of human interaction, both communicative and social, is initiations (McTear, 1985; Seibert, Hogan, & Mundy, 1982). Initiations come in a variety of forms and increase in sophistication and specification as children develop, from early joint attention behaviors such as alternating eye gaze to pointing/showing something of interest to another; to expressively requesting, commenting, and asking questions; and to engaging in elaborate social conversations (McTear, 1985; Seibert et al., 1982). This ability to spontaneously and independently direct and/or engage other individuals in interactions is something typically developing children appear to do early on and with great ease, quite saliently at approximately 9 months of age, when the first forms of intentional communication develop (Adamson, 1995; Bates, 1976; Lord & Paul, 1997). Children with other developmental disabilities, such as Down syndrome, also engage in initiations, albeit in a delayed fashion (McGee, Feldman, & Morrier, 1997; Sigman & Ruskin, 1999). However, the ability to initiate, which is usually taken for granted in typically developing children, is arguably one of the greatest challenges facing children diagnosed with autism spectrum disorders (ASDs) who appear to exhibit impairments in all forms of initiations (Krantz & McClannahan, 1993; Rogers, 2000; Zanolli, Daggett, & Adams, 1996). This is particularly important in light of research identifying initiations as a likely prognostic indicator for more favorable long-term outcomes (L.K. Koegel, Koegel, Shoshan, & McNerney, 1999).

DEFINITIONS

Defining *initiations* is a particularly difficult challenge because there are many different types of initiations, including initiations of joint attention (Bakeman & Adamson, 1984; Mundy & Gomes, 1996; Mundy, Sigman, Ungerer, & Sherman, 1986), initiations of requests (Linder, 1993; McTear, 1985), initiations via question asking (L.K. Koegel, Camarata, Valdez-Menchaca, & Koegel, 1998a; McTear, 1985; Taylor & Harris, 1995), initiations for play (Haring & Lovinger, 1989; Oke & Schreibman, 1990), and initiations for social conversation (Krantz & McClannahan, 1993; McTear, 1985). Each type of initiation consequently has a specific definition. However, as Landry, Smith, Miller-Loncar, and Swank (1997) discussed, the essence of all initiations is the independent formulation of social-communicative goals. That is, unlike responsiveness, in which other individuals (e.g., parents) provide children with a structure for organizing their social-communicative behaviors, initiations require children to independently form their own social-communicative goals without scaffolding from communicative partners. The authors further suggested that initiating may be a developmentally more difficult task than responding because of the lack of external support. In addition, many definitions in the literature include a temporal specification for a behavior to be considered an initiation (Strain, Kerr, & Ragland, 1979). For example, in order for a behavior to be considered an initiation, it must be emitted either 3 seconds before or after another person's motor, gestural, or verbal behavior (Strain et al., 1979). Other definitions in the literature simply define initiations as utterances that predict responses (McTear, 1985); yet others define initiations as behaviors (verbal or nonverbal) that children direct to others and are not preceded by instructions to talk (Breen & Haring, 1991; Hancock & Kaiser, 1996; Stone & Caro-Martinez, 1990). McTear (1985) subdivided initiations into three categories: questions, requests for action, and statements. McTear also subdivided reinitiations (utterances made if the first initiation fails to get a response from the listener) into four types: repeats, repeats with prosodic shift, repeats with attention getting, and attention-getting devices. Mueller, Bleier, Krakow, Hagedus, and Cournoyer (1977) showed that the frequency of attention-getting devices increases with age, suggesting a relationship with children's increasing communicative competence. Finally, McTear (1985) delineated that in order for an initiation to be successful, the speaker must be sure to obtain and maintain the listener's attention, construct an initiation appropriate to the listener's knowledge level, and be able to reinitiate if the first initiation was unsuccessful.

Despite the many different types of initiations and specific definitions, the key is that initiations are social-communicative behaviors—such as requests, questions, and comments—that children formulate independent of any external support from a communicative partner (Landry et al., 1997; McGee et al., 1997). Chapter 8 describes prelinguistic initiations in detail; therefore, the remainder of this chapter focuses on the development of verbal initiations and their relationship to, and coexistence with, nonverbal acts in typically developing children and the lack of initiations in children with autism.

VERBAL INITIATIONS IN TYPICALLY DEVELOPING CHILDREN

First words begin to emerge at approximately 1 year of age in typically developing children, and most typically developing children use several single words by 18 months of age (Bates, 1979; Linder, 1993; Seibert et al., 1982; Wetherby, Cain, Yonclas, & Walker, 1988). The literature has documented some particularly interesting and noteworthy findings about later verbal abilities in typically developing children. For example, several studies have documented a strong longitudinal association between joint attention abilities (i.e., initiating protodeclarative pointing, following gaze, and following pointing) and language abilities in the second year of life (Carpenter, Nagell, & Tomasello, 1998; Mundy & Gomes, 1996; Paul & Shiffer, 1991).

Initially, children with few words in their verbal repertoire are limited to initiating topics by pointing, holding out objects, or gesturing. However, as their vocabulary increases, children rely less on gestures to initiate (McLaughlin, 1998). Another interesting finding is that verbal initiations are used to communicate a wide range of intentions, including attention seeking (e.g., a child tugging on his or her mother's dress and saying "Mommy"), requesting objects (e.g., a child pointing to and/or saying "doggie" for a toy that he or she wants), requesting actions (e.g., a child rocking back and forth and/or saying "push" while sitting on a swing), commenting on objects (e.g., a child saying "ball" when seeing the object), commenting on actions (e.g., a child saying "down" as his or her father drops a toy), and greeting (e.g., waving good-bye as a parent leaves the house) (Bates, 1979; Garvey, 1975; Linder, 1993; McTear, 1985). Although these behaviors are dominant in typically developing children between 13 and 21 months of age, the behaviors may emerge as early as 10 to 11 months of age (Seibert et al., 1982). Furthermore, as noted by researchers (Halliday, 1979; McTear, 1985), children exhibit the ability to reinitiate at early ages, initially with vocalization repetition at as early as 9 months, followed by changes in intonation at as early as 15 months. Remarkably, 2-year-olds have been found to reinitiate 54% of the time following no responses to their initial initiation (Wellman & Lempers, 1977).

By 24 months of age, typically developing children exhibit an array of social-communicative initiations in their behavioral repertoire. By this time, children readily initiate joint attention bids to objects out of sight (Seibert et al., 1982). In addition, at this juncture in time, most children are able to request information through a variety of "wh-" questions (Adamson, 1995; Linder, 1993), initially by pointing and then by asking verbally (Lord & Paul, 1997; Tyack & Ingram, 1977). The ability to ask questions is a particularly important turning point in development because for the first time, children are using words to obtain new information about their environment and are self-initiating learning (Halliday, 1975; Meyer & Shane, 1973; Tyack & Ingram, 1977). Furthermore, one of the most common initiations is termed *requests for action* (also known as *directives*), which are defined as attempts to get the listener to perform a particular action (McTear, 1985). Children can initiate requests for actions in a variety of grammatical forms (directly or indirectly), such as "Mommy throw ball" or "Oh, not again."

By the time children are 2–3 years of age, they can introduce a topic and engage in a conversation of a few turns. Conversational skills are particularly impressive because they require the ability to take and assign turns, as well as the ability to reciprocally initiate and respond (McTear, 1985). It should be noted that for toddlers, novelty is an extremely important component that prompts them to initiate a topic (McLaughlin, 1998). However, by 5–6 years of age, children's discourse skills are similar to those of adults in that children not only can initiate topics but also can successfully maintain a conversational topic through a dozen turns and can use questions for a variety of pragmatic functions (Cook-Gumperz & Kyratzis, 2001; Hurtig, Ensrud, & Tomblin, 1982; Linder, 1993). Other conversational skills that have become refined at this age include the ability to add new information to a topic and to initiate the request for clarification of misunderstood utterances (Bates, 1976; McTear, 1985). In terms of reinitiations, researchers have found that children between 2 years, 10 months and 5 years, 7 months reinitiate within 2 seconds of their first initiation (Garvey & Berninger, 1981). Reinitiations are especially interesting because they suggest children's awareness of the discourse properties of their utterances (McTear, 1985).

Despite the fact that conversational skills are relatively unsophisticated until 5–7 years of age, it is important to note that the building blocks of conversations start as early as infancy (Locke, 1995; McTear, 1985). In fact, these early "conversational" interactions are referred to as *proto-conversations* (Bateson, 1975). Detailed analysis of early social-communicative interactions between infants and caregivers have revealed that the interactions possess elements of mature conversations, including turn taking with little overlap, in which infants and caregivers engage in conversation-like exchanges alternating between who initiates and who responds (Locke, 1995; McLaughlin, 1998; McTear, 1985). Snow (1977) analyzed the conversations between mothers and their babies and found that mothers treated their children's smiles, burps, and vocalizations as initiations and contingently responded to them. As their babies developed, mothers came to expect higher quality initiations. For example, at 3 months of age, mothers responded to simple burps, yawns, sneezes, and vocalizations. However, by 7 months, only vocalizations and babbling were responded to, and by 18 months, mothers expected their children to use words.

RATE AND FUNCTION OF INITIATIONS IN TYPICALLY DEVELOPING CHILDREN

Knowing when typically developing children begin to use and master different types of initiations is clearly important. However, equally important is understanding the relative frequency at which typically developing children use initiations and the functions that their initiations serve. In a study conducted by Wetherby and colleagues (1988), the quantitative use of intentional communication by children at the prelinguistic, one-word, and multiword stages was assessed. This study revealed that on average, typically developing children engaged in one communicative act per minute during the prelinguistic stage, two communicative acts per minute in the one-word stage, and five communicative acts per minute in the multiword stage. Furthermore, discourse analysis revealed that children in all three linguistic stages (prelinguistic, one-word, and multiword) showed more initiated than respondent acts. The percent of initiations also increased dramatically from the preverbal to verbal stages. In addition, children at all linguistic stages initiated communicative acts in each of the three categories of intentional communication (behavior regulation, social interaction, and joint attention). However, the majority of initiations fell in either the category of behavior regulation or joint attention during all three stages of language, with request action and comment being the overall most frequently used. Other studies have documented the functions of young children's initiations for a variety of developmental stages (Dore, 1974; Foster, 1979; Halliday, 1975; Tremblay, Strain, Hendrickson, & Shores, 1981; Wellman & Lempers, 1977). For example, Foster (1979) studied the development of initiation functions in children between 1 month and 2 years, 6 months. She found that initially, strategic initiations (those to which intent could be ascribed) primarily consisted of self-topics, whereby a child would try to direct attention to him- or herself—for example, by crying. Foster found that even the youngest children (between 1 and 5 months of age) used self-topic initiations, albeit infrequently. Next to develop were environmental-topic initiations, whereby children directed others' attention to objects in their immediate physical surroundings. Foster noted the earliest examples of these initiations at 5 months of age, as demonstrated by reaching behaviors. However, more salient forms developed by 1 year, 3 months, as exhibited by pointing. Finally, the ability to refer to objects not in the immediate environment (abstract-topic initiations) developed. The earliest examples of these initiations emerged around 1 year, 10 months but were more clearly established by 2 years, 6 months.

Other researchers have also investigated the quantity of initiations emitted by typically developing children. Tremblay and colleagues (1981) found that young typically developing preschoolers exhibited an average of 1 initiation every 2 minutes in an unstructured setting. Zanolli and colleagues (1996) found that 4- to 6-year-old typically developing children exhibited initiations toward each other approximately .5 times per minute during specific classroom activities (i.e., playing with blocks and toy cars, coloring, and using the water table). Finally, results obtained by McGrath, Bosch, Sullivan, and Fuqua (2003) indicated that in a 10-minute free-play session, 3- to 4-year-old children initiated toward each other an average of 5 times. Although these findings are very interesting, most used very small time samples (approximately 2 minutes).

Unfortunately, other than the few studies previously mentioned, very little information about the quantity of initiations in typical development is available in the literature. It is also important to note that few studies assessing the quantity of initiations have focused on peer-to-peer initiations (McGrath et al., 2003; Tremblay et al., 1981) and most have used very young children (McGrath et al., 2003; Trebmlay et al., 1981; Wetherby et al., 1988). Future research assessing the quantitative use of initiations in typically developing children is critical and should involve children at a variety of ages, across a variety of contexts, and for longer periods of time. Other researchers have also investigated the functions of initiations in toddlers (Dore, 1974; Halliday, 1975). For example, Halliday (1975) described a number of communicative functions used by toddlers, including interactional (establishing interactions with individuals), personal (expressing personal feelings), heuristic (inquiring about environment), regulatory (trying to control other's actions), instrumental (trying to obtain objects through others), informative (sharing knowledge with others), and imaginative (using words in play).

In terms of preschoolers, Tremblay and colleagues (1981) observed 60 3- to 5-year-old children across a 2-month period during free play. These researchers found that a majority of initiations exhibited by preschoolers served the following functions: rough-and-tumble play, sharing, play organization (e.g., "Let's play dolls"), assistance, affection, and questions. On a related note, Corsaro (1985) found that preschoolers between the ages of 2 and 4 years most frequently used imperatives and informative statements during peer play interactions.

INITIATIONS IN CHILDREN WITH AUTISM

This section discusses initiations in children with autism, including the presence of initiations in the behavioral repertoire of these children during infancy and early childhood, their role in screening and diagnosis, and their use in comparison with other populations of children.

Role of Initiations in Screening and Diagnosis of Autism

Several red flags of autism can be related to initiations, as shown in the following sections.

Difficulties with Nonverbal Initiations or Initiations of Joint Attention

Early on, children with autism may lack initiations in their behavioral repertoire, including initiations of joint attention (McArthur & Adamson, 1996; Mundy et al., 1986). For example, in a screening study of 41 18-month-old infants, Baron-Cohen, Allen, and Gillberg (1992) found that the Checklist for Autism in Toddlers (CHAT) reliably identified children at 18 months who later received diagnosis of autism at 30 months. Children who were identified as being at risk for autism at 18 months using the CHAT consistently demonstrated impairments in two or more of the following: lack of pretend play, lack of protodeclarative pointing, lack of social interest, lack of social play, and lack of joint attention. As the authors discussed, protodeclarative pointing (use of the index finger to indicate an object of interest to another person) and joint attention (showing or gaze monitoring in an attempt to direct or monitor the attention of another individual to an object or event of interest) are some of the earliest forms of initiations to develop in typically developing children. However, these behaviors are consistently absent or rare in children with autism as further substantiated by this screening study. Furthermore, according to the authors, knowing that these early forms of initiations are impaired in children with autism should increase successful identification at earlier ages by professionals, including pediatricians.

Lower Levels of Prelinguistic Initiations   By using studies of parental report, as well as retrospective analysis of home videotapes, researchers have been able to identify a number of behavioral characteristics exhibited by infants later diagnosed with autism (Ornitz, Guthrie & Farley, 1977; Stone & Lemanek, 1990; Wimpory, Hobson, Williams, & Nash, 2000). DeMeyer (1979) employed a semistructured parent interview to obtain retrospective reports of infant behaviors in children with autism and typically developing counterparts. The author identified that approximately half of the children with autism (52%) babbled less and that their babbling was qualitatively different from their siblings in comparison to typical developers. This is particularly important given that typically developing infants start using babbling as a means to initiate both communicative and social interactions with their caregivers at approximately 9 months of age (Cole & Cole, 2001).

Wimpory and colleagues (2000) found that parents reported that their infants who were later identified with autism had deficits in babbling with communicative intent. That is, unlike typically developing infants, who start to initiate babbling with their primary caregivers at as early as 4 months of age (Adamson, 1995; Cole & Cole, 2001), infants with autism, even at later ages, did not initiate babbling episodes with their caregivers.

Difficulties in Initiating Attention Seeking   Other behaviors differentiating autism from developmental delays in children, such as initiating attention-seeking gestures, have been documented in the literature (Kasari, Sigman, Mundy, & Yirmiya, 1990; Mundy, Sigman, & Kasari, 1990; Stone, 1998). Communicatively, infants and young children with autism do not generally attempt to attract attention to themselves through initiations such as showing, giving, and pointing (Mundy et al., 1990; Stone, 1998).

Difficulties with Child-Initiated Eye Contact   Children with autism appear to initiate eye contact less frequently to initiate joint attention interactions with adults (Mundy et al., 1986). This is particularly important in terms of early red flags, given how intertwined eye contact is in all social-communication, both nonverbal and verbal, for typically developing children.

Difficulty with Child-Initiated Social Interest   Children with autism tend to appear disinterested in novel events and actions of social interest. They may not come to a parent who calls their name or initiate an apparent interest in what is happening in their environments and may appear to have little interest in initiating or engaging in simple social games (Stone, 1998).

Difficulty with Imitation   Typically developing children often spontaneously imitate others, either immediately after an adult's action or sometime later. Poor imitation or lack of interest in imitating others is common in children with autism. It is interesting to note that many children will exhibit difficulty or a lack of interest in imitating others in a demand-type situation (e.g., teacher instruction to perform particular behavior) but will readily engage in echolalia when watching a preferred video. This may suggest an underlying motivational issue during less-preferred activities, rather than a generalized problem with the ability to imitate, for some children in the spectrum.

Summary   Researchers and practitioners agree that the advances being made in screening and diagnosis through the use of retrospective analysis only improve the opportunities for long-term positive outcomes for children with autism (Filipek et al., 1999; Rogers, 2000). Nevertheless, impairments in initiations for children with autism are not limited to deficits in prelinguistic and early social-communicative behaviors. Unfortunately, they are pervasive and affect many domains of social-communicative functioning. The following section discusses later verbal initiations that may be symptomatic of children with autism.

Verbal Initiations in Children with Autism

Various studies, described in the following subsections, offer target areas for improving verbal initiations in children with autism.

Initiations of First Words   One of the earliest parent report studies was conducted by Ornitz and colleagues (1977). These researchers used a written questionnaire to obtain developmental information from parents of children with autism and parents of typically developing children. Results revealed several interesting differences in infant behavior between the two groups. Communicatively, parents reported that 79% of typically developing infants used their first words by 16 months of age. This is in comparison with only 16% of children with autism. On a related note, 69% of typically developing infants initiated the use of first words to indicate a desire by 18 months, whereas only 10% of children later diagnosed with autism did so.

Similarly, DeMeyer (1979) found that only 48% of children with autism had first words by 12 months of age and that only half of these children used their first words meaningfully. This is in comparison with 82% of typically developing children, who used first words by 12 months.

Initiations of Meaningful First Words   Parents of the typically developing children report that their children have no difficulties using their words meaningfully. However, as previously noted in the study by DeMeyer (1979), children with autism often use words in ways that are not meaningful or are out of context. DeMeyer reported that 89% of children with autism used 15 or fewer words by 24 months of age, and most of these words were not meaningful. That is, the words often represented instances of echolalia.

Questions   As mentioned previously, by 24 months of age, typically developing children are beginning to combine words and use a variety of initiations, including asking "wh-" questions such as "Dat?" for "What's that?" (Linder, 1993). Children with autism often have few or no questions or information-seeking strategies in their communication repertoires. Unlike typically developing children, most children with autism have been found to initiate question asking infrequently (Hung, 1977; L.K. Koegel, 2000; Taylor & Harris, 1995; Wetherby & Prutting, 1984). When children with autism do initiate question asking, they rarely appear to do so for the purpose of requesting information, as most children do.

It should also be noted that some researchers have found that higher functioning verbal children with autism perseveratively and inappropriately ask questions in order to get attention and/or to initiate social interactions with others (Hurtig et al., 1982). For example, Hurtig and colleagues (1982) assessed the communicative function of question asking in higher functioning verbal children with autism. Results indicated that these children frequently asked questions to which they already knew the answer, suggesting that the function of question asking was not information gathering but a means to initiate social interactions. The authors hypothesized that this use of question asking reflected the children's limited repertoire of topic initiations and was comparable to the "insatiable" question asking displayed by typically developing 2- to 3-year-old children. Furthermore, the authors discussed that unlike most children with autism, who rarely initiate interactions with others, higher functioning children with autism appear to understand that question asking is a reliable tool for initiating because it obligates the listener to respond. This is especially promising because it suggests that the lack of verbal initiations in children with autism may be more directly related to language deficits rather than an intrinsic desire to avoid social-communicative interactions with others.

Child-Initiated Comments   Commenting is a common feature of typically developing children's language initiations (Linder, 1993). Although typically developing children often comment on items or actions in their environment, children with autism rarely do so. O'Neill and Happe (2000) examined the differences and similarities in commenting on something new among 22-month-old children with autism, typically developing children, and children with Down syndrome. The study consisted of presenting children with four trials of toys in which the first, second, and third trials contained the same toy and the fourth trial contained a different toy. Results revealed that typically developing children and children with Down syndrome initiated comments regarding the new item at relatively similar levels. The only difference was that children with Down syndrome initiated comments only to one person (i.e., the clinician) and that their typically developing peers initiated comments to both individuals in the testing room (i.e., the clinician and the mother). Conversely, the children with autism rarely initiated comments to others despite the fact that they engaged in equal amounts of vocalizations as the comparison peers. They directed these vocalizations to themselves, whereas the typically developing children and the children with Down syndrome initiated their vocalizations toward others for the purpose of commenting and sharing enjoyment.

Attention-Seeking Initiations   Studies have documented the fact that children with autism initiate attention-directing behaviors ("Mama, look!") significantly less frequently than typically developing children and children with developmental language delays (Landry & Loveland, 1989; Loveland & Landry, 1986). Furthermore, as mentioned previously, if children with autism do initiate attention-directing behaviors, it is more likely to be for the purpose of requesting rather than sharing enjoyment (Wetherby et al., 1988).

Summary   As a whole, the literature suggests that children with autism use language almost exclusively for requesting objects, requesting actions, and protesting (Wetherby & Prutting, 1984). The wide variety of initiations used by typically developing children are seen at lower levels or, in some cases, are completely lacking in the language of verbal children with autism.

SOCIAL INTERACTION INITIATIONS IN CHILDREN WITH AUTISM

It has been thoroughly documented in the literature that in comparison with both typically developing children and children with other developmental disabilities (e.g., Down syndrome), children with autism engage in far fewer social initiations with others, especially with siblings and other peers (Hauck, Fein, Waterhouse, & Feinstein, 1995; Knott, Lewis, & Williams, 1995; McGee et al., 1997; Oke & Schriebman, 1990; Ruble, 2001; Sigman & Ruskin, 1999). Specifically, in an assessment of play and social behaviors in preschool-age children with autism in inclusive school settings, L.K. Koegel, Koegel, Frea, and Fredeen (2001) found that in comparison with their typically developing peers, children with autism engaged in comparable levels of social interactions with adults but rarely or never engaged in social interactions with their peers.

Likewise, Hauck and colleagues (1995) found that children with autism and children with mental retardation differed in the quality, not quantity, of initiations toward adults. For the most part, children with autism made more behavior regulation initiations and fewer joint attention initiations toward adults, a finding consistent with other research (Sigman & Ruskin, 1999; Wetherby & Prutting, 1984). However, children with mental retardation initiated far more frequently toward peers than children with autism. Furthermore, Sigman and Ruskin (1999) documented that in comparison with children with Down syndrome, children with autism were less socially engaged with their peers because they infrequently initiated play bids, not because they were ignored by peers. It is interesting to note that Hauck et al. (1995) and Sigman and Ruskin (1999) found that the frequency of social interaction initiations was not predicted by severity of symptomatology but by cognitive and verbal abilities. In other words, children with autism who had more sophisticated language skills engaged in more initiations.

In terms of social interactions with siblings, Knott et al. (1995) identified that sibling dyads with a child with autism were marked by decreased interactions in contrast to sibling dyads with a child with Down syndrome. Most notably, children with autism spent less time in the same room with their siblings and imitated, responded to, and initiated communication toward their siblings less frequently than children with Down syndrome. This is in contrast with a later study conducted by El-Ghoroury and Romanczyk (1999), which found that children with autism appeared to initiate more often toward their siblings than to either parent. However, caution about these results is warranted for two reasons. First, as the authors suggested, parents may have attempted to compensate for their child's disability by constantly directing them in social interactions. Second, for a child initiation to be scored, there had to be no interaction occurring at the time. Because the parents maintained such high levels of interactions, the children had fewer opportunities to initiate, possibly distorting the results. Conversely, siblings in this study did not appear to try to compensate for the children's disabilities and rarely directed the children with autism. Consequently, the children with autism had many more opportunities to initiate and to have those initiations scored.

RATE AND FUNCTION OF INITIATIONS IN CHILDREN WITH AUTISM

As discussed earlier in this chapter, the functions of initiations among children with autism differ from those demonstrated by typically developing children and by children with other disabilities. That is, the initiations of children with autism primarily serve the function of requesting and protesting, whereas typically developing children and children with other disabilities exhibit a greater variety of initiation functions, with most being for the purpose of socializing (Wetherby, 1986). Similarly, the rate of initiations made by children with autism has been found to be distinctively different from that found among other children (Sigman & Ruskin, 1999). For example, Stone and Caro-Martinez (1990) assessed the initiation of spontaneous communicative acts by children with autism in natural school settings (i.e., special education classroom and cafeteria). The authors found that spontaneous communication was a rare event for these children. In fact, the children in this study initiated communication on average a mere three to four times per hour. Even more astounding is that one child did not initiate any communication during all 3 hours of observation. In contrast, typically developing children at the prelinguistic stage initiate communication more often than these older children did, with an average of one initiation per minute (Wetherby et al., 1988). In addition, only half of these children were ever observed to initiate their communicative acts to peers. Stone and Caro-Martinez also found that although the children with autism made initiations at particularly low rates, their initiations were primarily for getting attention and making comments about ongoing events. Knowing such information is important for the design of interventions.

In summary, the literature has clearly documented a pervasive impairment in the use of initiations by children with autism. The following section reviews the current state of knowledge on interventions designed specifically to address these deficits.

INTERVENTIONS TARGETING INITIATIONS IN CHILDREN WITH AUTISM

Although the literature offers no single explanation for the impairment of initiations in children with autism, it does present a consensus on the importance of and need for intervention (Guralnick & Neville, 1997; Hauck et al., 1995; Knott et al., 1995; Mundy et al., 1986; Rogers, 2000). Furthermore, the literature suggests several advantages to being able to initiate communication, including a probable increase in successful interactions, because the target individuals will have more control over interactions, increased independence, and increased frequencies of interaction (Gaylord-Ross & Haring, 1987; Haring & Lovinger, 1989; Jolly, Test, & Spooner, 1993; Weiss & Harris, 2001). In addition, increasing social-communicative initiations in children with autism is particularly important because social skills deficiencies during childhood have been found to be the single best behavioral predictor of adjustment problems in adulthood (Roff, 1961; Strain & Odom, 1986). Children who have successful peer interactions in childhood are less likely to experience subsequent social problems in adolescence and adulthood (McTear, 1985).

Over the years, interventions have targeted various types of initiations among children with autism, including joint attention (Whalen & Schreibman, 2003), play organization (Haring & Lovinger, 1989; Jolly et al., 1993; Stahmer, 1999), positive affect (Harris, Handleman, & Fong, 1987), affection (Charlop & Walsh, 1986), questions (L.K. Koegel et al., 1998; Taylor & Harris, 1995), requests (Charlop, Schreibman, & Thibodeau, 1985; Charlop & Walsh, 1986), greetings and social amenities (Matson, Sevin, Box, Francis, & Sevin, 1993; Jolly et al., 1993), social interaction (Haring & Lovinger, 1989; Pierce & Schreibman, 1995), and eye gaze (Charlop & Walsh, 1986; Harris, Handleman, & Fong, 1987). Overall, these interventions can be divided into three approaches: adult-mediated strategies, peer-mediated strategies, and child-initiated strategies (Jolly et al., 1993; Odom, Hoyson, Jamieson, & Strain, 1985; Odom & Strain, 1984; Oke & Schriebman, 1990; Strain & Timm, 1974). These strategies, as well as using appropriate peers and environments for intervention, are discussed next.

Adult-Initiated Strategies

In the first approach, adults serve as mediating and reinforcement agents between a child with autism and their typically developing peers (Strain & Odom, 1986). Moreover, the adult initiates each interaction with the child with autism and is also responsible for reinforcement delivery (Jolly et al., 1993; Weiss & Harris, 2001).

Peer-Mediated Strategies

In comparison, the second approach consists of teaching a typically developing peer to initiate, reinforce, and maintain ongoing interactions with a student with autism. Common intervention targets in peer-mediated strategies include sharing materials, organizing play episodes, and responding positively to the child with the disability (Jolly et al., 1993; Morrison, Kamps, Garcia, & Parker, 2001; Weiss & Harris, 2001). Strain and colleagues(1979) investigated some of the earliest peer-mediated strategies. They examined two approaches for implementing peer-mediated strategies and their effects on behavior change generalization in children with autism. First, a typically developing peer trainer was taught to prompt and reinforce two students with autism to socially interact with each other. In a second condition, the same peer trainer was instructed to initiate play overtures toward the students with autism. Results revealed that both approaches produced dramatic increases in the positive social behaviors (i.e., responses and initiations) of the children with autism; however, almost all improvements were in terms of responsivity as opposed to initiation. Furthermore, neither peer-mediated strategy resulted in sustained behavior change during the generalization sessions. That is, once the peer-mediated strategies were removed, the children with autism returned to baseline levels of initiations and responses.

Another common approach to peer-mediated strategies is peer tutoring (Sasso, Mitchell, & Struthers, 1986). In 2000, Laushey and Heflin expanded the use of peer tutoring to young children with autism and their typically developing peers in the form of a buddy system. Two children with autism and their typically developing peers in an inclusive school setting participated in this study. Each day, all students in the classroom were assigned a different daily buddy as a means to make new friends. All children were instructed to "stay, play, and talk" to their buddy during play periods in the classroom. A reversal design was implemented and revealed that the buddy system resulted in improved social skill use by all children, including the children with autism. The authors contended that in accordance with other research (Gresham, 1998), using a buddy system to train all children increases the likelihood that students with autism will have more opportunities to engage in generalized practice of social targets. Nonetheless, intervention gains were maintained at follow-up for only one child with autism.

Along the lines of peer tutoring, Pierce and Schreibman (1995) successfully taught typically developing peers to use the motivational procedures of Pivotal Response Treatment (PRT) to increase the social behaviors of two students with autism. Results revealed that both students with autism exhibited gains in their social behaviors (i.e., maintaining interaction and initiating) after intervention, generalized their behaviors to untrained peers, and maintained those gains at follow-up. The results of this study are especially important because this is one of the few studies in the literature to use naturalistic teaching procedures to increase initiations in children with autism.

Researchers also have enlisted siblings in the implementation of peer-mediated strategies (Celiberti & Harris, 1993; Hancock & Kaiser, 1996). Hancock and Kaiser

(1996) taught older siblings to implement milieu teaching procedures during play interactions with their younger siblings. Specifically, siblings were taught to use mand, mand-modeling, and reinforcement procedures. The study demonstrated that not only did the older typically developing siblings learn to effectively and correctly use the milieu teaching procedures but also that the target children also increased the frequency of their initiations. Moreover, both the typically developing siblings and the target children maintained their behavior changes at follow-up and generalized their skills to a new setting.

Child-Initiated Strategies

A third approach for increasing social initiations in children with autism is target child initiation training (Charlop & Walsh, 1986; Matson et al., 1993; Oke & Schreibman, 1990). With target child initiation training, a child with autism is taught skills to initiate and maintain interactions with peers, thus taking on an empowered role of initiator rather than just recipient (Jolly et al., 1998). In a two-part study, Oke and Schreibman (1990) empirically documented the importance of teaching children with autism how to initiate communication with peers. Specifically, peers were first taught to initiate communication with the child with autism, which resulted in initial increases in social behaviors in the target student. Nonetheless, as evident in other peer-mediated strategies, once peers decreased their rates of initiations, so did the child with autism. This was not remediated until target child training was introduced. That is, when the child with autism was taught how to initiate communication, his or her social responding increased again without the need for peer training. In addition, collateral changes in the target child's disruptive behaviors were only observed once he or she had been taught how to initiate communication with peers.

In terms of target child initiation training, the literature documents several procedures, including priming (Zanolli & Daggett, 1998; Zanolli et al., 1996), textual prompts and photographic activity schedules (Jolly et al., 1993; Krantz & McClannahan, 1993), and tactile prompts (Taylor & Levin, 1998). The effects of priming on the production of initiations by children with autism were assessed by Zanolli and Daggett (1998), who measured spontaneous initiations directed toward adults. Moreover, the authors examined the effects of reinforcement rate (high versus low) during priming sessions on the rate of spontaneous initiations during subsequent classroom activities. Results revealed that children consistently engaged in more spontaneous verbal initiations after high rates of reinforcement during priming sessions. According to Zanolli and Daggett, the results suggested that behavioral persistence produced by priming is dramatically influenced by previous rates of reinforcement, a contention that is consistent with findings from both basic and applied research regarding the influence of reinforcement on behavioral momentum (Nevin, Mandell, & Atak, 1983).

Shabani et al. (2002) assessed the effects of a tactile prompting device (i.e., a vibrating pager) on the verbal initiations of three children with autism during free play activities with typically developing peers. Prior to intervention, all three children responded to questions and initiations from adults; however, they rarely initiated communication with or played with peers. Results demonstrated that when the tactile

This photo sequence shows a child and his sister playing an interactive, highly preferred game. The game contains multiple pieces, making it easy for the children to take turns initiating language.

prompting device was used, all three children increased their frequency of verbal initiations toward peers. In addition, the three children also increased their responsivity to peers. When the prompting device was faded, however, only one child was able to partially maintain appropriate rates of verbal initiations.

Child-initiated strategies have also been employed to teach skills such as question asking. As mentioned previously, children with autism often ask few if any questions unless specifically taught this skill. L.K. Koegel et al. (1998) examined whether using motivational procedures to teach question asking to children with autism would result in generalization to other settings without additional teaching, prompting, and reinforcement. Specifically, children with autism who lacked verbal initiations were taught to ask "What's that?" in relation to objects that they had previously been unable to label. Results documented that the children not only learned to successfully ask "What's that?" when presented with such items but also exhibited generalization of spontaneous question asking to new settings and people (e.g., their homes, their mothers) with collateral gains in expressive vocabulary. Similarly, L.K. Koegel, Carter, and Koegel (2003) used motivational procedures to determine whether children with autism could spontaneously use a child-initiated query (i.e., "What happened?") as a pivotal response to facilitate the development of grammatical morphemes. Two children who lacked the use of temporal morphemes (i.e., those for regular past tense and irregular past tense) in their expressive language were taught to ask either "What happened?" or "What's happening?" in relation to the actions performed in child-preferred pop-up books. Both children learned their specific self-initiated strategy, as well as acquired and generalized the use of their targeted temporal morpheme.

Still other researchers have asserted that contextual effects can significantly contribute to the success of target child initiations. For example, Breen and Haring (1991) assessed the effects of contextual competence on social initiations. Specifically, the authors evaluated differences in the amount of initiations a target student made toward a typically developing peer when the dyad played a computer game familiar to the target student versus when they played an unfamiliar computer game. Results demonstrated that target students initiated 42% of the interactions when they played familiar games, whereas they initiated only 29% of the interactions when they played unfamiliar games. The authors contended that an analysis of social and physical contextual characteristics may be an especially helpful tool in facilitating target child initiations.

These findings are consistent with those from other studies, which have successfully used the strengths of children with autism to increase social interactions with typical peers (Baker, 2000). For example, Baker (2000) successfully increased the percentage of social interactions and joint attention behaviors exhibited by children with autism toward their typically developing siblings by incorporating the children's thematic ritualistic activities of into typical games. Furthermore, 1- and 3-month follow-up measures revealed maintenance of the social interaction and joint attention gains.

Hwang and Hughes (2000) reviewed the literature on social interaction training for children with autism between 1981 and 1997. The authors found 16 studies that focused on naturalistic interventions allowing the child with autism to take on the role of initiator. The naturalistic teaching techniques included contingent imitation (e.g., Harris et al., 1987), naturally occurring reinforcement (e.g., Pierce & Schreibman, 1995), time delay (e.g., Charlop et al., 1985; Taylor & Harris, 1995), and environmental arrangements (e.g., Thorp, Stahmer, & Schreibman, 1995). Although each teaching technique differed in a number of ways, all shared the common goal of providing trainer responses that were simple, predictable, and contingent upon child initiations. This review revealed many interesting findings, including the facts that few of the studies employed young preschool-age children with autism, most (69%) children in the studies exhibited verbalizations or echolalia, and very few studies either assessed or resulted in generalization and long-term maintenance. Moreover, the authors stated that future research should examine which combination of naturalistic teaching strategies is most useful with given groups of children with autism. For example, time delay alone may be an effective strategy to use with children who have functional language. For children with limited or no language, however, other naturalistic strategies, such as environmental arrangements, may need to be combined with time delay in order to increase initiation use.

Appropriate Peers and Environments for Intervention

A final consideration not only for target child initiation training but also for initiation training in general is the selection of appropriate peers for intervention. Strain and Odom (1986) identified a series of criteria for selecting appropriate candidates for participation in intervention at the preschool level, including children who exhibited compliance with requests made by teachers, had regular attendance, had age-appropriate play skills, had either no history or a positive history with the target child, were the target child's classmates, and expressed willingness to participate in interactions. Lord and Hopkins (1986) found that same-age typically developing children initiated communication more frequently with children with autism than younger typically developing children. In addition, unlike younger typically developing peers, same-age typically developing peers were better able to modify their initiations in ways that increased the likelihood of a response from the child with autism.

On a similar note, consideration should also be given to environmental components that may support training. For example, researchers have found that certain materials tend to be used more often by preschoolers in a cooperative fashion. For example, dolls, pretend housekeeping materials, cars, and blocks appear to be more conducive to social use, and therefore intervention, than items such as clay, crayons, and puzzles, which tend to be used more often during independent play (Kennedy & Itkonen, 1996; Strain & Odom, 1986; Zanolli & Daggett, 1998). Keeping such information in mind when developing initiation interventions may foster long-term positive outcomes.

CASE EXAMPLE

Anthony was diagnosed with autism when he was 2 years, 6 months. By the time the family was referred for services, he was 2 years, 9 months and used fewer than 10 consistent and functional words on a daily basis (e.g., *water, up, cookie*). Consequently, the initial goals of the program were to increase Anthony's motivation to respond and increase his production of functional verbalizations. Within 3 months of PRT intervention, Anthony consistently and functionally used several hundred words. In addition, he was beginning to combine words into simple two- and three-word utterances, primarily for the purpose of requesting, although he often made simple comments (e.g., "look water"). Approximately 5 months after the start of intervention, it became apparent that Anthony needed to be taught to ask self-initiated questions. His mother, Susan, was very excited about this prospect; although she was delighted with Anthony's progress, she eagerly anticipated the moment when her son would ask his first question. Susan longed for the time when Anthony would be able to share his interests with her and show a general curiosity. Based on Anthony's language development and his mother's desire to increase his initiations, the PRT clinician began to teach Susan the procedures of question asking, starting with "What's that?"

On the first day of introducing question asking, Susan was very excited. She had gathered all of the necessary materials (as highlighted in L.K. Koegel et al., 1999), including an opaque bag and a variety of highly desired reinforcers. Anthony, Susan, and the clinician sat on the floor of the playroom and proceeded with the first trial. Susan held out the opaque bag, looked into it, and prompted Anthony to say, "What's that?" Anthony did not ask, "What's that?"; instead, he proceeded to guess what was inside the bag. He said, "It's a ball." Again, Susan prompted him to ask her, "What's that?" but Anthony proceeded with more guesses: "It's a book. It's a bag." After a dozen or so trials of attempting to get Anthony to imitate the question "What's that?" with no success, the clinician attempted to help by varying the container (e.g., box, mailing envelope) or shortening the model to simply "That?" Nonetheless, Anthony continued to guess what was inside instead of imitating the question. (It should be noted that this is a frequently reported problem when question asking is first introduced; however, after a number of trials, most children quickly begin to imitate the modeled question). At this point in the session, Susan excused herself to go to the kitchen and check on lunch, which was in the oven. The clinician decided to continue with the trials and lie on the floor right in front of Anthony so that they were exactly at the same eye level. As the clinician leaned in, showed Anthony the opaque bag, and said, "Anthony, look at my mouth. Say, 'What's that?'" Anthony, in turn, leaned in closer and said, "Want a kiss?" They both broke into laughter and went off to tell Susan about the incredibly cute moment. After lunch and a few more trials, Anthony finally asked, "What's that?" He never stopped asking questions from that moment on. The next day, the clinician received a very excited call from Susan saying how they had gone to visit Anthony's father at work and that as they passed a soda machine, Anthony pointed and spontaneously asked, "What's that?" Anthony's parents and his PRT clinician continued to teach him a series of questions, and each subsequent question was considerably easier for Anthony to add to his repertoire.

Anthony is currently 7 years old and is fully included in second grade. He has friends, is invited to birthday parties, has play dates, plays soccer, and asks a lot of questions—his parents' favorite being, "Why do I have to go to bed?"

DISCUSSION OF CHAPTER CONCEPTS

As discussed throughout this chapter, the importance of initiations in development is undeniable. Not only are initiations a core feature of human social-communicative interactions (Adamson, 1995; McTear, 1985; Seibert et al., 1982), but they also are necessary for an individual to be considered a competent social communicator. Initiations are a necessary part of reciprocal interactions (Hurtig et al., 1982; Landry et al., 1997; Odom & Strain, 1984; Strain, 1983). Typically developing children appear to initiate communication early, with seemingly little effort or direct instruction from adults (Foster, 1979; McTear, 1985; Wetherby & Prutting, 1984). Although children with other disabilities, such as mental retardation or hearing impairments, may experience a delay in the development of their initiations, they nonetheless readily demonstrate a variety of initiations, including behavior regulation, joint attention, and social interaction (Antia & Dittillo, 1998; Hulsing, 1995; Kasari et al., 1990; McGee et al., 1997; O'Neill & Happe, 2000; Osterling, Dawson, & Munson, 2002). Conversely, children with autism appear to have difficulties initiating early in development (Baron-Cohen et al., 1992; Loveland & Landry, 1986; Osterling & Dawson, 1994; Wimpory et al., 2000), and research has thoroughly documented that these difficulties are pervasive across types of initiations and across communicative partners (e.g., adults, siblings, peers) (Hauck et al., 1995; Knott et al., 1995; Mesibov, 1983; Mundy et al., 1986). Moreover, research since the 1990s has concluded that without direct intervention, deficits in initiations are not ameliorated for children with autism (L.K. Koegel et al., 1999; Weiss & Harris, 2001). Given how pervasive impairments in initiations are for children with autism and the well-documented need for specific intervention, the collective body of literature reviewed and discussed in this chapter lead to a number of recommendations for intervention and future research.

DIRECTIONS FOR FUTURE RESEARCH

First, future lines of research directly investigating the exact nature and number of initiations in typically developing children would greatly increase knowledge of this phenomenon and provide special educators, researchers, and interventionists with invaluable guidance in developing age-appropriate interventions. For example, researchers such as McGee et al. (1997) discussed that the knowledge of how typically developing children exhibit particular behaviors is critical in establishing appropriate benchmarks for children with autism. Without an anchor for typical development, interventions for children with autism may inadvertently create other problems, such as inflated use of behaviors. That is, if typically developing 5-year-old children only initiate to peers on average twice per minute, teaching children with autism to initiate at higher levels can also be problematic. However, until more research on initiations in typically developing children with bigger sample sizes is conducted, such dilemmas cannot be thoroughly resolved.

Second, few initiation studies in the literature include very young children. Although some studies have worked with preschool-age children (cf. L.K. Koegel et al.,

1999), many of the studies that have demonstrated successful teaching of initiations have been delivered to either elementary-school age (between 5 and 10 years of age) or older children (Charlop et al., 1985; Oke & Schreibman, 1990; Zanolli & Daggett, 1998). This raises the question about the potential long-terms positive effects of beginning initiation training at earlier ages. Because autism can be identified as early as 18 months of age (Baron-Cohen et al., 1992), it would be interesting to assess whether an earlier incorporation of initiation training would prevent the pervasive deficit in initiations. Moreover, it would be interesting to assess whether targeting initiations earlier would change the developmental trajectory of these children and whether they would become less dependent on others for learning. Some research, such as that presented in Chapter 7, suggests that intervening with the motivational procedures of PRT may enable many children with autism to catch up with typically developing peers and change their developmental trajectory to a more age-appropriate one. The chapter authors recommend that initiation training be incorporated into intervention as soon as possible. For example, once children develop communicative intent and start to learn their first words, it is important to specifically provide instructional opportunities for them to initiate expressive language (e.g., waiting for a child to say "cookie" by using time delay rather than always asking the child what he or she wants). A variety of techniques can be used to target early initiations, including time delay (e.g., waiting) (Charlop et. al., 1985) and environmental arrangements (e.g., placing items in sight but out of reach) (Kaiser, Hancock, & Nietfeld, 2000). For more detailed guidelines, please refer to Table 1.1.

Third, relatively few studies have documented collateral gains when particular self-initiations (e.g., question asking) are taught to children with autism (L.K. Koegel et al., 1998). It is important to note that initiations in typically developing children seem to be the vehicle for self-learning and independence (McTear, 1985). With the trend toward target child initiation training, one should ask whether it is possible to identify pivotal initiations. That is, are there specific initiations that when targeted lead to collateral gains in untargeted areas and to further self-learning and independence for children with autism? A series of studies with promising results has been examining whether children with autism can be taught self-initiations as a pivotal response (L.K. Koegel et al., 2003; L.K. Koegel et al., 1998). In particular, in the first phase of a two-part study by L.K. Koegel et al. (1999), self-initiations were identified as a potential prognostic indicator for long-term favorable outcomes. That is, children who exhibited self-initiations at preintervention experienced more favorable outcomes (e.g., participation in fully inclusive classrooms, participation in after-school activities, positive interactions with peers) than children who demonstrated few or no self-initiations. In the second phase of the study, children who did not exhibit self-initiations at preintervention were taught a variety of child-initiated strategies (e.g., question asking, attention-seeking phrases). All children who participated in the second phase of the study learned to spontaneously use the child-initiated strategies and demonstrated collateral gains in a number of language and pragmatic arenas. More important, all children in the second phase of the study experienced long-term favorable outcomes. Unlike many previous intervention programs for children with autism, which relied almost entirely on adult-initiated teaching (whereby the child mainly responds to

This child loves letters, which can be used as natural reinforcers when he self-initiates a request for a letter.

questions or commands posed by the adult), child-initiated interventions enable children with autism to initiate their own learning interactions. Such studies provide great promise for target child training and for prospects of identifying pivotal initiations.

A fourth point of consideration is the fact that many initiation interventions available for children with autism continue to experience challenges with limited generalization and maintenance (Brady et al., 1984; Strain & Odom, 1986; Weiss & Harris, 2001). Some of this chapter's authors have conducted research targeting self-initiations in children with autism that has incorporated naturalistic and motivational teaching procedures and resulted in both generalization of skills and long-term maintenance (L.K. Koegel et al., 1998; L.K. Koegel et al., 1999; L.K. Koegel et al., 2003). Consequently, the chapter authors recommend that all initiation training, whether it is teaching initiations of first words or more complex social-communicative initiations, incorporate naturalistic and motivational procedures. Motivational procedures of PRT include the use of child choice, the interspersal of maintenance and acquisition tasks, task variation, and the use of natural reinforcers. Please refer to Chapter 1 for a more in-depth overview of PRT's motivational procedures.

A final area for further research relates to the involvement of families in initiation treatment. To date, few initiation studies for children with autism have incorporated family members, yet involving these individuals may have several advantages. For example, it may be advantageous to include siblings in intervention because during early childhood, sibling relationships provide a daily ongoing context for learning both language and social skills (Hancock & Kaiser, 1996; Powell & Gallagher, 1993; Stocker & Dunn, 1990). In addition, the interactions that family members have with children with autism can provide them with ongoing opportunities to practice and develop new skills. Furthermore, by incorporating both family members and other key social agents (e.g., teachers, tutors, specialists, typically developing peers) in initiation training, issues related to generalization across types or classes of interactants may be resolved. That is, some initiation research (Fredeen, 2002) has suggested that it may be necessary to incorporate general-case programming (Albin & Horner, 1988) and multiple-exemplar training (Brady et al., 1984; Breen, Haring, Pitts-Conway, & Gaylord-Ross, 1985; Stokes & Baer, 1977) to ensure that children with autism generalize initiations across types of interactants (e.g., adults, siblings, peers). Specifically, such findings have been demonstrating that when children with autism are taught to initiate expressive language with adults (e.g., to ask questions), they do not necessarily generalize their initiations to siblings and peers at similar levels. On the contrary, it appears necessary to teach initiations with all types of interactants (e.g., adults, siblings, peers) in order to ensure the best possible generalization and long-term maintenance. These findings may be related to the fact that different types of communicative partners may require different types of skills (L.K. Koegel et al., 2001). Accordingly, it is recommended that initiation training incorporate family members, typically developing peers, and other key social agents.

In summary, there seems to be a consensus in the literature on the importance of initiations in the habilitation of children with autism. Despite all the hard work that lies ahead, it is exciting to envision the impact that future initiation research will have on the long-term prognosis and outcome for children with autism.

III

Social Development

10

Working with Paraprofessionals to Improve Socialization in Inclusive Settings

Robert L. Koegel, Eileen F. Klein, Lynn Kern Koegel,
Mendy A. Boettcher, Lauren Brookman-Frazee, and Daniel Openden

This chapter is broad to reach the intended audience of a range of individuals—such as university students, parents, paraprofessionals, supervisors, and so forth—who are interested in supporting the social development of children with autism in inclusive settings. Children with autism are increasingly being included in typical settings— whether in school, after-school activities, or summer day camps. Consequently, the need for developing and implementing social interventions is essential. The literature suggests that without specialized training, paraprofessional support personnel who are trying to assist children with autism may engage in "hovering behavior," which can actually interfere with the children's social development in inclusive settings. Therefore, the purpose of the chapter is to describe interventions that paraprofessionals can implement to facilitate social interactions. These interventions are easy to learn and result in decreased hovering and increased social facilitation behavior and child socialization. Furthermore, once paraprofessionals learn these strategies, they can apply them to socialization situations for other children with autism.

BACKGROUND

In the past, children with autism and other developmental disabilities were enrolled in special classrooms, with little contact with their typically developing peers. (Karagiannis, Stainback, & Stainback, 1996; Kellegrew, 1995; Yell, 1998). In addition, the children were taught functional life skills, with little emphasis given to appropriate social interactions with peers without disabilities (Nietupski, Hamre-Nietupski, Curtin, & Shrikanth, 1997). However, when Congress passed the Education for All Handicapped Children Act of 1975 (PL 94-142)—and later legislation such as the Individuals with Disabilities Education Act (IDEA) of 1990 (PL 101-476), the Individuals with Disabilities Education Act Amendments of 1997 (PL 105-17), and the Individuals with Disabilities Education Improvement Act of 2004 (PL 108-446)—children with disabilities gained the right to an education in the least restrictive environment. A primary goal in the inclusion movement is to target children's social development (Harrower, 1999; Harrower & Dunlap, 2001). Although there is a trend toward the inclusion of children with disabilities in the general education classrooms in their neighborhood schools (L.K. Koegel, Koegel, Frea, & Fredeen, 2001) and a body of literature describing curricular adaptations exists, parents of children with disabilities are significantly less likely to have their children participate in community recreational activities in comparison with parents of children without disabilities (Ehrmann, Aeschleman, & Svanum, 1995). In addition, school programs often do not provide comprehensive social programs for children with disabilities.

Although paraprofessionals have played an important role in inclusion models (Giangreco, Edelman, & Broer, 2001; Giangreco, Edelman, Broer, & Doyle, 2001; Riggs & Mueller, 2001), research suggests that paraprofessionals often engage in hovering behavior, which may have negative effects on children's social development (Giangreco, Edelman, Luiselli, & MacFarland, 1997). Giangreco and colleagues found that this behavior can cause a number of problems for children with disabilities, including separating the children from their classmates and having a negative impact on peer interactions. Furthermore, other researchers have found a negative correlation between time spent interacting with adults and time spent interacting with peers during free play for both typically developing children and children with disabilities (Bronson, Hauser-Cram, & Warfield, 1997; Harper & McCluskey, 2003; L.K. Koegel et al., 2001).

In response to the study by Giangreco et al. (1997), Marks, Schrader, and Levine (1999) conducted a study to better understand the perspectives of paraprofessionals. They found that paraprofessionals tended to assume high levels of responsibility for managing the academic and behavioral needs of the children with disabilities because they did not want their students to "bother" the general education teacher and they wanted to represent the inclusion model well. These findings further support the call for more training for paraprofessionals and school personnel (Giangreco et al., 2001; Riggs & Mueller, 2001).

DESCRIPTION OF THE MODEL

This chapter presents training procedures for paraprofessionals that are designed to facilitate social interactions between children with autism and their typically developing peers and addresses concerns about hovering behavior that could limit social interactions. These procedures were implemented in a university-based summer camp program that children with and without autism attended in 1-week sessions. The paraprofessionals (i.e., the camp counselors) were trained by supervisors with expertise in inclusion, teaching social skills, and behavior management. Figure 10.1 shows that a team of people worked together with the families. The following sections describe the steps for using this training and intervention model.

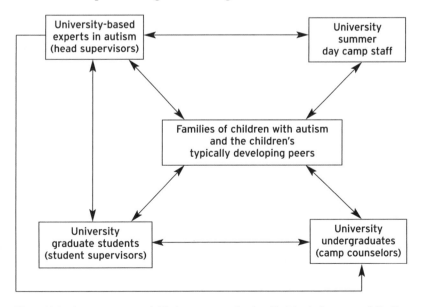

Figure 10.1. Summer camp model that uses paraprofessional training to improve socialization among children with autism.

Step 1: Establish a Baseline

In order to track progress and to assess the needs of a particular child with autism, it is important to collect a number of measures prior to starting the intervention. Baseline observations are critical to assess *exactly* how the child behaves in the *specific* environments targeted and how the typically developing peers behave in that setting. That is, the lunch table requires a different set of behaviors than a soccer field. Children act very differently while using the playhouse than they do while playing tetherball. Such areas analyzed in the program include the following:

1. *Communication:* In order to prompt social interactions, it is important for everybody, including both supervisors and paraprofessionals, to have an idea of a child's communicative level. Does the child speak in sentences or just use single words? Can the child ask questions or just make requests? Can the child carry on a conversation, or are interactions limited? Information about the child's communication can be gained from reports, interviews with others who know the child well (e.g., a parent, a teacher), and observations.

2. *Challenging behaviors:* A functional analysis is helpful in providing information relating to any inappropriate or disruptive behaviors that the child demonstrates. For example, some children use inappropriate behaviors to avoid tasks and social interactions, whereas others use inappropriate behaviors to initiate social interactions. Understanding why the problem behaviors are occurring helps in developing an individualized intervention program. Chapter 14 describes methods for conducting a functional analysis.

3. *Social skills:* Data on the child's level of socialization prior to intervention are important. Does the child spend all of his or her time alone, or does the child interact with peers? If the child interacts with peers, what percentage of the time is he or she interacting? Does the child "hang out" with peers by simply standing nearby and watching, or does the child actively participate in activities. Does the child talk with the other children or remain silent? If the child talks, what does he or she say? Does the child use the lingo and expressions that his or her peers use? All of these assessments of social behavior help in developing an individualized social program.

4. *Engagement in activities:* It is helpful to know which activities are easy for the child and which are more difficult. For example, if the children are playing basketball, it is necessary to assess whether the child with autism can dribble the ball, make baskets, and so forth. Likewise, if the children are using the swing at recess, it is important to determine whether the child can pump by him- or herself and push another child. Again, knowing to what extent the child with autism can participate in the activities is important for developing an appropriate program.

5. *Paraprofessional behavior:* Our research suggests that without training, paraprofessionals hover most of the time and provide few, if any, opportunities for socialization. Learning how to facilitate social interactions requires specialized training. It is important to monitor paraprofessionals' acquisition.

Step 2: Develop Individualized Goals for Each Child

Goal development is usually done by both head and graduate student supervisors based on behavioral observations and data collection. The baseline data are helpful for developing goals. The aim is to systematically increase the number of social interactions between the child with autism and his or her typically developing peers. Furthermore, it is important to increase the amount of time that the child with autism spends engaging in the activities of his or her typically developing peers. To assess change, it is necessary to monitor progress, which can be compared with the baseline measures, on a regular basis.

Step 3: Begin Training the Paraprofessional

It is helpful if the paraprofessional has an understanding of the procedures to be used. Suggested readings include the following;

- *How to Teach Pivotal Behaviors to Children with Autism: A Training Manual* (R.L. Koegel et al., 1989)

- *How to Teach Self-Management to People with Severe Disabilities: A Training Manual* (L.K. Koegel, Koegel, & Parks, 1992)

- *Increasing Success in School Through Priming: A Training Manual* (Wilde, L.K. Koegel, & Koegel, 1992)

- *Understanding Why Problem Behaviors Occur: A Guide for Assisting Parents in Assessing Causes of Behavior and Designing Treatment Plans* (Frea, L.K. Koegel, & Koegel, 1994)

In the original model described in this chapter, the student supervisors had obtained a master's degree and had approximately 6 years of experience working with children with developmental disabilities in inclusion settings. Initially, the training consisted of approximately 5 hours of daily direct supervision. The supervisors modeled the social facilitation techniques and provided in vivo feedback on the paraprofessionals' strengths and areas for improvement. After approximately 3 days, as the camp counselors gained experience and were implementing the appropriate procedures, the supervisors decreased the amount of direct supervision to approximately 2 hours per day. When the counselors started working with a new camper, the supervisor increased the supervision time to approximately 5 hours again. However, once the camper's individualized plan was in place and the paraprofessionals were integrating their previously acquired skills with the new individualized plan, the supervisors quickly decreased their supervision to approximately 2 hours per day.

Step 4: Implement the Program

Initially, the supervisors modeled effective methods of facilitating social interactions between campers with autism and their peers. Although all of the campers had individualized goals and, therefore, the feedback given to each support camp counselor was specific to their child's needs, the supervisors drew on intervention techniques from Pivotal Response Treatment (R.L. Koegel et al., 1989) and positive behavior support (L.K. Koegel, Koegel, & Dunlap, 1996).

Many different strategies were utilized to increase social interactions between the children with autism and their typically developing peers. All of the strategies were implemented with the goal of making the social interaction mutually reinforcing for both the child with autism and his or her typically developing peers (Baker, Koegel, & Koegel, 1998; Hurley-Geffner, 1995; Kennedy, 2001). Specific strategies were as follows:

1. *Develop sharing exchanges:* The first strategy was having the paraprofessional facilitate sharing exchanges. For example, if a typically developing child was interested in the snack belonging to a child with autism, the paraprofessional prompted the camper without a disability to ask for a snack trade. Likewise, the child with autism was taught to offer snacks to the peer. The likelihood of having opportunities for sharing was increased by asking parents of the children with autism to send their children to camp with special snacks, toys, and activities that could be shared or interesting items that could be passed around.

2. *Give opportunities to seek assistance from peers:* Hovering often occurs in situations for which assistance is needed: There is always a milk carton, a juice container that is hard to open or a jacket that is difficult to fasten. Yet, all of these situations provide ideal opportunities for the child with autism to learn to ask a peer for help. These situations not only provide a chance for peer–peer interactions but also reduce a child's dependence on paraprofessionals. Thus, the paraprofessionals in this program prompted the campers with autism to seek assistance from their peers–for example, with opening a snack container or unzipping a backpack.

3. *Increase meaningful verbal and nonverbal communication:* Regardless of the communication level of a child with autism, social conversation can be prompted. The paraprofessionals in this program prompted the children with limited verbal skills to point to an interesting item. It is always helpful to look for mutually reinforcing topics (e.g., trains) and activities so the interactions are more likely to continue on after the initial prompt. Both the child with autism and his or her peers can be prompted to engage in social interactions on an ongoing basis throughout the day.

4. *Implement buddy systems:* The program used a buddy system, which was a natural choice because children are great helpers. In almost any class, after-school activity, or camp setting, there are many opportunities for children to work together. The buddy system also increases safety in a group of children: It is easier to count 10 buddy pairs than to count 20 children. Buddies can help each other with school assignments, waiting in line, socialization, transitions, snack time, lunchtime, and bathroom breaks. Children can even teach each other new games such as Red Light/Green Light by being partners and making sure that their buddies follow the rules. Not only does the buddy system further decrease the child with autism's dependence on paraprofessionals but also all of the children benefit and have more fun.

5. *Provide social support:* Children with autism often need to be taught to engage in appropriate pragmatic behaviors. For example, cheering for a classmate who successfully hits a home run or giving a high-five to someone who aces a test are

subtle pragmatic behaviors that may not be picked up without special intervention. These positive social strategies can be prompted by paraprofessionals throughout the day and can result in positive interactions between peers.

6. *Provide opportunities for small talk:* There are numerous situations with opportunities for social engagement—not extensive conversations but simply small talk. A comment, compliment, or observation is in order at these times. Even a few words or a short sentence (e.g., "Cool shirt," "Awesome game") will do. For example, kids chat while they are lining up or waiting for the next activity to begin. Pointing out something fun that happened during gymnastics or complimenting a classmate on a new clothing item or hairstyle can begin a positive social interaction. Such proactive social engagement strategies can be prompted and encouraged throughout the day.

7. *Provide new games and activities:* Children always enjoy a new game or fun new activity. In the camp model, families and paraprofessionals provided new board games to use during free time. Selecting mutually reinforcing games creates additional opportunities for facilitating social interactions between children with autism and their typically developing peers. Of course, it is always helpful if a child with autism has had experience with a game before it is played. In such a case, especially if the child with autism has fairly good verbal skills, he or she may even be able to explain the rules to her peers.

8. *Use priming (Wilde et al., 1992):* As noted in the previous strategy description, it is often important for children with autism to be exposed to activities before they engage in these activities with their peers. Priming, a procedure that provides this exposure, has been shown to increase task engagement and decrease disruptive behavior during unfamiliar activities (Schreibman, Whalen, & Stahmer, 2000). A child with autism is generally primed the afternoon or evening before the activity is to occur to increase the probability that the child will successfully participate in the activity. For example, the night before a camper with autism has gymnastics class, the family may practice following the "gymnastics coach" (Mom) through a warm-up exercise; because of the familiarity of the routine, the child is more likely to follow the coach's directions in warm-ups the next day. Other examples of events to prime include new activities (e.g., karate), social situations (things to say during specific activities), and unusual events (a visit to a field trip location the day before the actual field trip).

Step 5: Measure Program Effectiveness

Evaluating the following critical areas is recommended to assess whether the program is effective:

1. *Paraprofessionals' hovering behavior:* In order to assess whether a paraprofessional is thoroughly trained, hovering behavior should be measured. As mentioned previously, some untrained paraprofessionals engage in hovering behavior constantly. Measuring hovering behavior can provide an idea whether an aide is helping a child with autism gain independence or requires more training.

2. *Paraprofessionals' social facilitation behavior:* Because the goal is for paraprofessionals to learn strategies for prompting prosocial behaviors, it is important to measure whether they are actively doing so. For instance, it is necessary to observe whether a paraprofessional takes advantage of all opportunities and prompts appropriate behaviors—that is, behaviors that the other children use. Similarly, it is important to note whether the prompting is frequent enough to be effective.

3. *Children's social behavior:* Obviously, the end goal is for the children with autism to learn and use social behaviors; thus, it is critical to measure whether this is happening. It is also important to measure whether the social behavior is prompted or spontaneous. Intervention needs to continue until the children learn to spontaneously use the prosocial behaviors.

4. *Children's affect:* An overarching goal of this model is for children with autism to be happy and enjoy their interactions. Therefore, it is always helpful to rate a child's interest, enthusiasm, and happiness. Use of affect scales (Baker et al., 1998; Dunlap & R.L. Koegel, 1980; see Figure 8.1) can help head supervisors assess whether activities are appropriate and in which activities the children with autism and their peers are most motivated to engage.

Findings

Prior to intervention, the paraprofessionals (i.e., the camp counselors) generally focused all of their attention on the child with autism to the exclusion of the other children. They often passively sat or stood next to their designated children (not talking to anyone or facilitating social interactions) or focused solely on the children with autism—for example, by holding hands or touching their children's heads.

However, once trained, the counselors learned to prompt their children to socially and verbally interact with peers; to prompt typically developing children to verbally interact with the campers with autism; to prompt social conversations; and to prompt children to cheer for each other, give high-fives, and engage in appropriate behavior during social games (e.g., Mother May I?, Connect Four).

Over time, as the social behavior of some of the children with autism became more fluent, the paraprofessionals were able to fade their prompts, so the campers with autism were socially engaged with their peers with little direct support. This finding is consistent with research demonstrating that children with autism can learn, relatively quickly, these positive reciprocal interactions with peers and appropriate social behavior (Baker et al., 1998). On a related note, the data from this model include affect measures, which indicated that the children with autism appeared to be enjoying the interaction with peers, as did typically developing peers.

Results

Prior to Intervention   Without training in how to facilitate social interactions among the campers with autism and their typically developing peers, the counselors exhibited high levels of hovering behavior and low levels of social facilitation. In addition, the campers with autism had low levels of social behavior. For example, research done prior to intervention showed that the counselors hovered consistently in

86%–100% of the intervals. Furthermore, they facilitated social behavior in 0%–3% of the intervals, and the children were engaged in social behavior for 0%–6% of the intervals.

Following Training   With training, the counselors decreased their hovering behavior and increased their facilitation of social behaviors among campers with autism and their typically developing peers. For instance, research revealed that with training, the counselors decreased their hovering behavior to approximately 0%–9% of the intervals, and their social facilitation behavior increased to 17%–89% of the intervals. The amount of social facilitation that counselors provided was highly dependent on the child's functioning level. When a camper with autism was engaged with peers, the counselors were encouraged to step back and continually monitor the interaction. Training the counselors in social facilitation behavior also had a collateral effect on the children's social behavior. Once the counselors had training in facilitating social behavior between the campers with autism and their typically developing peers, the percentage of intervals in which the campers with autism exhibited social behavior increased to 74%–91%.

Affect of Campers Prior to and Following Training   It is important to consider the social significance of training paraprofessionals in social facilitation behaviors. In this program, one method was to look at the happiness of the campers with autism and their typically developing peers. Prior to training the counselors, happiness ratings of the children with autism were consistently low, whereas their peers' ratings were consistently high. However, once the counselors were trained in social facilitation procedures, happiness ratings increased for the children with autism and matched those of their typically developing peers.

Case Example

Jose, a 4-year-old with autism, attended an inclusion preschool program during the school year. Jose was able to communicate in short but fluid sentences. In addition, he preferred interacting with adults instead of children. Jose loved to draw with markers, play with Lite-Brite, and play Red Light/Green Light. On the first day of camp, Jose was quiet and stuck close to Maria, his camp counselor. Maria quickly asked the head camp counselor to institute the buddy system that so all the campers had a partner to walk with to the first activity. With his buddy, Jose went to his first activity in the art room. Maria rearranged the art table to have only two marker baskets (instead of four) and reminded all of the children to ask each other to pass the marker baskets when they wanted to change color. This manipulation of the environment increased opportunities for social interaction among Jose and his peers.

As the camp week continued, Maria continually looked for opportunities to prompt social interactions throughout the day. For example, if Jose needed help opening a snack container, she prompted him to ask a friend. If Jose looked interested in another child's snack, she prompted Jose to ask his peer for a snack trade. Maria also used Jose's interest in Lite-Brite to create opportunities during free time. First, she prompted Jose to ask a friend to use the Lite-Brite with him. Then she taught them to take turns holding all the colored pegs and asking each other for a specific number of pegs. During the interaction, the two children would usually start talking about what kind of design they were going to make with the pegs. On the last day of the session, Jose went to the camp's "carnival" with his friends and shared in the fun and excitement with his friends. Jose's mother was so happy with her son's improved social interactions with peers that she signed him up for 2 more weeks of camp.

DISCUSSION OF CHAPTER CONCEPTS

This chapter has pointed out the importance and significance of training paraprofessionals to facilitate social behavior between children with autism and their typically developing peers. Although the children with autism in this program generally had social goals in their IEPs and the paraprofessionals were instructed to facilitate social interactions between the children with autism and their typically developing peers during baseline, these conditions did not seem to be sufficient to result in paraprofessional social facilitation behavior. Not only were the paraprofessionals not facilitating any social interactions but also, consistent with the results of other studies, they were hovering over their assigned campers and, at times, inhibiting social interactions (Giangreco et al., 1997). However, once the paraprofessionals received in vivo training on techniques for facilitating social interactions, the paraprofessionals' facilitation behavior increased; as a collateral effect, their hovering behavior decreased. These findings support a growing body of literature suggesting that paraprofessionals need training to conduct interventions for children with disabilities in inclusive settings (Aird, 2000; Dew-Hughes, Brayton, & Blandford, 1998; Downing, Ryndak, & Clark, 2000; Schepis, Ownbey, Parsons, & Reid, 2000).

In addition, numerous researchers have shown that social intervention programs increase the peer social interactions of children with autism (Brown, Odom, & Conroy, 2001; Frederickson & Turner, 2003; Gresham, 2000; Rogers, 2000; Shukla, Kennedy, & Cushing, 1999) and that affect improves when children with autism are engaged in social interactions with their typically developing peers. Data also suggest that it is possible to choose activities that are mutually reinforcing for children with autism and their peers without disabilities. These data further support past research suggesting that to develop relationships between children with and without disabilities, activities need to be mutually reinforcing (Baker et al., 1998; Hurley-Geffner, 1995; Kennedy, 2001).

DIRECTIONS FOR FUTURE RESEARCH

Increasing numbers of children with autism are included in community settings. In turn, it is important to examine the length of training needed for paraprofessionals, many of whom have different levels of skills, to implement social interventions with fidelity across children with different types of behavioral characteristics. Additional research might also look at the levels and types of support that children with varying behavioral characteristics and disabilities need to participate successfully and safely in community activities.

11

Play Dates, Social Interactions, and Friendships

Grace A. Werner, Laurie A. Vismara, Robert L. Koegel, and Lynn Kern Koegel

A hallmark and diagnostic criterion of autism is difficulties with socialization and communication. Although significant improvements in linguistic structures generally occur with intervention, deficits may linger in areas of social interaction, particularly in naturalistic environments such as in home and community settings. Specifically, children with autism may demonstrate difficulty with appropriately initiating and maintaining conversation, as well as with engaging in interactive play with peers. Motivational techniques such as those used in Pivotal Response Training (PRT) have been shown to improve social interactions with peers and simultaneously improve affect for all children involved. The purpose of this chapter is to illustrate how such motivational strategies may be successfully implemented during play dates to increase appropriate social communicative interactions between children with autism and their typically developing peers. These strategies are discussed in the context of developing a comprehensive social-skills package to develop and sustain friendships among children with autism and their typically developing peers.

BACKGROUND

An extensive body of research documents significant intervention gains in the treatment of autism (R.L. Koegel, Koegel, & McNerney, 2001; Lovaas, 1987; Ozonoff & Cathcart, 1998). However, deficits in social interaction have proven to be particularly complex and remain a challenge for professionals who work with individuals with autism (Weiss & Harris, 2001). Although numerous studies have documented increases in specific social behaviors, the need for additional social interventions that produce clinically significant changes remains strong (McGrath, Bosch, Sullivan, & Fuqua, 2003). In particular, fostering positive social interactions with typically developing peers has been identified as important in achieving these socially valid outcomes (McGee, Almeida, Sulzer-Azaroff, & Feldman, 1992; Odom & Strain, 1984; Pierce & Schreibman, 1997).

The important impact of peer relationships on social development and long-term positive outcomes has been well documented. Specifically, the literature suggests that peer rejection is associated with poor adjustment (Dodge et al., 2003; Laird, Jordan, Dodge, Pettit, & Bates, 2001) and that peer acceptance and friendship can serve as protective factors against loneliness and peer victimization for children who are at risk (Criss, Pettit, Bates, Dodge, & Lapp, 2002; Parker & Asher, 1993; Schwartz, Dodge, Pettit, & Bates, 2000). For children with autism in particular, difficulties with peer social interaction may result in social isolation (Frea, 1995; Howlin & Rutter, 1987; Mesibov, Shea, & Adams, 2001), and research shows that children with autism may be even more likely to experience loneliness and poor-quality friendships than their typically developing peers (Bauminger & Kasari, 2000). Furthermore, research suggests that socially isolated children are at risk for mental health difficulties as adults (Cowen, Pederson, Babigan, Izzo, & Trost, 1973; McHale, Dariotis, & Kauh, 2003). Thus, without intervention, children with autism may have limited experience with positive peer interactions and may be especially at risk for poor social outcomes.

This growing body of literature suggests the importance of creating opportunities for children with autism to engage in social interaction with their peers. In school settings, researchers have used strategies such as peer buddies (Laushey & Heflin,

2000), peer modeling and tutoring (Kamps et al., 1992), play groups (Wolfberg & Schuler, 1993), and peer networks (Kamps, Potucek, Lopez, Kravits, & Kemmerer, 1997) to provide opportunities for children with autism to interact with their typically developing peers. Although these social skills interventions have focused primarily on school settings, social opportunities may also be arranged in other natural settings such as homes, after-school programs, and parks (Wolfberg & Schuler, 1999). For typically developing children, inviting friends over to play after school is often a regular occurrence and can provide a context for the development of close friendships. These play dates have been suggested as a particularly important context for the practice of appropriate social skills and the development of friendships (Frankel & Myatt, 2003) and may be an important additional intervention context for children struggling with peer social interactions.

The literature suggests several variables that may be important in the facilitation of successful play dates. Environmental antecedents and contextual variables have been suggested to be particularly important in controlling social behavior with peers (Sasso, Mundschenk, Melloy, & Casey, 1998; Zanolli, 1997). For example, the use of choice and reinforcing activities has been shown to be an important motivational variable (R.L. Koegel, Dyer, & Bell, 1987; R.L. Koegel, O'Dell, & Koegel, 1987). In the context of play dates, activities need to be mutually reinforcing, both for the child with autism and for the typically developing peer(s). In order to promote reciprocal interactions, natural contingencies and shared control of reinforcers can be established such that interaction is necessary in order for the children to receive reinforcement from the activity (Kennedy & Itkonen, 1996). Building such cooperative arrangements into activities during play dates may help promote interaction by making available reinforcers contingent upon appropriate interactions. Short, structured play activities with support from a facilitator may be useful initially in promoting successful interactions (Wolfberg & Schuler, 1993). Support can then be faded as the children demonstrate increasing competence (Odom & Watts, 1991).

Research studying these strategies separately suggests improvement in some aspects of social interaction; however, the research provides little information about the broader impact of these components on meaningful peer relationships. Taken together, the use of mutually reinforcing activities, cooperative arrangements, and adult facilitation may help create an even more successful play date context and more clinically significant outcomes. Thus, this chapter discusses strategies for facilitating positive play date interactions. The components described in this chapter may be helpful in affecting broad aspects of social interaction during play dates, including reciprocal peer interactions, peer acceptance, and friendship as evidenced by unprompted peer invitations for social engagement and high levels of positive affect by both the children with autism and their typically developing peers.

INTERVENTION

The following steps can be introduced within the play date format to promote reciprocal social interaction between children and their peers. The strategies described can be combined into a package with the goal of providing contextual support for successful reciprocal interactions among the children.

Step 1: Pick a Playmate

In choosing appropriate playmates, it is helpful to ask a child's teacher and/or aide for recommendations on appropriate playmates from the classroom. Generally, teachers and aides are helpful in selecting children who share interests with the child and have the specific characteristics of maturity, humor, and perseverance. It is also helpful to unobtrusively observe the child and peers interacting in natural environments (e.g., school, extracurricular activities) to determine who the child interacts with in a positive and appropriate manner. In situations with a history of negative peer interactions, it may be helpful to find family friends or relatives or involve the child in recreational activities to provide opportunities to meet and interact with new peers. Then, as the child's social play improves, classmates can be selected.

Step 2: Plan the Play Date

When planning a play date, specific activities are planned ahead, and possibly even primed by exposing the child with autism to the activity in advance (L.K. Koegel, Koegel, Frea, & Green-Hopkins, 2003; Zanolli, Daggett, & Adams, 1996), in order to increase the children's anticipation and eagerness to participate in the activity. An organized activity also helps to promote continued social involvement during the play date. For example, having an ice cream party planned a few days in advance can give both the child with autism and the typically developing peer(s) something to look forward to as the activity approaches. Also, having a specific purpose for the play date

When setting up successful play dates, it is important to select activities that will be mutually reinforcing for each child. In this case, a cooking activity was selected to match the culinary interests of the children.

may prevent the child with autism from encountering potentially challenging social situations, such as deciding how to entertain the peer(s).

Second, selecting activities that are mutually reinforcing for both the child with autism and the typically developing peer(s) is important for increasing the children's motivation to participate and for encouraging further social interactions. This means choosing activities that all of the children will enjoy. It may be helpful to consult with the children's teachers and classroom aides, as well as the parents of the typically developing peer(s), in order to identify preferred activities the children may share. By considering the children's interests in selecting play date activities, these mutually reinforcing activities help to maintain the children's proximity and create a positive context for their joint participation and social conversation. Catering to common interests helps to ensure that all children have fun during the play date and that they will want to play together again on future occasions.

Third, priming may be helpful for the child with autism. Priming consists of previewing an activity in a nondemanding manner before it occurs. This familiarizes the child with the material and procedures, and it decreases off-task and disruptive behavior while improving engagement in appropriate behaviors. In the case of play dates, priming can give the child with autism an opportunity to be more skilled at the activity or even be the more knowledgeable participant in a new activity.

Step 3: Facilitate Interactions

Parents or other adults can facilitate reciprocal interactions during the play date by including cooperative arrangements. Research has shown that cooperative arrangements result in more frequent interactions among individuals than when such arrangements are not in place (Hyten & Burns, 1986; Kennedy & Itkonen, 1996). For play dates, cooperative arrangements consist of structuring the activity in such a way that the participation of each individual is critical to obtaining the positive outcome. For example, during a play date in which the children were baking cookies, each child brought a necessary item for making cookies (e.g., an essential ingredient, decorations, a favorite cookie cutter). This gave the children a reason to interact with each other from the start of the activity. Furthermore, cooperative arrangements were built into the play date activities such that the children's collaborative participation was required for a successful outcome. Natural contingencies, such as having the children jointly decide how to decorate each cookie and having them exchange the necessary materials, helped to maintain cooperative arrangements throughout the course of the play date.

Table 11.1 gives some ideas for planning play date activities that promote interaction. Some of these activities will be appropriate for the child with autism and a single peer, whereas other activities will be more appropriate for play dates involving multiple peers. The first column provides some ideas for fun play date activities. The second column gives specific examples of adding the structure of cooperative arrangements to facilitate additional interactions between children. These modifications help provide contextual support for positive play date interactions.

The combination of mutually reinforcing activities and cooperative arrangements can be used to facilitate verbal interactions between the children. The mutu-

This photo demonstrates the use of cooperative arrangements. Each child is provided with a portion of the activity's required components, making it necessary to interact in order to successfully complete the task objective (in this case, baking a cake).

ally reinforcing activities help to maintain the children's interest, and the cooperative arrangements set up specific opportunities for communication because one child will always have something that the other child needs to complete the activity. An adult should start the activity by dividing up the play materials to give the children a reason to interact and communicate with one another. One child can then be prompted to ask the other child for the play materials related to the activity. Having a peer fulfill this request reinforces the child's attempt at communication and motivates both children for additional communicative exchanges. This strategy may be optimal for children who have limited experience interacting with peers because even their simplest attempts are rewarded. As the child becomes more proficient at making these requests, other communicative functions (e.g., social comments) can be targeted in a similar way.

As noted in the preceding paragraph, an adult must be present to facilitate activities in the play date. An adult facilitator is important in deciding which communicative functions to teach and in implementing cooperative arrangements to promote reciprocal conversation. A facilitator can prompt many different kinds of communicative exchanges while the children are motivated to participate in the activity together. The facilitator's role is promoting interaction between the children, being especially careful to direct the children's conversation toward one another, rather than letting them communicate through the adult. Some examples follow for facilitating conversational skills.

Table 11.1. Play date activity ideas

Fun activities	Added contextual support
Swimming	Games in the pool (e.g., Marco Polo, underwater tea party, diving for treasures)
Eating ice cream	Making ice-cream sundaes together
Drawing	Playing Pictionary
Painting	Painting a mural together
Eating lunch	Playing social games while eating lunch (e.g., Telephone, I Spy)
Making individual art projects	Designing a collage together
Running around in the yard	Playing organized games (e.g., Chase, Hide and Seek, Freeze Tag, Red Light/Green Light, Red Rover)
Watching television	Playing charades or putting on a play
Playing with dolls	Putting on a puppet show
Going to the beach	Building a sand castle
Playing in the park	Engaging in organized activities or games (e.g., going on a treasure hunt, playing Duck, Duck, Goose)

Prompting Questions   While the children are playing, the facilitator can set up situations that require the children to ask each other questions. The facilitator should keep in mind that the children will be particularly motivated to ask each other questions if their questions have a clear purpose related to the activity. For example, if the children are playing a board game, the facilitator can prompt them to ask each other for the game pieces. While drawing, the children can be prompted to exchange markers or other art materials. It is important for the facilitator to be actively involved (especially in the initial stages) in order to give each child the needed materials to maintain social interaction. One rule of thumb is to try to anticipate what one child will want next and then to give that item to the peer(s) in order to encourage question asking. As the children become more accustomed to making initiations on their own, the facilitator can start stepping back to allow the children to interact spontaneously. One situation might involve questions while picking game board pieces to start a game:

Target child: "Can I have the green boy?"
    Peer: "Here. Can I have the purple?"
Target child: "Okay."

Another example involves questions while the children are engaged in drawing a picture together:

    Peer: "What marker do you want?"
Target child: "I want green. Do you want red?"
    Peer: "Yeah."

Prompting Comments   During an activity, the facilitator can prompt the children to make comments to each other. For example, before taking a turn while playing a board game, the facilitator can prompt either child to direct a comment to the other, such as delivering social praise (e.g., "Good job," "Cool"). Another example would be making basic comments regarding the game:

Target child: "It's your turn"
       Peer: "I'm catching up!"

The child making the comment is then reinforced by getting to continue playing. While making ice-cream sundaes, the children can be prompted to make social comments before receiving access to desired items (e.g., sprinkles, chocolate sauce). Another example might involve making basic comments on the appearance of the other's sundae:

Target child: "Yours looks good!"
       Peer: "I'm going to put a cherry on top."

Prompting Initiations for New Play Activities   It is important to keep the children motivated throughout the play date. Because the children's interests may change during the play date, teaching them to initiate changes in activity may be one way to maintain their enthusiasm in interacting with one another. If the facilitator notices one child losing interest (e.g., starting to walk away, picking up a new toy), that child can be prompted to invite the peer(s) to participate in a new activity. Examples follow for initiations of transitions and play idea suggestions, respectively:

       Peer: "Come with me"
Target child: "Okay, let's go"
       Peer: "Want to play trains?"
Target child: "I want Thomas!"
       Peer: "Here you go."

Step 4: Evaluate the Play Date's Success

In determining the effectiveness of the play date intervention package, it may be helpful to consider several variables. Depending on the child's current skill in social interactions and the specific intervention goals, some of these variables may be more relevant. Regardless of the chosen target behavior, monitoring some of the following variables is critical in evaluating the success of the intervention.

1. *Synchronous reciprocal interaction:* Because the goal is to promote high-quality social interactions, it is important to include measures that reflect this issue. In addition to measuring the occurrence of individual social behaviors (e.g., initiations, responses, nonverbal behaviors), it may be particularly advantageous to examine characteristics of the overall interaction. Specifically, measuring the amount of synchronous reciprocal interaction between the child and peer(s) may help to analyze the quality of their social overtures. *Synchronous reciprocal interaction* refers to the children's communicative and nonverbal behaviors being directed toward one another and related to one another's current interest (R.L. Koegel, Werner, Vismara, & Koegel, in press). For example, are the children engaged in the same activity and initiating and responding to one another? Are the interactions continuous and related to one another's behavior? This measurement of synchronous

reciprocal interaction helps to determine whether improvements have occurred in the children's abilities to exhibit and maintain high-quality social exchanges and provides information on the effectiveness of the play date intervention. Synchronous reciprocal interactions can be measured in intervals (e.g., how long the child engaged in the interaction) or by counting the number of interactions.

2. *Affect:* It is important to ensure that the children are really enjoying the play date interaction and having a lot of fun. Ratings of the children's enjoyment, interest, and comfort are a good index of the children's motivation to participate in the play date (R.L. Koegel, Bimbela, & Schreibman, 1996; R.L. Koegel & Egel, 1979; Schreibman, Kaneko, & Koegel, 1991). An affect rating scale (Baker, Koegel, & Koegel, 1998; Dunlap & Koegel, 1980; see Figure 8.1) may be useful in evaluating the children's interest, enthusiasm, and happiness during the play date. This can help evaluate the success of the play date through observing the children's eagerness to interact with one another. The children can be rated as they interact, or play dates can be videotaped (with parental permission) and scored later.

3. *Social validity outcomes:* It is also important to determine whether the play dates are having a long-term impact on the social and friendship development of the child with autism. Children with autism rarely have opportunities to interact with typically developing peers outside the school setting and often receive few, if any, invitations to participate in play dates, birthday parties, or sleepovers. One way to assess whether the play dates are improving the child's social network is by keeping track of the number of invitations from peers. It may take time to develop this history of positive interactions between the child and his or her peers. Once the number of invitations is increasing, this may mean that repeated positive experiences during play dates are being reciprocated. In this way, the social interaction itself can become naturally reinforcing to the children and can help sustain positive social exchanges.

Results

Research on this play date intervention package applied the previously noted strategies in working with children with autism to improve the quality of their social interactions with typically developing peers. Data from two children with autism (ages 8 and 9 years old) in their respective dyads with typically developing peers are presented next.

Prior to Intervention   Before participating in the play date intervention, both children spoke in phrases and sentences, using a wide variety of grammatical structures, but had difficulties with the pragmatic aspects of language. In particular, the children showed minimal responses to the comments and initiations of their respective peers, as well as difficulty with maintaining appropriate reciprocal social conversations. Consequently, they had difficulty initiating and maintaining social interactions and had no consistent friends. Without support, each of these children spent the majority of their recess time alone on the playground. In addition, they each had minimal contact with peers outside of school. For example, neither child participated in any extracurricular or recreational activities (e.g., camps, sports activities, after-school clubs). Also, the two children rarely extended or received invitations from peers to participate in typical social activities, such as play dates, birthday parties, and sleepovers.

During the few opportunities that these two children with autism did have to in-teract with typically developing peers from their respective classrooms, they were en-gaging in low levels of synchronous reciprocal interaction. For example, research prior to intervention showed that both children were only engaging in synchronous reciprocal interaction during 0%–40% of intervals, with no obvious trends. This find-ing indicated that the quality of their interactions with typically developing peers was very unstable and unpredictable, with limited evidence of social reciprocity. For ex-ample, while one typically developing peer was drawing a picture, the child with autism was busy reading a book, and there were few social exchanges of any kind. In another instance, when one typically developing peer commented on the picture made by the child with autism, he did not respond. This clearly showed low levels of synchronous reciprocal interaction within the dyad. In addition, affect scores for each separate dyad during these unsupported interactions were consistently in the neutral range for the children and their peers, indicating neutral ratings on domains of en-joyment, interest, and comfort during play interactions.

During Intervention   Once the play date intervention package was imple-mented, both children showed increases in high-quality interactions in their respec-tive dyads with typically developing peers. The combination of specific, mutually re-inforcing activities with facilitation of cooperative arrangements between the peers resulted in immediate increases in synchronous reciprocal interaction. For instance, research showed that with the support provided by the play date intervention pack-age, the children were engaging in synchronous reciprocal interaction during 70%–85% of intervals. This represented significant increases in levels of ongoing interaction between the peers during play dates. For example, during a play date for one of the children with autism, the child with autism and the typically developing peer were drawing pictures and initiating questions (e.g., "What are you drawing?") and com-ments (e.g., "I like your picture") to each other. There was also a reciprocal exchange of nonverbal behaviors, such as handing a marker to the other child or assisting the child in drawing. More important, these exchanges were also reciprocated by the peer (e.g., peer responded to question, made eye contact, smiled, used the marker offered by the other child). These were clear demonstrations of synchronous reciprocal inter-action because both children's verbal and nonverbal behaviors were directed toward one another within the social activity.

In addition, research revealed simultaneous increases in positive affect ratings within each dyad for both the children with autism and the typically developing peers. Specifically, affect scores on domains of enjoyment, interest, and comfort were consistently in the positive range for all children involved. The children were actively participating in social interactions and appeared comfortable, with frequent occur-rences of smiling and laughing.

Social Validity Outcomes   In addition to evaluating changes in synchronous reciprocal interaction and affect, data were gathered to determine whether the intervention was affecting the children's friendships with peers. In particular, the frequency of peer invitations were monitored throughout the course of intervention. The parents of the two children with autism kept track of the number of times each month that their children were invited to play at another peer's house. Prior to intervention, the parents reported that their children rarely received invitations from their peers. However, as play dates continued and synchronous reciprocal interaction improved, there was an increase in the number of these reciprocal invitations. For example, after several months of intervention, both families reported frequent interactions between the children and their respective peers, with the peers extending invitations at least one to two times per week. In addition to improved reciprocal interactions and higher positive affect, the play dates seemed to have resulted in typically developing peers making efforts to seek additional interactions with these children by inviting them over to play more often.

Case Example

Since her preschool years, Madison had been receiving intervention services for her diagnosis of autism. At 8 years of age, she continued to be enrolled in a full-inclusion classroom and excelled in numerous academic areas. She was able to communicate in full sentences and had an elaborate imagination. Despite her progress in these developmental domains, Madison continued to have difficulty interacting with her peers. For example, at school, while the other children played on the jungle gym or chased each other, Madison played alone in the sandbox. At lunch, she sat at her own table, eating her lunch with her back to the other children. She did not join her peers in playing house, jumping rope, or engaging in other games. If approached by another child, she rarely responded and usually walked away. At home, Madison had even fewer opportunities to interact with other children. Madison's mother was reluctant to invite other children over to her house. In the past, she had contacted other parents to arrange get-togethers, but her invitations were rarely accepted. Also, she saw how difficult it was for Madison to play with her peers for more than a few minutes, and she was afraid that if a play date did occur, the peer might not have a good time. At the same time, however, Madison's mother desperately wanted her daughter to experience a typical childhood, full of birthday parties, sleepovers, and meaningful friendships.

The first step in Madison's intervention program was to identify children to participate in play dates at Madison's house. Madison's teacher and classroom aide were asked to provide input in selecting appropriate play mates, such as children who were helpful or positive toward Madison. Initially, play dates were planned every other week. In addition, it seemed that a small group of children might have been motivated to go to theme-based parties, so these were planned on the alternate weeks. Based on observations at school and consultations with Madison's teacher and parents, the clinicians were able to identify a number of activities that Madison and her peers really enjoyed. Therefore, when organizing these play dates, the clinicians made sure to choose highly reinforcing activities that were specifically tailored to the interests of the children involved. For example, the clinicians learned that one peer loved to go bowling, so they planned a play date at the bowling alley. Other activities included ice cream and pizza parties, holiday theme parties, art and baking projects, and trips to the beach.

During these play dates, the clinicians purposely arranged situations that required the participation of each child. For instance, during a Halloween party, each child was given some of the materials needed to decorate one pumpkin and the children were asked to work together to decide on the design. With these cooperative arrangements, the children needed to communicate and interact with each other in order to complete the project. Using highly enjoyable activities also ensured their motivation to want to play together.

Because of the selection of activities and the support provided, the other children in the classroom started to hear about how much fun their peers were having at Madison's house. They heard about the trip to the bowling alley and saw the beaded necklaces that the girls had made, and they wanted to participate in all of the fun. What started off as just one or two children playing with Madison soon turned into all of the children asking to go over to her house to participate in the fun activities. Furthermore, as these play dates continued to occur, Madison and her peers became more fluid in interacting with each other. The peers' experience with the reinforcing activities, combined with Madison's increased proficiency in social areas, made the interactions themselves rewarding. Soon the peers became so excited about interacting with Madison that they began to ask their parents to invite Madison to their houses. Madison was soon being invited over by her new friends several times each week. Madison's mother was so happy that she had tears in her eyes as she was talking about all the birthday parties and sleepovers Madison was attending. For the first time, Madison's mother could see that her daughter was being accepted by her peers and treated like any other good friend.

When one of the chapter authors stopped by to see Madison after school one day, Madison was behaving in a completely different way. Instead of standing by the wall alone as she waited for her mother to pick her up, she was holding hands with two other girls, running, and laughing. Madison's friends were so out of breath from all the giggling that their mothers could hardly understand their pleas for yet another play date with Madison. Now Madison's mother does not have any trouble finding peers to come over. In fact, she has her hands full managing Madison's busy social calendar.

DISCUSSION OF CHAPTER CONCEPTS

Overall, the play date intervention package—which includes specific, mutually reinforcing activities; cooperative arrangements; and adult facilitation—can have a broad impact on measures of synchronous reciprocal social interaction and positive affect for children with autism. Additional social validation data from the chapter authors' research suggested an increased number of reciprocal invitations from peers as well.

Synchronous Reciprocal Interaction

The play date intervention package resulted in immediate and dramatic increases in the rates of unprompted synchronous reciprocal interaction for the children. Despite opportunities for interactions with peers before intervention, the children with autism could not sustain high-quality social interactions without support. With the support package, the children were better able to engage in these interactions at high levels. This provided evidence that intervention during play dates can promote high levels of synchronous interaction. It is important to note that following intervention, these interactions did not need to be directly prompted by the parent or clinician and that the children were engaging in these interactions spontaneously. This finding suggests that the use of specific, mutually reinforcing activities and cooperative arrangements, combined with the adult facilitation that was provided during the intervention, created the context for spontaneous social interactions to occur with increased frequency.

These increases in synchronous reciprocal interaction suggest that the children had at least some of the necessary skills for engaging in these appropriate reciprocal interactions and that the play date intervention package created a context that successfully supported these behaviors in a way that the free play with peers did not. This finding relates to literature on scaffolding (Schuler & Wolfberg, 2000; Wolfberg & Schuler, 1999) and on skill versus fluency deficits (Gresham, Sugai, & Horner, 2001).

Affect

In addition, there were higher levels of positive affect during supported play date sessions. Specifically, the children showed higher levels of enjoyment, interest, and comfort. This gave additional evidence that these children were enjoying the increased levels of interaction. This type of support may play an important role in promoting interactions that are viewed as fun and successful by both children. This is consistent with Frankel and Myatt (2003), who defined successful play dates as those containing continued mutually enjoyable interactions. Not only were the children engaging in social interaction, but the high affect ratings also suggest that the quality of their interactions, in terms of mutual enjoyment, had improved. This finding indicates that the children will want to engage in these types of interactions with each other again.

Reciprocal Invitations

The increased number of invitations from peers provided even more evidence that the play date intervention package may have resulted in typically developing peers wanting to spend more time with the children with autism. In turn, this finding suggested that the play dates may have had some impact on aspects of friendship development. Perhaps the children's increasing ability to participate in reciprocal interactions and the repeated positive experiences during play dates may have made the peers more interested in spending time with them. Indeed, Strain (2001) noted that in addition to proximity and participation, interactions must be reciprocal for friendship development to take place. This suggests that the high rates of synchronous reciprocal interaction may have been instrumental in the increases in peer invitations that were observed.

This collateral effect is particularly encouraging because friendship with peers was an important goal and a socially significant outcome for both children and their families but a difficult one that could not be directly targeted. Indeed, friendship has been viewed as an increasingly important goal and socially valid outcome for children with disabilities (Amado, 1993; Freeman & Kasari, 2002; Hurley-Geffner, 1995), both in school (Nickels, 1996; Strain & Schwartz, 2001) and home environments (Turnbull, Pereira, & Blue-Banning, 1999). The fact that this effect was not observed immediately following the start of intervention indicates that this type of effect may be clinically difficult to achieve and may take a considerable amount of time to develop. However, with continued efforts on the part of the children's families in arranging play dates with appropriate support, these reciprocal invitations continued to increase and maintained at a rate of approximately one to two per week.

Play dates have been suggested as a crucial context for peer interaction and friendship development. Parents of typically developing children report these as a regular occurrence for their children (Ladd & Hart, 1992; Newson & Newson, 1976). Frankel and Myatt (2003) estimated that children typically have approximately one to two play dates with peers per week and suggested that for children with friendship problems, having play dates occur less than once per week may not be sufficient. Some researchers have suggested that parent involvement in calling peers for play dates may result in more invitations to other peers' homes (Ladd, Hart, Wadsworth, & Golter, 1988). However, the parents of both children were regularly inviting peers over to play at their houses during the initial stages of intervention but only rarely got any invitations back, nor were many of these parents' attempts accepted. Over time and with continued play date interventions and increases in the quality of the play date interactions, invitations from peers began to increase to a more typical level for the children with autism. The fact that these invitations were eventually being initiated by peers is important because the literature suggests that peer status is better predicted by approaches of other children than by overall rates of peer interaction (Gresham, 1982). Thus, frequent interactions with peers may be poor predictors of high-quality peer relationships if these interactions are only initiated by the children with disabilities.

In summary, the play date intervention package described in this chapter had an impact on broad aspects of social interaction during play dates, including increased levels of synchronous reciprocal interaction and high rates of positive affect by both the children with autism and their typically developing peers. Additional social validity data indicated increasing numbers of peer invitations as a result of the play date intervention package. This study, which was conducted over an extended period of time, provides an in-depth analysis of the importance of contextual support in promoting high-quality play date interactions for children with autism. The low levels of synchronous reciprocal interaction before intervention showed that being in proximity to peers, whether in a full inclusion environment or by having friends over to "hang out," was not enough to promote high-quality interactions. It was not until the play date support was provided and increases in synchronous reciprocal interaction and higher affect were observed that the reciprocal invitations increased. This evidence supports the idea that numerous opportunities for social interaction may not result in the development of the high-quality social interactions so crucial for developing meaningful peer relationships. Some facilitation may be needed at first to support these high-quality interactions.

DIRECTIONS FOR FUTURE RESEARCH

Clearly, more research is important in further refining the components of the package and in adapting these techniques for use with a broad range of children. In addition, replication of these effects, including the increases in peer invitations that were observed, will provide more information about the many variables that contribute to the development of peer relationships for children with autism and will be helpful in continuing to develop increasingly successful interventions. However, these findings are promising in that they suggest that social intervention packages for use in the natural environment can have meaningful and lasting impacts on the development of high-quality peer interactions and relationships for children with autism.

IV

Reducing
Disruptive Behavior and
Broadening Children's Interests

12

Reducing
Ritualistic Behaviors and
Broadening Children's Interests

Robert L. Koegel, Jane Lacy Talebi, and Lynn Kern Koegel

This chapter discusses pivotal methods for reducing ritualistic behavior in children with autism and broadening the children's interests. The authors' general theory posits that the children's restricted interests are related to their giving these activities abnormally high placement in their reinforcement hierarchies. The hypothesis is that using transfer stimuli permits transitions to other reinforcers in the children's overall hierarchies. This is possible because the transfer stimuli function both to interrupt the reinforcement properties of the ritualistic objects and to direct the children to alternative reinforcers. Once the children make the transition away from the ritualistic objects and are exposed to new stimuli, these also have the potential to become reinforcing. (Note that this approach is similar to the pivotal role of teaching initiations described in Chapter 11.) Note that this may parallel the pivotal role of teaching initiations, except that previous chapters talked about the pivotal role of initiations with social interactions and this chapter refers to the role of initiations with potentially reinforcing stimuli in general. Thus, when the children begin interacting with the new stimuli, they have the opportunity to receive reinforcement from these items. This chapter discusses how to use transfer stimuli in conjunction with competing alternative reinforcers to reduce ritualistic behaviors and broaden children's interests.

BACKGROUND

One of the most prominent features of autism is the area of restricted interests and behaviors (American Psychiatric Association, 2000). This broad category includes stereotypic behavior, such as hand flapping or finger twirling, as well as a ritualistic interest in particular objects (Baron-Cohen, 1989; Simons, 1974). Both types of behaviors can cause major distress for the families of the children with autism and can severely limit the families' daily functioning (Reese, Richman, Zarcone, & Zarcone, 2003).

Ritualistic interest in a particular object can be conceptualized as an intense preoccupation with an object, during which a child becomes hyperfocused on the object and loses interest in other stimuli in the environment. It has been hypothesized that the ritualistic interest in objects often seen in children with autism may be a much more intense version of the interests that typically developing children have during early childhood (Bender & Schilder, 1940). Schultz and Berkson (1995) used the term *abnormal focused affections* to describe this same phenomenon of intense preoccupation with a specific object. To distinguish the phenomenon from obsessions and compulsions as defined in the DSM-IV, they included positive affect in their definition, as children who displayed these behaviors appeared to be particularly happy when around the ritualistic objects (Schultz & Berkson, 1995). In the same study, Schultz and Berkson investigated the possible relationship between ritualistic objects and stereotypic behavior and demonstrated that all participants who displayed abnormal focused affections toward a specific object also exhibited stereotypic behavior.

It is a strong possibility that stereotypic behavior, the second component in the restricted behavior category, is especially reinforcing to individuals with autism. These behaviors are also referred to as *self-stimulatory behaviors,* as they occur consistently and repetitively and appear to serve no other function other than giving the individual sensory feedback (Schreibman, 1988). In addition, research in this area has shown that little learning takes place when stereotypic behavior is also occurring (R.L. Koegel & Covert, 1972). Furthermore, children with autism do not play appropriately when engaged in stereotypic behavior (R.L. Koegel, Firestone, Kramme, & Dunlap, 1974), suggesting that such behavior is functionally incompatible with other interactions.

Thus, it may be particularly important to identify effective methods to interrupt an individual's stereotypic behavior or transfer his or her attention to a new stimulus, thus allowing the individual more appropriate and effective social and learning opportunities. Early research in the field sought to manage stereotypic behavior through methods such as overcorrection (Foxx & Azrin, 1973), time-out (Sachs, 1973), and shock (Baumeister & Forehand, 1972). Other more positive methods of reducing stereotypic behavior were seen in techniques such as vigorous physical exercise (Kern, Koegel, & Dunlap, 1984). Later research showed that stereotypic behavior can be managed effectively using self-management procedures. For instance, R.L. Koegel and Koegel (1990) showed that a comprehensive self-management package could effectively reduce an individual's stereotypic behavior. These low levels of stereotypic behavior maintained over time. In addition, Frea (1997) demonstrated that teaching individuals with autism to orient to external stimuli decreased the frequency of their stereotypic behavior. After the systematic fading of the teaching system, the participants continued to orient to external stimuli, suggesting that these more complex forms of stimulation had become more reinforcing than the stereotypic behavior. These latter studies suggest that once children are able to obtain reinforcement from other more appropriate stimuli, they no longer need the more primitive types of stimuli, such as self-stimulatory behavior.

An area that may be particularly relevant to this issue is the concept that interest in preferred objects might be arranged into individual reinforcement hierarchies. Dyer (1987) demonstrated that powerful external reinforcers specially assessed for each participant competed successfully with the reinforcement provided by stereotypic behavior. Results indicated that stereotypic behavior may fit into a larger reinforcement hierarchy with other reinforcers, with stereotypic behavior maintaining a higher place in the hierarchy if no other specially assessed reinforcers are identified for a participant. Dyer concluded with the suggestion that if a specially assessed reinforcer does not result in a decrease in the stereotypic behavior, external suppression of the stereotypic behavior should remove the competing reinforcement that the behavior provided to the participant and, thus, allow the participant to respond to the specially assessed reinforcement.

An approach using antecedent stimuli has been shown to be effective with other symptoms of autism. For example, past research has found that advance warning stimuli regarding transitions are effective in reducing aggressive behaviors, general problem behaviors, stereotypic behavior, and self-injurious acts in children with autism (Carr, Newsom, & Binkoff, 1980; Flannery & Horner, 1994; Mace, Shapiro, & Mace, 1998; Tustin, 1995). This chapter describes the use of transfer stimuli to help children make the transition away from highly preferred objects to other stimuli. In addition, it presents the hypothesis that during encounters in which children are not engaged in stereotypic behavior around ritualistic objects—and, thus, not as reinforced by rituals—the use of a positive, proactive approach will allow them to more readily make the transition to other stimuli.

Specifically, the authors' general theory posits that the individuals' restricted interests are related to an abnormally high placement of this activity in their reinforcement hierarchy. The hypothesis is that reducing the strength of the ritualistic object with a transfer stimulus that functions to both interrupt the reinforcement properties of the ritualisitc objects and to direct the children to an alternative reinforcer would permit transitions to other reinforcers in their overall hierarchy. In addition, the authors hypothesize that in encounters in which a child is not engaged in stereotypic behavior around the ritualistic object and, thus, not as reinforced by the ritual, he or she will more readily make the transition to other stimuli with the use of a positive, proactive approach.

INTERVENTION

The overall intervention consisted of two related intervention strategies that were based on the conceptual model's suggestion suggesting that stereotypic behavior occupied an abnormally high placement in the children's reinforcement hierarchies. To select the most relevant intervention strategy for a particular encounter, a decision tree (Figure 12.1 should be used by others who want to use the intervention) was employed by the mother of the demonstration child in this case example and a clinician noting the presence of stereotypic behavior before asking the child to leave the ritualistic object.

Intervention 1: Treatment When Stereotypy Is Occurring   If the stereotypic behavior was present before the request was made for the child to make the transition away from the ritualistic object, the transfer stimulus intervention was im-

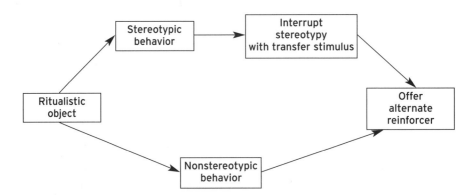

Figure 12.1.   The conceptual model used in the study to determine which intervention was most relevant for each encounter. Specifically, when the child was in front of the ritualistic object, he either exhibited stereotypic behavior or he did not. An intervention strategy was chosen based on whether stereotypic behavior was present. If he was exhibiting stereotypic behavior, the transfer stimulus and alternate reinforcer intervention was utilized to interrupt the stereotypy and have the child make the transition to a new reinforcer. If the child was not exhibiting stereotypic behavior before being requested to leave the ritualistic object, only an alternate reinforcer was offered, as there was no need to interrupt his behavior.

plemented first to interrupt the stereotypy. This intervention consisted of two primary parts:

1. *Present a transfer stimulus*: First, the transfer stimulus, which consisted of counting to 5, was implemented by the child's mother. This served to interrupt the stereotypy. Other examples of transfer stimuli include swinging the child, singing a favorite song, encouraging self-management, or using anything else that captures the child's attention.

2. *Present a competing alternate reinforcer*: The second step, following implementation of the transfer stimulus, was presenting a competing alternate reinforcer. In this example, the child was told that this would occur by someone saying, "I'm going to count to 5 and then we're going to go to the toy store [alternate reinforcer]." However, the child was not required to leave the desired activity or item until the transfer stimulus was complete. That is, an adult could implement the transfer stimulus intervention (i.e., counting) while standing in front of the ritualistic object and then proceeding to the alternate reinforcer immediately.

Intervention II: Treatment When Stereotypy Is Not Occurring

If the child was not exhibiting stereotypic behaviors, proactive techniques could be implemented immediately. In this case, the alternate reinforcer was presented and the adult and child proceeded to the alternate reinforcer immediately. For example, the adult got the child's attention and said, "We're going to the fast-food restaurant to get French fries [alternate reinforcer]," then proceeded to the alternate reinforcer.

Measurement

To adequately assess if the intervention had a meaningful effect on a child's behavior, several measures were collected:

1. *Leaving desired stimuli:* One measure recorded in the study was the amount of time it took a child to leave the desired stimulus. For instance, after the parent prompted the child to leave the object, the clinician started a timer and continued timing until the child had left the object. This took a number of different forms, including the child leaving the object willingly or the child being carried away by the parent.

2. *Exhibiting disruptive behavior:* Another recorded measure could be the amount of disruptive behavior exhibited by the child. *Disruptive behavior* can be defined as any behavior that interrupts the routines of the surrounding environment or of nearby people. Examples include a child's screaming, throwing him- or herself on the ground, running back to the desired object, crying, and throwing things in protest. It would be very simple to use the same interval recording system utilized for scoring responses to other stimuli.

3. *Responding to other stimuli*: Other stimuli can be defined as anything other than the ritualistic object of interest. In the study, these included the child's parent, the cli-

nician, other children in the environment, or other stimuli in the environment. Actions such as looking at, talking to, or running toward other stimuli were counted as responses. In a 10-second interval, if the child responded to other stimuli for the majority of the interval, then the code "other" was used.

CASE EXAMPLE

Julia, a 2-year, 8-month-old girl diagnosed with autism, showed an intense preoccupation with elevators and escalators. This ritualistic interest was present in most environments, including the doctor's office, office buildings, and hotels. It was especially noticeable in the shopping area that her family frequented several times per week. When Julia saw an elevator or escalator, she would run to it immediately and stand in front of it, pushing the buttons (as applicable) and talking excitedly to herself about the object. She would engage in stereotypic behavior, such as hand flapping or jumping. Julia would remain in front of the elevator, engaging in the behavior and not attending to anything her parents said to her. It was impossible to get her attention, and it seemed, at times, that the elevator or escalator was the only thing in her world. If her parents attempted to take her away from the elevator or escalator, Julia would begin crying. She would throw herself on the ground and have tantrums in front of the elevator or escalator. Unlike the tantrums of typically developing children, these tantrums continued even when Julia was presented with other fun objects. The result was Julia's parents having to drag her screaming and crying out of the shopping area. This distressing behavior forced them to end visits to the shopping area.

The initial goal of the intervention was to interrupt Julia's stereotypic behavior around the ritualistic object in an attempt to make the transition easier. This interruption was labeled a *transfer stimulus*. The transfer stimulus intervention consisted of two primary parts. First, the transfer stimulus (counting to 5) was implemented by Julia's mother. The second step was following the transfer stimulus with a competing reinforcer, such as French fries from a local eatery or a trip to the toy store at the end of the shopping area. These were chosen as alternate reinforcers because Julia had expressed a high level of interest in them in other settings and times with no accompanying self-stimulatory behavior. Specifically, Julia's mother was instructed to say, "I'm going to count to 5 and then we're going to go to the _____ [alternate reinforcer]". She implemented the intervention while standing in front of the ritualistic object and then proceeded to the alternate reinforcer immediately. Figure 12.2 presents an overall picture of the intervention.

A second goal of intervention involved teaching Julia's mother a procedure to use when Julia was not exhibiting stereotypic behavior. In this situation, she was instructed to offer an alternate reinforcer immediately before the stereotypic behavior started. If Julia was in front of the ritualistic object and not yet exhibiting self-stimulatory behavior, her mother would get her attention and offer an alternate reinforcer. This technique worked well. There were immediate improvements in Julia's behavior and her ability to make the transition away from the elevators and escalators (see Figures 12.3 and 12.4 for details about specific encounters). Not only did disruptive behavior decrease immediately but also Julia was able to leave an elevator or escalator in-

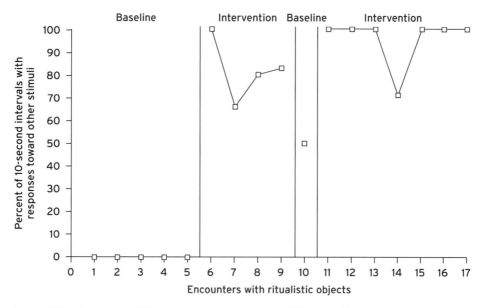

Figure 12.2. The percent of 10-second intervals in which the child engaged in responses to other stimuli rather than the ritualistic object when requested to leave the ritualistic object across 17 different encounters. During baseline sessions, the child did not respond to other stimuli at all (0%), whereas during intervention sessions, the child's responses to other stimuli rose to much higher levels (66%–100%).

dependently, without engaging in a tantrum or having to be dragged off. In addition, her attention to other stimuli, such as her mother or other reinforcers in the environment (e.g., the toy store), increased to very high levels (see Figure 12.5).

At the end of the intervention program, Julia's mother felt comfortable using both the transfer stimulus strategy and the proactive strategy in a variety of situations with Julia. She related feeling confident that she could address Julia's behavior in any context. For instance, she reported going to Julia's pediatrician for an annual check-up and using both procedures to help Julia go in and out of the building without her engaging in stereotypic or disruptive behavior.

Although Julia continues to show an interest in elevators and escalators, she is now able to make the transition away from these objects in a successful manner.

DISCUSSION OF CHAPTER CONCEPTS

This chapter has described how using a transfer stimulus in conjunction with an alternate reinforcer increases the responses to other stimuli in a child's environment, thereby temporarily rearranging the child's reinforcement hierarchy. That is, when a child is engaging in stereotypic behavior around a ritualistic object of interest, a transfer stimulus can be used in conjunction with a competing alternate reinforcing to effectively increase responses to other stimuli in his or her environment.

This chapter has further discussed a proactive technique, for use when stereotypic behavior is not present, to increase the responses to other stimuli in a child's environment. It appears that when a child is not engaged in stereotypic behavior around

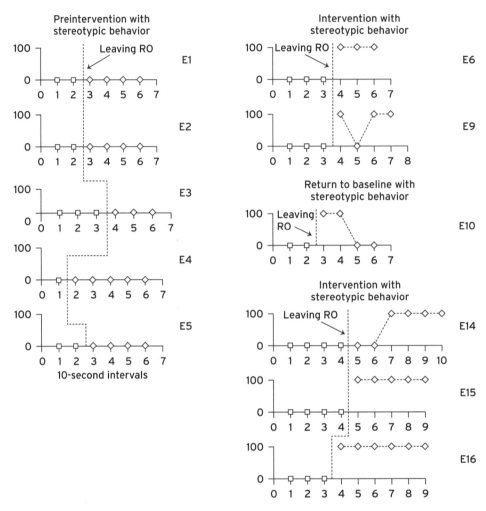

Figure 12.3. The child's responses to other stimuli during all encounters with the ritualistic object when stereotypic behavior took place. The far left panel shows the 10-second intervals with and without responses to other stimuli for each encounter during preintervention when the child exhibited stereotypic behavior before being requested to leave. This panel illustrates that the child never responded to other stimuli when requested to leave the ritualistic object, regardless of how many 10-second intervals passed. The panel on the far right shows the 10-second intervals with and without responses to other stimuli for each encounter after intervention when the child exhibited stereotypic behavior before being requested to leave. Because the child was exhibiting stereotypic behavior, the transfer stimulus intervention was utilized in all five of these encounters. The far-right panel shows that the child always responded to other stimuli after being requested to leave the ritualistic object. Also included in this panel is the return to baseline encounter (Session 10). (*Key:* E = encounters with the ritualistic object; RO = ritualistic object.)

the ritualistic object, competing alternative reinforcers are sufficient to allow the child to make a transition to other stimuli in the treatment setting. These results are in line with previous research in the positive behavior support field, suggesting that when possible, interventions should occur in the absence of problem behaviors (Carr et al., 2002). In this way, the problem behavior can be prevented from reoccurring in noncrisis times.

One conceptualization for this phenomenon regarding the transfer stimulus intervention strategy is associated simply with the notion of alternative reinforcers. Past research suggests that using objects that the child prefers as reinforcers increases his

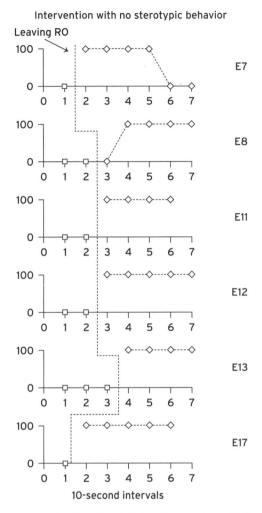

Figure 12.4. The child's responses to other stimuli during all encounters with the ritualistic objects when stereotypic behavior did not occur. Specifically, the figure shows the 10-second intervals with and without responses to other stimuli for each encounter after intervention when the child did not engage in any stereotypic behavior before being requested to leave. This figure illustrates that for each encounter, the child always responded to other stimuli immediately after being asked to leave the ritualistic object and offered an alternate reinforcer. (*Key:* E = encounters with the ritualistic object; RO = ritualistic object.)

or her motivation to engage in and complete a particular task (Dunlap et al., 1994; Moes, 1998). It is possible that offering a competing alternative reinforcer during intervention motivates a child to leave the preferred object upon request. However, it is more likely that an alternative reinforcer alone cannot help in having the child make the transition away from the ritualistic object. Thus, instead of an increase in the child's responses to other stimuli when offered an alternative reinforcer during preintervention sessions, which would be expected if the alternative reinforcer were the main explanation, the child's responses remained at same low levels as sessions in which no alternative reinforcer was offered. Furthermore, during preintervention sessions, the child often responded with high levels of disruptive behaviors (e.g., tantrums) upon leaving the ritualistic object.

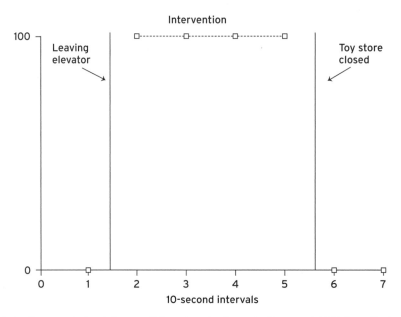

Figure 12.5.   The concept of a reinforcement hierarchy, using Encounter 7 as a model. This figure illustrates that upon implementation of the transfer stimulus and a request to leave the ritualistic object, the child immediately began responding to other stimuli. However, after the sixth interval, the alternate reinforcer was removed (i.e., the toy store was closed), and the child immediately began responding to the ritualistic object once again. This figure points to the importance of a salient alternate reinforcer as a component of the overall model discussed in the chapter.

A second, more likely, explanation for these findings may lie with the ability of the transfer stimuli to effectively interrupt the repetitive behaviors around the ritualistic object and to focus the child's attention on other stimuli. Previous research on using warning stimuli (i.e., those for signaling transitions) for children with autism demonstrates that such stimuli are effective in reducing disruptive behaviors, such as aggressive and stereotypic behavior (Carr et al., 1980; Tustin, 1995). The results of the study described in this chapter are consistent with these past results by suggesting that interrupting the stereotypic behavior with a transfer stimulus (i.e., counting to 5) may have allowed the child to focus on the other stimuli in the environment aside from the ritualistic object of interest. Research has demonstrated that children with autism often overselect to certain stimuli in their environments (Lovaas, Koegel, & Schreibman, 1979; Lovaas, Schreibman, Koegel, & Rehm, 1971). A specific, sometimes minor, part of the environment may gain control over the child's attention, preventing the child from attending to other stimuli in the environment (Schreibman & Koegel, 1982). In the study described in this chapter, however, the transfer stimulus was a necessary component of the intervention in that it helped focus the child's attention away from the object she was overselecting (i.e., elevator or escalator) to other stimuli in his environment (i.e., French fries or a visit to the toy store). With her attention on other reinforcers, the child was then able to make the transition away from the preferred object in an appropriate manner. This notion is further substantiated by the results pertaining to the findings from the second area of research regarding the proactive strategy to be used in encounters with no stereotypic behavior. It is apparent

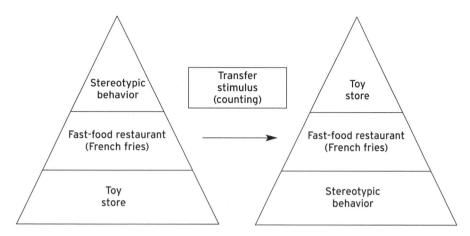

Figure 12.6.   Illustration of how a child's reinforcement hierarchy might be rearranged by using the transfer stimulus intervention.

that when the child was not engaged in stereotypic behavior before the request to leave, she made the transition away from the ritualistic object of interest much more easily.

Along these lines, past research regarding the reinforcement properties of various stimuli suggests that some stimuli may be more hierarchically reinforcing than others for an individual (Crespi, 1942; Dyer, 1987; Pihl & Greenspoon, 1969). It appears that when a child is not engaged in stereotypic behavior, he or she may be more readily reinforced by other stimuli. It is a strong possibility that the reinforcement hierarchy can be rearranged for just enough time to allow a calm transition away from ritualistic objects. In other words, by interrupting a stereotypic behavior, one may be able to lower its place in a child's reinforcement hierarchy, which allows other reinforcers to become motivating for the child (see Figure 12.6). Furthermore, interventions that are easily implemented in a community setting, such as the intervention described in this chapter's case example, are consistent with past research on the importance of implementing an intervention that improves a family's quality of life and has ecological validity (Carr et al., 2002).

DIRECTIONS FOR FUTURE RESEARCH

It may be valuable to measure parent and child affect both before and after intervention procedures. If the intervention is truly improving the family's quality of life, then affect should become more positive on the part of both mother and child during intervention. For more information, refer to the affect scales presented in Figure 8.1.

Further research is also needed to investigate if, along with increased experience with other reinforcers, the strength (or placement) of the other reinforcers would increase in the overall hierarchy and thus permanently remove the existence of the restricted interests. Although this chapter suggests that a child's reinforcement hierarchy can be rearranged on a temporary basis, it is worth investigating whether it is possible to make this more balanced/proportional arrangement permanent without eliminating the child's interest in the ritualistic object.

An additional important next step is to replicate these results with older children or adults with autism. In addition, assessing an individual's level of functioning to determine the practical implementation and relevance of such an approach would be helpful. Because restricted interests and behaviors form an area of stress for many families of children with autism, identifying techniques to broaden the children's interests and behaviors has both practical as well as theoretical significance.

13

Improving Social-Communication, Empathy, and Pragmatics in Individuals with Asperger Syndrome

Lynn Kern Koegel, Jane Lacy Talebi, Robert L. Koegel, and Cynthia Carter

This chapter describes procedures for improving empathic communicative responses in verbal children or adolescents with Asperger syndrome (AS) or high-functioning autism (HFA). As discussed later in this chapter, there is a lack of clear diagnostic criteria that differentiate AS and HFA. Therefore, the terms are used interchangeably in this chapter. However, when *AS* is used alone in the chapter, this indicates that no language delay is present. The chapter begins with an overview of AS, including history of the diagnostic label, primary clinical features, and the different diagnostic systems. It describes the use of self-management to increase social conversation skills and empathic social communicative responses. This intervention results in improved ratings of empathy and generalized improvements in other untreated pragmatic behaviors across conversational partners and environments. This chapter discusses the intervention in terms of improving the overall quality of social interactions for verbal children and adolescents diagnosed with AS or HFA.

OVERVIEW OF ASPERGER SYNDROME

The social difficulties apparent in individuals diagnosed with autism spectrum disorders (ASDs) can greatly interfere with all aspects of life (Mesibov, 1984; Rogers, 2000). The intervention literature reveals a variety of innovative interventions designed to remedy these social difficulties, with the ultimate goal being to help these individuals become more accepted in their given peer group. Children and adolescents who are accepted by their peers and experience stable friendships are more likely to have higher self-esteem levels, better academic functioning and motivation for school, and a happier state of mind (Cheng & Furnham, 2002; Savin-Williams & Berndt, 1990).

Thus, there is no doubt that intervention is critical for those who experience challenges in making and maintaining social relationships. However, the majority of the intervention studies in this area have focused on either very young children with autism or older children who are generally low functioning (Farmer-Dougan, 1994; Groden & Cautela, 1988; Haring, Breen, Pitts-Conway, Lee, & Gaylord-Ross, 1987; McConnell, 2002). This presents a dilemma when working with adolescents diagnosed with AS and HFA who are higher functioning than most individuals with ASDs in both the cognitive and language arenas (Volkmar & Klin, 2000). However, without intervention, social problems for individuals with AS and HFA generally increase with age, and by adolescence, individuals with AS and HFA can show significant difficulties (Gilchrist et al., 2001).

This is an important area for further study for several reasons. First, because adolescents with AS and HFA often have well-developed verbal skills and average cognitive functioning levels, they may be more susceptible than younger children with autism or lower-functioning individuals to the negative effects of social rejection or social isolation (Ghaziuddin, 2002). In addition, it may not be as easy to intervene in social situations and prompt successful social interactions with peers when dealing with adolescents who, due to their age, naturally resist adult intrusion or being labeled as different. As such, existing interventions should be examined closely for "goodness of fit" (Albin, Lucyshyn, Horner, & Flannery, 1996) with this population and changed to meet their needs, if necessary.

History of the Diagnosis

The term *Asperger syndrome* has been used interchangeably to describe several different groups, including individuals with HFA, adults with autism, or people with a syndrome that is completely separate from autism (Prior, 2003; Volkmar et al., 1996). Prevalence rates of AS have been estimated to range from 3.6 per 1,000 children to 2.5 per 10,000 children, depending on the strictness of the criteria used for classification (Ehlers & Gillberg, 1993; Fombonne, 2003a; Gillberg, 2002). This variable range indicates that until a consensus is reached on the exact definition and description of this group, it will be difficult to know precisely how common the disability truly is.

In 1944, Hans Asperger wrote of four young boys he had encountered in his clinical practice. He used the term *autistic psychopathy* to describe the boys' symptoms, which included a stilted, pedantic manner of speaking; inappropriate social behaviors; a restricted range of interests; and reported motor clumsiness (Frith, 1991). This description bore striking similarities to Leo Kanner's first description of childhood autism published in 1943. For instance, Asperger, a physician, and Kanner, a researcher, both believed the primary impairment for the children lay in the social area and observed stereotypic patterns of interests in their behaviors (Kugler, 1998). However, whereas Kanner noted a significant delay in language abilities, Asperger insisted that language development was typical in his sample, evidenced by a seeming mastery of the formal rules of language (Kugler, 1998). Other differences noted were apparent motor deficits in AS and different cognitive strengths, including higher levels of creativity and originality of thought in individuals with AS (Kugler, 1998).

Although Asperger continued to do clinical work and publish his findings throughout Europe for the remainder of his life, the term *Asperger syndrome* did not enter the consciousness of the American public, and consequently begin being used, until 1981, with an article written by Lorna Wing (1981). In this article, Wing reviewed Asperger's original paper and used her own research and clinical work to provide revisions to his definitions (Wing, 1981). These revisions included Wing's suggestion that AS may occur more frequently in females than originally noted by Asperger and the possibility of speech delay in AS (Wing, 1981). The article concluded with the notion that AS and autism share the same core symptom areas (Wing, 1981).

Main Clinical Features of AS

Circumscribed Interests   Individuals with AS often have a special area of interest on which they have accumulated a large amount of knowledge (Attwood, 2003; Volkmar & Klin, 2000). It has been estimated that more than 90% of children, adolescents, and adults with AS have some type of preferred or specialized interest (Attwood, 2003). Some experts suggest that the preferred interests often look developmentally appropriate when the individual is very young (Volkmar & Klin, 2000). However, as the child grows older, these interests may gradually begin looking increasingly inappropriate. For instance, the specific topics may become more atypical (e.g., memorizing the names of different cellular phone companies and all of their calling plans) or the individual may amass an excessive amount of facts on one topic (Volkmar & Klin, 2000).

Social Difficulties   Individuals with AS are typically isolated from their peer group. This often is not a result of withdrawing or some disinterest on their part (Volkmar & Klin, 2000). Individuals with AS often approach others to interact socially but use inappropriate or awkward strategies during this process. However, the opposite reaction (i.e., withdrawing from social interaction) can also be exhibited by a subgroup of individuals with AS (Shaked & Yirmiya, 2003).

In general, although individuals with AS may be able to verbally explain different emotions or social rules, they often appear unable to use their knowledge during natural social interactions in flexible ways (Klin, Sparrow, Volkmar, Cicchetti, & Rourke, 1995). Another area of difficulty relates to the content of their conversations. As stated previously, individuals with AS usually have a special topic of interest and use this topic often, or exclusively, in conversations with others. Because they also have difficulties cuing into the nonverbal signals of other people, individuals with AS may not know when it is an appropriate time to stop talking (Volkmar & Klin, 2000). For example, a teenager with AS who has trouble monitoring the reactions of others may engage a peer in a conversation about the different types of computer programs and talk for a half hour before noticing that the peer is either extremely bored or has already walked away.

Language Difficulties   Early speech development is usually not affected in AS (Volkmar & Klin, 2000). However, individuals with AS do experience extreme difficulties with the pragmatics of language (Shriberg et al., 2001). These can include improper regulation of voice volume, a monotone voice, a pedantic manner of speaking, and problems with expressing and interpreting nonverbal cues (Klin et al., 1995; Volkmar & Klin, 2000). In addition, conversational skills—such as introducing new topics, making transitions to different topics, or making relevant comments on another's story—can also be affected (Landa, 2000).

Diagnostic Systems

Different diagnostic systems use some of the previously described clinical symptoms and others to reach a diagnosis of AS. Some of these systems vary widely in their strictness and inclusion criteria. For example, before AS was recognized as a disorder by official psychological organizations in the early 1990s, researchers in the field used Hans Asperger's original descriptions to make their own definitions and criteria (Gillberg, 1989; Wing, 1981). One such example that has persisted throughout the years is Gillberg's criteria (Gillberg, 2002). It includes symptoms such as social impairment, compulsive routines, speech peculiarities, and motor clumsiness. This set of criteria is the only one in which AS can take precedence over autism when both criteria are met, based on clinical judgment.

A second, more formalized set of diagnostic criteria is found in the International Classification of Diseases and Disorders, Tenth Revision (ICD-10; see also the Clinical Modification, or ICD-10-CM), created by the World Health Organization (WHO,

1993; see also Gillberg, 2002). These criteria are hierarchical in nature in that autism takes diagnostic precedence even if criteria for AS are met as well. The ICD-10 definition of AS, which WHO included among its diagnostic categories for the first time in 1993, consists of eight primary symptoms and stipulates that three must be met by the individual in order to receive a diagnosis of AS.

The DSM-IV (American Psychiatric Association [APA], 1994) and DSM-IV-TR (APA, 2000) have presented the most recent criteria used to diagnose an individual with AS. The APA criteria are conceptually equal to those of the ICD-10, including the "precedence rule" of autism over AS (Volkmar et al., 1994; Volkmar, Klin, & Pauls, 1998). Again, similar to the ICD-10, only three symptoms from the listed eight must be met to receive a diagnosis of AS. Despite the DSM-IV-TR's seemingly thorough definitions and set-up, research has found that the DSM-IV-TR criteria for AS are unlikely to be met due to the precedence rule for a diagnosis of autism. For instance, Mayes, Calhoun, and Crites (2001) examined 157 children with clinical diagnoses of autism or AS. They found that none of the children in the sample met the DSM-IV-TR criteria for AS because they also exhibited symptoms that met the autism criteria. Ironically, Miller and Ozonoff (1997) examined Hans Asperger's original paper and found that all four of the participants described in his study met criteria for autism according to the DSM-IV-TR; therefore, they would not be classified as having AS according to the DSM-IV-TR. The results of these studies bring to question the usefulness of the current DSM-IV-TR criteria for diagnosing AS.

With all the different criteria systems used to diagnose AS, it is important to understand the level of consistency between systems. In other words, will a child be diagnosed differently depending on the criteria used? It is interesting to note that each set of criteria appears to identify differing numbers of children with AS (Ghaziuddin, Tsai, & Ghaziuddin, 1992; Leekam, Libby, Wing, Gould, & Gillberg, 2000). On the one hand, Leekam and colleagues (2000) showed that using the Gillberg criteria, 45% of a sample was identified as having AS. On the other hand, when the ICD-10 criteria were utilized, only 1% of the sample was shown to have AS. This discrepancy between systems reflects the problem in finding homogenous samples across sites for research purposes.

Another example of a discrepancy between systems involves the role of speech delay as defining criteria. Although Gillberg (2002) stipulated that speech delay may be present, the ICD-10 and the DSM-IV both require that there be no significant speech delay in order for a diagnosis of AS to be given. Subsequently, the question arises as to the validity of speech delay as a diagnostic marker. To attempt to answer this question, Mayes and Calhoun (2001) divided groups of children with AS and children with HFA into two groups: those with speech delay and those without. No significant differences, including on symptoms of autism, were detected between the two groups, indicating that absence of a speech delay may not be an effective way of distinguishing AS from autism. Furthermore, Volkmar et al. (1996) purported that although certain parts of speech development in AS may appear typical, there are other parts that are severely impaired, including pragmatics and conversational skills. These findings indicate that certain accepted diagnostic features may need to be reinvestigated in the near future. Indeed, leading researchers in the field have called for a revamping of the DSM-IV and the ICD-10, on the grounds that the criteria are too loose and lack important elements identified in the literature (Volkmar et al., 1996).

Changes in the Diagnostic Process

It has been suggested that clinicians are using definitions and criteria taken from their own clinical experience to make diagnoses rather than using a set of diagnostic criteria (Mayes et al., 2001). This mismatch between the clinical practice and the diagnostic systems presents a troubling gap. To remedy this discrepancy, experts in the field are examining the diagnostic criteria more critically. The role of speech development in autism and AS is one such example. The absence of a speech delay in AS has been touted as a distinguishing factor from autism. However, this is circular reasoning, as speech delay is also one of the criteria used to differentiate the two conditions and, as demonstrated in the previous section, may not predict diagnosis at all (Mayes et al., 2001). Instead, the emphasis is on finding clinical symptoms for AS that are not used as part of the diagnostic criteria, including course of the disorder, neurobiological markers, related disorders in the family, or response to intervention (Baron-Cohen & Hammer, 1997; Freeman, Cronin, & Candela, 2002; Klin, Volkmar, & Sparrow, 2000; Volkmar et al., 1998).

Attempts have also been made to form a valid and usable clinical interview to help clinicians screen for AS. Although these tools, such as the Asperger Syndrome Diagnostic Interview (ASDI; Gillberg, Gillberg, Rastam, & Wentz, 2001) or the Autism Spectrum Screening Questionnaire (ASSQ; Ehlers, Gillberg, & Wing, 1999), show good reliability and validity, they have yet to gain widespread use in the literature or clinical practice. In an effort to help close the gap between practice and research, it is important to decipher whether these screening tools are consistent with the features of the diagnostic systems.

Differential Diagnosis

AS bears a strong resemblance to several other disabilities discussed in the literature. Disorders with similar symptoms to AS include deficits in attention, motor control, and perception (DAMP), a diagnostic category discussed primarily in the European literature (Gillberg, 2002; Sturm, Fernell, & Gillberg, 2004); semantic-pragmatic disorder; and "schizoid" personality disorder, characterized by impairments in social interaction, atypical communication abilities, and emotional detachment (Klin & Volkmar, 2000). It is interesting to note that many of the similar disorders are rooted in different disciplines. It is possible that if an interdisciplinary approach were taken, the disorders would be more similar than first thought. Other major disorders with similarities to AS are discussed next.

Nonverbal Learning Disability (NLD)   Rourke (1995) described a sample of children with deficits in psychomotor coordination, nonverbal problem solving, and arithmetic, as well as an impaired ability to adapt to novel situations and interact socially with peers. Rourke also noted that this same group demonstrated intact rote verbal skills. These clinical observations were given credence when individuals with

NLD demonstrated a particular profile on intelligence tests (Rourke & Tsatsanis, 2000). Specifically, individuals with NLD generally show high verbal scores and lower performance scores on intelligence tests.

As far as etiology is concerned, in the original model, Rourke (1989) hypothesized that NLD develops if the white matter in a child's brain is underdeveloped or in some way damaged. More specifically, it was suggested that the primary brain region affected was the right hemisphere (Rourke, Del Dotto, Rourke, & Casey, 1990). This was hypothesized primarily because deficits in spatial or nonverbal functioning are typically observed in NLD, as opposed to relative strengths in verbal, routinized functioning, which are centered in the left hemisphere (Casey, Rourke, & Picard, 1991). The symptoms of NLD, including difficulty in social interaction, might manifest at any point in time when the damage occurs (Rourke, 1995).

Research has demonstrated that individuals with a number of disorders associated with damage to white matter (e.g., Williams syndrome, Turner syndrome, and fetal alcohol syndrome) show symptoms similar to those of NLD (Rourke, 1995). Although research has yet to solidly corroborate that individuals with AS have similar white matter damage in the right hemisphere of their brains (Ellis, Ellis, Fraser, & Deb, 1994; Ellis & Gunter, 1999), the striking clinical similarities between NLD and AS merit further investigation into Rourke's model. Indeed, looking at symptoms, it appears that AS and NLD have much in common, including difficulties with social interaction and nonverbal communication (Klin et al., 1995). In addition, some experts note that AS seems to follow the neuropsychological profile seen in the NLD model (Klin et al., 1995). For instance, some research has shown that individuals with AS exhibit a similar intelligence profile to those with NLD, exhibited by high verbal scores and low performance scores on intelligence tests (Ellis et al., 1994; Ghaziuddin & Mountain-Kimchi, 2004; Gillberg & Ehlers, 1998; Wing, 1998). With the increasing use of brain imaging technology, it is possible that the links between brain functioning and AS may be further clarified in the future.

Pervasive Developmental Disorder–Not Otherwise Specified (PDD-NOS)

PDD-NOS is a category typically reserved for those children who exhibit some impairments in social interaction, communication, and behaviors but who do not meet the outlined criteria for a diagnosis of classic autism. As such, this category consists of very different children, ranging widely in symptom manifestation, severity, and intellectual functioning (Klin et al., 1995). Research has demonstrated that, in general, when AS and PDD-NOS are compared, the social and communication impairments are more severe in AS, intellectual functioning is higher overall in AS, and there are fewer repetitive behaviors present in PDD-NOS (Klin et al., 1995; Volkmar et al., 1994).

Autism   Again, the lack of a gold standard for diagnostic criteria causes considerable confusion as to whether the differences between AS and autism represent qualitative or quantitative differences. Although controversial at the time of this book's publication, some research studies have detected a specific pattern on intelligence measures for individuals with AS. Specifically, the individuals tend to score better on the verbal portions of IQ tests, thus resulting in a discrepancy between verbal scores and performance scores (Ellis et al., 1994; Ghaziuddin & Mountain-Kimchi, 2004; Gillberg & Ehlers, 1998; Wing, 1998). It is interesting to note that the reverse pattern has been reported to be true for individuals with HFA (Gillberg & Ehlers, 1998). This neuropsychological pattern has the potential to be a distinguishing characteristic between the two disabilities, supporting the qualitative perspective of the two disorders. In addition, Ehlers and colleagues (1997) found that participants with AS performed worse than participants with autism on object assembly, coding, and block design. Even when full-scale IQ scores were controlled statistically, the differences between groups remained. These results are interesting in that they reveal a possible difference in cognitive profiles between the two groups. It should be noted, however, that these findings have been contradicted by other results indicating no difference in the cognitive profiles of individuals with AS and HFA (Reitzel & Szatmari, 2003). Some experts caution that it is still too early to accept this pattern as a distinguishing mark for AS and urge further research to clarify the issue (Ghaziuddin & Mountain-Kimchi, 2004; Reitzel & Szatmari, 2003).

Other researchers point to clinical differences between AS and autism. For instance, it has been noted by some that the social impairment in individuals with AS appears to be contained to interactions with peers, as opposed to the more global impairment in individuals with autism, which also affects their interactions with family members and adults (Szatmari, Bartolucci, & Bremner, 1989). In addition, research by Szatmari, Bryson, Boyle, Streiner, and Duku (2003) indicated that predictors of outcome may be different between AS and autism, with the relationship between early language skills and outcome being much stronger for individuals with autism.

Other research has supported the quantitative difference perspective, positing that AS differs from autism only in severity of symptoms, especially regarding cognitive levels. The underlying belief here is that AS actually is HFA (Mayes & Calhoun, 2003). In support of this notion, research has shown that as intelligence levels increase, symptoms of autism become less severe (Eaves, Ho, & Eaves, 1994; Miller & Ozonoff, 2000). These individuals with HFA, due to their higher cognitive levels, look very similar to individuals with AS, supporting the belief that the two disorders are one and the same. Indeed, recent research comparing groups of individuals with HFA and AS individuals have shown no significant differences between groups for current functioning, verbal language as a predictor of diagnosis, and motor functioning (Manjiviona & Prior, 1995; Mayes & Calhoun, 2001; Ozonoff, South, & Miller, 2000). Furthermore, individuals diagnosed with AS or HFA show the most discrepancies between each other in early childhood development, but can look very similar later in development (Ozonoff et al., 2000). Because these differences in functioning disappear by adolescence, the issue of which group has a better prognosis remains to be seen (Gilchrist et al., 2001; Howlin, 2003b; Ozonoff et al., 2000).

The actual differences between AS and HFA will remain unknown until the diagnostic criteria become more clear (Volkmar & Klin, 2000). As evidenced by the previously cited research studies, it is apparent that diverse samples and problems with the sampling procedures are confounding variables, leading to an inability to make any concrete conclusions about the differences between the two conditions at the time of this book's publication.

INTERVENTION

It is clear that intervention is important for individuals with AS, but it should be noted that social-communicative interventions are not meant to change the core personality of individuals or make these individuals conform to the standards of society (Klin & Volkmar, 2000). Indeed, the social model of disability contends that it is society that defines a disability, rather than the individual's physical or mental impairment, and this issue may be especially relevant for individuals with AS (Goodley, 2001; Molloy & Vasil, 2002). However, there are many detrimental effects for adolescents who experience rejection and failure with their peer group, including depression, anxiety, and negative self-evaluations (Egan & Perry, 1998; Ghaziuddin, Ghaziuddin, & Greden, 2002; Kim, Szatmari, Bryson, Streiner, & Wilson, 2000). Even though these negative effects may be caused in part by the values of an inflexible and rigid society, the fact remains that these adolescents continue to be socially isolated from their peer group. Effective interventions can provide adolescents with AS with strategies for enhancing their social lives, thereby promoting self-determination (Brown, Gothelf, Guess, & Lehr, 1998).

As the actual definition of *Asperger syndrome* is under intense debate, and because children with autism only relatively recently had the option of being included with their typically developing peers, few empirical studies have examined the effects of various types of interventions targeting this specific population of higher-functioning individuals. These interventions include computer-aided approaches, group approaches, and direct instruction techniques (Barnhill, Cook, Tebbenkamp, & Myles, 2002; Mishna & Muskat, 1998; Myles & Simpson, 2001; Silver & Oakes, 2001). However, there are many research studies looking at social-communicative interventions for individuals with a more classic diagnosis of autism or another disability. More research is necessary to assess whether these interventions would be effective for individuals with AS.

Social-communication interventions that have been used in past research and clinical practice for individuals with social difficulties include social stories, social scripts, social skills training groups, self-management programs, and peer-aided interventions (Breen, Haring, Pitts-Conway, & Gaylord-Ross, 1985; Broderick, Caswell, Gregory, Marzolini, & Wilson, 2002; Gray & Garand, 1993; Haring et al., 1987; L.K. Koegel, Koegel, Hurley, & Frea, 1992; R.L. Koegel & Koegel, 1990; Rogers & Myles, 2001). All of these interventions have been shown to have a positive effect on targeted social behaviors (Bledsoe, Myles, & Simpson, 2003; Breen et al., 1985; Broderick et al., 2002; R.L. Koegel & Frea, 1993). However, some of them, such as self-management techniques, are more appropriate for older and higher-functioning students.

Specifically, self-management is an ideal strategy because the intervention can be programmed to occur in the absence of an interventionist, thereby promoting independence on the part of the target individual. Developmentally speaking, adolescents—both those with and without disabilities—are in the midst of finding their own identity and becoming more independent from their parents or families (Tantam, 2003). In this way, self-management may appeal to adolescents because it emphasizes independence and self-control. Self-management has various applications (e.g., see

Chapter 15); the next section describes this procedure as it applies to improving empathetic responses among individuals with AS. For the purpose of this chapter, self-management techniques for children with HFA, who may have some difficulties with language structures, may require a few additional intervention components. Therefore, these techniques will be discussed and compared with those for individuals with AS whose structural language is intact.

Self-Management Intervention for Social Communication

A challenge in teaching social conversation to children or adolescents with autism is their lack or absence of empathic questions. That is, researchers have shown that the language functions of individuals with autism consist almost exclusively of requests and protests (Wetherby & Prutting, 1984). Other functions—such as information-seeking, bids for attention, and conversational initiations—may be used infrequently or not at all (L.K. Koegel, Camarata, Valdez-Menchaca, & Koegel, 1998b; Wetherby & Prutting, 1984). Thus, the challenges are twofold. First, the meaning of queries must be taught to children with autism. Second, the use of queries to maintain an ongoing interaction and to respond to a conversation must also be taught. For individuals with AS, the latter may only be necessary.

Research has found that teaching individuals with autism with mild to moderate impairments to self-manage social behaviors has resulted in collateral improvements in untreated social skills and generalized improvements in other pragmatic behaviors (L.K. Koegel et al., 1992; R.L. Koegel & Frea, 1993). In addition, this research suggested that in some cases, social behaviors involved with conversations might be part of a response class. Response classes represent topographically different behaviors that serve the same function for the individual. In other words, they are maintained by the same consequence (Carr, 1988; Sprague & Horner, 1994). That is, when one or more behaviors are treated, other behaviors within the same response class are expected to demonstrate a collateral change. Self-management has been developed as a procedure wherein an individual is taught to discriminate his or her own target behavior and then to record, or monitor, the occurrence of that target behavior. Self-management is designed to provide the individual with a technique that programs autonomy, independence, and the programmed occurrence of target behaviors in the absence of the interventionist's constant vigilance. These procedures, as well as generalized benefits in the area of pragmatics, are described in the next section of this chapter and in the case example.

General Procedures   Empathic responses can be taught to children and adults using self-management procedures. The general steps, described in L.K. Koegel, Koegel, and Parks (1992), are as follows:

1. Get ready

    a. Define behaviors

    b. Measure behaviors

    c.   Choose a reward

    d.   Select an initial goal

2.   Teach self-management

    a.   Gather materials

    b.   Identify the behavior

    c.   Record the behavior

    d.   Reward self-management

3.   Create independence

    a.   Increase the amount of time that the individual self-manages behavior

    b.   Fade the individual's reliance on prompts

    c.   Increase the number of responses necessary for a reward

    d.   Fade the presence of the treatment provider

4.   Teach self-management in additional settings

As noted in the preceding list, the first task is to prepare for the self-management. This requires developing a behavioral definition for the targeted behavior. For the intervention and research described in this chapter, the definition of an empathetic response is twofold. The individual has to look at *and* listen to the conversational partner and then make a verbal response or ask a related question. Prior to the start of intervention, a baseline is established to assess whether the response is in the student's repertoire and, if so, the frequency of the response. It is also necessary to assess which "wh-" questions the individual has in his or her repertoire. This is important for comparison as the individual's progress is tracked during intervention. In addition, rewards are determined, which can be given intermittently for appropriate empathetic response. The rewards that individuals choose range from receiving snacks or toys to going to the movies or a local coffee shop.

Once prepared, individuals are taught to self-manage their empathetic responses. Initially, they usually use wrist counters, (e.g., a golf counter available at a sports shop) that can record each response or a piece of paper with boxes for tally marks, initially. As they progress, it is possible to use time intervals, particularly with individuals who have AS. The intervention then differs for individuals who have AS and individuals who have autism because those with AS have more advanced language abilities. Thus, the programs are described separately.

Intervention for Individuals with AS   First, the goal of the intervention is explained to the person with AS: to have him or her listen to what the conversational partner says and then to respond with a statement or question showing interest in and/or concern about what the other person said. Based on preintervention observations, inappropriate behaviors are defined for each child. Specific inappropriate behaviors may include not responding to a conversational partner's questions, responding with an unrelated answer, leaving the area, and so forth. Other inappropriate behaviors may include physically turning from the conversation, demonstrating lack of eye contact, and so forth. The appropriate target behaviors of empathic responding within social conversations are the same for all participants (i.e., listening and then responding appropriately). Teaching self-management includes teaching the student to identify a behavior. The clinician models both the correct and incorrect responses for the individual. For example, the clinician says, "If I say 'I had a good weekend,' would a correct response be 'Do you have a Rolex watch?'?" These can be interspersed with correct target responses such as, "If I say, 'I had a good weekend,' would a correct response be 'What did you do over the weekend?'?"

Once the conversational partner can discriminate appropriate empathic responses on approximately 10 consecutive trials, he or she is asked to discriminate his or her own responses. For example, the clinician might say, "I had a huge lunch today," and the person with AS is asked to provide an appropriate response. If the individual responds with a reply such as, "What did you have for lunch?" he or she is given positive feedback and prompted to tally a point either on a piece of paper or a wrist counter. Likewise, the clinician asks for an inappropriate response to the same statement. If the individual responds, "Do you know what the exchange rate for the dollar is in China?" he or she is provided with positive feedback for appropriate discrimination. Again, at this stage, it is important to ensure that the person with AS understands the difference between appropriate and inappropriate responses. Next, the individual is ready to begin monitoring his or her own appropriate responses.

Generally, this process starts with individual responses. However, as the individual progresses and can accurately monitor a large number of responses, intervals are substituted so that the conversational flow is maintained. Specifically, the person with AS is given a preset countdown watch with an alarm that he or she uses to start and stop training intervals. At the end of the interval, the individual reports whether he or she displayed the appropriate communicative responses that were being taught. The individual marks a check on a preprinted form (or boxes for the tallies can simply be drawn on a piece of paper) if the communicative responses were appropriate during the interval. Once enough checks or "points" are gained, they are exchanged for one of the predetermined rewards chosen by the person with AS.

Intervention for Individuals with Autism Who Exhibit Language Difficulties   It should be noted individuals with autism generally have to be at least 5 years old, able to string a number of words together, and able to use a variety of grammatical structures (including the past tense) so the self-management intervention can be implemented. Unlike many people with AS, individuals with autism typically need some training on the use of grammatically correct appropriate questions. This is largely due to their language delays and lack of experience with social conversational discourse. For example, even after practice, many children with autism have difficulty using *did* and understanding that when the past tense of *do* is used, the verb reverts to the present. For example, they often ask, "Where did you went?" Although this particular question is likely to be understood by the conversational partner, it exemplifies the complexities of the English language and the challenges that individuals with language difficulties may experience. Furthermore, it is important to note that typical language developers learn to use these question forms properly through feedback from their parents and other adults. Only by using these forms regularly will individuals with autism be able to receive the necessary feedback to adjust their language accordingly. Also, some individuals with autism tend to repeat the same question. For example, if one says, "I saw a movie last night," a person with autism might reply, "What?" and then say, "What?" again if one followed up with, "I also had a snack at the theatre." With regular practice, however, most individuals with autism are able to generate appropriate and complete questions in response to conversational partners. Once they have some prompting and assistance, the previously described self-management steps can be followed.

Programming Self-Management in Additional Settings   Self-management programs for social conversation can be implemented in a number of settings. One advantage of self-management is its ease of generalization to other settings. Data from our center show that this program can be effective in generalized natural settings when it is implemented in a clinic room as well as in the individual's natural environment. That is, people who participate in this type of program are able to use self-management in natural settings such as school and home, even if the actual intervention did not take place in those settings.

Measurement   Several measures can be used to assess progress. The target behavior, which can be defined as any response relating to the conversational topic of the conversation partner, should be tracked. It is equally important to measure the overall appropriateness of the interaction. Finally, it is also necessary to measure the overall empathic reciprocity of the conversation. These elements are further described next.

Target Behavior   A 1-minute interval recording procedure or a score for each individual response can be used to measure the responses throughout baseline, intervention, and follow-up. Initially, individual responses will need to be scored, but as an individual progresses, time intervals can be recorded. Responses can be scored either as social-communicative responses relating to the conversation partner's conversational topic or an inappropriate/unrelated response. This data can provide a percentage of responses or intervals that are socially appropriate.

Appropriateness of Interaction Rating Scale   In addition to individual verbal responses, a subjective rating of appropriate conversational interaction can be scored. Generally, this is best accomplished by scoring representative videotaped segments (usually of at least 15 minutes) or by scoring an entire session by using a Likert-type scale to rate the participant's level of overall conversational interactions from 1 to 9, with 1 representing *very inappropriate interactions* and 9 representing *very appropriate interactions*.

Empathy Rating Scale   In addition, nonverbal empathic reciprocity can be scored prior to intervention, as well as during and after intervention. A good approach is to score randomly selected 15-minute videotape segments. Samples can be collected from each session, or if sessions are implemented frequently, probes can be collected periodically to assess progress. This measure also uses a Likert-type scale to rate the participant's level of empathic responses and overall nonverbal empathic reciprocity from 1 to 9, with 1 representing *very few empathic responses* and 9 representing *many empathic responses.*

Case Example

Jamie was a 20-year-old student at a local university who was majoring in mathematics. The top-scoring student in all of his classes, he had been diagnosed as having AS and had very little social interaction with other students. Jamie had been hospitalized three times for suicide attempts, and his mother reported that he rarely left his apartment and preferred to watch *Star Trek* movies during his free time. Jamie's mother contacted the clinic, but a staff member suggested that she give the clinic's contact information to Jamie so that he himself could arrange a visit if interested in intervention. Approximately a week later, Jamie e-mailed the clinic, expressing his interest in arranging a meeting. During the first visit, Jamie rarely made eye contact and only appeared interested in discussing *Star Trek* movies. Furthermore, his clothes were dirty, and he had not shaven or showered for several days. During this meeting, Jamie requested intervention and shared that he had no friends and experienced difficulty interacting with others his age.

Intervention began in a simulated living room area in the clinic. Initially, the clinician talked with Jamie about the importance of listening to another person and responding in a way that makes the other person believe that the listener is interested. Specifically, after demonstrating and discussing appropriate and inappropriate questions, clinicians began by making simple statements such as, "I saw a great movie last weekend," and suggesting that Jamie ask, "What did you see?" Other exercises included a clinician saying, "I went out of town over the weekend," and prompting Jamie to ask, "Where did you go?"

Within a few sessions, Jamie was able to respond appropriately to most questions. Another area of practice was having Jamie ask a relevant question while using appropriate eye contact. Once Jamie was able to discriminate the appropriate response, he began to monitor the responses using a golf counter that he discretely held in his hand.

Jamie rapidly learned to respond with interest to his clinician, and after a few months, he was able to do so for the entire hour of his session. However, he still had difficulty responding socially with unfamiliar people or to other college students. Thus, the next step was to systematically include unfamiliar college students in his interventions sessions. In order to do this systematically, the sessions were prearranged so that a college student would make statements similar to those practiced in previous sessions. For example, the student might say, "I'm taking such a difficult course this quarter," then pause so that Jamie could ask, "What class are you taking?" After each session, Jamie and his clinician discussed the conversation. After four sessions with unfamiliar college students, Jamie began to interact with new people more easily. At that point, his clinician also worked with him on initiations so that he could start a conversation if one was not ongoing. Jamie was given a variety of suggestions for simple conversation starters, such as asking about conversational partners' interests; bringing up sports; or asking conversational partners where they were from, what classes they were taking, what they were majoring in, or which interesting movies they had seen.

Within 3 months, Jamie was able to respond appropriately in social conversations greater than 80% of the time. In addition, his pragmatic scores and empathy were rated as *very appropriate*. In addition, Jamie began to shave, shower, and wear different outfits (these behaviors were not specifically targeted). Although he continued to show an interest in *Star Trek* movies, he no longer talked exclusively about this topic. Furthermore, he joined two campus clubs and began socializing more with other college students, particularly a woman who lived in his apartment building.

Jamie was a pleasure to work with, and intervention was facilitated by the fact that he was grateful for the assistance and strongly desired to learn how to socialize more effectively. The intervention assisted Jamie with learning how to engage in more reciprocal and empathetic conversations with his peers, which proved to be critical in developing friendships.

DISCUSSION OF CHAPTER CONCEPTS

For individuals with ASDs who have higher cognitive abilities and poor social functioning, the literature related to long-term outcomes is limited at the time of this book's publication. Indeed, the research shows mixed results depending on the life domain being examined. For example, individuals with AS often have good academic outcomes and average intelligence levels (Gillberg, 1991; Howlin, 2003b). However, they also report having few close friends and few romantic relationships or marriages (Engstrom, Ekstrom, & Emilsson, 2003; Orsmond, Krauss, & Seltzer, 2004; Venter, Lord, & Schopler, 1992). In regard to job satisfaction, adults with AS are often unemployed or do menial work that is beneath their true skills (Howlin, 2003a). These low levels of professional achievement may be a reflection of the difficulty that these individuals have in navigating the social subtleties of job interviews or social situations in the workplace and other community settings. Therefore, it is critical that they receive intervention for improving socialization.

The goal of the self-management is to teach independent responding, to improve the social interactions of individuals with ASDs, and to improve overall long-term prognoses. Self-management has been defined as a pivotal behavior, because when a person can self-regulate his or her behaviors, a number of other positive changes occur. In relation to social pragmatics, treated and untreated behaviors improve to more appropriate levels without the need for constant direct clinician intervention. This is consistent with previous research showing collateral or generalized changes across untreated behaviors when self-management was employed as a pivotal behavior to facilitate generalized broad improvements in individuals with autism (R.L. Koegel & Frea, 1993; R.L. Koegel, Koegel & Carter, 1999; Sprague & Horner, 1992). In summary, the overarching goal of PRT is to teach behaviors that normalize interactions with others. In addition, as discussed throughout this book, PRT is designed to be implemented in the natural environment. Self-management meets both of these goals.

This finding suggests that other response classes of behavior, especially social-communicative behaviors, may lend themselves to intervention as a group of related behaviors rather than as discrete, individual behaviors. This is also supported by previous research in the area of self-management (L.K. Koegel et al., 1992; R.L. Koegel & Frea, 1993; R.L. Koegel, Koegel, & Surratt, 1992) showing that this type of intervention may lead to increased independence. Furthermore, the act of self-management may naturally and inherently lend itself to generalization to untreated behaviors and to other settings and environments.

DIRECTIONS FOR FUTURE RESEARCH

As noted previously in this chapter, more research about defining characteristics of the subtypes of ASDs is warranted. A lack of clear definitions may be responsible for differential findings in studies such as IQ measures. More specific definitions may also help in better understanding areas of the brain that may be affected.

For addition, more research in the area of social behavior and empathy in children with AS and autism is necessary to better understand the both defining and intervening in this area, as well as to help improve inclusion for these individuals. It is important for individuals with AS as well as ASDs to have successful conversational interactions, which may be a first step toward social acceptance and the formation of meaningful relationships with others. Too frequently, less emphasis is placed on social relationships than on academic or functional skills, which may have long-term negative consequences for individuals with ASDs. More research involving the process of friendship development, techniques to improve social interaction, and interpersonal acceptance—regardless of ability level—is long overdue.

Combining Functional Assessment and Self-Management Procedures to Rapidly Reduce Disruptive Behaviors

Lynn Kern Koegel, Robert L. Koegel, Mendy A. Boettcher, Joshua Harrower, and Daniel Openden

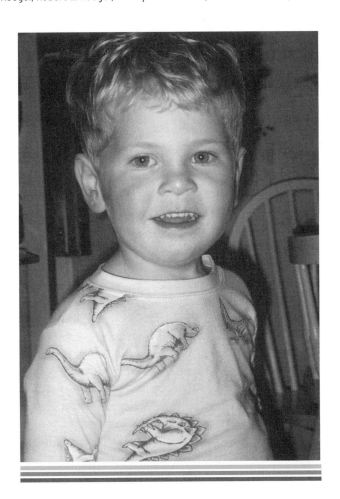

Many children with autism exhibit disruptive behaviors. Procedures such as teaching functionally equivalent replacement behaviors and self-management are frequently cited in the literature as effective in reducing these behaviors. This chapter describes how these two procedures can be effectively combined into a multicomponent treatment package to produce rapid reduction of problem behaviors and acquisition of fluent appropriate replacement behaviors. In addition, the chapter discusses how the use of these combined procedures can result in long-term maintenance of behavioral changes. Specifically, disruptive behavior quickly decreases when a self-management intervention is introduced. Simultaneously, it is critical that appropriate replacement behaviors be taught to facilitate long-term maintenance of behavioral improvements. Such multicomponent programs are critical for inclusive settings, in which immediate reduction of problem behaviors are necessary to maintain a placement in the least restrictive environment and fluent, sometimes complex, functionally equivalent replacement behaviors are crucial for long-term elimination of behavior problems.

BACKGROUND

Challenging behaviors, such as aggression and self-injury, cause great social concern and generally predict a very poor future. These behaviors rapidly lead to more restrictive school placements and typically limit the amount of time a student can enjoy inclusive community settings and activities. A number of technologies have been researched that beneficially affect the life quality among people with challenging behaviors, and a multicomponent intervention is recommended within a positive behavior support plan (Reid, 2000).

Functional assessment and self-management are two procedures that have been shown to be very effective in reducing challenging behaviors and increasing appropriate behaviors. Functional assessment, which is the process of identifying why problem behaviors occur and replacing these behaviors with functionally equivalent alternative replacement procedures (Durand & Carr, 1991, 1992; Horner & Carr, 1997; Horner et al., 1990; O'Neill, Horner, Albin, Storey, & Sprague, 1990; Sprague & Horner, 1995; Vaughn, Clarke, & Dunlap, 1997), has resulted in effective interventions that are likely to generalize over time, settings, and people. Epidemiological studies suggest that as many as 75%–80% of problem behaviors may have a communicative function (Derby et al., 1992; Iwata, Dorsey, Slifer, Bauman, & Richman, 1994); therefore, changes in behavior that occur when antecedent stimuli are addressed and functionally equivalent behaviors are taught can be quite dramatic (Wacker et al., 1998). However, the acquisition of a functionally equivalent replacement behavior and the decrease of behavior problems is less well understood and may vary across children. This may be due to a number of variables, such as how well established the problem behavior is, the efficiency of the problem and replacement behaviors, reinforcement schedules, the child's ability to tolerate a delay, and other environmental variables (L.K. Koegel, 2000). However, for most children, there will be a time period before the functionally equivalent replacement behavior is learned and used fluently and independently. This can be true especially for complex replacement behaviors such as fluent conversation. During this time, challenging behaviors are likely to continue to occur.

Self-management, which was introduced in Chapter 13 as an intervention for improving social communication, has been shown to be effective in reducing challenging behaviors. *Self-management* generally refers to a procedure in which people are taught to discriminate their own target behavior and record the occurrence or absence of that target behavior. Self-monitoring has been described as reactive (i.e., produces behavior change), and often this behavior change is seen immediately after implementation. Researchers have demonstrated that self-management can be an effective procedure, producing immediate decreases in disruptive and off-task behavior (L.K. Koegel, Harrower, & Koegel, 1999; R.L. Koegel & Koegel, 1990). Self-management does not address, however, the reasons why the behavior occurred, as does functional assessment.

Again, with the emphasis in the literature on broad quality of life changes, as opposed to laboratory demonstration of control of behavioral variables (Carr et al., 1999; Dunlap, Kern-Dunlap, Clarke, & Robbins, 1991), combined interventions are being sited as preferable to single interventions (Carr et al., 2002; Horner & Carr, 1997; L.K. Koegel, Koegel, Harrower, & Carter, 1999). Therefore, this chapter's specific purpose is to describe the use of functional assessment combined with self-management to reduce challenging behaviors and increase appropriate behaviors. These two procedures were chosen for several reasons. First, some complex functionally equivalent behaviors may not always be reinforced in the natural environment, especially when first being exhibited by the child. This can be especially problematic when disruptive behaviors continue to be reinforced in the natural environment. In addition, it may take time to teach replacement behaviors, and it may take even longer for them to actually result in the reduction of the problem behavior, as the problem behavior may remain more effective until the replacement behavior is efficient and being naturally reinforced. Thus, the self-management procedures can provide immediate reinforcement following a display of appropriate behavior; this strategy produces an immediate reduction in challenging behavior while replacement behavior is being taught to increase the likelihood of long-term durability.

INTERVENTION

Intervention targeting these areas consists of a two-phase treatment package; the following two subsections detail each.

Phase I: Self-Management

Self-management is a positive behavior support strategy. This strategy is used as an intermediary step to reduce problem behaviors while the functionally equivalent behaviors are being taught (Phase II). The specific self-management steps are detailed in Chapter 13. For this particular program, the children's targeted disruptive behaviors are defined. Then, preintervention baseline measurements are established. This can be accomplished either by taking videotapes of a child or collecting on-line (in vivo) data. Next, based on the preintervention data, intervals are selected that are a shorter time period than the intervals between disruptive behaviors. In other words, for the child's first intervals to be successful, it is necessary to begin with time intervals that are short enough for the child to experience success. Next, child-selected reinforcers are gathered that are provided as rewards for the child's successful intervals. Following these preparatory steps, the child is taught to self-manage. Initially, the child is taught to discriminate between the desired and undesired behaviors. After the child can identify appropriate and inappropriate behaviors, he or she is taught to tally intervals with appropriate behavior. Once the child is able to discriminate and monitor his or her behavior, steps to create independence are instated. Intervals are lengthened and added before a reward is provided. For example, a child with more frequent behavior challenges may begin with intervals of a few seconds, which are gradually increased to 10–15 minutes. Another child may be able to begin with intervals of several minutes, which can be gradually and systematically increased to a whole class period or even a whole day. In addition, the interventionist's prompts are faded so that the child is monitoring without the adult vigilance. Finally, the self-management is programmed to occur in other settings without the presence of the interventionist. Specifically, the monitoring devices (e.g., a wrist counter, a piece of paper with boxes for tallying, a repeat chronographic alarm watch) are sent with the child into additional settings, and the child is instructed to use the procedures in those settings. Regular validation checks are implemented in those settings (these do not have to be done by an interventionist) to ensure that the child is actually monitoring and exhibiting the target behaviors in those settings.

Phase II: Replacement Behaviors

Phase II consists of teaching the child to use functionally equivalent replacement behaviors. The first step of the functional assessment is to define the disruptive behaviors. Next, a baseline of the child's behaviors is established. As can be seen by the chart in Figure 14.1, the disruptive behavior is listed first, as well as the time and place where it occurred. Next, the chart contains a number of boxes so the clinician can check what happened before and what happened after the disruptive behavior. Finally, the clinician then hypothesizes why the disruptive behavior occurred. This step is critical to the process, as functionally equivalent replacement behaviors are developed based on the function of the behavior. Appropriate behaviors are specifically chosen to replace the problem behaviors, even though they are reduced using self-management procedures in Phase I. Replacement behaviors are important because they address the child's need for appropriate ways to communicate and improve the likelihood of long-term maintenance of reduced problem behaviors. The functional replacement behaviors are determined based on the functional assessment performed during baseline data collection. The functionally equivalent replacement behaviors are word phrases designed to serve the same purpose as the disruptive behavior noted during the preintervention assessments. The following section presents a more detailed explanation of the measures that can be used.

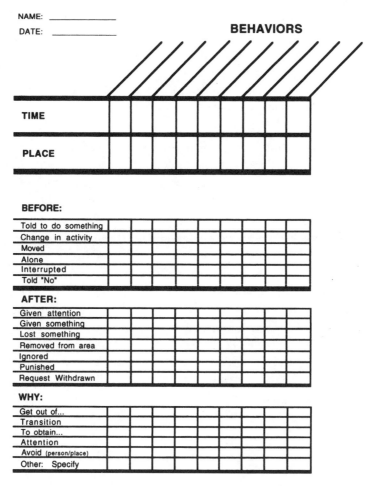

NAME: _____

DATE: _____

BEHAVIORS

TIME

PLACE

BEFORE:

| Told to do something |
| Change in activity |
| Moved |
| Alone |
| Interrupted |
| Told "No" |

AFTER:

| Given attention |
| Given something |
| Lost something |
| Removed from area |
| Ignored |
| Punished |
| Request Withdrawn |

WHY:

| Get out of... |
| Transition |
| To obtain... |
| Attention |
| Avoid (person/place) |
| Other: Specify |

Figure 14.1.   Sample functional assessment form. (From Koegel, L.K., Koegel, R.L., Kellegrew, D., & Mullen, K. [1996]. Parent education for prevention and reduction of severe problem behaviors. In L.K. Koegel, R.L. Koegel, & G. Dunlap [Eds.], *Positive behavioral support: Including people with difficult behavior in the community* [p. 13]. Baltimore: Paul H. Brookes Publishing Co.; reprinted by permission.)

Measures

Preintervention Measures   As always, prior to starting intervention it is important to collect data on a child's problem behaviors to assess whether an intervention is having the desired positive effect. It is helpful to collect these measures during typical daily activities. Data can be collected by anyone interacting with the child, such as the child's parent, teacher, or aide or a specialist who works with the child. In order to make consistency of recording more likely, a specific behavioral definition needs to be written for the child (see the example provided in the "Case Examples" section of this chapter). Once a clear definition is written, data collection can begin. The following measures are suggested.

Occurrence of Disruptive Behavior   The occurrences of disruptive behaviors can be counted during specific time periods, or the child can be videotaped (with the parents' permission) and the tapes can be analyzed later. The data on disruptive behavior can be collected in several ways. A frequency recording system, wherein each disruptive behavior is tallied, can be collected for a specified time period. If the child has lengthy tantrums, it may be easier to measure the duration of the behavior during designated time periods (e.g., recess, a 15-minute session, a class period).

Functional Assessment   Functional assessment of each disruptive behavioral incident can be recorded. These data are later used to determine appropriate functionally equivalent behaviors to teach in place of the inappropriate behaviors. As discussed previously, the problem behavior, the time it occurred, and setting where it occurred are recorded on the top of a form like the one shown in Figure 14.1. Next, what happened before and after the behavior and the likely function of the behavior are recorded in the box. Based on this data, an alternate appropriate behavior, which has the same function as the inappropriate behavior, can be taught.

Occurrence of Replacement Behaviors   Throughout the preintervention, intervention, and follow-up stages, it is important to collect data on the child's use of the replacement behavior. Long-term maintenance of problem-free behavior depends on the child's use of functionally equivalent behaviors. Each appropriate use of the replacement behavior can be recorded either throughout the day or during specified time periods. Data can be collected during baseline and throughout intervention and periodically after intervention is complete.

Case Examples

This chapter uses extended case examples to present a study that used the two-phase intervention program.

History and Data Collection   Kurt's and Trevor's families sought intervention for challenging behaviors. Each boy had received a diagnosis of autism from a licensed psychologist at a center for children with developmental disabilities; the diagnosis was made according to the criteria specified in the *Diagnostic and Statistical Manual for Mental Disorders* (DSM-IV-TR; American Psychiatric Association, 2000). According to parent, teacher, and child care provider report, both children had a documented history of behavior problems for at least 1 year across a variety of settings.

Data were collected in the children's regular intervention (special education pull-out programs), play, and educational settings. At baseline, other than verbal reprimands and time-out, no systematic interventions were in place for disruptive behaviors.

Trevor   Trevor was 5 years, 6 months when his school district called the clinic to intervene for his aggression. He was diagnosed with autism and demonstrated a language delay, although he was capable of combining up to five words to produce syntactically correct phrases. His vocabulary was in the ninth percentile, and his Language and Socialization scores on the Vineland Adaptive Behavior Scales (Sparrow, Balla, & Cicchetti, 1984) were below age level by 1 and 3 years, respectively. Trevor participated in a full-inclusion kindergarten classroom 5 days per week without an aide. He received speech and occupational therapy on a weekly basis in this setting. In addition to his delays, Trevor showed a lack of social initiations and difficulty with reciprocal social interaction in all settings as observed by the school psychologist, the clinicians, his speech-language specialist, and his teacher.

Trevor's overall challenging behaviors included frequently crashing tricycles into other children and their tricycles; bumping into other children with his shoulder; and poking and pushing other children while on the playground, while waiting in line, and during academic activities. Other aggressive behaviors at school included spitting at, hitting, and kicking other children. He also frequently engaged in inappropriate physical contact with his peers, such as excessive and inappropriate hugging and touching. Trevor's disruptive behaviors at school were so severe that he was at risk of being removed from this inclusive placement. At home, Trevor also engaged in frequent tantrums and noncompliance.

To start, data were collected in a variety of settings at Trevor's school. Academic conditions included activities such as cutting, coloring, identifying letters and numbers, listening to stories, and participating in group activities. Recess took place on a playground with both blacktop and grassy areas, and a variety of activities were available, such as sports, climbing equipment, bikes, slides, and swings. Again, other than verbal reprimands and time-out, no systematic interventions were in place for disruptive behaviors in these settings. These activities remained fairly stable throughout the school year.

For the purposes of data collection, disruptive behaviors were defined as instances of inappropriate contact with another child and aggressive behavior. Inappropriate contact was defined as any contact with another child (e.g., hugging, pushing). Generally, these behaviors caused an interruption of the other child's activity and drew attention (verbal or visual) away from the ongoing activity and toward Trevor. Each incident producing an interruption was recorded as a discrete event.

During the baseline time period, functional assessment procedures were implemented to determine functions of Trevor's disruptive behaviors at school. Each disruptive behavior recorded during baseline probes was analyzed for function according to the procedures in the manual *Understanding Why Problem Behaviors Occur: A Guide for Assisting Parents in Assessing Causes of Behavior and Designing Treatment Plans* (Frea, Koegel, & Koegel, 1994). The checklist shown in Figure 14.1 was used to record antecedents, behaviors, and consequences, as well as time and setting. These data were then used as the basis for forming hypotheses about functions of the disruptive behaviors. Functionally equivalent replacement behaviors, taught in Phase II of the intervention, were determined based on the hypotheses derived from these functional assessment procedures.

For Trevor, 93% of behaviors observed during baseline served the function of obtaining attention from or initiating social interactions with peers. Based on these data, appropriate replacement behaviors were developed that would allow Trevor to seek attention or initiate socially with his peers. After collecting this preintervention data, intervention began.

One initial self-management teaching session was conducted in the clinic for 1 hour. This setting consisted of a clinic room, which contained a table, several chairs, and various toys. All subsequent sessions were then conducted at Trevor's school, either in his classroom or during recess. Recess was targeted for the implementation of the intervention procedures, as most of his severe behavior problems occurred during that time. Functionally equivalent replacement behaviors were initially taught during one-to-one speech-therapy sessions in the school's small speech-therapy room, which contained a table and chairs. Following initial acquisition of the replacement behaviors in the one-to-one setting, Trevor's speech-language specialist conducted several sessions in the natural environment (i.e., during recess).

Kurt   Kurt was 5 years, 4 months at the start of intervention. Kurt initially participated in a community preschool without an aide but was asked to leave the preschool due to behavior problems. His parents subsequently enrolled him in another community preschool, where he was later assigned an aide because of his disruptive behavior. Kurt received weekly speech and occupational therapy in the preschool setting. The public school aide had no experience in developing or implementing a positive behavior support plan; therefore, despite frequent reprimands and time-outs, behavior problems were not decreasing.

Communicatively, Kurt demonstrated cognitive and language delays, although he was capable of syntactically correct phrases of up to three to four words. His scores on the Expressive One-Word Picture Vocabulary Test–Revised (Brownell, 2000) were in the 50th percentile, and he was unable to reach a basal on the Differential Abilities Scale (Elliot, 1990) due to motivation and attention difficulties. Kurt showed a lack of social initiations and age-appropriate reciprocal social interaction based on the data of trained observers such as his inclusion specialist, clinicians from the autism center, the school's speech-language specialist, and his teachers. Kurt's overall behavior problems, which were consistently exhibited across a variety of settings (e.g., clinic, home, school, community), included frequent yelling and inappropriate statements such as, "I hate this" and "You're stupid." Kurt's aggressive behaviors included hitting, kicking, and throwing toys at others. He also engaged in several daily temper tantrums that lasted 5–60 minutes and included crying, screaming, inappropriate verbal statements, hitting, kicking, and throwing objects. For the purposes of this study, only Kurt's yelling and inappropriate statements were targeted, as they were the most frequently displayed behaviors in the targeted setting and were often precursors to more severe behaviors.

The self-management procedures were taught and implemented in a living room setting for Kurt. The environment contained a variety of toys and games purchased from a local toy store. Kurt's parents interacted and played with him during these sessions, which lasted for an hour each and took place once per week.

Treatment Package Phase I: Self-Management   For both children, the self-management procedures were initially taught by a graduate student clinician and were eventually implemented by parents or teachers. Self-management procedures were taught according to the procedures in *How to Teach Self-Management to People with Severe Disabilities: A Training Manual* (L.K. Koegel, Koegel, & Parks, 1992). First, Trevor and Kurt were taught to recognize the target disruptive behaviors and correctly identify them. They were then taught to use a behavior recording chart (a small sheet of paper with boxes for tallying) and practiced identifying and accurately recording their own behaviors with feedback from the clinician. The children were then taught to perform these procedures when cued by a watch or timer rather than an adult. Finally, the children were taught to determine at specified times whether they had earned a reward for appropriate behavior. Once the each child was proficient at managing his own behavior, the adult implementing the intervention (i.e., clinician, parent, or teacher) faded his or her presence until the child was independently evaluating and recording his own behavior.

Over the course of intervention, both children's self-management intervals were gradually faded such that the children were managing their behavior with decreasing reliance on the intervention. Initially, Kurt was expected to self-manage his behavior for a very short period of time, such as 1–2 minutes, in order to receive a reward. Over the course of intervention, the length of these intervals was systematically increased. Specifically, if Kurt was successful in managing his behavior for 80% of intervals over the course of an entire session, the length of the intervals was increased by 1–2 minutes starting in the next session. This process continued until session probe number 18 (see Figure 14.2), at which point Kurt was only managing his behavior a couple of times during an entire session, depending on the length of the session (i.e., he was rarely observed engaging in self-management recording procedures during observation probes, which were shorter than his self-management intervals).

Initially, Trevor was expected to self-manage his behavior for short intervals as well (i.e., 5 minutes). These intervals were rapidly increased over the course of his

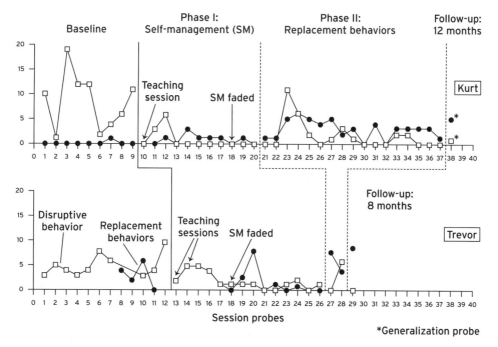

Figure 14.2. Frequency of disruptive and replacement behaviors across intervention.

school sessions to 30 minutes, based on the same criterion of 80% appropriate behavior. Using this same system of systematically increasing the length of the intervals, Trevor's intervals were increased until he was only required to record his behavior occasionally throughout the school day (i.e., a maximum of three times per day). Intervention continued in this manner until session probe number 17, when it became apparent that Trevor no longer required shorter intervals during the school day to maintain appropriate behavior. From this point forward, self-management was continued on a once-daily basis only, wherein Trevor was provided with a special treat at the end of each day if his behavior was appropriate for the entire day (see Figure 14.2). From this point forward, Trevor only evaluated his behavior once per day upon leaving school with his parents.

Treatment Package Phase II: Replacement Behaviors   The second part of the intervention package involved teaching the child the functionally equivalent replacement behaviors in conjunction with the ongoing self-management. The baseline data suggested that each child's disruptive behaviors primarily served the functions of trying to get help with a difficult task (Kurt) or to seek attention (Trevor). Therefore, Kurt was taught to ask for help when frustrated, and Trevor was taught appropriate phrases to initiate social interaction and seek attention. Although these phrases were relatively easy for the children to learn to say, it was more difficult to teach them to spontaneously use the behaviors when the need arose. Therefore, this phase of the treatment package targeted both initial acquisition of the phrases and spontaneous use of these phrases in natural contexts.

Kurt was taught appropriate phrases to seek help or ask for a break in frustrating situations, such as, "I need help," "Let's take a break," or "It's too hard." These phrases were taught and prompted during sessions until Kurt used them independently across a variety of activities and toys during his interactions with his parents. He continued to use his self-management program, as previously discussed, to maintain the decreases in his disruptive behavior during Phase II of intervention.

Trevor was prompted to use appropriate replacement phrases to seek attention from his peers, such as, "What are you doing?" and "Let's go play!" He was first taught these phrases in a one-to-one setting with his speech-language specialist at school. After several teaching sessions in her office, she implemented twice-weekly sessions during recess, wherein she prompted Trevor to use the phrases with his peers until he was using them spontaneously to seek attention. The total number of sessions in the natural environment was fewer than five over the course of approximately 2 weeks. Trevor then continued to receive self-management reinforcement from his parents at the end of the school day (as previously discussed) for appropriate behavior (i.e., self-management remained faded to the length of school day while he learned replacement behaviors).

Findings   A nonconcurrent multiple baseline design across participants (Barlow & Hersen, 1984) was employed with the two children across baseline and the two phases of intervention. The design gave the ability to control for history and maturation (Barlow & Hersen, 1984). Specifically, because intervention was started at different points in time after stable periods of the disruptive behaviors, the likelihood that maturation or other environmental variables (rather than the intervention) caused the effect was reduced or eliminated. Baseline probes were gathered over 9 sessions for Kurt and over 12 sessions for Trevor. Following baseline, probes continued to be gathered during Phases I and II. Self-management intervention probes were gathered over 11 sessions for Kurt and 14 sessions for Trevor. Replacement behavior intervention probes were gathered over 17 sessions for Kurt and 2 sessions for Trevor. A follow-up condition without any intervention was then conducted approximately 12 and 8 months, for Kurt and Trevor respectively, after intervention was terminated for each child. Follow-up consisted of 1 probe for each child.

Disruptive Behavior   Figure 14.2 shows the frequency of disruptive behaviors and appropriate replacement behaviors in a probe over the course of baseline and both phases of intervention for Kurt and Trevor. In the figure, open squares display the frequency of disruptive behaviors. Disruptive behaviors occurred frequently for both children during baseline, then were reduced to low levels during Phase I and remained low (with one exception for each child) during Phase II, as well as at follow-up.

Kurt   During baseline, disruptive behaviors occurred during all sessions for Kurt, with more than half of the probes containing 11 or more incidents (range: 11–19 for those probes). That is, Kurt had at least one disruptive incident and as many as 19 disruptive incidents during each 10-minute probe. Although Kurt's behavior during baseline was somewhat variable, there was no decreasing trend in the data. During Phase I, the frequency of disruptive behaviors decreased substantially (range: 0–6), with the last 8 probes in the phase (of 11 total probes) containing no disruptive behavior. During Phase II, the frequency of Kurt's disruptive behaviors remained low, with all but 2 probes containing less than three incidents of disruptive behavior (range: 0–3 for those probes). Finally, the frequency of disruptive behaviors for Kurt remained low at 12-month follow-up, with no incidents during the probe.

Trevor   During baseline, disruptive behaviors occurred during all probes for Trevor (range: 3–10 incidents). Trevor's behavior during baseline was somewhat variable; however, there was no decreasing trend in the data. In fact, there was a slight increasing trend. During Phase I, the frequency of disruptive behaviors decreased substantially (range: 0–5), with the last 10 probes typically at 1 or 0. During Phase II, the frequency of disruptive behaviors for Trevor remained at 0 during the first probe and increased in the second. The behaviors in this probe consisted of low-intensity incidents of nonaggressive contact; however, in a situation when Trevor was in close proximity to a large number of children (i.e., a crowd), Trevor demonstrated no disruptive behavior during the 8-month follow-up probe.

Appropriate Replacement Behaviors   The closed circles in Figure 14.2 show the frequency of appropriate replacement behaviors for both children across baseline, across both phases of treatment, and at follow-up. Appropriate replacement behaviors occurred with low frequency during baseline and Phase I, when only disruptive behaviors were being targeted. During Phase II, when appropriate replacement behaviors were taught, the frequency of the functionally equivalent behaviors increased substantially, and these treatment gains maintained at follow-up.

Kurt   Appropriate replacement behaviors occurred with low frequency during baseline (range: 0–1) and Phase I (range: 0–3) for Kurt. During Phase II, the frequency of appropriate replacement behaviors increased. All probes (except two) contained replacement behaviors, and the majority contained between 3 and 6 appropriate replacement behaviors. The frequency of appropriate replacement behaviors was maintained at 12-month follow-up for Kurt, with three appropriate replacement behaviors in the probe.

Trevor   Appropriate replacement behaviors for Trevor occurred with low frequency during baseline (range: 0–6). During Phase I, the frequency of these behaviors remained low, with all but 1 probe containing 0 to 2 appropriate replacement behaviors. During Phase II, the frequency of appropriate replacement behaviors increased. That is, probes contained replacement behaviors (range: 4–8). In addition, the frequency of appropriate replacement behaviors was maintained at the 8-month follow-up for Trevor, with 9 appropriate replacement behaviors in the probe.

Overall, Figure 14.2 shows that disruptive behaviors were reduced for both children during Phase I and were maintained at a low frequency during Phase II. In addition, these treatment gains were maintained at follow-up for both children. Furthermore, the frequency of appropriate replacement behaviors remained low or variable, but none occurred during many of the probes until training specific to replacement behaviors was implemented. At the end of intervention, disruptive behaviors remained low and appropriate replacement behaviors continued to be used by both children, with treatment gains appearing to maintain at follow-up.

Follow-Up   A follow-up data point was taken for each participant at 12 and 8 months postintervention. No intervention procedures were being implemented during these probes. For Kurt, all intervention procedures were faded when his sessions began occurring in a home-based, rather than the clinic-based, living room setting. At this point, Kurt no longer required the self-management intervention, and he needed only occasional reminders to use his functionally equivalent phrases at home. His 12-month follow-up data point was taken in the home, during interactions with his parents that were analogous to those that occurred in the previous sessions. No intervention procedures were used during this follow-up probe. For Trevor, intervention procedures were completely faded when the school year ended, and another one began without the presence of these procedures. Trevor's follow-up data point was taken approximately halfway through the following school year. No intervention procedures were used during this follow-up probe.

DISCUSSION OF CHAPTER CONCEPTS

The findings discussed in this chapter are consistent with the literature, which suggests that multicomponent interventions may be important to consider for reducing disruptive behaviors (Carr & Carlson, 1993; Kemp & Carr, 1995). To summarize the results presented in this chapter, self-management is an effective method to rapidly reduce the problem behaviors. Furthermore, teaching functionally equivalent behaviors provides children with an effective replacement for their disruptive behaviors, which may be important for long-term reductions of problem behaviors. As can be seen with the case examples, these treatment gains maintain across time when self-management is faded. It is likely that self-management more quickly reduces problem behaviors than replacement behavior training alone, as replacement behaviors may not be as efficient as problem behaviors until a high level of mastery or fluency is achieved (Horner & Day, 1991). The data from the chapter's case examples demonstrate that the participants were using few or no functionally equivalent replacement behaviors that served the same function as their disruptive behavior until teaching specific to these behaviors occurred. Overall, at the end of intervention, disruptive behaviors remained low and appropriate replacement behaviors continued to be used by both children, with treatment gains maintaining at follow-up.

DIRECTIONS FOR FUTURE RESEARCH

Literature in the area of self-management has shown that behavior change is typically rapid once intervention has been implemented (L.K. Koegel, Harrower, & Koegel, 1999; R.L. Koegel & Koegel, 1990). However, although self-management is an efficient intervention for quickly reducing problem behavior, it may be best used within the multicomponent treatment package for children with disruptive behaviors whose placements are at stake. Many studies that use self-management in isolation do not demonstrate durable long-term changes in behavior once self-management is faded (Gregory, Kehle, & McLoughlin, 1997; R.L. Koegel & Koegel, 1990; Ninness, Fuerst, Rutherford, & Glenn, 1991). The combination of self-management and teaching functionally equivalent communicative responses extends the literature in this area by demonstrating the effects of the multicomponent treatment on long-term durable behavior change (8–12 months).

Previous research also supports the notion that functional assessment is an important component of effective interventions, especially if treatment gains are to maintain over time. Furthermore, research in this area has demonstrated that if reductions in disruptive behavior are to occur as a function of teaching replacement behaviors, then the appropriate replacement responses must be equally or more efficient in securing reinforcement than the disruptive behavior (Horner & Day, 1991). The findings presented in this chapter demonstrate that reductions in problem behaviors, as well as increased use of functionally equivalent replacement behaviors, maintained over time after the self-management intervention was faded. These findings, together with previous research in this area, support the notion that self-management (the mechanism for initially reducing problem behavior in this case) in conjunction with an appropriate replacement behavior, could effectively decrease disruptive behavior and increase appropriate behavior over an extended period of time. Consistent with Horner and Day's findings, without the self-management, these relatively inefficient replacement behaviors may not have produced rapid changes. These ideas are also consistent with the literature on self-control and self-management for other populations as well. Baldwin and Baldwin noted that some behaviors require extensive self-control to gain significantly delayed reinforcement, which can help people "reach positive goals that enrich . . . [their] lives and make . . . [them] happier" (2001, p. 360).

Similarly, delayed reinforcement may also occur for behaviors that are on a thin schedule of reinforcement or are relatively inefficient, such as many socially appropriate behaviors. In these cases, teaching self-management to individuals with disabilities might be analogous to the self-control that most people demonstrate in sustaining appropriate responding over long periods of time to secure some types of delayed reinforcers. This responding typically involves complex behaviors, which may take time to teach. The results of this study may have addressed this issue, in that self-management may have provided intermediary reinforcement while complex, more efficient appropriate replacement behaviors were being learned. More research on the specific mechanisms that made these combined procedures effective is warranted.

In summary, this multicomponent intervention appeared to be an effective way to quickly reduce problem behaviors while teaching appropriate replacement behaviors to ensure long-term maintenance of the behavioral improvements. This multicomponent intervention addressed not only a method for efficiently reducing the problem behaviors but also taught the replacement behaviors that could be used to address the same behavioral functions and maintain treatment gains over time, leading to the participants' ability to function appropriately in inclusive settings. More research relating to the most effective multicomponent intervention plans may help children with autism and behavior issues make more rapid gains.

References

Adamson, L.B. (1995). *Communication development in infancy.* Madison, WI: Brown & Benchmark.

Adrien, J.L., Faure, M., Perrot, A., & Hameury, L. (1991). Autism and family home movies: Preliminary findings. *Journal of Autism and Developmental Disorders, 21*(1), 43–49.

Ainbinder, J.G., Blanchard, L.W., Singer, G.H.S., Sullivan, M.E., Powers, L., Marquis J., & Santelli, B. (1998). A qualitative study of Parent-to-Parent support for parents of children with special needs. *Journal of Pediatric Psychology, 23*, 99–109.

Aird, R. (2000). The case for specialist training for learning support assistants employed in schools for children with severe, profound and multiple learning difficulties. *Support for Learning, 15*(3), 106–110.

Albanese, A.L., San-Miguel, A.K., & Koegel, R.L. (1995). Social support for families. In R.L. Koegel & L.K. Koegel (Eds.), *Teaching children with autism: Strategies for initiating positive interactions and improving learning opportunities* (pp. 95–104). Baltimore: Paul H. Brookes Publishing Co.

Albin, R.W., & Horner, R.H. (1988). Generalization with precision. In R.H. Horner, G. Dunlap, & R.L. Koegel (Eds.), *Generalization and maintenance: Life-style changes in applied settings* (pp. 99–120). Baltimore: Paul H. Brookes Publishing Co.

Albin, R.W., Lucyshyn, J.M., Horner, R.H., & Flannery, K.B. (1996). Contextual fit for behavioral support plan: A model for "goodness of fit." In L.K. Koegel, R.L. Koegel, & G. Dunlap (Eds.), *Positive behavioral support: Including people with difficult behavior in the community* (pp. 81–98). Baltimore: Paul H. Brookes Publishing Co.

Amado, A.N. (Ed.). (1993). *Friendships and community connections between people with and without developmental disabilities.* Baltimore: Paul H. Brookes Publishing Co.

American Psychiatric Association. (1994). *Diagnostic and statistical manual of mental disorders* (4th ed.). Washington, DC: Author.

American Psychiatric Association. (2000). *Diagnostic and statistical manual of mental disorders* (4th ed., text rev.). Washington, DC: Author.

Anderson, S.R., Avery, D.L., DiPietro, E.K., Edwards, G.L., & Christian, W.P. (1987). Intensive home-based intervention with autistic children. *Education and Treatment of Children, 10*(4), 352–366.

Anderson, S.R., & Romanczyk, R.G. (1999). Early intervention for children with autism: Continuum-based behavioral models. *Journal of The Association for Persons with Severe Handicaps, 24*(3), 162–173.

Antia, S.D., & Dittillo, D.A. (1998). A comparison of the peer social behavior of children who are deaf/hard of hearing and hearing. *Journal of Children's Communication Development, 19*, 1–10.

Attwood, T. (2003). Understanding and managing circumscribed interests. In M. Prior (Ed.), *Learning and behavior problems in Asperger syndrome* (pp. 126–147). New York: The Guilford Press.

Azar, B. (1998). The development of tools for earlier diagnosis of autism is moving quickly. *American Psychological Association Monitor, 29*(11), 1–3.

Baghdadli, A., Picot, M., Pascal, C., Pry, R., & Aussilloux, C. (2003). Relationship between age of recognition of first disturbances and severity in young children with autism. *European Child and Adolescent Psychiatry, 12*, 122–127.

Bailey, D.B., Jr. (2001). Evaluating parent involvement and family support in early intervention and preschool programs. *Journal of Early Intervention, 24*(1), 1–14.

Bakeman, R., & Adamson, L.B. (1984). Coordinating attention to people and objects in mother–infant and peer–infant interaction. *Child Development, 55*(4), 1278–1289.

Baker, B.L. (1989). Parent training and developmental disabilities. *Monographs of the American Association on Mental Retardation, 13.* Washington, DC: American Association on Mental Retardation.

Baker, B.L., Lander, S.J., & Kashima, K.J. (1991). Effects of parent training on families of children with mental retardation: Increased burden or generalized benefit? *American Journal on Mental Retardation, 96,* 127–136.

Baker, M., Koegel, R.L., & Koegel, L.K. (1998). Increasing the social behavior of young children with autism using their obsessive behaviors. *Journal of The Association for Persons with Severe Handicaps, 23,* 300–308.

Baker, M.J. (2000). Incorporating children with autism's thematic ritualistic behaviors into games to increase social play interactions with siblings. *Journal of Positive Behavior Interventions, 2,* 66–84.

Baker, M.J., Koegel, R.L., & Koegel, L.K. (1998). Increasing the social behaviors of young children with autism using their obsessive behaviors. *Journal of The Association for Persons with Severe Handicaps, 23,* 300–308.

Baldwin, D. (1995). Understanding the link between joint attention and language. In C. Moore & C. Dunham (Eds.), *Joint attention: Its origins and role in development* (pp. 189–205). Mahwah, NJ: Lawrence Erlbaum Associates.

Baldwin, J.D., & Baldwin, J.I. (2001). *Behavior principles in everyday life* (4th ed.). Upper Saddle River, NJ: Prentice Hall.

Bambara, L.M., Ager, C., & Koger, F. (1994). The effects of choice and task preference on the work performance of adults with severe disabilities. *Journal of Applied Behavior Analysis, 27,* 555–556.

Baranek, G. (1999). Autism during infancy: A retrospective video analysis of sensory-motor and social behaviors at 9–12 months of age. *Journal of Autism and Developmental Disorders 29*(3), 213–224.

Barlow, D.H., & Hersen, M. (1984). *Single case experimental designs: Strategies for studying behavioral change.* New York: Pergamon.

Barnhill, G.P., Cook, K.T., Tebbenkamp, K., & Myles, B.S. (2002). The effectiveness of social skills intervention targeting nonverbal communication for adolescents with Asperger syndrome and related pervasive developmental delays. *Focus on Autism and Other Developmental Disabilities, 17,* 112–118.

Baron-Cohen, S. (1989). Do autistic children have obsessions and compulsions? *British Journal of Clinical Psychology, 28,* 193–200.

Baron-Cohen, S. (1995). *Mindblindness.* Cambridge, MA: The MIT Press.

Baron-Cohen, S., & Allen, J. (1992). Can autism be detected at 18 months? The needle, the haystack, and the CHAT. *Annual Progress in Child Psychiatry and Child Development,* 95–103.

Baron-Cohen, S., Allen, J., & Gillberg, C. (1992). Can autism be detected at 18 months? The needle, the haystack, and the CHAT. *British Journal of Psychiatry, 161,* 839–843.

Baron-Cohen, S., Cox, A., Baird, G., Swettenham, J., & Nightingale, N. (1996). Psychological markers in the detection of autism in infancy in a large population. *British Journal of Psychiatry, 168*(2), 158–163.

Baron-Cohen, S., & Hammer, J. (1997). Parents of children with Asperger syndrome: What is the cognitive phenotype? *Journal of Cognitive Neuroscience, 9,* 548–554.

Bates, E. (1976). *Language and context: The acquisition of pragmatics.* San Diego: Academic Press.

Bates, E. (1979). *The emergence of symbols: Cognition and communication in infancy.* San Diego: Academic Press.

Bates, E., Camaioni, L., & Volterra, V. (1975). The acquisition of performatives prior to speech. *Merrill-Palmer Quarterly, 21*(3), 205–226.

Bateson, M.C. (1975). Mother–infant exchanges: The epigenesis of conversational interaction. In D. Aaronson & R.W. Rieber (Eds.), *Developmental psycholinuistics and communication disorders: Annals of the New York Academy of Science, 263,* 101–112.

Baumeister, A.A., & Forehand, R. (1972). Effects of contingent shock and verbal command on body rocking of retardates. *Journal of Clinical Psychology, 28,* 586–590.

Baumgart, D., Brown, L., Pumpian, I., Nisbet, J., Ford, A., Sweet, M., Messina, R., & Schroeder, J. (1982). Principle of partial participation and individualized adaptations in educational programs for severely handicapped students. *Journal of the Association for the Severely Handicapped, 7,* 17–27.

Baumgartner, D., Bryan, T., Donahue, M., & Nelson, C. (1993). Thanks for asking: Parent comments about homework, tests, and grades. *Exceptionality, 4,* 177–183.

Bauminger, N., & Kasari, C. (2000). Loneliness and friendship in high-functioning children with autism. *Child Development, 71,* 447–456.

Bender, L., & Schilder, P. (1940). Impulsions: A specific disorder of the behavior of children. *Archives of Neurology and Psychiatry, 44,* 990–1008.

Bernheimer, L.P., Gallimore, R., & Weisner, T.S. (1990). Ecocultural theory as a context for the individual family service plan. *Journal of Early Intervention, 14*(3), 219–233.

Bernheimer, L.P., & Keogh, B.K. (1995). Weaving interventions into the fabric of everyday life: An approach to family assessment. *Topics in Early Childhood Special Education, 15*(4), 415–433.

Berry, J.W. (1997). Immigration, acculturation, and adaptation. *Applied Psychology: An International Review. 46*(1), 5–68.

Berry, J.W., Kim, U., Power, S., Young, M., & Bujaki, M. (1989). Acculturation attitudes in plural societies. *Applied Psychology: An International Review, 38*(2), 185–206.

Birenbaum, A., & Cohen, H.J. (1993). On the importance of helping families: Policy implications from a national study. *Mental Retardation, 31,* 67–74.

Bledsoe, R., Myles, B.S., & Simpson, R.L. (2003). Use of a social story intervention to improve mealtime skills of an adolescent with Asperger syndrome. *Autism, 7,* 289–295.

Blue-Banning, M.J., Turnbull, A.P., & Pereira, L. (2000). Group action planning as a support strategy for Hispanic families: Parent and professional perspectives. *Mental Retardation, 38*(3), 262–275.

Brady, M.P., Shores, R.E., Gunter, P., McEvoy, M.A., Fox, J.J., & White, C. (1984). Generalization of an adolescent's social interaction behavior via multiple peers in a classroom setting. *Journal of The Association for Persons with Severe Handicaps, 9,* 278–286.

Breen, C.G., & Haring, T.G. (1991). Effects of contextual competence on social initiations. *Journal of Applied Behavior Analysis, 24,* 337–347.

Breen, C.G., Haring, T.G., Pitts-Conway, V., & Gaylord-Ross, R. (1985). The training and generalization of social interaction during breaktime at two job sites in the natural environment. *Journal of The Association for Persons with Severe Handicaps, 10,* 41–50.

Bristol, M.M. (1984). Family resources and successful adaptation to autistic children. In E. Schopler & G.B. Mesibov (Eds.), *The effects of autism on the family* (pp. 289–310). New York: Kluwer Academic/Plenum Publishers.

Bristol, M.M., & Schopler, E. (1984). A developmental perspective on stress and coping in families of autistic children. In J. Blancher (Ed.), *Severely handicapped young children and their families* (pp. 91–141). San Diego: Academic Press.

Bristol-Power, M.M., & Spinella, G. (1999). Research on screening and diagnosis in autism: A work in progress. *Journal of Autism and Developmental Disorders, 29*(6), 435–438.

Broderick, C., Caswell, R., Gregory, S., Marzolini, S., & Wilson, O. (2002). "Can I join the club?" A social integration scheme for adolescents with Asperger syndrome. *Autism, 6,* 427–431.

Bronson, M., Hauser-Cram, P., & Warfield, M. (1997). Classrooms matter: Relations between the classroom environment and the social and mastery behavior of five-year-old children with disabilities. *Journal of Applied Developmental Psychology, 18,* 331–348.

Brookman-Frazee, L. (2004). Using parent/clinician partnerships in parent education programs for children with autism. *Journal of Positive Behavior Interventions, 6,* 195–213.

Brown, F., Gothelf, C.R., Guess, D., & Lehr, D.H. (1998). Self-determination for individuals with the most severe disabilities: Moving beyond chimera. *Journal of The Association for Persons with Severe Handicaps, 23,* 17–26.

Brown, W., Odom, S., & Conroy, M. (2001). An intervention hierarchy for promoting young children's peer interactions in natural environments. *Topics in Early Childhood Special Education, 21,* 162–175.

Brownell, R. (Ed.). (2000). *Expressive One-Word Picture Vocabulary Test–Revised.* Novato, CA: Academic Therapy Publications.

Bruinsma, Y. (2004). *Increases in joint attention behavior of eye gaze alternation to share enjoyment as a collateral effect of pivotal response treatment for three children with autism.* Unpublished doctoral dissertation, University of California, Santa Barbara.

Bruner, J. (1975). From communication to language. *Cognition, 3,* 255–287.

Bryan, T., Burstein, K., & Bryan, J. (2001). Students with learning disabilities: Homework problems and promising practices. *Educational Psychologist, 36*(3), 167–180.

Bryson, S.E., Clark, B.S., & Smith, I.M. (1998). First report of a Canadian epidemiological study of autistic syndromes. *Journal of Child Psychology and Psychiatry, 29,* 433–445.

Burton, D. (2002). *The autism epidemic: Is the NIH and CDC response adequate?* Opening statement at the April 18, 2002, hearing of the Committee on Government Reform, Washington, DC.

Calandrella, A.M., & Wilcox, J.M. (2000). Predicting language outcomes for young prelinguistic children with developmental delay. *Journal of Speech and Hearing Research, 42,* 915–924.

Callicott, K.J. (2003). Culturally sensitive collaboration within person-centered planning. *Focus on Autism and Other Developmental Disabilities, 18*(1), 60–68.

Camarata, S.M. (1995). A rationale for naturalistic speech intelligibility intervention. In S.F. Warren & J. Reichle (Series Eds.) & A.M. Fey, J. Windsor, & S.F Warren (Vol. Eds.), *Communication and language intervention series: Vol. 5. Language intervention: Preschool through the elementary years* (pp. 63–84). Baltimore: Paul H. Brookes Publishing Co.

Camarata, S.M. (1996). On the importance of integrating naturalistic language, social intervention, and speech-intelligibility training. In L.K. Koegel, R.L. Koegel, & G. Dunlap (Eds.), *Positive behavioral support: Including people with difficult behavior in the community* (pp. 333–351). Baltimore: Paul H. Brookes Publishing Co.

Campbell, S., Cannon, B., Ellis, J.T., Lifter, K., Luiselli, J.K., Navalta, C.P., & Taras, M. (1998). The May Center for Early Childhood Education: Description of a continuum of services model for children with autism. *International Journal of Disability, Development and Education, 45*(2), 173–187.

Carpenter, M., Nagell, K., & Tomasello, M. (1998). Social cognition, joint attention, and communicative competence from 9 to 15 months of age. *Monographs of the Society for Research in Child Development, 63*(Serial No. 255).

Carpenter, M., & Tomasello, M. (2000). Joint attention, cultural learning, and language acquisition: Implications for children with autism. In S.F. Warren & J. Reichle (Series Eds.) & A.M. Wetherby & B.M. Prizant (Vol. Eds.), *Communication and language intervention series: Vol. 9. Autism spectrum disorders: A transactional developmental perspective* (pp. 31–54). Baltimore: Paul H. Brookes Publishing Co.

Carr, E.G. (1982). Sign language. In R.L. Koegel, A. Rincover, & A.L. Egel (Eds.), *Educating and understanding autistic children* (pp. 142–157). San Diego: College-Hill.

Carr, E.G. (1988). Functional equivalence as a mechanism of response generalization. In R.H. Horner, G. Dunlap, & R.L. Koegel (Eds.), *Generalization and maintenance: Life-style changes in applied settings* (pp. 221–241). Baltimore: Paul H. Brookes Publishing Co.

Carr, E.G., & Carlson, J.I. (1993). Reduction of severe behavior problems in the community using a multi-component treatment approach. *Journal of Applied Behavior Analysis, 26*(2), 157–172.

Carr, E.G., Dunlap, G., Horner, R.H., Koegel, R.L., Turnbull, A.P., Sailor, W., Anderson, J.L., Albin, R.W., Koegel, L.K., & Fox, L. (2002). Positive behavior support: Evolution of an applied science. *Journal of Positive Behavior Interventions, 4*(1), 4–16, 20.

Carr, E.G., Levin, L., McConnachie, G., Carlson, J.I., Kemp, D.C., Smith, C.E., & McLaughlin, D.M. (1999). Comprehensive multi-situational intervention for problem behavior in the community: Long-term maintenance and social validation. *Journal of Positive Behavior Interventions, 1*(1), 5–25.

Carr, E.G., Newsom, C.D., & Binkoff, J.A. (1980). Escape as a factor in the aggressive behavior of two retarded children. *Journal of Applied Behavior Analysis, 13,* 101–117.

Casey, J.E., Rourke, B.P., & Picard, E.M. (1991). Syndrome of nonverbal learning disabilities: Age differences in neuropsychological, academic, and socio-emotional functioning. *Development and Psychopathology, 3,* 329–345.

Celiberti, D.A., & Harris, S.L. (1993). Behavioral intervention for siblings of children with autism: A focus on skills to enhance play. *Behavior Therapy, 24,* 573–599.

Charlop, M.H., Schreibman, L., & Thibodeau, M.G. (1985). Increasing spontaneous verbal responding in autistic children using a time delay procedure. *Journal of Applied Behavior Analysis, 18,* 155–166.

Charlop, M.H., & Trasowech, J.E. (1991). Increasing autistic children's daily spontaneous speech. *Journal of Applied Behavior Analysis, 24,* 747–761.

Charlop, M.H., & Walsh, M.E. (1986). Increasing autistic children's spontaneous verbalizations of affection: An assessment of time delay and peer-mediated procedures. *Journal of Applied Behavior Analysis, 19,* 307–314.

Charman, T., Swettenham, J., Baron-Cohen, S., Cox, A., Baird, G., & Drew, A. (1997). Infants with autism: An investigation of empathy, pretend play, joint attention, and imitation. *Developmental Psychology, 33*(5), 781–789.

Chen, D., Downing, J.E., & Peckham-Hardin, K.D. (2002). Working with families of diverse cultural and linguistic backgrounds: Considerations for culturally responsive positive behavior support. In J.M. Lucyshyn, G. Dunlap, & R.W. Albin (Eds.), *Families and positive behavior support: Addressing problem behavior in family contexts* (pp. 133–154). Baltimore: Paul H. Brookes Publishing Co.

Cheng, H., & Furnham, A. (2002). Personality, peer relations, and self-confidence as predictors of happiness and loneliness. *Journal of Adolescence, 25,* 327–339.

Cho, S., Singer, G.H.S., & Brenner, M. (2000). Adaptation and accommodation to young children with disabilities: A comparison of Korean and Korean American parents. *Topics in Early Childhood Education, 20*(4), 236–249.

Cho, S., Singer, G.H.S., & Brenner, M. (2003). A comparison of adaptation to childhood disability in Korean immigrant and Korean mothers. *Focus on Autism and Other Developmental Disabilities, 18*(1), 9–19.

Clarke, S., Dunlap, G., & Vaughn, B. (1999). Family-centered, assessment-based intervention to improve behavior during an early morning routine. *Journal of Positive Behavior Interventions, 1*(4), 235–241.

Cole, M., & Cole, S.R. (2001). *The development of children* (4th ed.). New York: Worth Publishers.

Connor, M. (1998). A review of behavioural early intervention programmes for children with autism. *Educational Psychology in Practice, 14*(2), 109–117.

Cook-Gumperz, J., & Kyratzis, A. (2001). Child discourse. In D. Schiffrin, D. Tannen, & H. Hamilton (Eds.), *A handbook of discourse analysis* (pp. 590–611). Malden, MA: Blackwell Publishers.

Cooper, C.R., & Denner, J. (1998). Theories linking culture and psychology: Universal and community-specific processes. *Annual Review of Psychology, 49,* 559–584.

Cooper, H., & Nye, B. (1994). Homework for students with learning disabilities: The implications of research for policy and practice. *Journal of Learning Disabilities, 27*(8), 470–479.

Cordisco, L.K., Strain, P.S., & Depew, N. (1988). Assessment for generalization of parenting skills in home settings. *Journal of The Association for Persons with Severe Handicaps, 3,* 202–210.

Corsaro, W.A. (1985). *Friendship and peer culture in the early years.* Westport, CT: Ablex Publishing Corporation.

Cowen, E.L., Pederson, A., Babigian, H., Izzo, L.D., & Trost, M.A. (1973). Long-term follow-up of early detected vulnerable children. *Journal of Consulting and Clinical Psychology, 41,* 438–446.

Crespi, L.P. (1942). Quantitative variations of incentive and performance in the white rat. *The American Journal of Psychology, 60,* 467–517.

Criss, M.M., Pettit, G.S., Bates, J.E., Dodge, K.A., & Lapp, A.L. (2002). Family adversity, positive peer relationships, and children's externalizing behavior: A longitudinal perspective on risk and resilience. *Child Development, 73,* 1220–1237.

Crnic, K.A., Greenberg, M.T., Ragozin, A.S., Robinson, N.M., & Basham, R. (1983). Effects of stress and social support on mothers and premature and full-term infants. *Child Development, 54,* 209–217.

Croen, L., Grether, J., Hoogstrate, J., & Selvin, S. (2002). The changing prevalence of autism in California. *Journal of Autism and Developmental Disorders, 32*(3), 207–215.

Cunningham, C. (1985). Training and education approaches for parents of children with special needs. *British Journal of Medical Psychology, 58,* 285–305.

Cutrona, C.E., & Russell, D.W. (1990). Type of social support and specific stress: Toward a theory of optimal matching. In B.R. Sarason, I.G. Sarason, & G.R. Pierce (Eds.), *Social support: An interactional view* (pp. 319–366). Hoboken, NJ: John Wiley & Sons.

Dawson, G., & Osterling, J. (1997). Early intervention in autism. In M.J. Guralnick (Ed.), *The effectiveness of early intervention* (pp. 307–326). Baltimore: Paul H. Brookes Publishing Co.

DeMyer, M.K. (1979). *Parents and children with autism.* Hoboken, NJ: John Wiley & Sons.

DeMyer, M.K., Barton, S., De Myer, W.E., Norton, J.A., Allen, J., & Steel, R. (1973). Prognosis in autism: A follow-up study. *Journal of Autism and Childhood Schizophrenia, 3,* 199–246.

Derby, K.M., Wacker, D.P., Sasso, G., Steege, M., Northup, J., Cigrand, K., & Asums, J. (1992). Brief functional assessment techniques to evaluate aberrant behavior in an outpatient setting: A summary of 79 cases. *Journal of Applied Behavior Analysis, 25*(3), 713–721.

Dew-Hughes, D., Brayton, H., & Blandford, S. (1998). A survey of training and professional development for learning support assistants. *Support for Learning, 13*(4), 179–183.

Dodge, K.A., Lansford, J.E., Burks, V.S., Bates, J.E., Pettit, G.S., Fontaine, R., & Price, J.M. (2003). Peer rejection and social information-processing factors in the development of aggressive behavior problems in children. *Child Development, 74,* 374–393.

Dore, J. (1974). Holophrases, speech acts, and language universals. *Journal of Child Language, 2,* 21–40.

Downing, J.E., Ryndak, D.L., & Clark, D. (2000). Paraeducators in inclusive classrooms. *Remedial and Special Education, 21*(3), 171–181.

Dunlap, G. (1984). The influence of task variation and maintenance tasks on the learning and affect of autistic children. *The Journal of Experimental Child Psychology, 37,* 41–64.

Dunlap, G., dePerczel, M., Clark, S., Wilson, D., Wright, S., White, R., & Gomez, A. (1994). Choice making to promote adaptive behavior for students with emotional and behavioral challenges. *Journal of Applied Behavioral Analysis, 24,* 505–518.

Dunlap, G., Dyer, K., & Koegel, R.L. (1983). Autistic self-stimulation and intertrial interval duration. *American Journal of Mental Deficiency, 88,* 194–202.

Dunlap, G., Foster-Johnson, L., Clarke, S., Kern, L., & Childs, K.E. (1995). Modifying activities to produce functional outcomes: Effects on the disruptive behaviors of students with disabilities. *Journal of The Association for Persons with Severe Handicaps, 20,* 248–258.

Dunlap, G., & Kern, L. (1993). Assessment and intervention for children within the instructional curriculum. In S.F. Warren & J. Reichle (Series Eds.) & J. Reichle & D.P. Wacker (Vol. Eds.), *Communication and language intervention series: Vol. 3. Communicative alternatives to challenging behavior: Integrating functional assessment and intervention strategies* (pp. 177–203). Baltimore: Paul H. Brookes Publishing Co.

Dunlap, G., & Kern, L. (1996). Modifying instructional activities to promote desirable behavior: A conceptual and practical framework. *School Psychology Quarterly, 11,* 297–312.

Dunlap, G., Kern-Dunlap, L., Clarke, S., & Robbins, F.R. (1991). Functional assessment, curricular revision, and severe behavior problems. In Social validity: Multiple perspectives [Special issue]. *Journal of Applied Behavior Analysis, 24*(2), 387–397.

Dunlap, G., & Koegel, R.L. (1980). Motivating autistic children through stimulus variation. *Journal of Applied Behavior Analysis, 13,* 619–627.

Dunst C.J., & Trivette, C.M. (1990). Assessment of social support in early intervention programs. In S.J. Meisels & J.P. Shonkoff (Eds.), *Handbook of early childhood intervention* (pp. 326–349). New York: Cambridge University Press.

Dunst, C.J., Trivette, C.M., Gordon, N.J., & Pletcher, L.L. (1989). Building and mobilizing informal family support networks. In G.H.S. Singer & L.K. Irvin (Eds.), *Support for caregiving families: Enabling positive adaptation to disability* (pp. 121–141). Baltimore: Paul H. Brookes Publishing Co.

Durand, V.M., & Carr, E.G. (1991). Functional communication training to reduce challenging behavior: Maintenance and application in new settings. In Social validity: Multiple perspectives [Special Issue]. *Journal of Applied Behavior Analysis 24*(2), 251–264.

Durand, V.M., & Carr, E.G. (1992). An analysis of maintenance following functional communication training. *Journal of Applied Behavior Analysis, 25*(4), 777–794.

Dworetzky, J.P. (1981). *Introduction to child development.* St. Paul, MN: West Publishing Company.

Dyer, K. (1987). The competition of autistic stereotyped behavior with usual and specially assessed reinforcers. *Research in Developmental Disabilities, 8*, 607–626.

Eaves, L.C., Ho, H.H., & Eaves, D. (1994). Subtypes of autism by cluster analysis. *Journal of Autism and Developmental Disorders, 24*, 3–22.

Education for All Handicapped Children Act of 1975, PL 94-142, 20 U.S.C. §§ 1400 *et seq.*

Egan, S.K., & Perry, D.G. (1998). Does low self-regard invite victimization? *Developmental Psychology, 34*, 299–309.

Ehlers, S., & Gillberg, C. (1993). The epidemiology of Asperger syndrome: A total population study. *Journal of Child Psychology and Psychiatry, 34*, 1327–1350.

Ehlers, S., Gillberg, C., & Wing, L. (1999). A screening questionnaire for Asperger syndrome and other high functioning autism spectrum disorders in school age children. *Journal of Autism and Developmental Disorders, 29*, 129–141.

Ehlers, S., Nyden, A., Gillberg, C., Dahlgren-Sandburg, A., Dahlgren, S.O., Hjelmquist, E., & Oden, A. (1997). Asperger syndrome, autism and attention disorders: A comparative study of the cognitive profiles of 120 children. *Journal of Child Psychology and Psychiatry, 38*, 207–217.

Ehrmann, L.C., Aeschleman, S.R., & Svanum, S. (1995). Parental reports of community activity patterns: A comparison between young children with disabilities and their nondisabled peers. *Research in Developmental Disabilities, 16*(4), 331–343.

Eiserman, W.D., Weber, C., & McCoun, M. (1995). Parent and professional roles in early intervention: A longitudinal comparison of the effects of two intervention configurations. *The Journal of Special Education, 29*, 20–44.

El-Ghoroury, N.H., & Romanczyk, R.G. (1999). Play interactions of family members towards children with autism. *Journal of Autism and Developmental Disorders, 29*, 249–258.

Elliot, C.D. (1990). *Differential Ability Scales.* San Antonio, TX: Harcourt Assessment.

Ellis, H.D., & Gunter, H.L. (1999). Asperger syndrome: A simple matter of white matter? *Trends in Cognitive Science, 3*, 192–200.

Ellis, H.D., Ellis, D.M., Fraser, W., & Deb, S. (1994). A preliminary study of right hemisphere cognitive deficits and impaired social judgments among young people with Asperger syndrome. *European Child and Adolescent Psychiatry, 3*, 255–266.

Englemann, S. (1980). *Direct instruction.* Englewood Cliffs, NJ: Educational Technology Publications.

Englemann, S., Becker, W.C., Carnine, D.W., & Gersten, R. (1988). The direct instruction follow through model: Design and outcomes. In Direct instruction: A general case for teaching the general case [Special issue]. *Education and Treatment of Children, 11*, 303–317.

Engstrom, I., Ekstrom, L., & Emilsson, B. (2003). Psychosocial functioning in a group of Swedish adults with Asperger syndrome or high-functioning autism. *Autism, 7*, 99–110.

Epstein, M.H., Munk, D.D., Bursuck, W.D., Polloway, E.A., & Jayanthi, M. (1999). Strategies for improving home-school communication about homework for students with disabilities. *The Journal of Special Education, 33*(3), 166–176.

Everard, P. (1987). An international perspective. In D.J. Cohen & A.M. Donnellan (Eds.), *Handbook of autism and pervasive developmental disorders* (pp. 743–748). Hoboken, NJ: John Wiley & Sons.

Farmer-Dougan, V. (1994). Increasing requests by adults with developmental disabilities using incidental teaching by peers. *Journal of Applied Behavior Analysis, 27*, 533–544.

Fenske, E.D., Zalenski, S., Krantz, P.J., & McClannahan, L.E. (1985). Age at intervention and treatment outcome for autistic children in a comprehensive intervention program. *Analysis and Intervention in Developmental Disabilities, 5*, 49–58.

Fenson, L., Dale, P., Reznick, J., Bates, E., Thal, D., & Pethick, S. (1994). Variability in early communicative development. *Monographs of the Society for Research in Child Development, 59*(5, Serial No. 242).

Fey, M. (1986). *Language intervention with young children.* Boston: Allyn & Bacon.

Filipek, P.A., Accardo, P.J., Baranek, G.T., Cook, E.H., Dawson, G., Gordon, B., Gravel, J.S., Johnson, C.P., Kallen, R.J., Levy, S.E., Minshew, N.J., Prizant, B.M., Rapin, I., Rogers, S.J., Stone, W.L., Teplin, S., Ruchman, R.F., & Volkmar, F.R. (1999). The screening and diagnosis of autistic spectrum disorders. *Journal of Autism and Developmental Disorders, 29*(6), 439–484.

Fine, M.J., & Gardner, A. (1994). Collaborative consultation with families of children with special needs: Why bother? *Journal of Educational and Psychological Consultation, 5*(4), 283–308.

Fisher-Polites, C. (2004). "PBS" spelled "friends." *Journal of Positive Behavior Interventions, 6*(3), 178–187.

Flannery, K.B., & Horner, R.H. (1994). The relationship between predictability and problem behavior for students with severe disabilities. *Journal of Behavioral Education, 4*(2), 157–176.

Fombonne, E. (1998). Epidemiological surveys of Autism. In F.R. Volkmar (Ed.), *Autism and pervasive developmental disorders* (pp. 32–63). New York: Cambridge University Press.

Fombonne, E. (2003a). Epidemiological surveys of autism and other pervasive developmental disorders: An update. *Journal of Autism and Developmental Disorders, 33*, 365–382.

Fombonne, E. (2003b). The prevalence of autism. *Journal of the American Medical Association, 289*(1), 87–89.

Foster, S. (1979). *From non-verbal to verbal communication: A study of the development of topic initiation strategies during the first two-and-a-half years.* Unpublished doctoral dissertation, University of Lancaster, England.

Foxx, R.M., & Azrin, N.H. (1973). The elimination of autistic self-stimulatory behavior by overcorrection. *Journal of Applied Behavior Analysis, 6*, 1–14.

Frankel, F., & Myatt, R. (2003). *Children's friendship training.* New York: Brunner-Routledge.

Frea, W.D. (1995). Social-communicative skills in higher-functioning children with autism. In R.L. Koegel & L.K. Koegel (Eds.), *Teaching children with autism: Strategies for initiating positive interactions and improving learning opportunities* (pp. 53–66). Baltimore: Paul H. Brookes Publishing Co.

Frea, W.D. (1997). Reducing stereotypic behavior by teaching orienting responses to environmental stimuli. *Journal for The Association of Persons with Severe Handicaps, 22*(1), 28–35.

Frea, W.D., Koegel, L.K., & Koegel, R.K. (1994). *Understanding why problem behaviors occur: A guide for assisting parents in assessing causes of behaviors and designing treatment plans.* Santa Barbara: University of California.

Fredeen, R. (2002). *Increasing social-communication initiations in preschool-age children with autism using pivotal response training.* Unpublished master's thesis, University of California, Santa Barbara.

Frederickson, N., & Turner, J. (2003). Utilizing the classroom peer group to address children's social needs: An evaluation of the Circle of Friends intervention approach. *The Journal of Special Education, 36*, 234–245.

Freeman, B.J., Cronin, P., & Candela, P. (2002). Asperger syndrome or autistic disorder? The diagnostic dilemma. *Focus on Autism and Other Developmental Disabilities, 3*, 145–151.

Freeman, B.J., Ritvo, E.R., Needleman, R., & Yokota, A. (1985). The stability of cognitive and linguistic parameters in autism: A five-year prospective study. *Journal of the American Academy of Child Psychiatry, 24*, 459–464.

Freeman, S.F.N., & Kasari, C. (2002). Characteristics and qualities of the play dates of children with Down syndrome: Emerging or true friendships? *American Journal on Mental Retardation, 107,* 16–31.

Frith, U. (1991). Asperger and his syndrome. In U. Frith (Ed.), *Autism and Asperger syndrome* (pp. 1–36). New York: Cambridge University Press.

Gabriel, R.L., Hill, D.E., Pierce, R.A., Rogers, S.J., & Wehner, B. (2001). Predictors of treatment outcome in young children with autism. *Autism: The International Journal of Research and Practice, 5*(4), 407–429.

Gallimore, R., Bernheimer, L.P., & Weisner, T.S. (1999). Family life is more than managing crisis: Broadening the agenda of research on families adapting to childhood disability. In R. Gallimore, L.P. Bernheimer, D. MacMillan, D. Speece, & S. Vaughn (Eds.), *Developmental perspectives on children with high-incidence disabilities* (pp. 55–80). Mahwah, NJ: Lawrence Erlbaum Associates.

Gallimore, R., Coots, J., Weisner, T., Garnier, H., & Guthrie, D. (1996). Family responses to children with early developmental delays: II. Accommodation intensity and activity in early and middle childhood. *American Journal on Mental Retardation,101*(3), 215–232.

Gallimore, R., Weisner, T.S., Bernheimer, L.P., Guthrie, D., & Nihira, K. (1993). Family responses to young children with developmental delays: Accommodation activity in ecological and cultural context. *American Journal on Mental Retardation, 98*(2), 185–206.

Gallimore, R., Weisner, T.S., Kaufman, S.Z., & Bernheimer, L.P. (1989). The social construction of ecocultural niches: Family accommodation of developmentally delayed children. *American Journal on Mental Retardation, 94*(3), 216–230.

Garfin, D., & Lord, C. (1986). Communication as a social problem in autism. In E. Schopler & G. Mesibov (Eds.), *Social behavior in autism* (pp. 237–261). New York: Kluwer Academic/Plenum Publishers.

Garvey, C. (1975). Requests and responses in children's speech. *Journal of Child Language, 2,* 41–63.

Garvey, C., & Berninger, G. (1981). Timing and turn taking in children's conversations. *Discourse Processes, 4,* 27–57.

Gaylord-Ross, R., & Haring, T.G. (1987). Social interaction research for adolescents with severe handicaps. *Behavior Disorders, 12,* 264–275.

Gaylord-Ross, R.J., Haring, T.G., Breen, C., & Pitts-Conway, V. (1984). The training and generalization of social interaction skills with autistic youth. *Journal of Applied Behavior Analysis, 17,* 229–247.

Ghaziuddin, M. (2002). Asperger syndrome: Associated psychiatric and medical conditions. *Focus on Autism and Other Developmental Disabilities, 17,* 138–144.

Ghaziuddin, M., Ghaziuddin, N., & Greden, J. (2002). Depression in persons with autism: Implications for research and clinical care. *Journal of Autism and Developmental Disorders, 32,* 299–306.

Ghaziuddin, M., & Mountain-Kimchi, K. (2004). Defining the intellectual profile of Asperger syndrome: Comparison with high-functioning autism. *Journal of Autism and Developmental Disorders, 34,* 279–284.

Ghaziuddin, M., Tsai, L.Y., & Ghaziuddin, N. (1992). Brief report: A comparison of the diagnostic criteria for Asperger syndrome. *Journal of Autism and Developmental Disorders, 22,* 643–649.

Giangreco, M.F., Edelman, S., & Broer, S. (2001). Respect, appreciation, and acknowledgement of paraprofessionals who support students with disabilities. *Exceptional Children, 67,* 485–496.

Giangreco, M.F., Edelman, S.W., Broer, S.M., & Doyle, M.B. (2001). Paraprofessional support of students with disabilities: Literature from the past decade. *Exceptional Children, 68,* 45–63.

Giangreco, M.F., Edelman, S.W., Luiselli, T.E., & MacFarland, S.Z.C. (1997). Helping or hovering? Effects of instructional assistant proximity on students with disabilities. *Exceptional Children, 64*(1), 7–18.

Gilchrist, A., Green, J., Cox, A., Burton, D., Rutter, M., & Le Couteur, A. (2001). Development and current functioning in adolescents with Asperger syndrome: A comparative study. *Journal of Child Psychology and Psychiatry, 42,* 227–240.

Gillberg, C. (1989). Asperger syndrome in 23 Swedish children. *Developmental Medicine and Child Neurology, 31,* 520–531.

Gillberg, C. (1991). Outcome in autism and autistic-like conditions. *Journal of the American Academy of Child and Adolescent Psychiatry, 30,* 375–382.

Gillberg, C. (2002). *A guide to Asperger syndrome.* New York: Cambridge University Press.

Gillberg, C., & Ehlers, S. (1998). High-functioning people with autism and Asperger syndrome. In E. Schopler, G.B. Mesibov, & L.J. Kunce (Eds.), *Asperger syndrome or high-functioning autism?* (pp. 79–106). New York: Kluwer Academic/Plenum Publishers.

Gillberg, C., Gillberg, C., Rastam, M., & Wentz, E. (2001). The Asperger syndrome (and high functioning autism) diagnostic interview (ASDI): A preliminary study of a new structured clinical interview. *Autism, 5,* 57–66.

Gillberg, C., Steffenburg, S., & Schaumann, H. (1991). Is autism more common now than ten years ago? *British Journal of Psychiatry, 158,* 403–409.

Gillberg, C., & Wing, L. (1999). Autism: Not an extremely rare disorder. *Acta Psychiatrica Scandinavia, 99,* 399–406.

Glascoe, F. (1998). *Collaborating with parents: Using parents' evaluation of developmental status to detect and address developmental and behavioral problems.* Nashville, TN: Ellsworth & Vandermeer Press.

Glascoe, F., & Dworkin, P. (1995). The role of parents in the detection of developmental and behavioral problems. *Pediatrics, 95*(6), 829–836.

Goodley, D. (2001). 'Learning difficulties', the social model of disability and impairment: Challenging epistemologies. *Disability and Society, 16,* 207–231.

Gray, C.A., & Garand, J.D. (1993). Social Stories: Improving responses of students with autism with accurate social information. *Focus on Autistic Behavior, 8,* 1–10.

Gray, K.M., & Tonge, B.J. (2001). Are there early features of autism in infants and preschool children? *Journal of Paediatrics and Child Health, 37*(3), 221–230.

Gregory, K.M., Kehle, T.J., & McLoughlin, C.S. (1997). Generalization and maintenance of treatment gains using self-management procedures with behaviorally disordered adolescents. *Psychological Reports, 80*(2), 683–690.

Gresham, F.M. (1982). Social skills instruction for exceptional children. *Theory Into Practice, 21,* 129–133.

Gresham, F.M. (1998). Social skills training: Should we raze, remodel, or rebuild? *Behavioral Disorders, 24,* 19–25.

Gresham, F.M. (2000). Best practices in social skills training. In A. Thomas & J. Grimes (Eds.), *Best practices in school psychology IV* (Vol. 2, pp. 1029–1040). Bethesda, MD: National Association of School Psychologists.

Gresham, F.M., & MacMillan, D.L. (1998). Early intervention project: Can its claims be substantiated and its effects replicated? *Journal of Autism and Developmental Disorders, 28,* 5–13.

Gresham, F.M., Sugai, G., & Horner, R.H. (2001). Interpreting outcomes of social skills training for students with high-incidence disabilities. *Exceptional Children, 67,* 331–344.

Groden, J., & Cautela, J. (1988). Procedures to increase social interactions among adolescents with autism: A multiple baseline analysis. *Journal of Behavioral Therapy and Experimental Psychiatry, 19,* 87–93.

Guralnick, M.J. (Ed.). (1997). *The effectiveness of early intervention.* Baltimore: Paul H. Brookes Publishing Co.

Guralnick, M.J., & Neville, B. (1997). Designing early intervention programs to promote children's social competence. In M.J. Guralnick (Ed.), *The effectiveness of early intervention* (pp. 579–610). Baltimore: Paul H. Brookes Publishing Co.

Halliday, M.A.K. (1975). *Learning how to mean: Explorations in the development of language.* New York: Arnold.

Halliday, M.A.K. (1979). One child's protolanguage. In M. Bullowa (Ed.), *Before speech: The beginning of interpersonal communication* (pp. 171–190). New York: Cambridge University Press.

Hancock, T.B., & Kaiser, A.P. (1996). Siblings' use of milieu teaching at home. *Topics in Early Childhood Special Education, 16,* 168–190.

Handleman, J.S., & Harris, S.L. (2001). *Preschool education programs for children with autism.* Austin, TX: PRO-ED.

Handleman, J.S., Harris, S.L., Celiberti, D., Lilleheht, E., & Tomchek, L. (1991). Developmental changes of preschool children with autism and normally developing peers. *Infant-Toddler Intervention, 1,* 137–143.

Haring, T.G., Breen, C.G., Pitts-Conway, V., Lee, M., & Gaylord-Ross, R. (1987). Adolescent peer tutoring and special friend experiences. *Journal of The Association for Persons with Severe Handicaps, 12,* 280–286.

Haring, T.G., & Lovinger, L. (1989). Promoting social interaction through teaching generalized play initiation responses to preschool children with autism. *Journal of The Association for Persons with Severe Handicaps, 14,* 58–67.

Harkness, S., & Super, C.M. (1995). Culture and parenting. In M.H. Bornstein (Ed.), *Handbook of parenting: Biology and ecology of parenting* (Vol. 2, pp. 211–234). Mahwah, NJ: Lawrence Erlbaum Associates.

Harper, L., & McCluskey, K. (2003). Teacher–child and child–child interactions in inclusive preschool settings: Do adults inhibit peer interactions? *Early Childhood Research Quarterly, 18,* 163–184.

Harris, S.L., & Handleman, J.S. (2000). Age and IQ at intake as predictors of placement for young children with autism: A four to six-year follow-up. *Journal of Autism and Developmental Disorders, 30*(2), 137–142.

Harris, S.L., Handleman, J.S., & Fong, P.L. (1987). Imitation of self-stimulation: Impact on the autistic child's behavior and affect. *Child and Family Behavior Therapy, 9,* 1–21.

Harris, S.L., Handleman, J.S., Gordon, R., Kristoff, B., & Fuentes, F. (1991) Changes in cognitive and language functioning of preschool children with autism. *Journal of Autism and Developmental Disorders, 21,* 281–290.

Harris, S.L., Wolchik, S.A., & Weitz, S. (1981). The acquisition of language skills by autistic children: Can parents do the job? *Journal of Autism and Developmental Disorders, 11,* 373–384.

Harrower, J. (1999). Educational inclusion of children with severe disabilities. *Journal of Positive Behavior Interventions, 1,* 215–230.

Harrower, J., & Dunlap, G. (2001). Including children with autism in general education classrooms. *Behavior Modification, 25,* 762–784.

Harry, B. (2002). Trends and issues in serving culturally diverse families of children with disabilities. *The Journal of Special Education, 36*(3), 131–138.

Hauck, M., Fein, D., Waterhouse, L., & Feinstein, C. (1995). Social initiations by autistic children to adults and other children. *Journal of Autism and Developmental Disorders, 25,* 579–595.

Hinton, L.M., & Kern, L. (1999). Increasing homework completion by incorporating student interests. *Journal of Positive Behavior Interventions, 1*(4), 231–234.

Ho, M.K. (1987). *Family therapy with ethnic minorities.* Thousand Oaks, CA: Sage Publications.

Horner, R.H., & Carr, E.G. (1997). Behavioral support for students with severe disabilities: Functional assessment and comprehensive intervention. *Journal of Special Education. Special Issue: Research in Severe Disabilities, 31*(1), 84–109.

Horner, R.H., & Day, M.H. (1991). The effects of response efficiency on functionally equivalent competing behaviors. *Journal of Applied Behavior Analysis, 24*(4), 719–732.

Horner, R.H., Dunlap, G., Koegel, R.L., Carr, E.G., Sailor, W., Anderson, J.A., Albin, R.W., & O'Neill, R.E (1990). Toward a technology of "non-aversive" behavioral support. *Journal of The Association for Persons with Severe Handicaps, 15*(3), 125–132.

Horner, R.H., Todd, A.W., Lewis-Palmer, T., Irvin, L.K., Sugai, G., & Boland, J.B. (2004). The School-Wide Evaluation Tool (SET): A research instrument for assessing school-wide positive behavior support. *Journal of Positive Behavior Interventions, 6,* 3–12.

Howlin, P. (2003a). Longer-term educational and employment outcomes. In M. Prior (Ed.), *Learning and behavior problems in Asperger syndrome* (pp. 269–293). New York: The Guilford Press.

Howlin, P. (2003b). Outcome in high-functioning adults with autism with and without early language delays: Implications for the differentiation between autism and Asperger syndrome. *Journal of Autism and Developmental Disorders, 33,* 3–13.

Howlin, P., & Rutter, M. (1987). *Treatment of autistic children.* Hoboken, NJ: John Wiley & Sons.

Hoyson, M., Jamieson, B., & Strain, P.S. (1984). Individualized group instruction of normally developing and autistic like children: A description and evaluation of the LEAP curriculum model. *Journal of the Division of Early Childhood, 8,* 157–181.

Hulsing, M.M. (1995). Analysis of successful initiations of three children with hearing loss mainstreamed in kindergarten classrooms. *Language, Speech, and Hearing Services in Schools, 26,* 45–57.

Hulsing, M.M., Luetke-Stahlman, B., Loeb, D.F., Nelson, P., & Wegner, J. (1995). Analysis of successful initiations of three children with hearing loss mainstreamed into kindergarten classrooms. *Language, Speech, and Hearing Services in Schools, 26,* 45–57.

Hung, D.W. (1977). Generalization of "curiosity" questioning behavior in autistic children. *Journal of Behavior Therapy and Experimental Psychiatry, 8,* 237–245.

Hurley-Geffner, C.M. (1995). Friendships between children with and without developmental disabilities. In R.L. Koegel & L.K. Koegel (Eds.), *Teaching children with autism: Strategies for initiating positive interactions and improving learning opportunities* (pp. 105–125). Baltimore: Paul H. Brookes Publishing Co.

Hurth, J., Shaw, E., Izeman, S.G., Whaley, K., & Rogers, S.J. (1999). Areas of agreement about effective practices among programs serving young children with autism spectrum disorders. *Infants and Young Children, 12,* 17–26.

Hurtig, R., Ensrud, S., & Tomblin, J.B. (1982). The communicative function of question production in autistic children. *Journal of Autism and Developmental Disorders, 12,* 57–69.

Hwang, B., & Hughes, C. (2000). The effects of social interaction training on early social communicative skills of children with autism. *Journal of Autism and Developmental Disorders, 30,* 331–343.

Hyten, C., & Burns, R. (1986). Social relations and social behavior. In H.W. Reese & L.J. Parrott (Eds.), *Behavior science: Philosophical, methodological, and empirical advances* (pp. 163–183). Mahwah, NJ: Lawrence Erlbaum Associates.

Iacono, T.A., Chan, J.B., & Waring, R.E. (1998). Efficiency of a parent-implementation early language intervention based on collaborative consultation. *International Journal of Communication Disorders, 33*(3), 281–303.

Individuals with Disabilities Education Act (IDEA) Amendments of 1997, PL 105-17, 20 U.S.C. §§ 1400 *et seq.*

Individuals with Disabilities Education Act (IDEA) of 1990, PL 101-476, 20 U.S.C. §§ 1400 *et seq.*

Individuals with Disabilities Education Improvement Act of 2004, PL 108-446, 20 U.S.C. §§ 1400 *et seq.*

Iovannone, R., Dunlap, G., Huber, H., & Kincaid, D. (2003). Effective educational practices for students with autism spectrum disorders. *Focus on Autism and Other Developmental Disabilities, 18,* 150–165.

Iwata, B.A., Dorsey, M.F., Slifer, K.J., Bauman, K.E., & Richman, G.S. (1994). Toward a functional analysis of self-injury. In N.A. Neef (Ed.), Functional analysis approaches to behavioral assessment and treatment [Special issue]. *Journal of Applied Behavior Analysis, 27*(2), 197–209.

Janney, R., & Snell, M.E. (2004). *Modifying schoolwork* (2nd ed.). Baltimore: Paul H. Brookes Publishing Co.

Jenkins, S., Stephens, B., & Sternberg, L. (1980). The use of parents as parent trainers of handicapped children. *Education and Training of the Mentality Retarded 15*(4), 256–263.

Jolly, A.C., Test, D.W., & Spooner, F. (1993). Using badges to increase initiations of children with severe disabilities in a play setting. *Journal of The Association for Persons with Severe Handicaps, 18,* 46–51.

Kaiser, A.P., Hancock, T.B., & Nietfeld, J.P. (2000). The effects of parent-implemented enhanced milieu teaching on the social communication of children who have autism. *Early Education and Development, 11*(4), 423–446.

Kalyanpur, M., & Harry, B. (1997). A posture of reciprocity: A practical approach to collaboration between professionals and parents of culturally diverse backgrounds. *Journal of Child and Family Studies, 6*(4), 487–509.

Kaminsky, L., & Dewey, D. (2001). Sibling relationships of children with autism. *Journal of Autism and Developmental Disorders, 31,* 399–410.

Kamps, D.M., Leonard, B.R., Vernon, S., Dugan, E.P., Delquadri, J.C., Gershon, B., Wade, L., & Folk, L. (1992). Teaching social skills to students with autism to increase peer interactions in an integrated first-grade classroom. *Journal of Applied Behavior Analysis, 25,* 281–288.

Kamps, D.M., Potucek, J., Lopez, A.G., Kravits, T., & Kemmerer, K. (1997). The use of peer networks across multiple settings to improve social interaction for students with autism. *Journal of Behavioral Education, 7,* 335–357.

Karagiannis, A., Stainback, S., & Stainback, W. (1996). Historical overview of inclusion. In S. Stainback and W. Stainback (Eds.), *Inclusion: A guide for educators* (pp. 17–28). Baltimore: Paul H. Brookes Publishing Co.

Kasari, C. (2002). Assessing change in early intervention programs for children with autism. *Journal of Autism and Developmental Disorders, 32*(5), 447–461.

Kasari, C., Sigman, M., Mundy, P., & Yirmiya, N. (1990). Affective sharing in the context of joint attention interactions of normal, autistic, and mentally retarded children. *Journal of Autism and Developmental Disorders, 20,* 479–497.

Kellegrew, D.H. (1995). Integrated school placements for children with disabilities. In R.L. Koegel & L.K. Koegel (Eds.), *Teaching children with autism: Strategies for initiating positive interactions and improving learning opportunities* (pp. 127–146). Baltimore: Paul H. Brookes Publishing Co.

Kellegrew, D.H. (2000). Constructing daily routines: A qualitative examination of mothers with young children with disabilities. *The American Journal of Occupational Therapy 54*(3), 252–259.

Kemp, D.C., & Carr, E.G. (1995). Reduction of severe problem behavior in community employment using an hypothesis-driven multicomponent intervention approach. *Journal of The Association for Persons with Severe Handicaps, 20*(4), 229–247.

Kennedy, C. (2001). Social interaction intervention for youth with severe disabilities should emphasize interdependence. *Mental Retardation and Developmental Disabilities Research Reviews, 7*, 122–127.

Kennedy, C.H., & Itkonen, T. (1996). Social relationships, influential variables, and change across the life span. In L.K. Koegel, R.L. Koegel, & G. Dunlap (Eds.), *Positive behavioral support: Including people with difficult behavior in the community* (pp. 287–304). Baltimore: Paul H. Brookes Publishing Co.

Kern, L., & Dunlap, G. (1998). Curricular modifications to promote desirable classroom behavior. In J.K. Luiselli & M.J. Cameron (Eds.), *Antecedent control: Innovative approaches to behavioral support* (pp. 289–307). Baltimore: Paul H. Brookes Publishing Co.

Kern, L.K., Koegel, R.L., & Dunlap, G. (1984). The influence of vigorous versus mild exercise on autistic stereotyped behaviors. *Journal of Autism and Developmental Disorders, 14*, 57–67.

Kim, J.A., Szatmari, P., Bryson, S., Streiner, D.L., & Wilson, F.J. (2000). The prevalence of anxiety and mood problems among children with autism and Asperger syndrome. *Autism, 4*, 117–132.

Kim, Y.T., & Lombardino, L.J. (1991). The efficacy of script contexts in language comprehension intervention with children who have mental retardation. *Journal of Speech and Hearing Research, 34*(4), 845–857.

Klin, A., Sparrow, S.S., Volkmar, F.R., Cicchetti, D.V., & Rourke, B.P. (1995). Asperger syndrome. In B.P. Rourke (Ed.), *Syndrome of nonverbal learning disabilities: Neurodevelopmental manifestations* (pp. 93–118). New York: The Guilford Press.

Klin, A., & Volkmar, F.R. (2000). Treatment and intervention guidelines for individuals with Asperger syndrome. In A. Klin, F.R. Volkmar, & S.S. Sparrow (Eds.), *Asperger syndrome* (pp. 240–266). New York: The Guilford Press.

Klin, A., Volkmar, F.R., & Sparrow, S.S. (2000). *Asperger syndrome.* New York: The Guilford Press.

Knott, F., Lewis, C., & Williams, T. (1995). Sibling interaction of children with learning disabilities: A comparison of autism and down's syndrome. *Journal of Child Psychology and Psychiatry, 36*, 965–976.

Koegel, L.K. (1995). Communication and language intervention. In R.L. Koegel & L.K. Koegel (Eds.), *Teaching children with autism: Strategies for initiating positive interactions and improving learning opportunities* (pp. 17–32). Baltimore: Paul H. Brookes Publishing Co.

Koegel, L.K. (2000). Interventions that facilitate communication in autism. In Treatments for people with autism and other pervasive developmental disorders: Research perspectives [Special issue]. *Journal of Autism and Developmental Disorders, 30*(5), 383–391.

Koegel, L.K., Camarata, S.M., Valdez-Menchaca, M., & Koegel, R.L. (1998a). Setting generalization of question-asking by children with autism. *American Journal on Mental Retardation, 102*, 346–357.

Koegel, L.K., Camarata, S.M., Valdez-Menchaca, M., & Koegel, R.L. (1998b). Teaching children with autism to use self-initiated strategy to learn expressive vocabulary. *American Journal on Mental Retardation, 102*.

Koegel, L.K., Carter, C.M., & Koegel, R.L. (2003). Teaching children with autism self-initiations as a pivotal response. *Topics in Language Disorders, 23*, 134–145.

Koegel, L.K., Harrower, J.K., & Koegel, R.L. (1999). Support for children with developmental disabilities in full inclusion classrooms through self-management. *Journal of Positive Behavior Interventions, 1*(1), 26–34.

Koegel, L.K., & Koegel, R.L. (1995). Motivating communication in children with autism. In E. Schopler & G.B. Mesibov (Eds.), *Learning and cognition in autism* (pp. 73–87). New York: Kluwer Academic/Plenum Publishers.

Koegel, L.K., Koegel, R.L., Bruinsma, Y., Brookman, L., & Fredeen, R. (2003). *Teaching first words.* Santa Barbara: University of California.

Koegel, L.K., Koegel, R.L, & Dunlap, G. (Eds.). (1996). *Positive behavioral support: Including people with difficult behavior in the community.* Baltimore: Paul H. Brookes Publishing Co.

Koegel, L.K., Koegel, R.L., Frea, W. D., & Fredeen, R.M. (2001). Identifying early intervention targets for children with autism in inclusive school settings. *Behavior Modification, 25*, 745–761.

Koegel, L.K., Koegel, R.L., Frea, W., & Green-Hopkins, I. (2003). Priming as a method of coordinating educational services for students with autism. *Language, Speech, and Hearing Services in Schools, 34,* 228–235.

Koegel, L.K., Koegel, R.L., Harrower, J.K., & Carter, C.M. (1999). Pivotal Response Intervention I: Overview of approach. *Journal of The Association for Persons with Severe Handicaps, 24*(3), 174–185.

Koegel, L.K., Koegel, R.L., Hurley, C., & Frea, W.D. (1992). Improving social skills and disruptive behavior in children with autism through self-management. *Journal of Applied Behavior Analysis, 25,* 341–354.

Koegel, L.K., Koegel, R.L., Kellegrew, D., & Mullen, K. (1996). Parent education for prevention and reduction of severe problem behaviors. In L.K. Koegel, R.L. Koegel, & G. Dunlap (Eds.), *Positive behavioral support: Including people with difficult behavior in the community* (pp. 3–30). Baltimore: Paul H. Brookes Publishing Co.

Koegel, L.K., Koegel, R.L., & Parks, D.R. (1992). *How to teach self-management to people with severe disabilities: A training manual.* Santa Barbara: University of California.

Koegel, L.K., Koegel, R.L., Shoshan, Y., & McNerney, E. (1999). Pivotal response intervention II: Preliminary long-term outcome data. *Journal of The Association for Persons with Severe Handicaps, 24*(3), 186–198.

Koegel, L.K., Valdez-Menchaca, M., & Koegel, R.L. (1994). Autism: Social communication difficulties and related behaviors. In V.B. Van Hasselt & M. Hersen (Eds.), *Advanced abnormal psychology* (pp. 165–187). New York: Kluwer Academic/Plenum Publishers.

Koegel, R.L., Bimbela, A., & Schreibman, L. (1996). Collateral effects of parent training on family interactions. *Journal of Autism and Developmental Disorders, 26*(3), 347–359.

Koegel, R.L., Camarata, S.M., & Koegel, L.K. (1994). Aggression and noncompliance: Behavior modification through naturalistic language remediation. In J.L. Matson (Ed.), *Autism in children and adults: Etiology, assessment, and intervention* (pp. 165–180). Pacific Grove, CA: Brooks/Cole.

Koegel, R.L., Camarata, S., Koegel, L.K., Ben-Tall, A., & Smith, A. (1998). Increasing speech intelligibility in children with autism. *Journal of Autism and Developmental Disorders, 28,* 241–251.

Koegel, R.L., & Covert, A. (1972). The relationship of self-stimulation to learning in autistic children. *Journal of Applied Behavior Analysis, 5,* 381–387.

Koegel, R.L, Dunlap, G., Richman, G., & Dyer, K. (1981). The use of specific orienting cues for teaching discrimination tasks. *Analysis and Intervention in Developmental Disabilities, 1,* 187–198.

Koegel, R.L., Dyer, K., & Bell, L.K. (1987). The influence of child-preferred activities on autistic children's social behavior. *Journal of Applied Behavior Analysis, 20,* 243–252.

Koegel, R.L., & Egel, A.L. (1979). Motivating autistic children. *Journal of Abnormal Psychology, 88*(4), 418–426.

Koegel, R.L., Firestone, P.B., Kramme, K.W., & Dunlap, G. (1974). Increasing spontaneous play by suppressing self-stimulation in autistic children. *Journal of Applied Behavior Analysis, 29,* 521–528.

Koegel, R.L., & Frea, W.D. (1993). Treatment of social behavior in autism through the modification of pivotal social skills. *Journal of Applied Behavior Analysis, 26*(3), 369–377.

Koegel, R.L., & Koegel, L.K. (1990). Extended reductions in stereotypic behavior of students with autism through a self-management treatment package. *Journal of Applied Behavior Analysis, 23*(1), 119–127.

Koegel, R.L., Koegel, L.K., & Brookman, L.I. (2003). Empirically supported pivotal response interventions for children with autism. In A. Kazdin & J. Weisz (Eds.), *Evidence-based psychotherapies for children and adolescents* (pp. 341–357). New York: The Guilford Press.

Koegel, R.L., Koegel, L.K, & Carter, C.M. (1999). Pivotal teaching interactions for children with autism. *School Psychology Review, 28*(4), 576–594.

Koegel, R.L., Koegel, L.K., Frea, W.D., & Smith, A.E. (1995). Emerging interventions for children with autism: Longitudinal and lifestyle applications. In R.L. Koegel & L.K. Koegel (Eds.), *Teaching children with autism: Strategies for initiating positive interactions and improving learning opportunities* (pp. 1–15). Baltimore: Paul H. Brookes Publishing Co.

Koegel, R.L., Koegel, L.K., & McNerney, E.K. (2001). Pivotal areas in intervention for autism. *Journal of Clinical Child Psychology, 30*(1), 19–32.

Koegel, R.L., Koegel, L.K., & Schreibman, L. (1991). Assessing and training parents in teaching pivotal behaviors. *Advances in Behavioral Assessment of Children and Families, 5,* 65–82.

Koegel, R.L., Koegel, L.K., & Surratt, A.V. (1992). Language intervention and disruptive behavior in preschool children with autism. *Journal of Autism and Developmental Disorders, 22*(2), 141–153.

Koegel, R.L., O'Dell, M.C., & Dunlap, G. (1988). Producing speech use in nonverbal autistic children by reinforcing attempts. *Journal of Autism and Developmental Disorders, 18*(4), 525–538.

Koegel, R.L., O'Dell, M.C., & Koegel, L.K. (1987). A natural language paradigm for teaching nonverbal autistic children. *Journal of Autism and Developmental Disorders, 17,* 187–199.

Koegel, R.L., & Schreibman, L. (1977). Teaching autistic children to respond to simultaneous multiple cues. *Journal of Experimental Child Psychology, 24,* 299–311.

Koegel, R.L., Schreibman, L., Britten, K.R., Burke, J.C., & O'Neill, R.E. (1982). A comparison of parent training to direct child treatment. In R.L. Koegel, A. Rincover, & A.L. Egel (Eds.), *Educating and understanding autistic children* (pp. 260–279). San Diego: College-Hill Press.

Koegel, R.L., Screibman, L., Good, A., Cerniglia, L., Murphy, C., & Koegel, L.K. (1989). *How to teach pivotal behaviors to children with autism: A training manual.* Santa Barbara: University of California.

Koegel, R.L., Schreibman, L., Johnson, J., O'Neill, R.E., & Dunlap, G. (1984). Collateral effects of parent-training on families with autistic children. In R.F. Dangel & R.A. Polster (Eds.), *Behavioral parent-training: Issues in research and practice* (pp. 358–378). New York: The Guilford Press.

Koegel, R.L., Schreibman, L.M., Loos, L., Dirlich-Wilhelm, H., Dunlap, G., Robbins, F.R., & Plienis, A.J. (1992). Consistent stress profiles in mothers of children with autism. *Journal of Autism and Developmental Disorders, 22,* 205–216.

Koegel, R.L., Symon, J.B., Koegel, L.K. (2002). Parent education for families of children with autism living in geographically distant areas. *Journal of Positive Behavior Interventions, 4*(2), 88–103.

Koegel, R.L., Werner, G.A., Vismara, L.A., & Koegel, L.K. (in press). The effectiveness of contextually supported play date interactions between children with autism and typically developing peers. *Research and Practice for Persons with Severe Disabilities.*

Koegel, R.L., & Wilhelm, H. (1973). Selective responding to the components of multiple visual cues. *Journal of Experimental Child Psychology, 15,* 442–453.

Koegel, R.L., & Williams, J.A. (1980). Direct vs. indirect response-reinforcer relationships in teaching autistic children. *Journal of Abnormal Child Psychology, 4,* 537–547.

Krantz, P.J., MacDuff, M.T., & McClannahan, L.E. (1993). Program participation in family activities for children with autism: Parents' use of photographic activity schedules. *Journal of Applied Behavior Analysis, 26,* 137–138.

Krantz, P.J., & McClannahan, L.E. (1993). Teaching children with autism to initiate to peers: Effect of a script-fading procedure. *Journal of Applied Behavior Analysis, 26,* 121–132.

Kugler, B. (1998). The differentiation of autism and Asperger syndrome. *Autism, 2,* 11–32.

Kyratzis, A. (1998). Narrative identity: Preschoolers' self-construction through narrative in the same-sex friendship group dramatic play. *Narrative Inquiry, 9,* 427–455.

Ladd, G.W., & Hart, C.H. (1992). Creating informal play opportunities: Are parents' and preschoolers' initiations related to children's competence with peers? *Developmental Psychology, 28,* 1179–1187.

Ladd, G.W., Hart, C.H., Wadsworth, E.M., & Golter, B.S. (1988). Preschoolers' peer networks in nonschool settings: Relationship to family characteristics and school adjustment. In S. Salzinger, J.S. Antrobus, & M. Hammer (Eds.), *Social networks of children, adolescents, and college students* (pp. 61–92). Mahwah, NJ: Lawrence Erlbaum Associates.

Laird, R.D., Jordan, K.Y., Dodge, K.A., Pettit, G.S., & Bates, J.E. (2001). Peer rejection in childhood, involvement with antisocial peers in early adolescence, and the development of externalizing behavior problems. *Development and Psychopathology, 13,* 337–354.

Lake, J.F., & Billingsley, B.S. (2000). An analysis of factors that contribute to parent-school conflict in special education. *Remedial and Special Education, 21*(4), 240–251.

Landa, R. (2000). Social language use in Asperger syndrome and high-functioning autism. In A. Klin, F.R. Volkmar, & S.S. Sparrow (Eds.), *Asperger syndrome* (pp. 125–155). New York: The Guilford Press.

Landry, S.H., & Loveland, K.A. (1989). The effect of social context on the functional communication skills of autistic children. *Journal of Autism and Developmental Disorders, 19,* 283–299.

Landry, S.H., Smith, K.E., Miller-Loncar, C.L., & Swank, P.R. (1997). Responsiveness and initiative: Two aspects of social competence. *Infant Behavior and Development, 20,* 259–262.

Laski, K.E., Charlop, M.H., & Schreibman, L. (1988). Training parents to use the Natural Language Paradigm to increase their autistic children's speech. *Journal of Applied Behavior Analysis, 21,*(4), 391–400.

Laushey, K.M., & Heflin, L.J. (2000). Enhancing social skills of kindergarten children with autism through the training of multiple peers as tutors. *Journal of Autism and Developmental Disorders, 30,* 183–192.

Leekam, S., Libby, S., Wing, L., Gould, J., & Gillberg, C. (2000). Comparison of ICD-10 and Gillberg's criteria for Asperger syndrome. *Autism, 4,* 11–28.

Lewy, A., & Dawson, G. (1992). Social stimulation and joint attention in young autistic children. *Journal of Abnormal Child Psychology, 20*(6), 555–566.

Lincoln, Y.S., & Guba, E.G. (1985). *Naturalistic inquiry.* Thousand Oaks, CA: Sage Publications.

Linder, T.W. (1993). *Transdisciplinary Play-Based Assessment: A functional approach to working with young children* (Rev. ed.). Baltimore: Paul H. Brookes Publishing Co.

Locke, J.L. (1995). Development of the capacity for spoken language. In P. Fletcher & B. MacWhinney (Eds.), *The handbook of child language* (pp. 278–302). Malden, MA: Blackwell Publishers.

Lord, C. (1995). Follow-up of two-year-olds referred for possible autism. *Journal of Child Psychology & Psychiatry, 36*(8), 1365–1382.

Lord, C., & Hopkins, J.M. (1986). The social behavior of autistic children with younger and same-age nonhandicapped peers. *Journal of Autism and Developmental Disorders, 16,* 249–262.

Lord, C., & Paul, R. (1997). Language and communication in autism. In D. Cohen & F. Volkmar (Eds.), *Handbook of autism and pervasive developmental disorders* (pp. 195–225). Hoboken, NJ: John Wiley & Sons.

Lord, C., & Pickles, A. (1996). Language level and nonverbal social communicative behaviors in autistic and language-delayed children. *Journal of the American Academy of Child and Adolescent Psychiatry, 35,* 1542–1550.

Lord, C., Rutter, M., Goode, S., Heemsbergen, J., Jordan, H., Mawhood, L., & Schopler, E. (1989). Autism Diagnostic Observation Schedule: A standardized observation of communicative and social behavior. *Journal of Autism Developmental Disorders, 19,* 185–212.

Lord, C., & Schopler, E. (1989). The role of age at assessment, developmental level, and test in the stability of intelligence scores in young autistic children. *Journal of Autism and Developmental Disorders, 19,* 483–489.

Lord, C., & Schopler, E. (1994). TEACCH services for preschool children. In S. Harris & J. Handleman (Eds.), *Preschool education programs for children with autism* (pp. 15–36). Austin, TX: PRO-ED.

Lotter, V. (1966). Epidemiology of autistic conditions in young children: 1. Prevalence. *Social Psychiatry, 1,* 124–137.

Lovaas, O.I. (1977). *The autistic child: Language development through behavior modification.* New York: Irvington.

Lovaas, O.I. (1987). Behavioral treatment and normal education and intellectual functioning in young autistic children. *Journal of Consulting and Clinical Psychology, 55*(1), 3–9.

Lovass, O.I., Berberich, J.P., Perloff, B.F., & Schaeffer, B. (1966). Acquisition of initiative speech in schizophrenic children. *Science, 151,* 705–707.

Lovaas, O.I., Koegel, R.L., & Schreibman, L. (1979). Stimulus overselectivity in autism: A review of research. *Psychological Bulletin, 86*(6), 1236–1254.

Lovaas, O.I., Koegel, R.L., Simmons, J.Q., & Long, J.S. (1973). Some generalization and follow-up measures on autistic children in behavior therapy. *Journal of Applied Behavior Analysis, 6,* 131–166.

Lovaas, O.I., & Schreibman, L. (1971). Stimulus overselectivity of autistic children in a two stimulus situation. *Behavior Research and Therapy, 9,* 305–310.

Lovaas, O.I., Schreibman, L., Koegel, R.L., & Rehm, R. (1971). Selective responding by autistic children to multiple sensory input. *Journal of Abnormal Psychology, 77,* 211–222.

Loveland, K.A., & Landry, S.H. (1986). Joint attention and language in autism and developmental language delay. *Journal of Autism and Developmental Disorders, 16,* 335–349.

Lucyshyn, J.M., Albin, R.W., & Nixon, C.D. (1997). Embedding comprehensive behavioral support in family ecology: An experimental single-case analysis. *Journal of Consulting and Clinical Psychology, 65*(2), 241–251.

Lucyshyn, J.M., Horner, R.H., Dunlap, G., Albin, R.W., & Ben, K.R. (2002). Positive behavior support with families. In J.M. Lucyshyn, G. Dunlap, & R.W. Albin (Eds.), *Families and positive behavior support: Addressing problem behavior in family contexts* (pp. 3–43). Baltimore: Paul H. Brookes Publishing Co.

Lutzker, J.R., & Campbell, R. (1994). *Ecobehavioral family interventions in developmental disabilities.* Belmont, CA: Brooks/Cole Thomson Learning.

Lutzker, J.R., Huynen, K.B., & Bigelow, K.M. (1998). Parent training. In V.B. VanHassett & M. Herson (Eds.), *Handbook of psychological treatment protocols for children and adolescents* (pp. 467–500). Mahwah, NJ: Lawrence Erlbaum Associates.

Lutzker, J.R., & Steed, S.E. (1998). Parent training for families of children with developmental disabilities. In J.M. Briesmeister & C.E. Schaefer (Eds.), *Handbook of parent training: Parents as co-therapists for children's behavioral problems* (2nd ed., pp. 281–307). Hoboken, NJ: John Wiley & Sons.

Lutzker, J.R., Steed, S.E., & Huynen, K.B. (1998). Ecobehavioral treatment of challenging behaviors. *Journal of Developmental and Physical Disabilities, 10*(4), 349–363.

Mace, A.B., Shapiro, E.S., & Mace, F.C. (1998). Effects of warning stimuli for reinforcer withdrawal and task onset on self-injury. *Journal of Applied Behavior Analysis, 31,* 679–682.

Mandell, D., Listerud, J., Levy, S., & Pinto-Marti, J. (2002). Race differences in the age at diagnosis among medicaid-eligible children with autism. *American Academy of Child and Adolescent Psychiatry, 41*(12), 1447–1453.

Manjiviona, J., & Prior, M. (1995). Comparison of Asperger syndrome and high-functioning autistic children on a test of motor impairment. *Journal of Autism and Developmental Disorders, 25,* 23–39.

Marks, S.U., Schrader, C., & Levine, M. (1999). Paraeducator experiences in inclusive settings: Helping, hovering, or holding their own. *Exceptional Children, 65*(3), 315–330.

Markus, J., Mundy, P., Morales, M., Delgado, C.E.F., & Yale, M. (2000). Individual differences in infant skills as predictors of child-caregiver joint attention and language. *Social Development, 9*(3), 302–315.

Masur, E.F., & Ritz, E.G. (1984). Patterns of gestural, vocal, and verbal imitation performance in infancy. *Merrill-Palmer Quarterly, 30*(4), 369–392.

Matson, J.L., Benavidez, D.A., Compton, L.S., Paclawskyj, T., & Baglio, C.S. (1996). Behavioral treatment of autistic persons: A review of research from 1980 to the present. *Research in Developmental Disabilities, 17,* 433–465.

Matson, J.L., Sevin, J.A., Box, M.L., Francis, K.L., & Sevin, B.M. (1993). An evaluation of two methods for increasing self-initiated verbalizations in autistic children. *Journal of Applied Behavior Analysis, 26,* 389–398.

Mayes, S.D., & Calhoun, S.L. (2001). Non-significance of early speech delay in children with autism and normal intelligence and implications for DSM-IV Asperger's disorder. *Autism, 5,* 81–94.

Mayes, S.D., & Calhoun, S.L. (2003). Relationship between Asperger syndrome and high-functioning autism. In M. Prior (Ed.), *Learning and behavior problems in Asperger syndrome* (pp. 15–34). New York: The Guilford Press.

Mayes, S.D., Calhoun, S.L., & Crites, D.L. (2001). Does DSM-IV Asperger's disorder exist? *Journal of Abnormal Child Psychology, 29,* 263–271.

McArthur, D., & Adamson, L.B. (1996). Joint attention in preverbal children: Autism and developmental language disorder. *Journal of Autism and Developmental Disorders, 26,* 481–496.

McCabe, M.A., & Uzigiris, I.C. (1983). Effects of model and action on imitation in infancy. *Merrill-Palmer Quarterly, 29*(1), 69–82.

McCall, R.B., Parke, R.D., & Kavanaugh, R.D. (1977). Imitation of live and televised models by children one to three years of age. *Monographs of the Society for Research in Child Development, 42* (Serial No. 173).

McClannahan, L., & Krantz, P. (1997). The Princeton Child Development Institute. In S. Harris & J. Handleman (Eds.), *Preschool education programs for children with autism* (pp. 15–36). Austin, TX: PRO-ED.

McClannahan, L., Krantz, P., & McGee, G. (1982). Parents as therapists for autistic children: A model for effective parent training. *Analysis and Intervention in Developmental Disabilities, 2,* 223–252.

McConkey, R., Mariga, L., Braadland, N., & Mphole, P. (2000). Parents as trainers about disability in low income countries. *International Journal of Disability, Development and Education, 47*(3), 309–317.

McConnell, S.R. (2002). Interventions to facilitate social interactions for young children with autism: Review of available research and recommendations for educational intervention and future research. *Journal of Autism and Developmental Disorders, 32,* 351–372.

McEachin, J.J., Smith, T., & Lovaas, O.I. (1993). Long-term outcome for children with autism who received early intensive behavioral treatment. *American Journal on Mental Retardation, 97*(4), 359–372.

McGee, G.G., Almeida, M.C., Sulzer-Azaroff, B., & Feldman, R.S. (1992). Promoting reciprocal interactions via peer incidental teaching. *Journal of Applied Behavior Analysis. Special Issue: The education crisis: Issues, perspectives, solutions, 25,* 117–126.

McGee, G.G., Daly, T., & Jacobs, H.A. (1994). The Walden Preschool. In S. Harris & J. Handleman (Eds.), *Preschool education programs for children with autism* (pp. 15–36). Austin, TX: PRO-ED.

McGee, G.G., Feldman, R.S., & Morrier, M.J. (1997). Benchmarks of social treatment for children with autism. *Journal of Autism and Developmental Disorders, 27,* 353–364.

McGee, G.G., Jacobs, H.A., & Regnier, M.C. (1993, Winter). Preparation for families for incidental teaching and advocacy for their children with autism. *OSERS News in Print,* 9–13.

McGee, G.G., Krantz, P.J., & McClannahan, L.E. (1985). The facilitative effects of incidental teaching on preposition use by autistic children. *Journal of Applied Behavior Analysis, 18*(1), 17–31.

McGee, G.G., Morrier, M.J., & Daly T. (1999). An incidental teaching approach to early intervention for toddlers with autism. *Journal of The Association for Persons with Severe Handicaps, 24*(3), 133–146.

McGee, G.G., Morrier, M.J., & Daly, T. (2001). The Walden Early Childhood Programs. In J.S. Handleman & S.L. Harris (Eds.), *Preschool education programs for children with autism* (pp. 157–190). Austin, TX: PRO-ED.

McGrath, S.B., Bosch, S., Sullivan, C.L., & Fuqua, R.W. (2003). Training reciprocal social interactions between preschoolers and a child with autism. *Journal of Positive Behavior Interventions, 5,* 47–54.

McHale, S.M., Dariotis, J.K., & Kauh, T.J. (2003). Social development and social relationships in middle childhood. In R.M. Lerner, M.A. Easterbrookes, & J. Mistry (Eds.), *Handbook of psychology: Vol. 6. Developmental psychology* (pp. 241–265). Hoboken, NJ: John Wiley & Sons.

McHale, S.M., Sloan, J., & Simeonsson, R.J. (1986). Sibling relationships of children with autism, mentally retarded, and nonhandicapped brothers and sisters. *Journal of Autism and Developmental Disorders, 16,* 399–413.

McLaughlin, S. (1998). *Introduction to language development.* San Diego: Singular Publishing Group.

McLean, J.E., & Snyder-McLean, L.K. (1978). *A transactional approach to early language training.* Columbus, OH: Charles E. Merrill.

McLean, L.K. (1990). Communication development in the first two years of life: A transactional process. *Zero to Three, 11,* 13–19.

McTear, M.F. (1985). *Children's conversations.* Malden, MA: Blackwell Publishers

Mesibov, G.B. (1983). Current perspectives and issues in autism and adolescence. In E. Scholper & G.B. Mesibov (Eds.), *Autism in adolescents and adults* (pp. 37–53). New York: Kluwer Academic/Plenum Publishers.

Mesibov, G.B. (1984). Social skills training with verbal autistic adolescents and adults: A program model. *Journal of Autism and Developmental Disorders, 14,* 395–404.

Mesibov, G.B., Adams, L.W., & Klinger, L.G. (1997). *Autism: Understanding the disorder.* New York: Kluwer Academic/Plenum Publishers.

Mesibov, G.B., Shea, V., & Adams, L.W. (2001). *Understanding Asperger syndrome and high functioning autism.* New York: Kluwer Academic/Plenum Publishers.

Meyer, W.J., & Shane, J. (1973). The form and function of children's questions. *Journal of Genetic Psychology,* 285–296.

Miles, M.B., & Huberman, A.M. (1994). *Qualitative data analysis: An expanded sourcebook* (2nd ed.). Thousand Oaks, CA: Sage Publications.

Miller, J.F. (1981). *Assessing language production in children.* Boston: Allyn & Bacon.

Miller, J.N., & Ozonoff, S.A. (1997). Did Asperger's cases have Asperger's disorder? A research note. *Journal of Child Psychology and Psychiatry, 38,* 247–251.

Miller, J.N., & Ozonoff, S.A. (2000). The external validity of Asperger disorder: Lack of evidence from the domain of neuropsychology. *Journal of Abnormal Psychology, 109,* 227–238.

Miller, W.R., & Seligman, M.E.P. (1975). Depression and learned helplessness in man. *Journal of Abnormal Psychology, 84,* 228–238.

Minnes, P.M. (1988). Family resources and stress associated with a developmentally handicapped child. *American Journal of Mental Retardation, 93,* 184–192.

Mishna, F., & Muskat, B. (1998). Group therapy for boys with features of Asperger syndrome and concurrent learning disabilities: Finding a peer group. *Journal of Child and Adolescent Group Therapy, 8,* 97–114.

Moes, D. (1995). Parent education and parenting stress. In R.L. Koegel & L.K. Koegel (Eds.), *Teaching children with autism: Strategies for initiating positive interactions and improving learning opportunities* (pp. 79–93). Baltimore: Paul H. Brookes Publishing Co.

Moes, D. (1998). Integrating choice making opportunities within teacher assigned academic tasks to facilitate the performance of children with autism. *Journal of The Association for Persons with Severe Handicaps, 23,* 319–328.

Moes, D.R., & Frea, W.D. (2000). Using family context to inform intervention planning for the treatment of a child with autism. *Journal of Positive Behavior Interventions, 2*(1), 40–46.

Moes, D.R., & Frea, W.D. (2002). Contextualized behavioral support in early intervention for children with autism and their families. *Journal of Autism and Developmental Disorders, 32*(6), 519–533.

Molloy, H., & Vasil, L. (2002). The social construction of Asperger syndrome: The pathologizing of difference? *Disability and Society, 17,* 659–669.

Morrison, L., Kamps, D., Garcia, J., & Parker, D. (2001). Peer mediation and monitoring strategies to improve initiations and social skills for students with autism. *Journal of Positive Behavior Interventions, 3,* 237–250.

Mueller, E., Bleier, M., Krakow, J., Hagedus, K., & Cournoyer, P. (1977). The development of peer verbal interaction among two-year-old boys. *Child Development, 48,* 284–287.

Muhlenbruck, L., Cooper, H., Nye, B., & Lindsay, J. (2000). Homework and achievement: Explaining the different strengths of relation at the elementary and secondary school levels. *Social Psychology of Education, 3,* 295–317.

Mullen, K.B., & Frea, W.D. (1995). A parent–professional consultation model for functional analysis. In R.L. Koegel & L.K. Koegel (Eds.), *Teaching children with autism: Strategies for initiating positive interactions and improving learning opportunities* (pp. 175–188). Baltimore: Paul H. Brookes Publishing Co.

Mundy, P. (1995). Joint attention, social-emotional approach in children with autism. *Development and Psychopathology, 7,* 63–82.

Mundy, P., & Crowson, M. (1997). Joint attention and early communication: Implications for intervention with autism. *Journal of Autism and Developmental Disorders, 27,* 653–676.

Mundy, P., & Gomes, A. (1996). Individual differences in joint attention skill development in the second year. *Infant Behaviour and Development, 21,* 469–482.

Mundy, P., & Markus, J. (1997). On the nature of communication and language impairment in autism. *Mental Retardation and Developmental Disabilities Research Reviews, 3,* 343–349.

Mundy, P., Sigman, M., & Kasari, C. (1990). A longitudinal study of joint attention and language development in autistic children. *Journal of Autism and Developmental Disorders, 20*(1), 115–128.

Mundy, P., Sigman, M., & Kasari, C. (1994). Joint attention, developmental level, and symptom presentation in young children with autism. *Development and Psychopathology, 6,* 389–401.

Mundy, P., Sigman, M., Ungerer, J., & Sherman, T. (1986). Defining the social deficits of autism: The contribution of non-verbal communication measures. *Journal of Child Psychology and Psychiatry, 27*(5), 657–669.

Mundy, P., & Stella, J. (2000). Joint attention, social orienting, and communication in autism. In S.F. Warren & J. Reichle (Series Eds.) & A.M. Wetherby & B.M. Prizant (Eds.), *Communication and language intervention series: Vol. 9. Autism spectrum disorders: A transactional developmental perspective* (pp. 55–77). Baltimore: Paul H. Brookes Publishing Co.

Mundy, P., & Willoughby, J. (1998). Nonverbal communication, affect, and social-emotional development. In S F. Warren & J. Reichle (Series Eds.) & A.M. Wetherby, S.F. Warren, & J. Reichle (Vol. Eds.), *Communication and language intervention series: Vol. 7. Transitions in prelinguistic communications* (pp. 111–133). Baltimore: Paul H. Brookes Publishing Co.

Myles, B.S., & Simpson, R.L. (2001). Understanding the hidden curriculum: An essential social skill for children and youth with Asperger syndrome. *Intervention in School and Clinic, 36,* 279–286.

National Research Council. (2001). Educating children with autism. In C. Lord & James P. McGee (Eds.), *Committee on Educational Interventions for Children with Autism.* Washington, DC: National Academy Press.

Nelson, K. (1986). *Event knowledge: Structure and function in development.* Mahwah, NJ: Lawrence Erlbaum Associates.

Nevin, J.A., Mandell, C., & Atak, J.R. (1983). The analysis of behavioral momentum. *Journal of the Experimental Analysis of Behavior, 39,* 49–59.

Newson, J., & Newson, E. (1976). *Seven years old in the home environment.* Hoboken, NJ: John Wiley & Sons.

Nickels, C. (1996). A gift from Alex—The art of belonging: Strategies for academic and social inclusion. In L.K. Koegel, R.L. Koegel, & G. Dunlap (Eds.), *Positive behavioral support: Including people with difficult behavior in the community* (pp. 123–144). Baltimore: Paul H. Brookes Publishing Co.

Nietupski, J., Hamre-Nietupski, S., Curtin, S., & Shrikanth, K. (1997). A review of curricular research in severe disabilities from 1976 to 1995 in six selected journals. *The Journal of Special Education, 31,* 36–55.

Nihira, K., Weisner, T.S., & Bernheimer, L.P. (1994). Ecocultural assessment in families of children with developmental delays: Construct and concurrent validities. *American Journal on Mental Retardation, 48(5),* 551–566.

Ninness, H.C., Fuerst, J., Rutherford, R.D., & Glenn, S.S. (1991). Effects of self-management training and reinforcement on the transfer of improved conduct in the absence of supervision. *Journal of Applied Behavior Analysis, 24*(3), 499–508.

Odom, S.L., Hoyson, S., Jamieson, B., & Strain, P.S. (1985). Increasing handicapped preschoolers social interactions: Cross-setting and component analysis. *Journal of Applied Behavior Analysis, 18,* 3–16.

Odom, S.L., & Strain, P.S. (1984). Peer-mediated approaches to promoting children's social interaction: A review. *American Journal of Orthopsychiatry, 54,* 544–557.

Odom, S.L., & Watts, E. (1991). Reducing teacher prompts in peer-mediated interventions for young children with autism. *The Journal of Special Education, 25,* 26–43.

Oke, N.J., & Schreibman, L. (1990). Training social initiations to a high-functioning autistic child: Assessment of collateral behavior change and generalization in a case study. *Journal of Autism and Developmental Disorders, 20,* 479–497.

O'Neill, D.K., & Happe, F.G.E. (2000). Noticing and commenting on what's new: differences and similarities among 22-month-old typical developing children, children with Down syndrome and children with autism. *Developmental Science, 3,* 457–478.

O'Neill, R.E., Horner, R.H., Albin, R.W., Storey, K., & Sprague, J.R. (1990). *Functional analysis of problem behavior: A practical assessment guide.* Sycamore, IL: Sycamore Publishing Company.

Ornitz, E.M., Guthrie, D., & Farley, A.H. (1977). The early development of autistic children. *Journal of Autism and Childhood Schizophrenia, 7*(3), 207–229.

Orsmond, G.I., Krauss, M.W., & Seltzer, M.M. (2004). Peer relationships and social and recreational activities among adolescents and adults with autism. *Journal of Autism and Developmental Disorders, 34,* 245–256.

Osterling, J., & Dawson, G. (1994). Early recognition of children with autism: A study of first birthday home videotapes. *Journal of Autism and Developmental Disorders, 24*(3), 247–257.

Osterling, J., Dawson, G., & Munson, J. (2002). Early recognition of 1-year-old infants with autism spectrum disorder versus mental retardation. *Development and Psychopathology, 14,* 239–251.

Overmier, O.B., & Seligman, M.E.P. (1967). Effects of inescapable shock upon subsequent escape and avoidance learning. *Journal of Comparative and Physiological Psychology, 63,* 28–33.

Ozonoff, S., & Cathcart, K. (1998). Effectiveness of a home program intervention for young children with autism. *Journal of Autism and Developmental Disorders, 28,* 25–32.

Ozonoff, S., South, M., & Miller, J.N. (2000). DSM-IV-defined Asperger syndrome: Cognitive, behavioral, and early history differentiation from high-functioning autism. *Autism, 4,* 29–46.

Parker, J.G., & Asher, S.R. (1993). Friendship and friendship quality in middle childhood: Links with peer group acceptance and feelings of loneliness and social dissatisfaction. *Developmental Psychology, 29,* 611–621.

Parsons, M.B., & Reid, D.H. (1995). Training residential supervisors to provide feedback for maintaining staff teaching skills with people who have severe disabilities. *Journal of Applied Behavior Analysis, 28,* 317–322.

Parsons, M.B., Reid, D.H., & Green, C.W. (1996). Training basic teaching skills to community and institutional support staff for people with severe disabilities: A one day program. *Research in Developmental Disabilities, 17,* 467–485.

Patton, M.Q. (1987). *How to use qualitative methods in evaluation.* Thousand Oaks, CA: Sage Publications.

Patton, M.Q. (1990). *Qualitative evaluation and research methods* (2nd ed.). Thousand Oaks, CA: Sage Publications.

Paul, R., & Shiffer, M.E. (1991). Communicative initiations in normal and late-talking toddlers. *Applied Psycholinguistics, 12,* 419–431.

Piaget, J. (1959). *The language and thought of the child.* London: Routledge and Kegan Paul.

Pierce, G.R., Sarason, I.G., & Sarason, B.R. (1996). Coping and social support. In M. Zeidner & N.S. Endler (Eds.), *Handbook of coping: Theory, research, applications* (pp. 434–451). Hoboken, NJ: John Wiley & Sons.

Pierce, K., & Schreibman, L. (1995). Increasing complex social behaviors in children with autism: A review. *Journal of Applied Behavior Analysis, 28,* 285–295.

Pierce, K., & Schreibman, L. (1997). Using peer trainers to promote social behavior in autism: Are they effective at enhancing multiple social modalities? *Focus on Autism and Other Developmental Disabilities, 12,* 207–218.

Pihl, R.O., & Greenspoon, J. (1969). The effect of amount of reinforcement on the formation of the reinforcing value of a verbal stimulus. *Canadian Journal of Psychology, 23,* 219–225.

Plienis, A.J., Robbins, F.R., & Dunlap, G. (1988). Parent adjustment and family stress as factors in behavioral parent training for young autistic children. *Journal of the Multihandicapped Person, 1,* 31–52.

Powell, T.H., & Gallagher, P.A. (1993). *Brothers and sisters: A special part of exceptional families* (2nd ed.). Baltimore: Paul H. Brookes Publishing Co.

Powers, M.D. (1992). Early intervention for children with autism. In D.E. Berkell (Ed.), *Autism: Identification, education, and treatment* (pp. 225–252). Mahwah, NJ: Lawrence Erlbaum Associates.

Prior, M. (2003). *Learning and behavior problems in Asperger syndrome.* New York: The Guilford Press.

Prizant, B.M., & Wetherby, A.M. (1987). Communicative intent: A framework for understanding social-communicative behavior in autism. *Journal of American Academy of Child and Adolescent Psychiatry, 26*(4), 472–479.

Raghavan, C., Weisner, T.S., & Patel, D. (1999). The adaptive project of parenting: South Asian families with children with developmental delays. *Education and Training in Mental Retardation and Developmental Disabilities, 34*(3), 281–292.

Randall, P., & Parker, J. (1999). *Supporting the families of children with autism.* Hoboken, NJ: John Wiley & Sons.

Reese, R.M., Richman, D.M., Zarcone, J., & Zarcone, T. (2003). Individualizing functional assessments for children with autism: The contribution of perseverative behavior and sensory disturbances to disruptive behaviors. *Focus on Autism and Other Developmental Disabilities, 18,* 89–94.

Reid, D.H. (2000). Enhancing the applied utility of functional assessment. *Journal of The Association for Persons with Severe Handicaps, 25,* 241–244.

Reid, D.H., Rotholz, D.A., Parsons, M.B., Morris, L., Braswell, B., Green, C.W., & Schell, R.M. (2003). Training human service supervisors in aspects of PBS: Evaluation of a statewide, performance-based program. *Journal of Positive Behavior Interventions, 5,* 35–46.

Reitzel, J., & Szatmari, P. (2003). Cognitive and academic problems. In M. Prior (Ed.), *Learning and behavior problems in Asperger syndrome* (pp. 35–54). New York: The Guilford Press.

Reynolds, B.S., Newsom, C.D., & Lovaas, O.I. (1974). Auditory overselectivity in autistic children. *Journal of Abnormal Child Psychology, 2,* 253–263.

Riggs, C., & Mueller, P. (2001). Employment and utilization of paraeducators in inclusive settings. *Journal of Special Education, 35,* 54–74.

Ritvo, E.R., Freeman, B.J., Pingree, C.B., Mason-Brothers, A., Jorde, L.B., Jenson, W.R., McMahon, W.M., Petersen, P.B., Mo, A., & Ritvo, A. (1989). The UCLA–University of Utah epidemiologic survey of autism: Prevalence. *American Journal of Psychiatry, 146*(2), 194–199.

Robbins, F.R., Dunlap, G., & Plienis, A.J. (1991). Family characteristics, family training, and the progress of young children with autism. *Journal of Early Intervention, 15*(2), 173–184.

Robins, D.L., Fein, D., Barton, M.L., & Green, J.A. (2001). The modified checklist for autism in toddlers: An initial study investigating the early detection of autism and pervasive developmental disorders. *Journal of Autism and Developmental Disorders, 31*(2), 131–151.

Roff, M. (1961). Childhood social interactions and young adult bad conduct. *Journal of Abnormal and Social Psychology, 63,* 333–337.

Rogers, M.F., & Myles, B.S. (2001). Using social stories and comic strip conversations to interpret social situations for an adolescent with Asperger syndrome. *Intervention in School and Clinic, 36,* 310–313.

Rogers, S.J. (1998). Empirically supported comprehensive treatments for young children with autism. *Journal of Clinical Child Psychology, 27*(2), 168–179.

Rogers, S.J. (2000). Interventions that facilitate socialization in children with autism. *Journal of Autism and Developmental Disorders, 30*(5), 399–409.

Rogers, S.J., Hall, T., Osaki, D., Reaven, J., & Herbison, J. (2001). The Denver Model: A comprehensive, integrated educational approach to young children with autism and their families. In J.S. Handleman & S.L. Harris (Eds.), *Preschool education programs for children with autism* (pp. 95–134). Austin, TX: PRO-ED.

Rogers-Adkinson, D.L., Ochoa, T.A., & Delgado, B. (2003). Developing cross-cultural competence: Serving families of children with significant developmental needs. *Focus on Autism and Other Developmental Disabilities, 18*(1), 4–8.

Rourke, B.P. (1989). *Nonverbal learning disabilities: The syndrome and the model.* New York: The Guilford Press.

Rourke, B.P. (Ed.). (1995). *Syndrome of nonverbal learning disabilities: Neurodevelopmental manifestations.* New York: The Guilford Press.

Rourke, B.P., Del Dotto, J.E., Rourke, S.B., & Casey, J.E. (1990). Nonverbal learning disabilities: The syndrome and a case study. *Journal of School Psychology, 28,* 361–385.

Rourke, B.P., & Tsatsanis, K.D. (2000). Nonverbal learning disabilities and Asperger syndrome. In A. Klin, F.R. Volkmar, & S.S. Sparrow (Eds.), *Asperger syndrome* (pp. 231–253). New York: The Guilford Press.

Ruble, L.A. (2001). Analysis of social interactions as goal-directed behaviors in children with autism. *Journal of Autism and Developmental Disorders, 31,* 471–482.

Ruef, M.B., Turnbull, A.P., Turnbull, H.R., & Poston, D. (1999). Perspectives of five stakeholder groups: Challenging behaviors of individuals with mental retardation and/or autism. *Journal of Positive Behavior Interventions, 1*(1), 43–58.

Russell, D., Cutrona, C.E., Rose, J., & Yurko, K. (1984). Social and emotional loneliness: An examination of Weiss's typology of loneliness. *Journal of Personality and Social Psychology, 46*(6), 1313–1321.

Sachs, D.A. (1973). The efficacy of time-out procedures in a variety of behavior problems. *Journal of Behavior Therapy and Experimental Psychiatry, 4,* 237–242.

Salend, S.J., & Taylor, L.S. (2002). Cultural perspectives: Missing pieces in the functional assessment process. *Intervention in School and Clinic, 38*(2), 104–112.

Sameroff, A.J. (1975). Transactional models of early social relations. *Human Development, 18,* 65–79.

Sameroff, A.J. (1987). The social context of development. In N. Eisenburg (Ed.), *Contemporary topics in development* (pp. 273–291). Hoboken, NJ: John Wiley & Sons.

Sameroff, A.J., & Chandler, M. (1975). Reproductive risk and the continuum of caretaking causality. In F. Horowitz (Ed.), *Review of child development research: Vol. 4* (pp. 187–244). Chicago: University of Chicago Press.

Sameroff, A.J., & Fiese, B. (1990). Transactional regulation and early intervention. In S. Meisels & J. Shonkoff (Eds.), *Early intervention: A handbook of theory, practice, and analysis* (pp. 119–149). New York: Cambridge University Press.

Sameroff, A.J., & Fiese, B. (2000). Models of development and developmental risk. In C.H. Zeanah, Jr. (Ed.), *Handbook of infant mental health* (2nd ed., pp. 3–19). New York: The Guilford Press.

Sanders, M.R. (1996). New directions in behavioral family intervention with children. In T.H. Ollendick & R.J. Prinz (Eds.), *Advances in clinical child psychology: Vol. 18* (pp. 283–329). New York: Kluwer Academic/Plenum Publishers.

Sanders, M.R., & Dadds, M.R. (1982). The effects of planned activities and child management procedure on parent training: An analysis of setting generality. *Behavior Therapy, 13,* 452–461.

Sanders, M.R., & Glynn, T. (1981). Training parents in behavioral self-management: An analysis of generalization and maintenance. *Journal of Applied Behavior Analysis, 14,* 223–237.

Santarelli, G., Koegel, R.L., Casas, J.M., & Koegel, L.K. (2001). Culturally diverse families participating in behavior therapy parent education programs for children with developmental disabilities. *Journal of Positive Behavior Interventions, 3*(2), 120–123.

Santelli, B., Turnbull, A.P., Lerner, E., & Marquis, J. (1993). Parent to Parent programs: A unique form of mutual support for families of persons with disabilities. In G.H.S. Singer & L.E. Powers (Eds.), *Families, disability, and empowerment: Active coping skills and strategies for family interventions* (pp. 27–57). Baltimore: Paul H. Brookes Publishing Co.

Sasso, G.M., Mitchell, V.M., & Struthers, E.M. (1986). Peer tutoring versus structured interaction activities: Effects on the frequency and topography of peer initiations. *Behavioral Disorders, 11,* 249–259.

Sasso, G.M., Mundschenk, N.A., Melloy, K.J., & Casey, S.D. (1998). A comparison of the effects of organismic and setting variables on the social interaction behavior of children with developmental disabilities and autism. *Focus on Autism and Other Developmental Disabilities, 13,* 2–16.

Savin-Williams, R.C., & Berndt, T.J. (1990). Friendship and peer relations. In S.S. Feldman & G.R. Elliott (Eds.), *At the threshold: The developing adolescent* (pp. 277–307). Cambridge, MA: Harvard University Press.

Schepis, M.M., Ownbey, J.B., Parsons, M.B., & Reid, D.H. (2000). Training support staff for teaching young children with disabilities in an inclusive preschool setting. *Journal of Positive Behavior Interventions, 2*(3), 170–178.

Schneider, P., & Gearhart, M. (1988). The ecocultural niche of families of with mentally retarded children: Evidence from mother–child interaction studies. *Journal of Applied Developmental Psychology, 9*(1), 85–106.

Schopler, E., & Reichler, R.J. (1971). Parents as cotherapists in the treatment of psychotic children. *Journal of Autism and Childhood Schizophrenia, 1,* 87–102.

Schopler, E., Short, A., & Mesibov, G. (1989). Relation of behavioral treatment to "normal functioning": Comment on Lovaas. *Journal of Consulting and Clinical Psychology, 57,* 162–164.

Schover, L.R., & Newsom, C.D. (1976). Overselectivity, developmental level, and overtraining in autistic and normal children. *Journal of Abnormal Child Psychology, 4,* 289–298.

Schreibman, L. (1988). *Autism.* Thousand Oaks, CA: Sage Publications.

Schreibman, L. (2000). Intensive behavioral/psychoeducational treatments for autism: Research needs and future directions. *Journal of Autism and Developmental Disorders, 30*(5), 373–378.

Schreibman, L., Charlop, M.H., & Koegel, R.L. (1982). Teaching autistic children to use extra stimulus prompts. *Journal of Experimental Child Psychology, 33*, 475–491.

Schreibman, L., Kaneko, W.M., & Koegel, R.L. (1991). Positive affect of parents of autistic children: A comparison across two teaching techniques. *Behavior Therapy, 22*(4), 479–490.

Schreibman, L., & Koegel, R.L. (1982). Multiple-cue responding in autistic children. In J. Steffen & P. Karoly (Eds.), *Advances in child behavioral analysis and therapy: Vol. II. Autism and severe psychopathology* (pp. 81–99). Lexington, MA: D.C. Heath & Co.

Schreibman, L., & Koegel, R.L. (2005). Training for parents of children with autism: Pivotal responses, generalization, and individualization of interventions. In E.D. Hibbs & P.S. Jensen (Eds.), *Psychosocial treatments for child and adolescent disorders: Empirically based strategies for clinical practice* (2nd ed., pp. 605–631). Washington, DC: American Psychological Association.

Schreibman, L., Koegel, R.L., & Craig, M.S. (1977). Reducing stimulus overselectivity in autistic children. *Journal of Abnormal Child Psychology, 5*, 425–436.

Schreibman, L., Stahmer, A.C., & Pierce, K.L. (1996). Alternative applications of pivotal response training: Teaching symbolic play and social interaction skills. In L.K. Koegel, R.L. Koegel, & G. Dunlap (Eds.), *Positive behavioral support: Including people with difficult behavior in the community* (pp. 353–371). Baltimore: Paul H. Brookes Publishing Co.

Schreibman, L., Whalen, C., & Stahmer, A. (2000). The use of video priming to reduce disruptive transition behavior in children with autism. *Journal of Positive Behavior Interventions, 2*, 3–11.

Schuler, A.L., & Wolfberg, P.J. (2000). Promoting peer play and socialization: The art of scaffolding. In S.F. Warren & J. Reichle (Series Eds.) & A.M. Wetherby & B.M. Prizant (Vol. Eds.), *Communication and language intervention series: Vol. 9. Autism spectrum disorders: A transactional developmental perspective* (pp. 251–277). Baltimore: Paul H. Brookes Publishing Co.

Schultz, T.M., & Berkson, G. (1995). Definition of abnormal focused affections and exploration of their relation to abnormal stereotyped behaviors. *American Journal on Mental Retardation, 99*(4), 376–390.

Schwartz, D., Dodge, K.A., Pettit, G.S., & Bates, J.E. (2000). Friendship as a moderating factor in the pathway between early harsh home environment and later victimization in the peer group. *Developmental Psychology, 36*, 646–662.

Segall, M.H., Lonner, W.J., & Berry, J.W. (1998). Cross-cultural psychology as a scholarly discipline: On the flowering of culture in behavior research. *American Psychologist, 53*(10), 1101–1110.

Seibert, J.M., Hogan, A.E., & Mundy, P.C. (1982). Assessing interactional competencies: The Early Social-Communication Scales. *Infant Mental Health Journal, 3*, 244–245.

Seligman, M.E.P. (1972). Learned helplessness. *Annual Review of Medicine, 23*, 407–412.

Seligman, M.E.P., Klein, D.C., & Miller, W.R. (1976). Depression. In H. Leitenberg (Ed.), *Handbook of behavior modification* (pp. 168–210). New York: Appleton-Century-Crofts.

Seligman, M.E.P., & Maier, S.F. (1967). Failure to escape traumatic shock. *Journal of Experimental Psychology, 74*, 1–9.

Seligman, M.E.P., Maier, S.F., & Geer, J. (1968). The alleviation of learned helplessness in the dog. *Journal of Abnormal and Social Psychology, 73*, 256–262.

Shabani, D.B., Katz, R.C., Wilder, D.A., Beauchamp, K., Taylor, C.R., & Fischer, K.J. (2002). Increasing social initiations in children with autism: Effects of a tactile prompt. *Journal of Applied Behavior Analysis, 35*, 79–83.

Shah, K. (2001). What do medical students know about autism? *Autism, 5*(2), 127–133.

Shaked, M., & Yirmiya, N. (2003). Understanding social difficulties. In M. Prior (Ed.), *Learning and behavior problems in Asperger syndrome* (pp. 104–125). New York: The Guilford Press.

Sheinkopf, S.J., & Siegel, B. (1998). Home-based behavioral treatment of young children with autism. *Journal of Autism and Developmental Disorders, 28*(1), 15–23.

Shriberg, L.D., Paul, R., McSweeney, J.L., Klin, A., Cohen, D.J., & Volkmar, F.R. (2001). Speech and prosody characteristics of adolescents and adults with high-functioning autism and Asperger syndrome. *Journal of Speech, Language, and Hearing Research, 44*, 1097–1115.

Shukla, S., Kennedy, C., & Cushing, L. (1999). Intermediate school students with severe disabilities: Supporting their social participation in general education classrooms. *Journal of Positive Behavior Support, 1,* 130–140.

Siegel, B., Pliner, C., Eschler, J., & Elliott, G.R. (1988). How children with autism are diagnosed: Difficulties in identification of children with multiple developmental delays. *Journal of Developmental and Behavioral Pediatrics, 9*(4), 199–204.

Sigman, M., & Ruskin, E. (1999). Continuity and change in the social competence of children with autism, Down syndrome, and developmental delays. *Monographs of the Society for Research in Child Development, 64*(Serial No. 256).

Siller, M., & Sigman, M. (2002). The behaviors of parents of children with autism predict the subsequent development of their children's communication. *Journal of Autism and Developmental Disorders, 32*(2), 77–89.

Silver, M., & Oakes, P. (2001). Evaluation of a new computer intervention to teach people with autism or Asperger syndrome to recognize and predict emotions in others. *Autism, 5,* 299–310.

Simons, J.M. (1974). Observation on compulsive behavior in autism. *Journal of Autism and Childhood Schizophrenia, 4,* 1–10.

Singer, G.H.S., Goldberg-Hamblin, S.E., Peckham-Hardin, K.D., Barry, L., & Santarelli, G.E. (2002). Toward a synthesis of family support practices and positive behavior support. In J.M. Lucyshyn, G. Dunlap, & Albin, R.W. (Eds.), *Families and positive behavior support: Addressing problem behavior in family contexts* (pp. 155–183). Baltimore: Paul H. Brookes Publishing Co.

Singer, G.H.S., Irvine, A.B., & Irvin, L.K. (1989). Expanding the focus of behavioral parent training: A contextual approach. In G.H.S. Singer & L.K. Irvin (Eds.), *Support for caregiving families enabling positive adaptation* (pp. 85–102). Baltimore: Paul H. Brookes Publishing Co.

Singer, G.H.S., Marquis, J., Powers, L.K., Blanchard, L., Divenere, N., Santelli, B., Ainbinder, J.G., & Sharp, M. (1999). A multi-site evaluation of Parent to Parent programs for parents of children with disabilities. *Journal of Early Intervention, 22*(3), 217–229.

Singer, G.H.S., & Powers, L.E. (1993a). Contributing to resilience in families: An overview. In G.H.S Singer & L.E. Powers (Eds.), *Families, disability, and empowerment: Active coping skills and strategies for family interventions* (pp. 1–25). Baltimore: Paul H. Brookes Publishing Co.

Singer, G.H.S., & Powers, L.E. (1993b). *Families, disability, and empowerment: Active coping skills and strategies for family interventions.* Baltimore: Paul H. Brookes Publishing Co.

Skinner, D., Rodriguez, P., & Bailey, D.B. (1999). Qualitative analysis of Latino parents' religious interpretations of their child's disability. *Journal of Early Intervention, 22*(4), 271–285.

Smith, C.B., Adamson, L.B., & Bakeman, R. (1988). Interactional predictors of early language. *First language, 8,* 143–156.

Smith, T. (1999). Outcome of early intervention for children with autism. *Clinical Psychology: Science and Practice, 6*(1), 33–49.

Snow, C.E. (1977). The development of conversation between mothers and babies. *Journal of Child Language, 4,* 1–22.

Soodak, L.C., & Erwin, E.J. (2000). Valued member or tolerated participant: Parents' experiences in inclusive early childhood settings. *Journal of The Association for the Persons with Severe Handicaps, 25*(1), 29–41.

Sparrow, S.S., Balla, D.A., & Cicchetti, D.V. (1984). *Vineland Adaptive Behavior Scales.* Circle Pines, MN: American Guidance Service.

Spradlin, J.E., & Brady, N.C. (1999). Early childhood autism and stimulus control. In P.M. Ghezzi, W.L. Williams, & J.E. Carr (Eds.), *Autism: Behavior analytic perspectives* (pp. 49–65). Reno, NV: Context.

Sprague, J.R., & Horner, R.H. (1992). Covariation within functional response classes: Implications for treatment of severe problem behavior. *Journal of Applied Behavior Analysis, 25*(3), 735–745

Sprague, J.R., & Horner, R.H. (1994). Covariation within functional response classes: Implications for treatment of severe problem behavior. In T. Thompson & D.B. Gray (Eds.), *Destructive behavior in developmental disabilities: Diagnosis and treatment. Sage focus editions: Vol. 170* (pp. 213–242). Thousand Oaks, CA: Sage Publications.

Sprague, J.R., & Horner, R.H. (1995). Functional assessment and intervention in community settings. In Self-injury in developmental disabilities: Neurobiological and environmental mechanisms [Special issue]. *Mental Retardation and Developmental Disabilities Research Reviews, 1*(2), 89–93.

Stahmer, A.C. (1995). Teaching symbolic play skills to children with autism using pivotal response training. *Journal of Autism and Developmental Disorders, 25*(2), 123–141.

Stahmer, A.C. (1999). Using pivotal response training to facilitate appropriate play in children with autistic spectrum disorders. *Child Language Teaching and Therapy, 15,* 29–40.

Stahmer, A.C., & Schreibman, L. (1992). Teaching children with autism appropriate play in unsupervised environments using a self-management treatment package. *Journal of Applied Behavior Analysis, 25,* 447–459.

Stiebel, D. (1999). Promoting augmentative communication during daily routines: A parent problem-solving intervention. *Journal of Positive Behavior Interventions, 1,* 159–169.

Stocker, C., & Dunn, J. (1990). Sibling relationships in childhood: Links with friendship and peer relationships. *British Journal of Developmental Psychology, 8,* 227–244.

Stokes, T., & Baer, D. (1977). An implicit technology of generalization. *Journal of Applied Behavior Analysis, 10,* 349–367.

Stone, W.L. (1998). Autism in infancy and early childhood. In D. Cohen & F. Volkmar (Eds.), *Handbook of autism and pervasive developmental disorders* (pp. 266–282). Hoboken, NJ: John Wiley & Sons.

Stone, W.L., & Caro-Martinez, L.M. (1990). Naturalistic observations of spontaneous communication in autistic children. *Journal of Autism and Developmental Disorders, 20,* 437–453.

Stone, W.L., & Lemanek, K.L. (1990). Parental report of social behaviors in autistic preschoolers. *Journal of Autism and Developmental Disorders, 20,* 513–521.

Stone, W.L., & Yoder, P.J. (2001). Predicting spoken language level in children with autism spectrum disorders. *Autism, 5*(4), 341–361.

Strain, P.S. (1983). Identification of peer social skills for preschool mentally retarded children in mainstreamed classrooms. *Applied Research in Mental Retardation, 4,* 369–382.

Strain, P.S. (2001). Empirically based social skill intervention: A case for quality-of-life improvement. *Behavioral Disorders, 27,* 30–36.

Strain, P.S., & Cordisco, L.K. (1994). LEAP preschool. In S.L. Harris & J.S. Handleman (Eds.), *Preschool education programs for children with autism.* Austin, TX: PRO-ED.

Strain, P.S., Kerr, M.M., & Ragland, E.U. (1979). Effects of peer-mediated social initiations and prompting/reinforcement procedures on the social behavior of autistic children. *Journal of Autism and Developmental Disorders, 9,* 41–54.

Strain, P.S., & Odom, S. L. (1984). Peer social-initiations: Effective intervention for social skills development of exceptional children. *Exceptional Children, 52,* 543–551.

Strain, P.S., & Odom, S.L. (1986). A comparison of peer-initiation and teacher antecedent interventions for prompting reciprocal social interaction of autistic preschoolers. *Journal of Applied Behavior Analysis, 19,* 59–71.

Strain, P.S., & Schwartz, I. (2001). ABA and the development of meaningful social relations for young children with autism. *Focus on Autism and Other Developmental Disabilities, 16,* 120–128.

Strain, P.S., & Timm, M.A., (1974). An experimental analysis of social interaction between a behaviorally disordered preschool child and her classroom peers. *Journal of Applied Behavior Analysis, 7,* 583–590.   .

Sturm, H., Fernell, E., & Gillberg, C. (2004). Autism spectrum disorders in children with normal intellectual levels: Associated impairments and subgroups. *Developmental Medicine and Child Neurology, 46,* 444–447.

Sue, D.W. (1981). *Counseling the culturally different.* Hoboken, NJ: John Wiley & Sons.

Sugai, G., & Horner, R.H. (2002). The evolution of discipline practices: School-wide positive behavior supports. *Child & Family Behavior Therapy, 24,* 23–50.

Sugai, G., Horner, R.H., Dunlap, G., Hieneman, M., Lewis, T.J., Nelson, C.M., Scott, T., Liaupsian, C., Sailor, W., Turnbull, A.P., Rutherford, H.R., Wickham, D., Wilcox, B., & Ruef, M. (2000). Applying positive behavior support and functional behavioral assessment in schools. *Journal of Positive Behavior Interventions, 2,* 131–143.

Symon, J.B. (in press). Expanding interventions for children with autism: Parents as trainers. *Journal of Positive Behavior Interventions*.

Szatmari, P., Bartolucci, G., & Bremner, R. (1989). Asperger's syndrome and autism: Comparison of early history and outcome. *Developmental Medicine and Child Neurology, 31*, 709–720.

Szatmari, P., Bryson, S.E., Boyle, M.H., Streiner, D.L., & Duku, E. (2003). Predictors of outcome among high-functioning children with autism and Asperger syndrome. *Journal of Child Psychology and Psychiatry and Allied Disciplines, 44*, 520–528.

Tantam, D. (2003). The challenge of adolescents and adults with Asperger syndrome. *Child and Adolescent Psychiatric Clinics of North America, 12*, 143–163.

Taylor, B.A., & Harris, S.L. (1995). Teaching children with autism to seek information: Acquisition of novel information and generalization of responding. *Journal of Applied Behavior Analysis, 28*, 3–14.

Taylor, B.A., & Levin, L. (1998). Teaching a student with autism to make verbal initiations: Effects of a tactile prompt. *Journal of Applied Behavior Analysis, 31*, 651–654.

Taylor, G.R. (2001). Parental involvement in writing individual education plans. In G.R. Taylor (Ed.), *Educational interventions and services for children with exceptionalities: Strategies and perspectives* (2nd ed., pp. 220–228). Springfield, IL: Charles C Thomas.

Thorp, D.M., Stahmer, A.C., & Schreibman, L. (1995). Effects of sociodramatic play training on children with autism. *Journal of Autism and Developmental Disorders, 25*, 265–282.

Timm, M.A. (1993). The regional intervention program: Family treatment by family members. *Behavioral Disorders, 19*(1), 34–43.

Tomasello, M. (1988). The role of joint attentional processes in early language development. *Language Sciences, 11*, 69–88.

Tomasello, M. (1995). Joint attention as a social cognition. In C. Moore & P. Dunham (Eds.), *Joint attention: Its origins and role in development* (pp. 103–130). Mahwah, NJ: Lawrence Erlbaum Associates.

Tomasello, M., Mannle, S., & Kruger, A. (1986). The linguistic environment of one to two year old twins. *Developmental Psychology, 22*, 169–176.

Tomasello, M., & Todd, J. (1983). Joint attention and lexical acquisition style. *First Language, 4*(12), 197–211.

Tremblay, A., Strain, P.S., Hendrickson, J.M., & Shores, R.E. (1981). Social interactions of normally developing preschool children: Using normative data for subject and target behavior selection. *Behavior Modification, 5*, 237–253.

Turnbull, A.P., Blue-Banning, M., Turbiville, V., & Park, J. (1999). From parent education to partnership education: A call for a transformed focus. *Topics in Early Childhood Special Education, 19*(3), 164–172.

Turnbull, A.P., Pereira, L., & Blue-Banning, M.J. (1999). Parents' facilitation of friendships between their children with a disability and friends without a disability. *Journal of The Association for Persons with Severe Handicaps, 24*, 85–99.

Turnbull, A.P., & Ruef, M. (1996). Family perspectives on problem behavior. *Mental Retardation, 34*(5), 280–293.

Tustin, R.D. (1995). The effects of advance notice of activity transitions on stereotypic behavior. *Journal of Applied Behavior Analysis, 28*, 91–92.

Tyack, D., & Ingram, D. (1977). Children's production and comprehension of questions. *Journal of Child Language, 4*, 211–224.

Vaughn, B.J., Clarke, S., & Dunlap, G. (1997). Assessment-based intervention for severe behavior problems in the natural family context. *Journal of Applied Behavior Analysis, 30*(4), 713–716.

Vaughn, S., Schumm, J.S., & Kouzekannani, K. (1993). What do students think when their general education teachers make adaptations? *Journal of Learning Disabilities, 26*, 545–555.

Venter, A., Lord, C., & Schopler, E. (1992). A follow-up study of high-functioning autistic children. *Journal of Child Psychology and Psychiatry, 33*, 489–507.

Volkmar, F.R., & Klin, A. (2000). Diagnostic issues in Asperger syndrome. In A. Klin, F.R. Volkmar, & S.S. Sparrow (Eds.), *Asperger syndrome* (pp. 25–71). New York: The Guilford Press.

Volkmar, F.R., Klin, A., & Pauls, D. (1998). Nosological and genetic aspects of Asperger syndrome. *Journal of Autism and Developmental Disorders, 28*, 457–463.

Volkmar, F.R., Klin, A., Schultz, R., Bronen, R., Marans, W., Sparrow, S., & Cohen, D.J. (1996). Asperger's syndrome. *Journal of the American Academy of Child and Adolescent Psychiatry, 35,* 118–123.

Volkmar, F.R., Klin, A., Siegel, B., Szatmari, P., Lord, C., Campbell, M., Freeman, B.J., Cicchetti, D.V., Rutter, M., Kline, W., Buitelaar, J., Hattab, Y., Fombonne, E., Fuentes, J., Werry, J., Stone, W., Kerbeshian, J., Hoshino, Y., Bregman, J., Loveland, K., Szymanski, L., & Towbin, K. (1994). Field trial for autistic disorder in DSM-IV. *American Journal of Psychiatry, 151,* 1261–1367.

Vygotsky, L.S. (1962). *Thought and language.* New York: Press & Willey.

Wacker, D.P., Berg, W.K., Harding, J.W., Derby, K.M., Asmus, J.M., & Healy, A. (1998). Evaluation and long term treatment of aberrant behavior displayed by young children with disabilities. *Journal of Developmental and Behavioral Pediatrics, 19*(4), 260–266.

Warren, S.F., Yoder, P.J., & Leew, S.V. (2002). Promoting social-communicative development in infants and toddlers. In S.F. Warren & J. Reichle (Series Eds.) & H. Goldstein, L.A. Kaczmarek, & K.M. English (Vol. Eds.), *Communication and language intervention series: Vol. 10. Promoting social communication: Children with developmental disabilities from birth to adolescence* (pp. 121–149). Baltimore: Paul H. Brookes Publishing Co.

Webster-Stratton, C. (1997). From parent training to community building. *Families in Society, 78,* 156–171.

Weisner, T.S., & Garnier, H. (1992). Nonconventional family life-styles and school achievement: A 12-year longitudinal study. *American Educational Research Journal, 29*(3), 605–632.

Weiss, M.J., & Harris, S.L. (2001). Teaching social skills to people with autism. *Behavior Modification, 25,* 785–802.

Weiss, R.S. (1974). The provision of social relationships. In Z. Rubin (Ed.), *Doing unto others* (pp. 17–26). Upper Saddle River, NJ: Prentice-Hall.

Weld, E.M., & Evans, I.M. (1990). Effects of part versus whole instructional strategies on skill acquisition and excess behavior. *Journal of Applied Behavior Analysis, 14,* 449–463.

Wellman, H.M., & Lempers, J.D. (1977). The naturalistic communicative abilities of two-year olds. *Child Development, 48,* 1052–1057.

Wetherby, A.M. (1986). Ontogeny of communicative functions in autism. *Journal of Autism and Developmental Disorders, 16*(3), 295–315.

Wetherby, A.M., Cain, D.H., Yonclas, D.G., & Walker, V.G. (1988). Analysis of intentional communication of normal children from the prelinguistic to the multiword stage. *Journal of Speech and Hearing Research, 31,* 240–252.

Wetherby, A.M., & Prizant, B.M. (1999). Enhancing language and communication development in autism: Assessment and intervention guidelines. In D. Berkell Zager (Ed.), *Autism: Identification, education, and treatment* (pp. 141–174). Mahwah, NJ: Lawrence Erlbaum Associates.

Wetherby, A.M., & Prizant, B.M. (Vol. Eds.). (2000). *Autism spectrum disorders: A transactional developmental perspective.* Baltimore: Paul H. Brookes Publishing Co.

Wetherby, A.M., & Prutting, C.A. (1984). Profiles of communicative and cognitive social abilities in autistic children. *Journal of Speech and Hearing Research, 27,* 364–377.

Whalen, C., & Schreibman, L. (2003). Joint attention training for children with autism using behavior modification procedures. *Journal of Child Psychology and Psychiatry, 44*(3), 456–468.

Whiting, B., & Edwards, C. (1988). *Children of different worlds: The formulation of social behavior.* Cambridge, MA: Harvard University Press.

Whiting, J., & Whiting, B. (1975). *Children of six cultures: A psychocultural analysis.* Cambridge, MA: Harvard University Press.

Wilcox, M.J., Hailey, P.A., & Ashland, J.E. (1996). Communication and language development in infants and toddlers. In M.J. Hanson (Ed.), *Atypical infant development* (pp. 365–402). Austin, TX: PRO-ED.

Wilde, L.D., Koegel, L.K., & Koegel, R.L. (1992). *Increasing success in school through priming: A training manual.* Santa Barbara: University of California.

Wilhelm, H., & Lovaas, O.I. (1976). Stimulus overselectivity: A common feature in autism and mental retardation. *American Journal of Mental Deficiency, 81,* 227–241.

Williams, J.A., Koegel, R.L., & Egel, A.L. (1981). Response–reinforcer relationships and improved learning in autistic children. *Journal of Applied Behavior Analysis, 14,* 53–60.

Wimpory, D.C., Hobson, R.P., Williams, M.G., & Nash, S. (2000). Are infants with autism socially engaged? A study of recent retrospective parental reports. *Journal of Autism and Developmental Disorders, 30,* 525–536.

Wing, L. (1981). Asperger's syndrome: A clinical account. *Psychiatric Medicine, 11,* 115–130.

Wing, L. (1998). The history of Asperger syndrome. In E. Schopler, G.B. Mesibov, & L.J. Kunce (Eds.), *Asperger syndrome or high-functioning autism?* (pp. 11–28). New York: Kluwer Academic/Plenum Publishers.

Wing, L., & Gould, J. (1979). Severe impairments of social interaction and associated abnormalities in children: Epidemiology and classification. *Journal of Autism and Developmental Disorders, 9*(1), 11–29.

Wolf, M.M., Risley, T., & Mees, H. (1964). Application of operant conditioning procedures to the behaviour problems of an autistic child. *Behaviour Research and Therapy, 1,* 305–312.

Wolfberg, P.J., & Schuler, A.L. (1993). Integrated play groups: A model for promoting the social and cognitive dimensions of play in children with autism. *Journal of Autism and Developmental Disorders, 23,* 467–489.

Wolfberg, P.J., & Schuler, A.L. (1999). Fostering peer interaction, imaginative play and spontaneous language in children with autism. *Child Language Teaching and Therapy, 15,* 41–52.

Wood, M. (1995). Parent–professional collaboration and the efficacy of the IEP process. In R.L. Koegel & L.K. Koegel (Eds.), *Teaching children with autism: Strategies for initiating positive interactions and improving learning opportunities* (pp. 147–174). Baltimore: Paul H. Brookes Publishing Co.

World Health Organization. (1993). *The ICD-10 Classification of Mental and Behavioural Disorders: Diagnostic criteria for research.* Geneva: Author.

Yeargin-Allsopp, M., Rice, C., & Karapurkar, T. (2003). Prevalence of autism in a US metropolitan area. *Journal of the American Medical Association, 289*(1), 49–55.

Yell, M. (1998). *The law and special education.* Upper Saddle River, NJ: Prentice Hall.

Yoder, P.J., & Davies, B. (1992). Do children with developmental delays use more frequent and diverse language in verbal routines? *American Journal of Speech and Hearing Research, 36*(1), 83–97.

Yoder, P.J., Spruytenburg, H., Edwards, A., & Davies, B. (1995). Effect of verbal routine contexts and expansions on gains in the mean length of utterance in children with developmental delays. *Language, Speech, and Hearing Services in Schools, 26*(1), 21–32.

Yoder, P.J., & Warren, S.F. (2001). Relative treatment effects of two prelinguistic communication interventions on language development in toddlers with developmental delay vary by maternal characteristics. *Journal of Speech and Hearing Research, 44,* 224–237.

Yoder, P.J., Warren, S.F., Kim, K., & Gazdag, G.E. (1994). Facilitating prelinguistic communication skills in young children with developmental delay II: Systematic replication and extension. *Journal of Speech and Hearing Research, 37,* 841–851.

Zanolli, K. (1997). The environmental antecedents of spontaneous social behavior. In D.M. Baer & E.M. Pinkston (Eds.), *Environment and behavior* (pp. 219–228). Boulder, CO: Westview Press.

Zanolli, K., & Daggett, J. (1998). The effects of reinforcement rate on the spontaneous social initiations of socially withdrawn preschoolers. *Journal of Applied Behavior Analysis, 31,* 117–125.

Zanolli, K., Daggett, J., & Adams, T. (1996). Teaching preschool age autistic children to make spontaneous initiations to peers using priming. *Journal of Autism and Developmental Disorders, 26,* 407–422.

Zhang, C., & Bennett, T. (2003). Facilitating the meaningful participation of culturally and linguistically diverse families in the IFSP and IEP process. *Focus on Autism and Other Developmental Disabilities, 18*(1), 51–59.

Zionts, L.T., Zionts, P., Harrison, S., & Bellinger, O. (2003). Urban African American families' perceptions of cultural sensitivity within the special education system. *Focus on Autism and Other Developmental Disabilities, 18*(1), 41–50.

Index

Tables and figures are indicated by *t* and *f*, respectively.